Analysis analysed

Analysis analysed

When the map becomes the territory

Fred Plaut

London and New York

First published 1993
by Routledge
11 New Fetter Lane, London EC4P 4EE

Simultaneously published in the USA and Canada
by Routledge
29 West 35th Street, New York, NY 10001

© 1993 Fred Plaut

Typeset in Stempel Garamond by Michael Mepham, Frome, Somerset
Printed and bound in Great Britain by
Biddles Ltd, Guildford and King's Lynn

British Library Cataloguing in Publication Data
A catalogue record for this book is available from the British Library.

Library of Congress Cataloging in Publication Data
Plaut, Fred.
  Analysis analysed / Fred Plaut.
  p. cm.
  Includes bibliographical references and index.
  1. Psychoanalysis—Philosophy. I. Title.
  [DNLM: 1. Psychoanalytic Theory. 2. Psychoanalytic Therapy.
  WM 460 P721a]
  RC506.P58 1993
  150.19'5–dc20
  DNLM/DLC
  for Library of Congress   92–49187
                                                            CIP

ISBN 0–415–00789–5

To the memory of Evelyn
and with love for Helga

Contents

List of illustrations ix
Preface xi
Acknowledgements xix

Part I Analysis analysed
Introduction 1

1 Faith in analysis 3

2 The dream of analysis, mutuality and the romantic vision 18

3 Can it be analysed? 38

4 Concerning results 58

5 The patient speaks: analytic comments 75

Part II Learning from experience
Introduction 99

6 The autonomous ritual 101

7 'What do you actually do?' 118

8 Object constancy or constant object? 135

9 The psychopathology of individuation 145
  I Gordon's paradise 145
  II Celia's cross 172

Part III Analysis mapped
Introduction 187

10 The map: metaphor and reality 189

11 Analytic maps: the tools 208

12 Analytic maps: a pilot study   251

13 Some reflections on the Klein–Jungian hybrid   284

14 Where does analysis stand?   306
   I Answering a serious objection to mapping   306
   II Putting it on a map   322

   Epilogue   342
   Bibliography   346
   Name index   353
   Subject index   000

Illustrations

8.1	Worship of the phallus	138
8.2	Phallic amulet found in London 1842	139
9.1	*Coco de mer* tree	153
9.2	*Coco de mer* fruit	154
9.3	Gordon's Crest of the Seychelles	171
10.1	Europe in the shape of a woman	196
11.1a	Schematized T in O map	210
11.1b	Zonal map	211
11.2	Christian *mappa mundi*	212
11.3	Triora Stela	213
11.4	Daniel's dream	217
11.5	*Pilgrim's Progress*	218
11.6	Map of matrimony	219
11.7	*Treasure Island*	220
11.8	Paradise Design, Prague	226
11.9	Paradise symbol, enlarged	227
11.10	Beatus map	228
11.11	Paradise symbol, Hereford	229
11.12	Prehistoric design, Kivik	231
11.13	Labyrinth, Hereford	236
11.14	Paradise and world	238

11.15	Conception in the labyrinth?	245
11.16	How to draw a labyrinth	249
12.1	Analyst's and patient's expectations	253
12.2	Analyst's and patient's assessments	255
12.3	A patient's itinerary	258
12.4	A failed thematic map	260
12.5–7	Three dream maps	264
12.8	The interactional map of analysis	271
12.9 12.10	Details of 12.8	275
12.11	Directional changes in the labyrinth	282
14.1a	Bion's invariant	318
14.1b	A modification	318
14.2	Celestial map	324
14.3	Where does analysis stand?	329
14.4	From daydreams to Utopia	339

Preface

This book is meant for analysts of all 'schools' as well as psychotherapists and lay-persons with some knowledge of the subject. The personal view from which it is written is derived from my first having undergone a Jungian analysis and training, and quite a lot later a Freudian psychoanalysis. In between there were many friendly discussions with colleagues from different 'schools' and countries – mostly in London. The addition is important, because I believe that the setting and local climate exert a considerable influence on the product. But as for maps, I did not become interested until I came to England from South Africa after the Second World War. There I had completed the medical studies begun in Germany. My interest in psychiatry had begun when I was thirteen and heard a psychiatrist talk about his work. Army psychiatry re-aroused it. Postgraduate study in London was combined with analysis which became increasingly important, and really led to a new beginning and to the adoption of England as my third home. Shortly after my arrival there I saw a road map in a junk-shop the like of which I had not seen before and managed to buy it. The seventeenth-century map showed the road from London to Portsmouth. These details are only important when I look back and realize how disorientated I had been at the time. I certainly needed a map but was only aware of the aesthetic appeal of this one. Many years were to pass before I became seriously interested in maps and collected some, making friends with salesmen and cartobibliographers.

I had not intended to move again but then my circumstances changed and in 1986 I left for Berlin where I had not lived before but had made friends with colleagues. There I found working conditions for analysts very different from those I had known in London. Analysing and supervising now on a reduced scale gave me time to ponder over and review how my work had developed from a new perspective. It made me want to write down what I had gleaned without it becoming anything like a volume of 'Collected Papers'. I hope that my analysis of analysis has come at the right time to be shared with others.

For the moment however, I have to return to the London of the 1950s and 1960s which was particularly conducive to exchanges between psychoanalysts and analytical psychologists (Jungians). There was Anna Freud, Melanie Klein,

Paula Heimann, Winnicott, Michael and Enid Balint, and Bion. Gerhard Adler, Leopold Stein, John Layard and Michael Fordham were representative of the Jungian side. In Zürich I had had a memorable meeting with Jung in 1952. His interpretation of a dream of mine evoked a spontaneous and vivid reaction in him.

It could be said that my frequent references to eminent analysts are of historical and parochial interest only and that I was influenced by them. True, but so were and are many analysts and psychotherapists worldwide. And 'influence' along with 'suggestion' belongs to the various neglected aspects of analysis which are mentioned in all three parts of the book. The 'Klein–Jungian hybrid', see Chapter 13, is a particular example of it.

These circumstances are the background against which I examine some basic assumptions and aims of both psychoanalysis and analytical psychology, as pioneered by Freud and Jung and elaborated by successive generations. When my comments refer to 'analysis' I mean this to apply both to psychoanalysis and to analytical psychology. Where this is not the case, they have been separated out. As each part of the book is introduced separately, I can be brief in my description of the main features.

The aim of the book is to clarify what analyis is about. It is not a book about analysis. What prompts me to analyse analysis at the present time is that a general 'shaking of the foundations' is being felt in analytical circles. The sceptical reviewing and questioning that is going on arises largely from within the profession itself and is still on the increase. The reasons for the unease are various and manifold. *First* and foremost is the questionable relation between 'global' aims of analysis and its demonstrable effect. We can no longer expect individual case reports to be a satisfactory criterion. *Second*, what *in detail* is the connection between the various steps of the analytic procedure and its ultimate outcome? *Third*, by what criteria and methods is this to be judged? There is as yet no agreement about the procedure. The methods of observation and recording and the research design needed present an extremely intricate problem. *My hope is to facilitate the various lines of research by finding relevant perspectives and better means of communication.*

I set about it by examining and illustrating the text, matrix and context of analysis. Many of the 'neglected aspects' to which I refer belong to the matrix and the context. Let the *'text'* consist of various analytical theories and techniques which have been formulated and gathered into a body of knowledge to which extensions and modifications are constantly being added, while others are superseded. This process is not only of historical interest; it throws light on analysis itself as a living organism. As such it must have a context. But today the overriding question which needs to be studied is whether the organism can survive while undergoing metamorphoses to adapt to the 'climatic' changes to which it has also contributed. For example, the world in which everybody knows about unconscious motivation, Freudian slips and the like, is no longer as ignorant as it had been. Alternatively, the practical value of analysis as a psychotherapeutic method could become absorbed into the general body of psychotherapy and cease to have its separate existence. Another way of survival is by what I shall refer to as the 'air roots', meaning the hard-to-define social and cultural connections of analysis with the western way of life, such as its subtle effect on general education, the dramatic arts and biographical studies.

I have made it my job to question some common overinterpretations of the text. These concern the indiscriminate use of global concepts in analytical psychology, such as 'the opposites' and 'individuation' or 'ego strength' and 'the transitional object' in psychoanalysis. The rule-of-thumb dream interpretation according to which the analyst must be found somewhere in the dream is equally reprehensible. Any technical term that becomes of central significance is in danger of losing meaning altogether by being overworked. For example, 'projective identification' is 'in' at the moment. So is 'shame'. So is 'the holding of the regressed' patient', or 'baby', by the 'mother-analyst'. Although Winnicott's 'transitional object' has weathered well, this has not prevented misuse. Each term is utterly convincing; when first coined it holds the centre of the stage for a greater or lesser time and is hailed like a 'new breakthrough'. Which does not mean that the new understanding changes the ultimate outcome of analyses. But while it works it fans enthusiasm and keeps the trust in analysis alive. When doubts arise, as they must, the faith in the work is really put to the test. This is the subject of the *first chapter* and turns up again in various places, notably in the *last chapter*.

The psychological problematic of this area depends not only on the analytic understanding but must also include the social and cultural context, as I pointed out in a paper entitled 'The presence of the third' (Plaut, 1990). The very large 'philosophical' coinage would not be justified if the psychological background and *matrix* of analysis could be ignored as having no longer anything to do with the daily work. But I think that the matrix makes itself felt in several ways, one of which has already been mentioned, that is the quest for comprehensive, global terms, whether expressed as theories, techniques or aims. The longing for universals, such as 'wholeness' in our field, speaks of mankind's longing for a unified state of being.

Similarly unquestionable is the faith analysts profess in 'change', also known as 'transformations'. It too must be regarded as part of the matrix. It looks as if the whole potency of analysis had become fixated on this objective. Psychoanalysis expects that by going further and further back into the beginnings of an individual's life it will advance our knowledge of mental processes *and* result in better and more effective analysis. On the Jungian side the same benefit is expected from the realization of archetypal patterns and symbols supported by alchemical and mythological parallels. The process of interaction between the patterns and the 'self' is believed to generate transformations. Psychoanalytically, change signifies the establishment of a sound personality structure, equipped to withstand the warring instincts, and to face reality with its blows and misfortunes. In any event 'change' implies change for the better, closer to the aim of developing into a complete or mature person. Change can happen on the scale of an individual session in which a cogent symbol appeared, or a 'mutative' interpretation was given after an intuition or the countertransference has opened the analyst's vision. Or, again, change may be seen in a series of such occurrences or steps taken. All are based on the belief and subsequent observation of improvement, because something has 'changed' and the analyst – or, more modestly – the analysis has brought about the change. At favourable moments evidence of the change can be supported by case illustrations meant to allay any lingering doubt. It is true that hoped for desirable and convincing changes *do* occur. Only such changes are, in my view, less specific than theoreticians would have it. The feeling of mutual understanding, regardless of the specifics, brings about a favourable change in the analytic climate. The change *begins* very often when the analyst has had a new 'insight', which incidentally increases or renews his/her empathy with the patient.

My tendentious description is aimed at the single-mindedness of the analytic orientation. But at the same time I want to illuminate part of the matrix and *the most neglected area of analysis*, that is *the unchanging nature of people* who can only become more and more themselves, that is what they are and have been from the beginning. The acceptance of 'no change' leads to an alternative matrix. Before this becomes acceptable – and that really would constitute a change – we hope to change both ourselves, our circumstances and our patients. Here success is, at best, limited. At least, that is how it often seems to the onlooker to whom the meagreness of what can be regarded as proof is in inverse proportion to the ingenuity and inner consistency of various analytical theories. The same can be said about the vast volume of analytical literature, compared with the small number of publications that attempt to convey what it is like to be undergoing an analysis, that is to be the patient. This absence is a source of wonderment when one considers that every analyst has been through the mill and may have written learned books and papers about the analyses of patients, see also Chapter 5, 'The patient speaks'. I attribute the lack to a number of reasons. One is that to be in analysis is much like being in a dream, as I elaborate in Chapter 2. Although one can write down dreams and everybody can be counted upon to know what dreaming is like, there remains something slightly shameful for educated western people to take their dreams or analysis seriously. Maybe it is because as dreamers and patients we have no control over what happens to us and to be in control, 'mastery', is the basic power ideal of our society. Freud was utterly different. Being his own analyst, he had the courage to publish many of his dreams together with his own interpretations and in support of his theory. Jung in his turn was the only analyst who has publicly stated – not in detail, it is true, but in principle – that as changes occur in the patient, so does the analyst change. By rejecting 'mastery' both made themselves masters.

What else is 'change'? In Chapter 7 I make out a case for the continuity of a theme in a person's psychology and call it the constant object. This is illustrated in Chapter 9 with the example of unanalysed persons and figures but also patients who had had some analysis. The thesis in brief is that to become fully aware of unchanging patterns in one's personality and to make the best of one's limitations is the kind of change that analysts do *not* refer to when they describe how a patient was 'changed' by analysis. This is in curious contrast to the observation analysts make about each other – provided that the other analyst is not one's former patient – namely that the colleague has 'not changed'. Some quite openly admit, with a mixture of resignation and despair, that they have not changed. *What it all amounts to is that 'change' or 'transformation' without differentiation and criteria has no meaning outside its own frame of reference.* Nor is it any help to call the unchangeable characteristics 'unanalysable', since this can imply that at some time in the future, possibly with improved analytical techniques, the characteristics will become analysable, that is subject to change. Innate traits will never be analysed away. The best one may hope for is that they will be turned to good account. The worst, that we will become caricatures of ourselves.

I think that the belief in transformations is, like that in a panacea or an Utopia, a recurring archetypal theme; about which more in Chapter 14 where I argue the psychological necessity to make allowance for such an area. It belongs to the matrix from which analysis was born and from which it has not altogether freed itself. It is confusing that 'changes' which benefit the patient *do* occur in or after analysis but sometimes also without. Whether they occur because of it and as the result of specific interventions or fortuitously is hard to tell. But my impression is that the chances are greater, if we do not expect too much or try too hard to bring changes about. Before leaving the examples of what is meant by the matrix from which universals and the desire for transformations originate, later to be reflected by analysis, here is another example of the matrix affecting the text. It can be seen when analysis is looked on as a ritual as outlined in Chapter 6. In a later chapter, 11, the ritual is represented on an inner map, the labyrinth. It symbolizes our journey and meanderings from life to death and leaves space for central encounters of which analysis may be one.

Let us now turn to the *context*, that is those parts which surround the text and throw light on its meaning, except that the context also influences analytical practice directly. I have looked at the context, from a social and cultural point of view. For example, the frequency of sessions is not only dependent on the geographical distance between analyst and patient, but also on the financial resources available. It cannot be said to be irrelevant, if the analyst's ideal and rule is to see patients, say five times a week. That rule is or was grounded in the matrix in as much as hypnosis had been the forerunner of analysis. This was at a time when hospitalized patients were hypnotized at least once a day. At any rate, I show grounds for the conclusion that the way analysis is practised, that is its technique and management, indicates the meaning it has for the individual practitioner and the patient. Frequency of sessions, then, is part of the context to which the attitudes referred to respectively as 'classical' and 'romantic' make their contribution; four to five sessions per week when 'classical' and where money is no object, while once or twice a week is sufficient for the 'romantic' analyst and the less well-off patient.

As a cultural phenomenon analysis operates in the space between 'worlds' which have been variously named 'external' and 'psychological' reality, or the realm of the material and the spiritual, the individual and the collective. It does its work by focusing on processes which, for convenience's sake, can be further divided into intrapsychic and interpersonal. Both come together in the distinctive relationship called the 'transference'. In as much as analysis tries to mediate between these various worlds it is in competition with the function of *institutionalized* religion, in contrast to mysticism. But to mediate one has to take up a position and have an orientation and a point of view for which I adopted Bion's term 'vertex', because that does not depend on the sensory perception 'sight'. It is mystical in its focus on the unknown. To be together or at-one with it should, according to Bion, be the analyst's aim.

A further example of the cultural context is seen when there is no room for analysis because the group, family, tribe or other community count for infinitely more than the individual. The effect of such social circumstances is similar to times of starvation when analysis lacks the necessary infrastructure.

In Part I, with mainly the text of analysis in mind, I question some of the basic tenets and aims and then proceed to compare the aims with the results. In the present state of our ignorance about the results only subjective impressions can be given, not the least important of which is what patients have to say.

In Part II the questioning is continued but the emphasis is on what I learned as an analyst by not taking anybody's word for granted. This concerns mainly Jung's concept of the opposites as the source of psychic energy and the conjunction of opposites as the chief ingredient of individuation. In Chapters 7, 8 and 9, I introduce an alternative and to my mind more realistic route to our becoming what we are, or 'self-realization'.

I have made it clear that I think very little of case illustrations because they are all too often designed to support a theory or technique and usually end in a *QED*. It has been argued that case illustrations are only meant to show how a given analyst works. But this is plainly a prevarication. First, an analyst's working method or technique is of no interest to others unless it is meant to advance or bear out a point of theory. Second, what analysts *can communicate* is restricted to *what they sincerely believe* they do. The patient's responses to the analyst's interpretations are presented by the analyst and are quoted in support of the point the analyst is making. The patients themselves are not reporting, nor is anybody else bearing out the analyst's statement. *What I believe the analyst's technique does communicate is his/her attitude to the work*. And here the informed reader must be the judge. When in Chapter 7 I give a longer case description, I do so not with the purpose of confirming a theoretical point, but to illustrate that what I actually do is far more determined by the contingencies of the moment than by the implementation of a theoretical point of view. Although I admit the need to have one, I often fail to implement it.

Part III departs from anything I have previously published. I put forward the tentative idea that maps can be used as a medium of orientation in and communication about analysis. It is not, or not yet, a way of bringing cognition to bear on data derived from unconscious manifestations of the unknown ('unconscious'). But mapping could be a staging post on the way to making analysis more widely known. In Chapter 12 an analytical map is applied to an individual analytical situation, while in Chapter 14 a selective survey map shows where analysis may be standing today. Here inner and outer worlds, text, matrix and context are brought together in map format.

Debatable as both text and context are, words are not the only means by which we can become more conscious of what is going on, nor are emotions and intuitions. A different way by which we orientate ourselves is the sense of location, space and movement (kinaesthesis) by which we relate ourselves to the environment. I refer to it as 'spatiality'. Mapping is a way of using this sense and of recording the experience. As the context can make no sense to anyone ignorant of the text, so the map can only tell us *about the experience of analysis* which changes when it is brought together with the actual living of it. That, as every hiker knows, is true of all maps. Like other maps too, a map that attempts to reflect an analytical moment is a combination of a preconceived map in the head of the analyst and/or patient and the meeting, merging or conflicting with an event. At any rate, a map that has been used by a traveller is no longer the same as it had been.

In Chapter 14 I show that the island position in which analysis takes place favours the formation of illusions which are such a common phenomenon in the course of analysis. While the intention is to turn these to good account, the very disposition to projections, identifications and illusions to which we are all prone, can lead to very real discoveries. At the same time, however, they bring us close to the shores of Utopia.

My interest in mediaeval maps and mapping in general may tempt readers to a comparison with Jung's involvement with alchemy. There is some truth in this because I have a feeling of fellowship with the generations of map makers who set out with geometricized world images in their minds and then had to settle for the increasingly complex and asymmetrical realities of discovery. The major difference however is that mapping and analysing have nothing in common except that they are both cultural activities. A common purpose may be found in the search for truthful orientations. Some early maps do resemble cosmic mandalas and other symmetrical structures which, in my view, lead to tranquillizing illusions, but really inhibit discovery. But early maps are by no means the only and certainly not the most useful map category which can help in communicating about analysis. Details are found in Chapter 12 where other important map categories are illustrated.

To return to the beginning: the interchanges between satisfaction and frustration, which are called, after Bion, the invariant in analysis, find their counterpart in the vacillations between faith and doubt. This became the major theme of the book in which I embark to discover what analysis may be about and how to share what I found.

Chapters 1 to 5 have not been published before, nor have Chapters 10 to 14. The four chapters constituting Part II are edited and enlarged versions of papers which were previously published (see also Acknowledgements).

Acknowledgements

The familiar expression of thanks to persons 'without whose help this book could not have been written' was never more aptly used than here.

Every author has a context and I am acutely aware of mine. Writing as I do from Berlin and in the language I am most familiar with, I consider myself to have been extremely fortunate to have found the right conditions for gathering my thoughts and feelings and adding ideas not previously expressed. For without Helga Anderssen I would not have left London where I had worked as an analyst for forty years. But I had made friends with colleagues in Berlin previously and made new ones. Having got there and started on the book I had the extraordinary good fortune to find a super secretary in Sandy Hayman. More about her contribution in a moment.

The leading member of my supporting team was Andrew Samuels who looked through my writing without ever quite despairing, although I gave him plenty of opportunity. My thanks are profound and heartfelt.

Matthias von der Tann has been an enormous help as empathic and knowledgeable commentator as well as resourceful computer tutor, always on the spot. In both capacities he has earned my respect and gratitude. This is the occasion to thank the many friends, colleagues and family in both cities for having been patient and supportive during my long labour.

I further want to thank Francis Herbert of the Royal Geographical Society and Catherine Delano-Smith of the University of Nottingham for their advice with cartographical material.

Many thanks to David Stonestreet of Routledge for his encouragement and patience from start to finish.

Sandy Hayman has not only given loyally and unstintingly of her time and energy but also compiled the bibliography. I cannot thank her enough.

Helga's help has been beyond praise. In addition to her common sense and sound judgement she has been of immense practical help. She has suffered patiently and sometimes impatiently, but always lovingly. No one could ask for more.

The following are acknowledged: lines from T. S. Eliot's *The Cocktail Party* by kind permission of Faber & Faber Ltd, London. Etimologia de Cardeña by courtesy of the Real Academia de la Historia Biblioteca, Madrid. Gordon's Crest of the Seychelles by courtesy of School of Oriental and African Studies, University of London. Map of Matrimony by courtesy of the Geography and Map Division, Library of Congress, Washington, D.C. Paradise Symbol from Isidore of Spain's map in the Vatican Library (B.V.A. VAT. Lat.6018, f64v–65) enlarged and redrawn.

I am grateful to Kiepenheuer & Witsch Verlag for allowing me to publish lines from Heinrich Böll's 'Brief an einen jungen Katholiken'; Fischer Taschenbuch Verlag for allowing me to quote lines from the German translation of Gardiner's book entitled *Der Wolfsmann vom Wolfsmann;* and Routledge for their permission to quote from the English translation of Obholzer's *The Wolf Man*. My thanks are also due to the editors of the *Journal of Analytical Psychology* for allowing me to republish with emendations material now in Chapters 6, 7, and 8 and to the editor of *Analytische Psychologie* for allowing me to republish the English version of 'General Gordon's paradise'.

Part I

Analysis analysed

INTRODUCTION

In Part I I highlight some of the assumptions that form the background of analytical practice. The first chapter deals with the balance of faith and doubt which is taken up in detail throughout the book. Brief reference is made to the requirements for becoming an analyst and to the general expectations people have who come to analysis.

In the second chapter the analysis of dreams as the cornerstone of all kinds of analysis, whether 'Freudian', 'Jungian', 'Kleinian' etc. is discussed. The differences between these 'schools' are given less emphasis than the general trend towards 'mutuality' between patient and analyst, and the leaning toward the 'romantic' vision. It is suggested that whatever the similarity between dreaming and analysing may be, the 'classic' vision and cognitive methods are today not receiving enough attention.

In Chapter 3 some objections and difficulties are mentioned which would seem to make it impossible to proceed. Foremost among these are the dissensions. If analysts cannot agree among themselves, is there a sufficiently homogeneous body of knowledge left to investigate? The question makes it necessary to go into detail concerning the context such as the causes, meanings and aims of analysis.

Chapter 4 continues to examine the connection between the context and the outcome of analysis. Attention is drawn to the bizarre situation in which the protagonists of rival 'schools' and 'visions' implicitly assert to have discovered the better version of the truth without being able to demonstrate better results. The basic difficulties of assessing results in analysis are gone into.

In Chapter 5 patients have their say. Here it has been necessary to go back into the history of psychoanalysis in order to crystallize something about a fundamental triangular relationship between the analyst, the origins of theory and the patient.

Chapter 1

Faith in analysis

In this book I want to concentrate on aspects of analysis that have received less attention than I think they deserve. As a man-made rather than a natural phenomenon, analysis cannot be separated from the person who practises it, the analyst. But that is only the first of many complex interactions which make it necessary to design methods of research into the analytic process itself, that is to analyse analysis.

I want to begin obliquely by comparing analysis to two other cultural phenomena – religion and art. My comparison will be limited to western culture and I intend to highlight some common elements and make use of the differences in order to create a three-dimensional picture.

Religion, art and analysis – all three stem from the same matrix within the psyche. To come to fruition, all three depend on the *faith* of devoted practitioners. What it is precisely that they have faith in, is less important than the capacity to have faith at all. The same would apply to the process of scientific discovery. *It is faith in the unseen but it is not blind faith.*

Faith is a word that has religious overtones, in contrast to trust which we use when one can test who or what is trustworthy. Faith, on the other hand, is more independent of circumstances, you either have or have not got it although, here again, you can lose it. When it is there we can entertain hope. The capacity to have either trust or faith can be ruined by unfavourable circumstances, especially early in life. In one case I can think of, this seems to have happened when, as a young child, the patient was overburdened by adult responsibilities. Seduced by praise for being already grown-up, his (other) ability to play imaginatively was ruined together with the capacity for symbolic realizations (Milner, 1955, Plaut, 1966). No doubt there are earlier and more severe adverse conditions which can be the origin of not being able to have trust or faith. Here are some examples of the evolution from trust to faith in the development of analysis.

Freud (1920) observed a 1½-year-old boy and his *'Fort! Da!'* ('Gone! There!') play with a reel and string, which symbolized his actual mother's departure and return. The boy pretended to have her under his control (*SE 18*:

p. 15). By believing the reel represented his mother whom he could get rid of and whose return he could manipulate by pulling at the string, the boy could create the comforting illusion that he had his mother 'on a string'.

Winnicott (1941) made observations on the 'spatula game' of a child about the same age and came to a similar conclusion but with a significant addition. The child threw the spatula on the floor; it was picked up for him. This process was repeated many times. It seemed as if the child was experimenting with the loss of the actual mother, but by doing so he was also testing the relation between her and the mother *inside* him without excessive fears that she may not return (Winnicott, 1952). The young child's experiment can be taken as the necessary preliminary to a gradual change from imaginary triumph to the development of non-controlling expectancy, that is faith.

Bion took the matter a step further when he introduced his 'act of faith' which is expected of the analyst and depends on the disciplined denial of 'memory and desire' (Bion, 1970). He saw in faith a scientific state of mind that makes analysis possible, a *'primary methodological principle'*, as Eigen rightly observed (Bion, 1970, Eigen, 1981). In my view Bion's demand closely resembles that which is made on the patient who is asked to trust and share free associations and other spontaneous mental activity with the analyst and to forgo immediate gratifications.

The examples indicate an evolution of faith within the analytic project: Freud had faith in his intuition when he 'saw' the connection between an external event and the child's play. Winnicott emphasized the importance of the child's internal mother reflected in the experiments with the spatula. And, finally, Bion saw the analyst's capacity to be without supporting sensory evidence such as sight and other sensual images of memory as an act of faith.

The psychological starting point of this evolution can be taken back to William James who, at the beginning of the century, wrote in his *The Varieties of Religious Experience* that 'treating these [religions] as purely subjective phenomena without regard to their "truth", we are obliged, on account of their extraordinary influence upon actions and endurance, to class them amongst the most important *biological* functions of mankind' (James, 1902, emphasis added). James sees the biological worth of religious experiences in the increased spiritual strength of the person who experiences them.

Jung had been well aware that the subject of faith was one of theology's traditional battlegrounds. In contrast to Freud he stressed the symbolic in myths, including the Bible. Placing *his* faith in this realization, he made discoveries concerning the cultural and therefore psychological importance of symbolical truth. For Jung, faith became, not a matter of sentiment, but of reasoned necessity, where reason and necessity was given the same status as James's 'biological function'. Humanity, Jung wrote, needed the improbability of religious statements in order to arrive at a totally different spiritual reality, 'superimposed on the sensuous and tangible actuality of this world' (*CW* 5: para. 336). Thus Jung, James and Bion travelled by different routes to arrive at much the same conclusion concerning the spiritual *and* practical value of faith.

In a lighter vein, I would suggest that games which parents play with young children, such as 'fly away Peter, fly away Paul' and later, versions of 'hide-and-seek' can be seen as exercises in losing–finding–doubting–trusting. So is the letting oneself fall backward, the body rigid, into reliable arms. The thrill that accompanies the game every time it is repeated suggests that trust, like faith, does not become absolute.

The relevance of faith would have been strenuously denied when psycho-analyis went through its historic birth-pangs at the beginning of the century: separation from traditional wisdom concerning human nature and the estab-lishment of the new discipline on a 'scientific' basis were the priorities. But if we reflect that both analysis and religion offer sustenance and moral guidance to humanity in its divided state, needing food but unable to live by bread alone, the functional similarity is undeniable. What is more, both analysis and religion demand something in return for the help they offer.

These rituals and sacrifices were *essential* if either analysis or religion is to be truly effective. However, we must accept that, save in certain details, such as the confessional element, the similarities between analysis and religion are balanced by profound differences. The differences are consequent upon dif-fering origins: divine revelation in one case and a unique observational viewpoint and technique in the other.

But the rise of psychology itself is, in turn, a historical and cultural phe-nomenon representing a modern attempt to give explanation, order and meaning to a welter of behavioural manifestations. As such it fulfils an orien-tating and guiding function within the sphere of all human activities.

The maps which religions provide give clear guidelines for the conduct of believers. To stick to it in all circumstances requires faith. Analysts by contrast abhor giving guidance and advice; patients should find out for themselves. In practice withholding guidance can make patients all the keener to spot what the analyst 'really thinks'. Analysts, on the other hand, have a theoretical point of view enabling them to make observations and to give interpretations. To do so requires a measure of faith considering that objective proof is not possible. It requires even more faith to apply our theories to ourselves, to practise as we preach. Do we also expect our patients, as the living evidence of our work – 'our results' – to confirm our theoretical expectations? If such evidence has not been forthcoming what was the whole exercise about? Does analysis provide an order or cosmos that gives sense and meaning to an otherwise chaotic universe? Whatever the answer to these questions, faith or trust is required of all analysts who are able to sustain doubt. This precondition to discovery is forgotten as soon as a hypothesis has been 'proved' and becomes elevated to the status of a theory.

As regards the *results and implicit promises* held out by religion and analysis, again these are comparable; healing or whole-making via salvation – redemption by the grace of God on the one hand and, on the other, whole-making or healing by self-realization (individuation) in the case of Jungian analysis. Both sets of goals are based on the same hopeful idea regarding the possibility of transformation and relative curability (if not perfectability) of the individual person. It must be added that both systems offer explanations of man's behaviour, limitations and fate.

With such uncomfortably close similarities it is small wonder that the Church, as the representative of religion, saw something like heresy in analysis and that analysts, in their competitive turn, regarded religion as superstitious mumbo-jumbo. However, in time the antagonism has decreased and the earlier, absolute incompatibility has shifted. Does the *rapprochement* mean that both analysis and religion have come to recognize their practical limitations?

The observations on the *different origins of religion and analysis* can be extended to a consideration of the status of the founders of both, whether they be merely human or human and divine. The addition of the divine element makes a mighty difference as regards the authority vested in the founder or pioneer. In due course it becomes easier to question the theoretical statements of a scientific pioneer than the divinely inspired word of a religious teacher or rabbi. For the authority of God's seed is absolute, whether incarnated as in the biblical word or in God's representative on earth. The word becomes dogma, the teaching doctrine leaving no room for doubt.

Despite their being of ordinary birth, with no claim to special status other than their genius, pioneers like Freud and Jung had authority attributed to them by their patients, pupils and successors. This projected authority has been accompanied by a great deal of admiration and even adulation from their followers and so the Word (or the words) frequently cited and quite properly treated with respect became for a while indubitable to their followers. (Quite rightly, in as much as pioneers are ahead of their time.)

Detractors, on the other hand, have not been slow to call these manifestations by other names: discipleship and indoctrination. What is true is that the original discoveries have been confirmed and added to by the first generation of pupils, subtly and gently questioned by their offspring (the second generation) and treated with some impatience and even a measure of iconoclasm by subsequent generations, but never with total disrespect.

THE POET'S WISDOM, A COMPARISON

We have looked at the practical implications of faith in religion and analysis. How about the other source of wisdom that is expressed in images and metaphors, that is poetry? Analysts are sometimes credited with knowing more about human nature than other people. This is not altogether true, nor is it true of other members in the helping professions such as psychotherapists, healers, doctors or priests.

Yet it would be instructive to know what gave rise to this reputation. It could be an extension of humanity's search for omniscience and infallibility which is exemplified in religion. The fallacy of analytic omniscience is at once exposed when we compare what the analyst offers as knowledge or truth with the wisdom of great poets and dramatists. As Winnicott in 'Fear of breakdown' put it:

> Naturally if what I have to say has any truth in it this will already have been dealt with by the world's poets, but the flashes of insight that come into poetry cannot absolve us from our painful task of getting step by step from ignorance towards our goal.
>
> (Winnicott, 1974)

So the poet's statement owes something to an intuitive flash or even a revelation; it strikes a chord and rings true for everybody. The poet must, of course, also have the gift to express the vision cogently. Despite the apparent ease and spontaneity of the poet's communication, we may be sure that it also owes a lot to hard work. However, the work is of a different order to that of the analyst, for the poet works alone. Analytic knowledge, on the other hand, is arrived at by a painstaking procedure and, more often than not, takes years to bring to a conclusion. In addition, the long labour with its moments of truth is the product of collaboration between two people. Such struggles are not easily forgotten. Although analysts and patients have their flashes of intuition too, it is precisely because of the painstaking pedestrian approach that such moments tend to have a lasting effect. Furthermore, the whole process of un- or dis-covery is linked with events in the person's life, past and present. Analytic discovery is not like a chord that has been struck in an insulated room, but rather more like the resonance of a bell emitting vibrations into the surrounding territory. The very fact that analysis is proceeding often affects other persons, not only those immediately connected with the patient.

Compared to the analyst's, the poet's burden of responsibility is impersonal and comparatively light. Although the imagery created enriches us at the time of encounter, its vitalizing effect may not last in spite of its profundity. The solace offered is a by-product of the poet's art, although poets too presumably need to know that they can make us 'feel better', in touch with ourselves and all humanity. But the precise influence of their vision and voice on our daily lives is not their primary concern.

In many respects then, the analyst is much more ambitious than the poet and patients rightly expect more than entertainment, solace or uplift. They hope to be listened to and understood, and, further, that their disease be alleviated in a manner that they can eventually follow with their conscious minds even though they will have to let the 'unconscious' lead the way. This means that patients can link whatever troubles them with possible causes which lie beyond their control – for example the behaviour of parents. Such discovery and partial explanation of troubles often makes the patient feel easier because it reduces the sense of guilt and failure. This effect, desirable as it is, does not usually last. The reason is that the alleviation of pressingly painful feelings only touches on the fringes of what the patient is really curious about: him- or herself in relation both to the world outside and to the core of being, the inner world, the soul. Therefore, the patient is actually striving for the same truth or wisdom for which the poet searches. The analyst who uses metaphoric language borrows poetic truth. But the 'poeticization' of analysis is something that the patient has to experience in his/her own way and time. It is a curious situation in which the analyst, perhaps agog with anticipation and a sense of awe, is waiting for the patient to move beyond the literal reality of a world which he/she does not usually question. This transition depends upon intense effort requiring qualities of endurance and, hence, a high degree of motivation to discover and move into unknown territory.

Perhaps analysis owes its place in our culture to the widespread limitation that we cannot get to these inaccessible, poetic, awe-inspiring places without a companion and guide. The patient's developing relationship to the analyst–guide is crucial to understanding the distance travelled, the direction of the journey and to entertaining ideas about the possible destination.

THE ANALYST'S WORK AND LIFE

The analyst's initial function is, apparently, to point out blind spots to their patients and so enable them to see more clearly where formerly they were floundering blindly. In this way patients become aware of some of the origin of their impediments. Subsequently there is often an influx of energy that enables patients to realize latent potentialities. At first, this might be in terms of socially desirable goals, earning (more) money, becoming potent and able to love, starting a family. Alternatively, the patient can see his/her task as one of becoming reconciled to his/her limitations including, eventually, death. It is this second kind of realization, which usually follows the more social developments, that has aroused the suspicion and opposition of the 'establishment'. What goes on may run counter to what is considered 'healthy'. The patient has now become 'difficult' as the result of his/her analysis and may even give up a good job, leave spouse and family and become introspective. In short, patients appear to have taken leave of their senses – and all in order to fulfil themselves!

What is all this navel-gazing, this self-indulgence *for* anyway? And why is the patient *still* going to see this man or woman?

What has happened to the patient is that the freeing effects of analysis have produced brand-new problems: social insecurity and emotional conflicts, perhaps between old loyalties and exciting new prospects. The patient begins to wonder whether to persevere or give up analysis.

Meanwhile, the analyst will be asking him/herself whether the intervention has, in fact, caused more upheaval than the results could possibly justify. They may take refuge in their theories as well as past experience. They will also check their findings for clues from the unconscious, such as their own and the patient's dreams, and maybe their dreams 'about' the patient. (But *who* is the patient in the dream?) If matters really do look fraught, the analyst will consult a colleague or a group of colleagues who could help to sort out their own involvement in a situation which has become problematic. These remarks will bring the word 'transference' to the lips of anybody who has ever read anything about analysis and 'countertransference' to those who are even more knowledgeable, but see also p. 277, below, under 'mutual transference'.

I am using these concepts here merely to indicate in a general way the extraordinarily close connection between the *work* and the *person* who is doing it, bearing in mind Jung's apocryphal remark: 'It's not what you know but who you are that matters'. Indeed, the inseparability of what the analyst has learned in his/her own analysis and training from the evolving person he/she hopes to become or remain may be seen as the distinguishing characteristic of the profession. Here again, we may make comparisons with the poet or artist whose association between the work and life is equally close but less self-conscious.

So, when I speak of the dilemmas and hazards that face the analyst, I am also portraying the essential element of faith in analysis, the intricacies of which are my main theme. Here I can only comment on some main features such as *the transference*. It is so called because something is transferred from the timeless, dream-like world of one person in his/her cultural sphere to another person, or even a whole group of 'others' (family, tribe, race, nation). To make matters more complicated, there is always a grain of truth in these 'projected' views of the other.

Add to this the eternal demand for cure and panaceas, and it comes as no surprise that traditional illusions should insinuate themselves time and again into analysis. Of course, we are too sophisticated to promise a cure but we may well imply that something equally good or better can happen in analysis. Although not untrue, the implication becomes a lie, simply because it distracts from the *focus* of analysis: the discovery of emotional truth which causes upheaval, requires reorientation and does, at times, become unbearable. According to Bion such lies are mobilized to prevent what may become a 'catastrophic change ' (Bion, 1970). The analyst has the responsibility of weighing up that risk against the liberating effect of no longer having to live a lie and to gain a new orientation.

Moreover, lies serve the purpose of carrying any excessive emotional charge away from oneself to an apparently safe area, the 'other'. Inevitably it is the analyst who happens to become the target of such projections, whether in terms of approach or fear and repulsion, of love or hatred, or both. Analysts have to bear being the containers of powerful emotional charges. They do so with the help of theories which explain and defuse these 'projectiles' – but not altogether. Something always sticks and cannot be got rid of. Analysts know how to 'interpret' a situation and its origins; to do so is their proper job. At the same time they have to admit that the routine use of such knowledge is their first line of defence. The second line would be by retaliating in kind.

Once the rampart is breached, analysts have to find other means of preserving their togetherness and personal integrity. In a subtle but inexorable way they are exposed to the cumulative effect of projectiles, much as a dentist is exposed to the virus that causes the common cold. The dentist acquires an immunity; analysts must not, for this would deprive them of their working sensibility, knocking out their alarm bells and making them even more likely to fall victim to the dangers of psychic blindness or 'infection', as Jung called it (*CW 16*: para. 365, see p. 52 , below).

I have been trying to demonstrate certain aspects of analysis, and convey the nature of the work and the demands it makes. The principle of the New Testament story of the beam and the mote holds good. But the repeated and detailed therapeutic use requires a sympathetic as well as a theoretical understanding of the phenomenon which goes beyond moral exhortation. To add some flesh and blood, and also to give an indication of the analyst's second line of defence, I want to compare the ordinary breadwinner's return home tired and irritable after work with that of a chauvinistic analyst who has a wife and family. In addition to wanting to know, before all else, why the bicycle has been left by the front door and by whom, and why the dinner is not ready, the analyst may be tempted to offer his/her partner and family explanations for their behaviour which – being 'unconscious' – they had not even thought of. That is to say the analyst will give them the 'real' reasons for their regrettable conduct and ignore their explanations, regarding these as mere rationalizations and refusal to be 'conscious' and contrite.

Bearing this family scenario in mind, we can understand (a) why the tired analyst may continue his/her interpretations after office hours and thereby misuse his/her technical know-how to let off steam. The accused will have far less comeback than if they had been cursed in plain language; (b) the psychic infection may spread. Should the partner be equipped with the same weapons, perhaps be an analyst too, such discord could result in a futile running battle; (c) patients who have recently acquired the 'lingo' are far more likely to indulge in such power-games than those who have learnt better or found a better model in their analyst. One may hope that the analyst will recognize the danger of losing the boundary between the working and the private relationship. But the temptation persists simply because of the absorbing and often irritating nature of analytic work. The pressures on the analyst as a person are such that he/she may show a tendency to preach, if only by repetition of the same interpretation. But these 'slip-ups' are trifling compared with the much more serious temptation to fulfil a patient's apparent need for sexual love to which I shall return at the end of this chapter.

Not being automatons, analysts constantly have to adjust their own requirements according to whether they are in the professional or private environment. This switching back and forth is much more demanding than in most other jobs because both, environment as well as emotional, demands may look and feel very similar. A 'persona' offers no protection either at home or at work. As the boundary between the two areas becomes at times hazy there is a danger of losing one's bearings. Not to do so requires vigilance. But a vigilant person is neither relaxed nor spontaneous. There is no lasting solution to this problem. Analysts have to live with it. It means 'living dangerously'. The challenge and anxiety it involves is, in my view, one of the hidden attractions of the job. The snag is that if anxiety and insecurity increase beyond a certain point, there is the danger that the boundaries may break down. The question therefore arises: Why become an analyst?

MOTIVES, COST AND HAZARDS

As members of the human species, we are not only equipped with the same physical features and appetites but are also unable to live cut off from emotional and spiritual nourishment. This statement is meant to cover the whole area of quasi-instinctual curiosity, ranging from wanting to know how we and the world around us function, to speculations about the reasons why we operate as we do – often in such contradictory ways. This curiosity combined with intelligence is our common heritage. But the particular question arises why some people should want to become analysts although there are easier ways of earning a living.

Nearly all analysts I asked agreed that the choice of their profession was largely determined by their own psychology. This includes the wish to find out about themselves and others, Klein's *'epistemophilic instinct'*. Analysts have little option but to become and remain explorers of the inner world and for this they need to *stay* as well as to *have* patients. Of course, the psychological factor plays a part in the choice of many professions where there is an individual option. But I cannot think of any other vocation in which an archetypal self-image, in our case the mythological motif of the 'wounded healer', plays so marked a part.

The preconditions for becoming an analyst include an academic qualification (usually in medicine or psychology) plus clinical experience with patients or clients in one of the helping professions. This makes it rare for an analyst to qualify much before the age of forty.

Having qualified, analysts will require periodic further analysis throughout their working life which usually means for the rest of their life, for few analysts totally retire. The expenditure on 'maintenance and running repairs' is therefore considerable. In addition, there is the time and expense required to keep abreast of professional developments. Less obvious and frequently neglected is the analyst's need to keep free time for the social and emotional side of life. If they do not deliberately cater for this, the pressures of the demands described earlier threaten to cause a break in personal boundaries and spoil analytic work. Although I am unable to make exact comparisons between the divorce statistics for analysts and other professional groups, my impression is that the divorce – or separation – rate for analysts is high; analysts do not seem to differ in this respect from other professional groups. But then, analysis is not primarily concerned with establishment values unless the analysis is paid for by insurance schemes, in which case rehabilitation to work and other socially desirable aims become priorities (see results, p. 63, below). It is however concerned with the whole human being and the fulfilment of its potential through relationships with others leading to well-being. Therefore the absence of psychiatric symptoms and the ability to work cannot be the sole adequate yardstick by which to measure the analyst's, any more than anyone else's, health. The psychological determinants that lead to the choice of the profession make it imperative not only to practise deliberate disciplined self-analysis but also periodic 'check-ups' by a colleague. The more so, as the results of even the longest 'super-analysis' are of uncertain duration. Although analysts know this, they are inclined to neglect their own maintenance as if they were somehow exempt.

In terms of money, a full-time analyst in private practice working, say, forty hours per week and taking the necessary eight weeks' holiday per year, earns less than a senior general practitioner or a not-so-senior consultant in the UK National Health Service, and less than a dentist can earn in many countries. This is still a good income, but to put the figure into proportion one has to add the considerable capital sum he has to lay out for his own analysis and training, often taking as long as seven years.

When I write about the hazards of the analytic profession, I am not referring to external dangers such as physical or slanderous attacks which are, in any case, rare. It is to more intrinsic vocational hazards of the job that I want to draw attention. My hope is that, in this way, I shall throw further light on the nature of analysis itself. The vocational hazards of being an analyst are, in turn, linked with the original choice of that profession. A two-fold, even paradoxical, situation will serve as example to illustrate many detailed problems. Without the wish to succeed, to help patients in terms of relieving their anxieties and furthering their personal development and preferably both, no one would want to become an analyst. Without the ability to surrender that wish and to remain what has been called a 'participant observer', one does not become an analyst. Analysis, compared with other forms of psychotherapy, attempts to be 'non-directive'. Analysts in training who had been in one of the caring professions before (social workers, doctors, nurses) often have difficulty not to tell patients 'What is good (or bad) for them'. It becomes easier to abstain if one can tolerate one's own doubt.

It is not surprising if, at the end of a long analysis, patients who did not set out with the intention of becoming analysts discover that they are attracted to the profession. In order to stick to the avowed aim of analysis, to uncover unconscious motivation as well as to uncover links and to find new meaning, this wish must first be looked at as an expression of identification with the analyst. Some analysts in training say quite openly that they want to become 'members of the same club' in order not to lose the analytic relationship. Inasmuch as this is an expression of separation anxiety, it is an inadequate motive for becoming an analyst. However, the patient who wants to become an analyst may have another non-specific reason like just wanting to belong, to acquire a group (or 'we') identity which in our urban society is not easily come by.

But in the long run, there lurk much more insidious vocational hazards, as we saw above. Some stem from doubts in the value of the work. First, the analyst may come to doubt the curative value of insight in relation to the patient's disease. For, however deep the insight might be, experienced on the gut level and not merely intellectually, characteristic behaviour patterns still tend to reassert themselves. They are like a person's fate – by which I mean that the repetition of typical behaviour forms a theme which may continue throughout a person's life, like a signature tune or 'leitmotiv'. What is more, such patterns are known to persist through successive generations as, for example, fear of the opposite sex expressed in the form of contempt, until finally there is no further offspring. The recognition of such patterns is important in order to learn what cannot be changed by analysis but possibly modified by an implicit 'philosophical' attitude. This is not just resignation on my part but a view based on repeated observations. To draw an analogy: if coronary disease runs in a family, affecting mostly the males, it would be better to arrange one's life in accordance with that possibility rather than to counter-act it, say by taking strenuous exercise. Counter-measures, as we know from Greek tragedy, are apt to produce exactly what we are trying to avert. If however the counter-measure, let us suppose heart surgery, is successful and fate has apparently been mastered, is this going to increase a person's capacity for faith or their belief in the omnipotence of technique? The question is put in order to highlight the difference which a successful surgical result alone cannot decide.

SPECIFIC REQUIREMENTS

A specific demand on analysts is for a kind of *double vision*; they have to look at all the clinical data and phenomena as expressions of a suffering fellow-being but *also* from a highly selective and therefore detached analytic point of view which makes links between the parts that make up or are derived from the whole.

The selective analytic viewpoint is the outcome of theories and observations which started as intuitions into which the pioneers put their faith. And faith is still required by practising analysts today because the territory discovered cannot by its very nature be as unambiguously demonstrated as, for example, a relatively unchanging geographical feature. The prominent contributions to the selective analytic viewpoint from which analysts make their observations are:

1   the reconstruction of childhood memories with special emphasis on repressed events and desires and, hence, on what was and has remained repressed, because painful or forbidden. Freud's 'psychic apparatus' applies to this contribution;
2   the growth or development of the personality expressed in terms such as integrating and individuating processes including Jung's views on symbols and their effect frequently in association with alchemical and religious parallels;
3   closely linked with the foregoing is the quest for meaning and creativity.

But faith in the analytic point of view is, as stated, not faith in the efficacy of the method, nor in the ability to cure or 'help' (whatever help may mean). *Analysts need to have faith in faith itself.* It may not move mountains but it will help him to go on searching for truth, to make small discoveries about links between causes and patterns, about meanings and psychic transformations whereby psychologically appropriate responses to interventions can be recognized. Also, by rejecting the illusory aspects of religion analysts may, paradoxically, appreciate a person's need for illusion, at least from time to time. At all events, analysts have to tread carefully when feeling they must disillusion, because they are sure to be treading on someone's dreams. It is a common beginner's mistake to want to disillusion patients in order to demonstrate the value of some correct but at that moment inappropriate application of theory.

T. S. Eliot spoke the poet's truth when he wrote, in *East Coker*, 'Human kind cannot bear very much reality'. What is more, when the pendulum of our emotions has reached the point of maximum excursion it may, of its own accord, begin to swing in the opposite direction. The psyche's self-correcting tendency may be better aided by our ability to wait, than by our interventions. It is at this point that the analyst who took up the job because of his/her own need to help others by making them see and change the error of their ways is liable to become stuck. Anxiety may take the form of wanting to do something rather than to do nothing and watch patiently.

For reasons such as these, some people who train to become analysts may never get there or, having been trained, discontinue to analyse and practise some other and quicker form of therapy in the hope that it will yield demonstrable results comparatively quickly. One has to remember that all therapies, whether physical or psychological, new, rediscovered or ancient have their initial successes often based on the 'charisma' of the initiator but followed in due course by professional disappointment. Such disillusionment is expressed by the recurrent rule: 'one third cured, one third improved, one third not improved or worse'. Even then, any criteria by which results are assessed must include the length of time that has elapsed since treatment ended (see 'results',

p. 63). The practitioner's assessment of what the effective agent was may also change as the range of observations and techniques evolves.

Initial success of any therapeutic method is doubtless due to the enthusiastic vision of the pioneer and their followers or team. Mesmer's magnet seemed to lose its healing power after ten years. Freud, in the early days of psychoanalysis, became disappointed when the patient's condition was still no better after four months. Now, no analyst is unduly alarmed when the original complaint persists after four years. All this goes to show how subtle and incisive is the *distinction between enthusiasm and faith*. One could compare it with the difference between being in love and loving. It is confusing that cures achieved under the protective veil of enthusiasm should be attributed to faith-healing before either enthusiasm or faith have been tested by doubt.

There is an ever-ready market for enthusiastic healers as well as for a proliferating number of psychotherapies. They all have their successes, but in the long run the above 'rule of three' applies. A population's appetite for experimenting with new therapies, either one at a time, or several in combination, seems unlimited. This applies particularly in the wealthier countries with highly developed technology. The number of consumers of therapies seems to increase with the number of therapies available – at least up to a point. Certainly, there are more enthusiasts than persons who are capable of sustained faith. The lie due to enthusiasm – and here again I do not mean deliberate dishonesty – is that certain realities are omitted from the simplified account. The resulting lie is far more easily swallowed than the multifaceted sober truth discovered by a long and faithful search.

WHY SHOULD PEOPLE STILL WANT ANALYSIS?

In answer to this question I want to return to my earlier attempt to envision analysis as one of a number of significant cultural phenomena. If we take analysis together with religion and poetry, we become aware of a common implicit assumption: the individual, each single person alive, represents the unit of highest value in a democratic system. *In theory*, at least, that is the political credo in which analysis, western religion and poetry flourish. But there can be little doubt that *in practice* in many countries analysis is the privilege of the few. The privilege is not just restricted by financial, educational or intellectual endowment, but by a gift which is harder to define. Some minimum standard of infant-care seems necessary to lay the foundations out of which the capacity can be born to entrust oneself to an exploration without guaranteed benefit. For it to flourish, no matter what terrible, destructive events happened later in life and were suffered by the individual, a long-lasting process of repair akin to a labour of love is needed. Analyses take such a long time because they include both a technical, step-by-step process, and the relatively unselfish devotion or love called *agape*. The sex of the couple, analyst and patient, is not the decisive factor. It is their getting to know and trust each other in depth.

The baring of soul which is required is impossible to tolerate unless it goes hand-in-hand with the building up of trust in the human being. When this reaches the level of faith that is constantly exposed to doubt, the analytic work has been creative in spite of our nearly equally great potential to destroy it. This delicately poised balance suggests another reason why analysis takes such a long time and why it costs so much, not just in terms of money but also of devotion. On the debit side this is also why, in isolated persons, the analytic relationship can become indissoluble.

We shall return to the subject of devotion in two places. One is in Chapter 8 in connection with a person's relation to constant objects. The other is in the last chapter where devotion is regarded as the individual's psychological contribution to the area of cultural activities. Analysis is regarded as part of this domain in which there is no room for 'mastery' and self-aggrandisement.

Nevertheless, it is well known that transgressions do occur in analysis when power is abused in the form of an incestuous relationship. How is this possible? The symbol of sexual union evokes such an overwhelming response that it induces a confusion with ordinary carnal love (fucking). It is a confusion that in some persons, and in all of us sometimes, leads to an inability to distinguish between symbolic and literal reality (see also p. 157 below). When sex between analyst and patient occurs, the symbolic unification of body and soul has regrettably been misinterpreted, and wrongfully and harmfully enacted. The presence of an incest taboo enshrined in the ethics of the analytic profession demonstrates the need to establish special safeguards. Even then, sexual 'acting out' has by no means been eliminated. The absence of a culturally and socially accepted ritual that could mediate between instinctual fulfilment and symbolic realization is a topic that I addressed in a paper entitled 'Where have all the rituals gone?' (Plaut, 1975, see pp. 101–17, below).

When the analysis of an individual brings into being the faith and love necessary for the achievement of its goals, an implicit, non-verbal message is constellated. The analyst feels the better for having met the patient together with the unfulfilled part of life and usually this is mutual even when details about the analyst's life remain unspoken. Such effects cannot be mass-produced, nor has every person who reaches such a meeting point got there by means of analysis. Before analysis existed, the experience of persons who got there would have been called 'religious' because a suitable climate for person-ality-unification was provided by religious experiences. However, when religion demanded blind, unquestioning faith it had, of course the *opposite* effect. Jung's position is in agreement with Unamuno's statement 'Faith which does not doubt is dead faith' (Unamuno, 1967). The reader who will go on to subsequent chapters cannot remain unaware of my own doubts regarding analysis. *In fact this book is a justification of analysis by doubt, rather than by faith.*

From what I said it must be obvious why so many psychotherapies flourish which offer short cuts as seen from the standpoint of analysis. That they have something to offer, that the results of each one may seem similar or even superior to those of analysis, I do not doubt. As long as the experience these therapies provide is brought back into context and becomes part of a unifying process, it is valuable. In this respect analysis, marriage and religion all offer similar and comparable opportunities. (The three are of course not mutually exclusive.)

I do not see why weekend workshops which pillage the slowly acquired analytic experience should not be enjoyed. Analysis, with all its dignity, offers no sensual enjoyments. Although it sets out to liberate the person from narrow inhibitions, the practice of analysis itself involves an ascetic discipline and makes corresponding demands on both analyst and patient. Its rewards are the discoveries of both fictions and truths about enjoyable states of psychic realism. Free from both starry-eyed optimism and depressive hopelessness, analysis need not be without humour and joy.

Chapter 2

The dream of analysis, mutuality and the romantic vision

No analyst can be in practice for very long without becoming aware of the numerous ramifications and links of his/her craft with other disciplines. Experts from too many areas such as religion, literature, anthropology, theology, philosophy, sociology, as well as psychology and psychiatry, have drawn our attention to the influence that analysis has had on their work. It would therefore be possible to use any of these disciplines and show that the unintentional, implicit, peripheral effect has been so profound as to justify calling analysis a socio-cultural phenomenon. In short, it has, in one way or another, influenced life in western society. This socio-cultural enterprise exists alongside psychoanalysis as a 'cure' or therapy of neurotic ailments. What has become of Freud's clinical intentions is one key issue in my reflections. The other is to consider the effect of the socio-cultural frame, supposedly peripheral on analysis itself – *the interaction between the periphery and the centre of analysis.*

But how can one know what is central? Obviously, it is not enough to call any aspect of analysis, its practice, technique or theoretical concepts, central. When trying to relate some of my own papers to recent literature, it struck me that the interest in the dream had not changed much since Freud wrote his 'Interpretation of Dreams' at the turn of the century. True, attitudes and views on dreams and the dreamer have been subject to many variations, but interest in the dream as a central phenomenon in analysis has not waned. This interest seemed, therefore, a suitable invariant to take as a starting and viewing-point from which to survey some characteristic features of analysis as a theory.

Dreaming and analysing have much in common. Despite the obvious differences between the dream's spontaneous occurrence and the deliberate activity of engaging in analysis, I shall argue that, in practice, analysing today resembles dreaming in some essential respects. And the gerund (ending in '-ing') is bound to tell us something essential about the nouns 'dream' and 'analysis'.

This statement would have been heretical at the turn of the century when psychoanalysis was the instrument whereby dreams were investigated for their unconscious content and meaning and interpreted according to Freud's theory of infantile sexuality. At that time the analyst was the observer who was able to decode the hidden meaning of dreams. A detached frame of mind was optimal for this task. The decoding and interpreting of the dream was deemed successful when it confirmed the theory.

After these opening remarks, readers could not be blamed if they expected to find reports, interpretations and comments on dreams and their dreamers. Instead, for now, I must restrict all that undoubtedly evocative colour in order to concentrate on the *role* of dreams in the practice of analysis. Because it is this that has served as a model or prototype for all analysis.

In the business of analysing, it is essential that along with theory, technique and practice the whole person of the analyst should be involved as Jung put it (*CW 16*: para. 198). But we should not assume that the detached observing–recording had been altogether abandoned. However, the more engaged stance will prevail – at least most of the time – when we are trying to understand the patient's dreams or in analysing any other communication. In other words, many analysts now believe that their observations of dreams must be accompanied by the personal capacity to enter the dream with the help of their own associations, while the patient who re-enters the dream has the chance to relive it. This leads to a kind of interactive communication that is different from the one-sided interpretation that had been standard practice. As the result of this change of heart (as much as of anything else) there is now a better feeling of partnership between analyst and patient. And because the analyst also dreams, sometimes even 'about' the patient, and tries to understand his dreams by the same means as he interprets the patient's dreams, he knows that for this if for no other reason he is 'as much in the analysis' as the patient (Jung, ibid.).

I believe that the increasingly humanised partnership between the analyst and patient, of which dream analysis is but one example, has also compounded the difficulty of defining what *analysis* is: *it has become just as hard to define as it is to delineate a dream*. Like the dream, analysis is a conglomerate, composed of different parts that may be seen to articulate with each other, but the links vary according to the theoretical standpoint adopted (see Preface). In general, it can be said that both dream and analysis are built on shifting sand. Dreamlike analytic theory and corresponding interpretations may be totally convincing when first proposed, but tend to become less so or undergo alterations and distortions as they struggle to fit in with the circumstances in which the dream is recounted or the theory applied. To continue with my simile: the structures built on such uncertain foundations may look solid and provide effective shelter, though the building itself is of a temporary and ephemeral construction.

But while the increasing difficulty in defining the boundaries and complexities of both dream and analysis made the situation more uncertain than it had seemed in the early days, it was also accompanied by a growing humanization exemplified by the analyst's acknowledged participation in dream analysis and the whole analytic process. From having been a participating observer, but still a 'scientist', the analyst seems to have turned into an observing participator. Differently put, the dream, as central phenomenon of analysis, which in all its elusive significance had always been the subject of a vast literary interest, seems to have *exerted a powerful influence on the very instrument, analysis*, which had been designed to observe and decode it.

To this day the dreamer, the interpreting analyst and the dream still make their appearance in almost every clinical paper. In view of the close association, it is not very surprising that analysis should have become more dream-like and that the dream is no longer seen as the model that typifies neurotic symptom-formation as Freud had postulated. Along with this change, the division of mental processes into 'primary', as in dreaming (primitive, instinctual, wish-fulfilling), and 'secondary', as when we are fully awake (rational, reality-adapted) thinking (see p. 21, below) became relativized. The possibility and usefulness of distinguishing sharply between illusion and reality has become doubtful.

It is not that the cogency of Freud's terms summarizing the characteristics of 'primary process thinking', *'condensation'*, *'displacement'* and *'symbolization'*, is in serious doubt. But in many respects they fail to do justice to the significance of much of the dream's content and even more so to the structure and importance of the dream. Jung observed that a fourfold structure similar to that of a drama could be detected in quite a number of dreams (*CW 8*: para. 561f). He further differentiated between several types of dream, for example the trifling residue of a day's undigested contents and the 'big' dream of supra-personal or even 'prophetic' meaning (*CW 8*: para. 555). More fundamental than any of these refinements and relevant to the present comparison between events in dreams and in analysis was Jung's approach to the dream as couched in an image-language that did not have to be decoded and unmasked, but could be understood just as it was. The dream meant what it said, neither more nor less. It was therefore only a question of finding a key to its understanding. According to Jung a key, if not *the* key, could be discovered by someone with knowledge of symbolisms gathered from mythology and so forth. If various forms of art also spoke their image-language and achieved their effect by means of 'illusion', did not the dream with its frequent metaphoric allusions and symbolic expressions resemble an artistic creation?

Jung had early on drawn attention to the value of the 'transcendent function', that operated between conscious and unconscious realms (*CW 8*: para. 131f). Later Winnicott was to postulate something similar in the form of 'transitional phenomena' (Winnicott, 1958). Evidently, clear definitions between the regions in which the mind was supposed to operate were not borne out by the analytic observation of children and the analysis of adults. From then on the instrument, analysis, could no longer be accurately focused. It was as if it had become contaminated by frequent contact and long association with too many dreams.

As I want to plead for the separation of analysing from dreaming in order to gain clarity about the issues that are blurring the relationship, I first need to substantiate my claim that the two have become intertwined. For the sake of convenience some common characteristics have been enumerated together as follows: the experience, memory, psychodynamic explanation, vicissitudes of regression, language and interpretation.

First, we will examine *the experiential level*. Although dreams are chiefly experienced in terms of images, there is also a 'just so' mode of dreaming by which the dreamer simply knows without being able to explain how. This resembles the analyst's intuitions, the predecessors of their hypotheses and theoretical formulations by the light of which they make their observation. The precondition in both instances seems to be that sharply focused attention on known facts or 'reality' is temporarily switched off. At any event, people frequently come out of an analytic session feeling as 'if they had been in a dream'. This does not seem to depend on whether they had been using the couch or a chair. Although many have no option but to plunge straight back into their workaday lives, those who can afford a quiet interval have reported feeling the benefit of coming together again. This presupposes that they have been 'in a different world', or 'like on an island', which does not imply that the experience had been blissful; far from it. It only means letting oneself become aware of living in two worlds that must be linked with each other. If dreams were nature's attempt to bridge the gap, it was the job of analysis to bring the patient's two worlds closer together by improving and strengthening that bridge. The analyst had brought the dream to the fore and made it into an ally, somewhat restive perhaps, but needed for the job. After analysis, dreams would become the former patient's chief instrument of self-analysis.

Another aspect that makes the dream experience comparable to undergoing analysis is that both take place under circumstances that are defined by a ritualistic frame. The routine of going to sleep, perchance to dream, and the analytic routines of entering the consulting room at the appointed time, lying down (or sitting in a certain chair) for a definite time then leaving the room again to return to the world outside, can in both cases be regarded as facilitating the transaction. In both instances too we notice the outstanding attribute of any ritual, which is to provide help in the crossing of a threshold from one state of being to another. (See also rituals, p. 114.)

The obvious difference in experiencing dreams and analysis is of course the routine sharing of the patient's dreams. I mention this here in passing because of its far-reaching consequences on the dream itself and the analytic relationship in particular. If, for example, the patient's recounting of dreams should deteriorate into a ritualized deflection of unpleasant problems and yet remain unnoticed, the analysis would become a sham.

On the level of *psychodynamic explanation*, regression can be regarded as the common denominator. In general the term means returning to a previous state. In terms of thinking processes it means going back from 'secondary' to 'primary' (see p. 20, above). The earlier vague judgement had been that secondary thinking was to replace the primary kind and that patients would be cured, if they would only be reasonable and use the second mode as the analyst did when he interpreted dreams.

The curious situation with which patients were expected to cope was that, on the one hand, their regression to the dreaming-primary process-level of thinking was asked for by the analyst who was obviously interested in dreams. Had not the patients on the couch been encouraged to abandon their logical, secondary thought processes in favour of playing with free associations? On the other hand, patients had to become accustomed to the translation of their raw material, the dream, into the demanding verbal explanations of analysis. While this often felt frustrating, the bargain seemed acceptable to most patients, or to all patients most of the time.

The next characteristic is *dreams and the vicissitudes of regression*. While a degree of regression would thus be regarded as optimal for analysis some patients seemed to *like* being in a state of regression enjoying an 'oceanic feeling' in preference to the 'ordeal of return' in which they should utilize the benefits of analytic insights the better to live in the ordinary world. The refusal was recognized and suitably explained in terms of the patient's history. Analysts were in agreement that it was not a matter of moral weakness, but of a trauma or traumas that had befallen the patient early on in life. But they were divided about the analytic technique in the case of patients afflicted by 'latent psychosis', or with 'borderline' and 'narcissistic' personalities who might regress beyond the bounds of what was analytically desirable into florid mental illness. Some, like Jung, had had a lot of psychiatric experience. Although keenly interested in dream symbolisms occurring in psychotic patients, he was worried about saying or doing anything that might encourage the patient's absorption in dreams, lest they extend into hallucinosis and occupy still more space in waking life. In certain patients, however, in the later stages of analysis, Jung encouraged patients to 'objectify' their dream images, notably by painting. Being able to look at the product would strengthen the bridge between the patient's ego and the fascinating image. The action of making the latter visible would render it more accessible to the person's self. In this way 'objectivation' could reduce or even replace dreaming when this seemed desirable (*CW 18*: para. 399). Others like Winnicott who, with his pediatric background, knew a lot about infancy saw that regressive states could with very careful management, by 'holding' the patient, be turned to therapeutic advantage (Winnicott, 1965). Balint however had learnt to recognise the warning signals and distinguished accordingly between 'benign' and 'malignant' forms of regression (Balint, 1968). Bion again seemed to meet the danger by proposing that the analyst should take an ascetic attitude to dream images as to all other 'sensa' that turn up in analysis. Rather than comparing whole configurations he dismantled images into 'elements' and observed how they articulate and change. Characteristically he demanded that the analyst should abandon notes, records and all kinds of attempts to recall previous events and instead develop '*a dream-like memory*' (Bion, 1970); see also our consideration of memory, below.

Whatever we may think of the merit of these statements, they strengthen my assertion that the relationship between analysis, work on dreams and states of regression has remained central. What has changed are views on the significance of regression. From something that was inevitable in dreams and during the analytic session but otherwise undesirable, regression became a concept with marked therapeutic implications. What is more to the point, some positive aspects of regression are now seen as a form of lessened ego-control, thus making room for self-expression. An example is condensation, meaning the merging of time-and-space-boundaries which brings about the merging of dream images and their combination into new composites. Where Freud had spoken of an 'artistic intertwining', analysts after him have emphasized the dream's creative potentialities (*SE 4*: p. 285). All this foreshadows what I shall refer to as the romantic vision of analysis (see below, p. 33).

The language by which analyst and patient communicate often bears a significant similarity to *the 'language' of dreams*. Because we remember our dreams usually by their visual imagery, it is when *words* are *used in a dream* that they are all the more memorable. This is not only on account of neologisms, contractions and double meanings, but also because of the employment of figures of speech such as metaphors. Once used, these easily become a shorthand expression by which patient and analyst can refer to certain dream events that have acquired an agreed significance much like the in-words used in families. Although analytic communications by metaphor are frowned upon by some analysts as encouraging 'collusion', when it comes to *writing about analysis*, the writings of the pioneers as well as their successors abound with figures of speech. (The general index to Freud's works lists about 450 metaphors. No doubt this contributed to making his writings at once pleasurable and persuasive.) It looks as though the metaphorical language of dreams which obviously cannot be stopped by analysis turns up again when it comes to statements *about* dreams or analysis. For example, Fordham's model of integrating and de-integrating phases of the self is deliberately abstract but communicated on a descriptive image level, involving comparisons with inspiration – expiration, systole and diastole, ebb and flow and the like (Fordham, 1957).

However, it is in the *unspoken* but deeply felt language of the dream, and its bodily and emotional elements that we recognize another striking similarity with some silent moments of analysis.

Then there is *the memory of dreams* in analysis. Analysts are very familiar with the causes of *not* remembering and of distortions of memory as based on the defensive mechanism of *repression* which plays a cardinal role in psychoanalytic theory. How then do we re-member, re-call and re-produce the past when the present involves two people who meet in specific circumstances?

Let us first agree that nothing can bring back the past, although the renewed physical presence of the patient in the consulting room makes the best possible substitute. On this all analysts I asked were agreed. But they were divided over what would be the next best method. Some would not trust their memory at all and needed notes and/or mechanical recordings. Most relied on a mixture of recollections supported by notes. Others, like myself, felt that discussion among friendly colleagues and with the usual safeguard of anonymity provided a suitable climate for remembering. What does this suggest regarding the psychological process of remembering? Could the customary notion that memory operates quasi-photographically be mistaken? Are the prefixes at the beginning of verbs connected with memory misleading? Let us assume the patient had a dream. In the session the patient tells the dream or what he/she can remember but possibly also with additions and omissions that make the dream into an acceptable story. Then the analyst makes notes about the dream or what he/she has taken in of it. When it comes to discussing or publishing the dream the parts that have been understood are highlighted, more especially those that support points of theoretical interest. How can we know how much there is left of the dream as dreamt? If memories and dreams can lead to associations and amplifications, is not the reverse also possible? This, after all, is what happens when we say that something has 'broken' a dream. If the surroundings and the setting of the consulting room were designed to promote associations and so forth, are the latter not likely to facilitate *a fresh construction that only resembles 'memories'*? This does not mean that memories are fantasies in the sense of mere fanciful inventions. On the contrary, the stuff that memories are built on has to be in keeping with reality to some extent, as without it we would be unable to benefit from any experience such as crossing the road. Although the 'bricks' are old, memory is largely a present construct, very much influenced by present interest and intentions. This is a neglected factor in analytic communications as Hirschberg's excellent paper 'Remembering: Reproduction or Construction?' confirmed (Hirschberg, 1989).

Finally, we come to *the interpretation of dreams*. What holds good for dream interpretation holds good for the interpretation of other material that is reported or directly observed in analytic sessions. But analysts no longer follow the line of demarcation between the dream's manifest content and the true meaning resulting from a translation into the latent content. Meltzer even wants to change interpretation to 'formulation' (Meltzer, 1984). As I understand it, this means a change in the analyst's role from that of a translator who promulgates the authorized version to one who formulates a point of view. In that way, the analyst surrenders some of the authority which adhered to the role of his predecessor who in days of old made known what the messages from on high signified. The modern counterpart is always glad to have the dreamer's help in adding to and confirming the interpretation and is almost as glad if he/she vehemently rejects it, indicating 'resistance'. But it seems more than doubtful whether all the power with which the analyst is willy-nilly endowed can be abrogated even if he/she only 'formulates'. This point leads to the problem of suggestion in analysis and will be taken up below (see p. 69).

To sum up, a change in dream interpretation has been accompanied by a change in the *analyst's attitude* to the patient. This change has been more noticeable in psychoanalysis which has moved closer to Jung's position. It means looking at dreams as sources of *direct information* about psychic processes. Spelling the meaning out has become optional. True, one or more keys, such as mythology, would still be required to elucidate that information. But that still is a very different attitude from the one that informed the analyst-detective having to get the better of the so-called 'dream-censor' who had cleverly hidden the true meaning behind an innocuous looking 'manifest content'.

UNDERSTANDING DREAMS IN THE LIGHT OF THE MUTUAL TRANSFERENCE

Having considered some characteristic features that dreaming and analysing have in common, we must now return to the obvious difference. When the patient had told a dream, he/she is expected to enter the aura of the dream by allowing a drift to a zone between daytime thinking and a cast of mind, somewhat similar to dreaming, which favours free associations and the like. Analysts are expected to be receptive to this state by responding to it with the kind of *unfocused attention* that Freud has described in metaphorical terms, such as 'freely hovering' attention, the well-polished mirror and 'blank screen'. How has it come about that this apparently contradictory demand developed a bias in favour of the observing participator, implying a shift of emphasis from observation to participation?

I already referred to the primary and secondary thought processes which, in practice, it is not always possible to distinguish, anymore than it is to maintain the distinction between manifest and latent dream content. The establishment of an intermediate zone between conscious and unconscious such as Jung's 'transcendent function', and Winnicott's area between fantasy and reality, the 'transitional phenomena' (see p. 137), are all changes from the firm distinctions and boundaries as originally conceived. The later conceptualizations had become necessary because observations showed the existence of thoughts that were not available to consciousness at the moment, and yet their easy and spontaneous retrieval indicated that it was not due to repression either. The new developments could therefore be looked at as an enlargement of the hypothetical area of the mind which Freud had called the *'preconscious system'*. But there seems little doubt that the shift referred to had been made possible by the new concepts concerning intermediate states, see above, which favoured the analyst's participation. Here was a space for imaging jointly.

But by far the most important contribution to participating came from a *revision of the transference which could now include the countertransference*.

Let us start with how things had been when it was possible to formulate opposite points of view on the interpretation of dreams and the role of the transference.

An old psychoanalytic rule of thumb was that *the analyst* in some guise appeared in every patient's dream and must be sought out and interpreted accordingly. This contrasts with Jung's position that dream interpretation should be undertaken on the 'subjective' as well as on the 'objective' level. The former means much the same as 'intrapsychic' and implies that all figures in the dream were reflections of *the patient's* psyche or parts of it. He/she was, so to speak, held responsible for what happened in the dream. If the patient was reluctant to see it that way, Jung sometimes said: 'Whose dream is it, yours or mine?' (personal communication).

Although both instances are very crude, they exemplify that there was a time when there were clearly defined boundaries between the dreamer and the interpreting analyst. What seems to have happened is that these boundaries became blurred. A certain merging occurred around the edges and the reason for it is in my view that the meaning of countertransference has changed. To anticipate the conclusion: the transference now seems to include the counter-transference or, differently put, the latter has become part of the former.

Credit must be given to Jung, not only for having differentiated, as mentioned, between different types of dream, but also for having shown that the counter-transference could be useful to the analyst as 'a highly important organ of information' (*CW 8*: para. 519, *CW 16*: para. 163). Previously it had been generally regarded as a nuisance inasmuch as the patient's projections were answered by the analyst's counter-projections. Jung's work on the subject dates back to before 1916, when the first English translation of 'The Psychology of Dreams' appeared. (The last expanded version was published as 'General Aspects of Dream Psychology' in 1948 (*CW 8*: para. 443f).)

First among the psychoanalysts to take up the thesis was Heimann when she wrote 'The psychoanalyst's countertransference is an instrument of research into the patient's unconscious' (Heimann, 1950). Heimann, like other psychoanalysts after her had probably not read Jung: at any rate he is not mentioned. In the long run and in most instances it does not matter 'who said it first'. What matters is that mutuality in the transference implies a new working relationship between the partners. This view has by no means found general acceptance. For example, an analyst who is looking for evidence of 'resistance' in a dream will interpret differently from one who on the basis of mutuality works with the patient towards a joint understanding. Among the post-Jungians who have worked on this, Fordham (1957) and Dieckmann (1979) are probably the best known. The revision implies that information not only about the patient's state, but also about the state of the analyst's psyche can become available. This particularly concerns contents that were previously *not unconscious on account of 'repression'* but *unknown* in their full significance – and will probably become so again later. Jung considers this kind of unconsciousness 'through mere lack of realization' and regards the dream content as having been selected by the conscious situation of the dreamer in order to make up for or 'compensate' for his incomplete awareness (*CW 8*: para. 477). From this point of view it becomes possible to see that the conscious content of a situation and the transference stand in a reciprocal relationship to each other. The transferred content is to begin with the patient's projection of undigested material. Maybe it was expressed by ill-health and/or unhappy relationships. Now by 'working through', it becomes the common property in which both parties have their personal interest – hence, *mutual transference*.

The mutual transference, an example

I abandoned case illustrations or vignettes in support of a point I wish to make because of the various falsifications which are introduced but not acknowledged by that method. It must therefore be understood that instead of writing about a single patient I am writing about *the patient as if he or she were the representative* of a number of patients sharing the common characteristic which I now wish to highlight. More truthfully 'the patient' is a composite fictitious figure invented by me for the present purpose.

I shall refer to the present theme as *'separation anxiety'*, although the label cannot possibly do justice to the richness of living and deeply felt images that give rise to the term. One of the patients expressed what others had probably felt: I had words at my disposal for states of mind that felt uncontrollable to her. Because I had the ability to use words, she felt that I was, unlike her, in control of the situation. For that reason alone it seems desirable that there should be *more understanding* of dreams *than interpretation*. The exception to the rule would be when there is too much 'mutuality' (see below, p. 276), and a new separating definition of the analyst's function has to be found.

On the previous occasion I had *reacted against*, 'counter', the transference when I believed that I could assuage distrust by giving a personal article as a token of my reliability. I do not doubt that the token had been given with sincere sympathy. My own anxiety at the time made me focus on her inability to trust. I think 'separation anxiety' could not have emerged without this preliminary 'false' step. But it is also possible that my action delayed the arrival of the next phase.

This happened when the patient had had a series of erotic dreams in relation to other women before she dreamt that her mother was in bed with her which seemed a satisfying experience. In another dream about the same time there was the visual image of a nipple which she felt had penetrated her vagina. At the time of these dreams she had difficulty with her child, who developed distressing symptoms of anxiety unless she could sleep in mother's bed. Then a further dream occurred in which the patient could hear noises coming from her parents' bedroom.

I think that she could not have dreamt, remembered and told me these dreams without there having developed considerably more trust than there had been in the opening phase of the analysis. But I feel certain that the separation anxiety became the focus that had activated the transference reaction within myself which I call 'mutual'. Childhood memories and anxiety dreams were aroused which brought my own separation anxieties back to life. I had known about these from my previous analyses, but not as vividly and cogently as I could 'remember' in the present context. This seemed to me a newly constructed memory (see p. 24 above), rather than the re-emergence of a re-repressed content. The appearance of the mutual transference took me by surprise. I did not tell the patient about it, in case the mutuality would increase and become an illusory togetherness and thought it sufficient that she felt relieved after telling me her dreams. She was not too afraid to tell me that she felt 'better', but still worried that this could imply separation by my stopping the analysis.

Now the theme of separation and the anxieties connected with it affected us both and was in that sense mutual. But 'mutual' does not mean 'in the same way'. It needs underscoring that both the origin and manifestations were different (cf. Chapter 12, The Thematic Centre, p. 276).

I greeted my anxieties like an old acquaintance whom at first I was not altogether pleased to see, but later on was glad to get to know better. It was quite a discovery. I could appreciate afresh Jung's statement made in 'On the nature of dreams': *'The unconscious is the unknown at any given moment'* (*CW* 8: para. 469). And I was also glad that it was now possible to assist the patient in a way I had not been able to when I only knew that this anxiety was lurking underneath her persona, trying to break through by means of her symptoms which had distressed us and had prompted the action to which I referred.

The patient, on the other hand, reacted to her dreams with embarrassment and consternation before she felt relief. There were no associations other than the obvious relevance of her own child's behaviour. I did not interpret because I felt that the dreams *were* the interpretation we had been waiting for while she had longed for the emotional and bodily closeness she had needed from her mother, a longing she could not even admit to herself. There had been 'good reasons' why her mother could not supply this when it was needed and also for the patient to swallow her frustration and anger and to play along, feigning to be self-contained. The closeness she had not experienced she could neither accomplish nor let go. My own separation anxiety was of different origin and had, so far as I know, begun later in life. Yet our *separate* experiences of *the same theme* in the course of the analysis was good enough to effect a mutual transference. It would go without saying that I did not tell the patient about my own story, were it not for my wanting to emphasize the *separateness in mutuality*. I am grateful to Winnicott for having formulated that it is part of the maturational processes and certainly an essential capacity that analysts have to develop in order to be alone, especially in the presence of the patient

(Winnicott, 1965). Paradoxically perhaps, this increases the mutuality of transference, however different the mode of expression may be.

The meaning of 'mutual' and varying views on mutuality

An apology is due to the reader for having added yet another adjective to those already in existence for differentiating between special kinds of transference and countertransference. Thus we find 'illusory' and 'syntonic' (Fordham, 1957), as well as 'complementary' and 'concordant' (Racker, 1968, Lambert, 1981) and 'archetypal' among the terms in use. The latter can be traced back to Jung (CW 16: para. 381n), that is to say in addition to the popular terms 'positive' and 'negative' which give us no information beyond the most noticeable feeling tone. The advantage of 'mutual' is that it is an ordinary word compared with adjectives that start with the prefixes 'syn-' or 'con-', suggesting that there could be the kind of togetherness between the participants that analysts refer to by the pejorative word 'identification' because it can lead to the illusion of a 'symbiotic relationship'. 'Mutual', on the other hand, means 'possessed, entertained, or *done by each* towards or with regard *to the other*': it therefore comes very close to 'reciprocal', a word that can be applied to acts of friendliness as well as hostility (*Shorter Oxford English Dictionary*, emphasis added). However, the words by themselves are not patent-right nor safeguard against misuse. All this would not matter if the mutuality that pervades Jung's dialectical procedure 'where the therapist enters into relationship with another psychic system both as questioner and answerer' were not such a delicate problem on which all interpretations and indeed unspoken reactions hinge (*CW 16*: para. 8).

Although the word does not figure in Jung's writings, I have used mutuality here in connection with our understanding of the transference in general and of dreams in particular. In the example I gave, I referred to the coinciding of the patient's separation anxiety with vivid memories and dreams from my own childhood. There are indeed quite a number of hypotheses and descriptive terms in Jung's work which would explain the close connection between psychological events that go on in one person and affect another. The reason why this should be so is that the concept of the archetype is central to his work. Linked with it are the '*complexes*' (see below) which determine the affect with which the archetypes are experienced by the individual. (For details and definitions the reader is referred to *A Critical Dictionary of Jungian Analysis* by Samuels, Shorter and Plaut, 1986). It is also not uncommon that the affectively toned complex of one person touches off that of another who will react to it in his own way. When this occurs in daily life, understanding is swept away by emotions. But in analysis the exchanges that take place must be looked at in detail because emotional reactions alone cannot be relied upon to lead to a deeper understanding of oneself in relation to another person, including their and one's own 'dreams', both in the literal and metaphorical sense. Analysts try to deduce some generally valid laws (theory) from detailed observations, as scientists would, in order to increase the range of their empathic understanding. Unfortunately, this is a complicated matter because the observations do, in turn, depend on personality factors and preconceived notions which determine the angle of approach. (See also concepts of cure and global aims, below p. 53.) No matter what the analyst's theoretical position with regard to the mutuality of the enterprise, its success will largely depend on whether his/her theoretical viewpoint is so well integrated with his/her personality that (a) he/she need not think about it when working and (b) can nevertheless abandon it when the observations no longer seem to fit. These general remarks should be borne in mind when I introduce some theoretical divisions among post-Jungians and psychoanalysts concerning the present subject. There are some distinctions, which seem trivial at or shortly after the time they are made. For example, Jung speaks of complexes as 'splinter psyches' (*CW 8*: para. 203). Others are striking. For instance the complex is referred to as 'the architect of dreams and symptoms' (*CW 8*: para. 210). Also: 'complexes are splinter psyches' (ibid: para. 203). Among more recent formulations we find the complex seen as a 'part-self' (Fordham, 1979) and as a 'sub-personality' which Redfearn prefers (Redfearn, 1985). For example, some post-Jungians actually make use of the concept 'complex' while others seem no longer to find it of practical use. Foremost among the protagonists of the concept is Dieckmann whose recent *Komplexe* presents a comprehensive review (Dieckmann, 1991). Analysts are further divided according to whether they lean more towards the 'archetypal school' for whom the complex is a variant that stands, so to speak, between the archetype and the individual, or whether they tend more towards the 'developmental school', as I do. Whether such differences will remain important in historical perspective remains to be seen. Meanwhile the conflicts strengthen my plea for a graphic method of representation such as mapping which could clarify the divisions by making their origin and context visible. However, the concept of mutuality has roots in both camps.

First, it acknowledges the human disposition to react to the important events of life with patterns of behaviour that are ubiquitous and typical of our species, for example by behaving in accordance with a mythological motif or by the institution of rituals (see p. 103). Therefore, when a recurring theme is recognized and reflected in the transference the question analysts would ask themselves in the first place is not how pathological the patient's enactment is, but what personal knowledge they have of the pattern or theme that has become manifest.

Second, the variations on the theme are characteristic of the individual and shaped, not only by the environment, nor by the varying strength of instinctual drives and their interaction with hypothetical structures or agencies such as the ego and the self. An increasingly important addition to theory is that during psychic growth objects, or rather their representation in image form, become internalized and that fantasy plays an important part in this process. By means of pro- and introjections the object relations would play a decisive role in the individual's relationship to other persons.

Therefore the first, archetypal aspect of mutuality encompasses the universe of the human species. As such it is the unvarying background of all encounters. But the way we encounter our objects in and through the presence of another person is individually determined. It is *the combination* which makes the mutuality of real encounters possible as when:

Ships that pass in the night, and speak each other in passing.
Only a signal shown and a distant voice in the darkness.
(Longfellow)

Here the ship is both the unknown person, the 'other', as well as the (inner) object projected on to him/her. The 'speaking each other' may be seen as the archetypal background of meeting in the night. Signal and distant voice are our limited means. But the content of the meeting can often be better understood as the product of a person's history and cultural setting, that is developmentally. This is frequently the case, especially at the beginning of an analysis when the projected content appears unilaterally rather than mutually determined (see Figs 12.1, p. 253 and 12.2, p. 255). This view is closer to psychoanalysis than to archetypal psychology in general and the *'object relations'* theory ('British School') in particular.

However, the mutuality which I described in my example could also be 'explained' by an affinity of complexes, or as being due to one (or all) of the following: *'primitive identity'* ('participation mystique') or any other kind of 'identification' with the patient, or, as the result of the patient and I having moved into a certain *archetypal field* represented symbolically in dreams, both the patient's and my own. This would be in keeping with Dieckmann's finding when he and his co-workers explored the area of countertransference (Dieckmann, 1980). Thus in the example I gave it can be said that the 'archetype of separation' which Strauss postulated in her paper was activating the unconscious of both patient and analyst (Strauss, 1964). Or, again, the phenomenon could be understood as an example of Jung's 'synchronicity', events that coincided in time and were connected to each other by the agent of meaning.

Although Jung refers to *synchronicity as an 'acausal connecting principle'*, it is conceived of as being ultimately due to the special affective charge that surrounds archetypes and complexes (*CW 8*: paras 816–968). This charge is thought to restrict and heighten the focus of attention in one area and thereby to lower it in others where it becomes dimmed and produces what Jung following Janet (1903) called an 'abaissement du niveau mental.' It 'gives the unconscious a favourable opportunity to slip into the vacated space' (*CW 8*: para. 841). What in my example 'slipped in' was the painfulness of separation which I had not noticed at the time when I had been preoccupied with the patient's lack of trust. It was this that became the common meaning or the 'connecting principle'. 'Meaning', it could be argued, then takes the place of the cause, although in a rather subjective and exclusive sense of the word.

The reason why the views on mutuality are important in the work bears repeating: it is because the analyst is in a one-to-one situation about which he/she *can and may* only communicate to a very limited extent. Therefore it may help if I sketch in the development of the views mentioned which preceded the *object-relations* theory of psychoanalysis *and* of *'synchronicity'* in analytical psychology as follows.

When 'Über psychische Energetik und das Wesen der Träume' appeared in 1928, later to become 'General Aspects of Dream Psychology', Jung had developed (within the context of dream interpretation on the 'subjective', intrapsychic level) *an object relations hypothesis* (*CW 8*: paras 518–24). There he set out to give a psychological rather than a parapsychological explanation of phenomena. What he called the 'object-imago' must be understood as the early equivalent term for the modern 'internal object' or 'object-representation', now simply referred to as *the object*. Interestingly enough, the way Jung describes the various steps that lead to the self identifying with the object correspond exactly to the intro- and projective processes that object relations theory made use of at a later date. Jung realized the dangerous consequences of interpreting dreams on this intrapsychic level (see above, p. 28), most particularly in the case of patients we now refer to as borderline or narcissistic personality disorders.

Usually this kind of interpretation was 'somewhat disagreeable', as Jung put it. It touched on a person's shadow and conveyed that the fault is not in the stars, but that it is 'in ourselves that we are underlings'. Now such interpretations can be little short of disastrous for patients in the condition mentioned. Jung compares their situation with that of a person in a 'primitive' state of mind in whom there exists an identity between self and object. It is analogous to that of a 'primitive' whose objects, whether fetishes or ancestors, have, by a process of identification, acquired 'magical qualities'. A psychological interpretation of how this has come about would be tantamount to taking the objects away, thereby undermining the basis of that person's existence (ibid.). A modern approximation of Jung's hypothesis can be found in Kohut's 'self-objects' (Kohut, 1971).

But whatever happens to a destroyed *object*? Jung considers that it becomes a 'ghost', that is to say it goes on existing in an intangible form and exerts an influence on the subject 'which cannot be distinguished from psychic phenomena' (op. cit.). At this point one can sense the beginning of what was to become the principle of 'synchronicity' twenty-four years later. Here Jung's view differs radically from Winnicott's who thought it desirable that the destroyed object should become 'real'. If, for example, the object had been the analyst, the analyst should, at the end of the analysis be allowed to exist outside the patient's life; the former (internal) object having served its purpose should be granted *'externality'*. The object as such, that is the formerly inner object, had thereby ceased to exist. It had been *replaced by reality* (Winnicott, 1971). But maybe that was all the more necessary after the patient had been in as deep a state of dependence as Winnicott's management of the 'false self' in a state of transition to a 'true self' demanded (op. cit.). Or, to translate these concepts into Jung's terminology: the patient has acquired an effective *persona* to cope with life in an apparently independent way but continues to suffer as my patient did from the isolating effect of not being able to remove the actor's mask. To resume growth as a human being the patient will first have to become in some respect like a naked and dependent babe. This may account for Winnicott's hope that the analyst *as an object* representing a surrogate mother will disappear for good by becoming 'real'.

I think the different views on the fate of objects as seen in the late works of both Jung and Winnicott *is* of far-reaching consequence to the question of mutuality both during and after analysis. *During analysis* Jung's object-imago has, as we saw, an archetypal component, something that is not only of personal, but also of general validity. Individuals, by becoming aware of their historical and cultural setting, ancestry included, can discover where they truly live. They are not quite alone in their individuality, not 'all their own work', nor that of their parents. It is *the analyst's attitude* more than anything else that conveys to patients that they, as much as the analyst, are members of the same human family. What is more, *after analysis* they will be members *of a special family*, that is the group of analysed people to which the analyst also belongs. So the analyst as an object cannot altogether vanish. Something mutual, not just a ghostly internalized object, nor yet an 'external' analyst and patient will remain for quite some time. On the social level we are suspended between an I- and we-identity and need the balance as Elias in *The Society of Individuals* calls it (Elias, 1987). In our context this means that mutuality is precarious: the 'we' or 'us' group of analysed people does confront analysts and patients alike with the choice between the élitism of a clique and the isolationism of not belonging anywhere.

With these differing views regarding *the nature of mutuality* on the one hand, and the relationship between individuals and their objects on the other in mind, we are now ready to resume the job in hand and *consider how the amalgam of dreaming and analysing could be divided into separate parts*. The next section is intended to emphasize my plea that it is time cognitive methods (not to be mistaken for 'objective') found a place in thinking and reporting about the analytic process. Imaging and dreaming together in the romantic vein have had their own way for too long.

THE ROMANTIC VISION OF ANALYSIS

Searching for a dimension that could make 'mutuality' a critical rather than an ideal concept, it struck me that the basic attitude analysts bring to their work is every bit as important as the patient's basic assumption about analysis in relation to him/herself. *But what is a basic attitude?* How, and by whom, can it be determined? If, according to Strenger, there is a classic and a romantic vision of analysis, this could be a useful starting point (Strenger, 1989). Several objections arise against such a division, just because it is a division and analysts don't, as already mentioned, like to be labelled, especially not when a certain aura surrounds the label.

For instance, 'classic' could be associated with right, good, and 'romantic' with wrong, bad. Alternatively, many analysts might like to claim that they belong to both camps and thereby relativize the situation, and domesticate it, from the start. This would prevent the recognition of an otherwise useful division concerning attitudes that easily escapes notice. Again, it could be argued that the basic attitude must be part of the analyst's personality which, as Jung and others after him have pointed out, is more important than the theory to which the analyst subscribes. But 'basic attitude' is, I feel, a shade more precise than 'personality'.

The reason for referring to Strenger's paper is that it deepens my impression of the prevailing trend in analysis which favours the romantic vision. I think this is especially true of 'Jungian analysis'. If that be so, the danger of the useful tension between the two 'attitudes' being lost would mean a loss to analysis as a whole. Therefore, let us look at some details. Strenger quotes from Hulme's early paper: 'The view which regards men as a well, a reservoir full of possibilities I call romantic; the one which regards him as a very finite and fixed creature, I call classic' (Hulme, 1924).

Strenger puts Freud as the embodiment of the classic attitude, Ferencszi and Kohut as typical representatives of the romantic stance. I think an example of what an attitude is would be better than a definition. It may also throw light on the connection between a theoretical viewpoint and an attitude, if I were to put side by side two definitions of 'the unconscious'.

Freud: 'The unconscious, that is the "repressed"' (in 'Beyond the Pleasure Principle', 1920, and in the context of 'repetition compulsion').

(*SE 18*: p. 19)

Jung: 'The unconscious is the unknown at any given moment', see above (in 'General Aspects of Dream Psychology' and with special reference to 'the dreams compensating function').

(*CW 8*: para. 469)

These *ad hoc* quotations show the classic, 'reductive' attitude from which Freud's theory of repression stems. According to Strenger it points to a pessimistic view of human nature. Classicists would call it realistic. Jung's definition is functional. The psyche seen as a self-regulating system is definitely a romantic notion. One can sense the 'reservoir full of possibilities' that typifies the romantic stance. It informs Jung's work and that of most post-Jungians, myself included. Theirs is an optimistic view that sees the rich tapestry of phenomena of psychological experiences which express the unique individuality of the person. For Jung, as for Kohut, the highest stage of development is a cohesive self. Jung refers to 'self realization' and the process of 'individuation'. Although the importance of the individual is the tacit assumption on which all analysis is based, the romantic attitude in particular stresses the perfectibility of human nature.

There is further an enthusiasm that easily gathers around concepts of mutuality, such as the combined transference–countertransference which I described. The same holds good for symbols of the self that appear spontaneously such as mandalas (magic circles) do in dreams. Again, enthusiasm is easily aroused by synchronistic phenomena such as the wisdom contained in the metaphors with which the *I-Ching* (Chinese oracle) answers the questioner's state of mind (see also below, p.112).

Whatever the basic attitude, I agree with Strenger when he writes that the analyst inevitably transmits it to the patient. It 'colours all his interventions'. According to him, the patient will experience 'every interpretation on the background of the general attitude the analyst emanates' (Strenger, ibid.). It is particularly well conveyed by the analyst's voice to which the patient would listen the more acutely when unable to see the speaker's face and figure.

Let us return to the line-up behind the two visions. The mention of some of the most important names of the post-Freudian era to which Strenger refers would lead us too far here. (Surprisingly, Jung is not mentioned.) The polarization itself must determine the search for a mixed stance which in practice is probably more common than the extremes. Take Winnicott for example. In his attitude he was no doubt on the side of the romantics, wanting to find the 'true self' even if this means what I refer to as 'crazy creativity'. But then again, in the description of how he envisages the end of the analysis, we see the realism characteristic of classic analysis (see 'object usage' above, p. 32).

Balint, in his chapter 'Character analysis and new beginning', can appreciate the balance between two assertions derived from opposite camps (Balint, 1952). He quotes analysts on the question of whether our work can change character by changing a person's capacity to love (and hate). Some say you can, other equally experienced analysts according to Balint say the opposite. He writes that when this happens, as it frequently does among research workers, the question referred to has probably never been formulated precisely enough.

Here the enthusiasm engendered by the romantics can lead to short-term success. But in general it seems to me that the larger units, such as the Jungian and the Kohutian 'self' and Winnicott's 'true self', are more easily idealized than smaller ones such as the ego which also had its run in American ego psychology. We further recall Freud's 'ideal-ego'. But there is no such thing as an 'ideal self', because *Jung's 'self' is always an ideal*. Hence the merit of Fordham's 'deintegrates of the self' as a counterbalance (Fordham, op. cit.).

Of course, any concept can be idealized, even the search for psychic reality and the hatred of it. The 'absolute truth', Bion's 'O', in its unattainability leads to idealization (Bion, 1965). Although Bion in his astringency amounting to asceticism despises 'sensa', he has nevertheless put 'reverie' on the map. It refers to the mother's capacity to contain and transform the infant's raw, undifferentiated, 'beta elements' into shaped mental images. The idea of being able to fulfil this transforming, mothering function is, as Meltzer puts it, 'something essentially mysterious' (Meltzer, 1984). It seems a fascinating idea to analysts who it would seem take 'reverie' as if it were a technique of tranformation. Here the romantic begins to verge on the sentimental. The 'too much mutuality', referred to earlier, threatens the separateness of the partners which is equally essential, if analysis is to lead to an ending. Identification, and hence mutual idealization, is one way to describe the danger. This is also illustrated by Bion's concept of relationships expressed as 'symbiotic' in contrast to 'commensal'. This means 'a relationship in which two objects share a third to the advantage of all three'. The advantage to the third is hard to see unless we enter the realm of mystical rites as Jesus did when breaking bread and commanded his disciples: 'Take this and eat: this is my body'. (The New English Bible, Matthew 26: 26) (Bion, 1970). The image of commensal is people being at the same table and, presumably, eating off it. They remain, nevertheless, different people with different kinds of mental digestion even though they may partake of the same dream. The boundary between symbiotic and commensal is always critical, meaning that it is easily lost in which case mutuality reaches a state of *illusory sameness*. We all know this from having been in love. This is the point where *the analysis of the dream* as traditional medium of participation *can threaten to become 'the dream of analysis'*. I think this danger is very real today. The romantic's apotheosis of intuition is best epitomized by Meltzer: 'While listening to your dream I had a dream.' It is an abbreviated statement and he did *not* make it to the patient. But I have no difficulty in imagining other analysts who would, and would deplore the intrusiveness of that suggestion.

The question therefore arises if anything can be done to redress the balance by strengthening the classic vision, as without the necessary tension between the two basic attitudes, analysis, under the sway of the romantic vision, is in danger of getting swamped in a welter of images and *ad hoc* theoretical formulations. The romantic vision incorporates what Jungian analysts refer to as the 'Eros' principle and I agree that during analytic therapy this must be so. But on reflecting about what we do and aim at and how we can soberly communicate about it, 'Logos' would not be left out.

To return to my plea for some cognitive processing: in the third part of the book I suggest how mapping could help in recording observations according to the theoretical viewpoint adopted. As a method it is sufficiently far removed from the observed data, but not as abstract as the philosophical and mathematical thinking behind Bion's grid.

Just how far my thesis is removed from what I judge the mainstream of

'Jungian analysis' to be is shown by a paper a colleague wrote nine years before Strenger on much the same topic.

In his 'Romantic and classical views of analysis' Redfearn linked the romantic view with the primal relationship (Redfearn, 1980). 'Primal' implies something that is there right at the beginning, like in 'primordial image' or 'primal scream', something that is based on the individual's earliest experience. It is deduced that the analyst in this situation plays the role of the 'holding mother' who 'fits in' with the infant-patient. 'Primal' in terms of relationship is also close to Winnicott's 'nursing couple'. That is a patient who although adult, lives close to first things involving, 'the primal material of analysis, namely ego death and the realities, blood, faeces, slime, water etc. of being born and giving birth' (Redfearn, ibid.). This type of patient brings paintings, poetic writing and dreams to the analytic session. 'I felt myself a privileged witness of a profoundly integrative process in her', writes Redfearn in describing one such patient (ibid.). He distinguishes between such 'primal seekers' and 'primal-avoiders', the former being frequently associated with Jungian analysis.

Redfearn is well aware of the polarization, if not caricaturization he undertakes here in order to make his point. This particularly applies when he describes the second type of patient for whom a 'working relation' is the right analytic procedure and who is best suited for a classical Freudian analysis. Nevertheless the patient he uses as example related to him much more as a person than the first who was an artistic woman. In principle, Redfearn allows both types of patient and analyst to be of equal value. But twice he warns of analysts who impose their worlds on their followers and patients (ibid.). Fair enough. However, it is hard to see how the holding analyst-mother, who in the primal relationship fits in with the infant-patient and in whose analysis he felt a 'privileged witness', could possibly be at one and the same time imposing his world on the patient. So as it cannot be Redfearn who does the imposing, he must be writing about the other type of analyst. Without actually saying so, Redfearn shows his own bias towards the romantic view and the primal relationship.

I hope that this chapter has shown why I favour the classical vision which does not prevent me from flirting with 't'other dear charmer' (with apologies to John Gay, *The Beggar's Opera*).

Chapter 3

Can it be analysed?

Before continuing with the obstacles that prevent clarifying what analysis is about, I should like to deal with a possible objection to the undertaking as a whole. It goes something like this.

'By trying to unravel the compound of analysis, its theories, techniques, observations and its unique experiential quality you are in danger of bringing a conscious procedure to bear on something in which unconscious processes, the realm of the imagination, of intuition and empathy, play a major, if undefinable, role.'

While respecting this point of view I consider it outdated. Since to be an analyst has become a more or less recognized profession, the 'winged life' (with apologies to Blake's 'Joy') that inspired it at the turn of the twentieth century has become thoroughly earthed by institutionalization. The enthusiasm that was prevalent when analysts had to struggle to keep alive no longer inspires the profession as it did when analysis was a 'movement'. But the clock cannot be turned back. When there was such an analytic movement a temporary consensus about the essence of analysis existed because the theory was simple, the sense of discovery and hopes of cure ran high. Success was comparatively quickly achieved. And although it is true that analysis as a whole is more than the sum of its constituent parts, I feel it is time to review various aspects of analysis that may be called peripheral because they form the frame or setting within which it takes place but are none the less influential. After that has been done, it will, I hope, be possible to hazard an informed guess as to what it is that holds the whole contraption together despite all its strains and stresses. I shall begin by asking the question: *How can analysis be analysed when it cannot even be defined*?

The moment we take a close look at the phenomenon of analysis we can trace some of its components as having originated from older sources of knowledge about human beings. The idea of the 'Unconscious' predated Freud (Ellenberger, 1970). Also, the use of the couch goes back to hypnosis. It is not really surprising that after barely a hundred years the parentage of the new-comer should still be clearly visible.

Seen from the historic angle, analysis may appear as a blend of religion, neuro-psychiatry and philosophy; its roots reach down to mythology and anthropology. In addition, there are links with psychology, psychiatry and social science. When it comes to illustrative parallels with literature and especially poetry, we note that analysts have drawn on this source of wisdom from the start. Winnicott acknowledged these connections when he wrote that, if there was any truth in what he had to say, it would already have been dealt with by the world's great poets. He added, however, that such flashes of intuitive insights were not enough for the step-by-step labour of analysis (Winnicott, 1974). Much of the originality of analysis therefore depends on the method of application or technique which, to be credible, hence effective, has to become an integral part of the analyst's personality.

There are other background factors which are liable to escape notice in the hurly-burly of the daily analytic work. I draw attention to some of these in three short papers entitled 'What do you actually do?' (as asked by laymen) and 'What do we actually do?' (too rarely asked by analysts) (see pp. 118–134), while in the 'The presence of the third' I show that the socio-cultural environment is yet another factor, the influence of which on analytic work is often underestimated (Plaut, 1990). There I postponed looking into differences in analytic viewpoint which vary not only according to 'schools', but with the ideological climate at different geographical locations. These will be referred to in the chapter 'Where does analysis stand?' (p. 306).

Behind all the questions about the background and practice of analysis as a socio-cultural phenomenon in our time there are, as mentioned, two basic assumptions without which that phenomenon would be unthinkable. The first is the indubitable importance of the individual in our civilization; the other concerns the equally unquestionable belief in progress, meaning here the continuous evolution towards the improvement of mankind: an assumption that was, as Ellenberger reminds us, dear to Janet whose influence on Freud, but also on Jung, can hardly be overestimated (Ellenberger, 1970). Together these points constitute a whole category of influential 'thirds' which keep analysis going. Intangible, yet weighty when taken together, these factors account for the almost unsurmountable difficulty of making a comprehensive statement about the phenomenon and practice of analysis. In other respects, analysis may fairly claim to have repaid some of its indebtedness: analytic understanding has deepened and enriched the very roots from which it has sprung. In addition, it has opened up new perspectives and insight in other fields, such as art history, literary criticism, social sciences and politics.

I draw attention to the *reciprocity between the roots and ramifications of analysis* at the outset, because if one thought of analysis exclusively as a *psychotherapeutic method*, it could easily be forgotten that its linking function between the humanities existed virtually from the start.

At all events, as a psychotherapeutic method, analysis cannot be separated from its cultural context and climate. For example, commissions of psycho-analysts have sat for years and years in order to define analysis proper from analytical psychotherapy: all to no avail (references in Cremerius, 1984). (I shall use 'analysis' to cover all psychotherapeutic methods which are based on the concepts of Freud and Jung and subsequent generations of analysts unless I consider that the differences warrant pointing out.)

There are a number of reasons why no unanimity on such an important issue has been reached. If I start to enumerate those which seem most relevant here, I shall also have begun to answer the question: '*So, what do I mean by "analysing analysis"*'? Let us start with some reflections. When we cast our minds back to the beginnings of psychoanalysis, we can hardly escape the conclusion that the moment of epoch-making discoveries has passed.

Compared with Freud's 'Interpretation of Dreams' (1900) and 'The Psychopathology of Everyday Life' (1901) on the one hand, and Jung's 'Transformations and Symbols of the Libido' (1912), later renamed 'Symbols of Transformation', all subsequent discoveries have been less seminal. This is not to say that subsequent pioneering work has been less important to practising analysts. But the knowledge contained in those works has become absorbed into the repertoire of reasonably well-educated people in our culture and students of analysis still use these books for reference. Post-Freudian (Brown, 1961) and post-Jungian (Samuels, 1985) writings are not only by definition but also ideologically unthinkable without the early researches and discoveries that have put analysis on the map. However, the period of 'extending' the pioneering work has also passed (see below, p.41f).

We can marvel at the vision of those who pioneered analysis. But had vision not been combined with tenacity, their brain-children would not have survived. Both Freud and Jung fought with grim determination for their survival. By 'their' I mean their own as well as that of their work: the one without the other has become unimaginable. But they were both dependent on a circle of loyal supporters, Freud, first on the scene, more obviously so than Jung. One has only got to recall 'The Committee' and the seven rings which Freud presented to the seven men around him, in order to sense again the desperate need for affirmation. Jung did not surround himself with an old guard. Instead, he seems to have attracted intelligent women as followers and admirers. Neither he nor Freud brooked opposition. Of course, they were no more single-minded nor less obsessed by their vision than, say, Galileo, Columbus or Pasteur who all had to make use of *the passion of their convictions* to bring their work to fruition. But the analysts were – and still are – at a disadvantage: there is no mathematical, nor directly physically observable and measurable proof of their findings. The discoveries they made depended on affirmation by patients and colleagues who were enthused or antagonized by the new light they had shone into the dark continent of the mind. Causes and connections, as well as motivations and meanings of human behaviour ignored or condemned in the past, now led to a new understanding of our frailties. Opposition from the 'Establishment' was, not surprisingly, formidable: what was feared was amorality as the result of the discovery of infantile sexuality.

In fact, it was a *new morality* that was dawning. But that took some time to sink in. In other words, analysis had a direct effect on the upbringing of children and thereby on civilization itself. It is important to recall these beginnings in order to appreciate that Freud and his followers were in very real danger of being treated as heretics or insane.

But there were also psychological dangers of a different order, such as Bion has shown, i.e. the relation between the visionary or mystic and the Establishment is fraught: on the one hand, with the burden of Messianic hope, and on the other with destructive envy; a phenomenon that is not restricted to our field of research (Bion, 1970). The visionaries themselves live in fear lest their mission should fail. Their anxiety is not restricted to open opposition: what they and their followers fear even more is betrayal by someone in their midst, a Judas. Hence precautions must be taken. But since we are here dealing with mythologies, these precautions invariably fail. For example, without Christ's betrayal and its consequences Christianity would not have become a world religion.

Analysts should not have been surprised if they remained subject to such laws as they had discovered. Freud's secret 'Committee' only worked up to a point: Adler and Steckel had already defected when it was founded, Jung, who never became a member of it, broke with Freud, shortly after the foundation. The historic 'split' furthered separate development. Although the history of the defections can be read up in detail in Jones's book on Freud's life and work and in Gay's *Freud, A Life in our Time*, it bears repeating in the present context, because the 'splits' among analysts have continued right up to the present (Jones, 1953, Gay, 1988). A balanced and liberal view on 'The significance of the dissidents for psychoanalysis' had recently been written by Cremerius, a senior German psychoanalyst (Cremerius, 1984).

The opponents of analysis rejoiced: dissensions meant that since analysts could not ever agree among themselves, they need not be taken seriously anyway. Analysts who have witnessed and survived these highly charged upheavals that for a time at least divided their ranks into friends and foes, can, in retrospect, regard these divisions as a sign of further growth. At any rate, all parties are liable to claim that they are either loyal because they follow their founder both in the letter as well as the spirit, or because they are *extending* the original discoveries into new areas, leaving the foundations, however, untouched. Both claim the father's blessing.

True, differences in personality and personal premises (see p. 39) also add to the rivalry today just as much as ever. Then, as now, the dissidents, having gathered enough strength and support, will issue a declaration of independence much to the indignation of the establishment. After the splitting process has been repeated enough and the distance from the founding fathers has increased by a few generations, the phenomenon loses the element of shocked surprise and becomes something of a routine. After a time, the painful ideological splits yield to the soothing awareness of a pluralistic development.

My sweeping statement about the time of the epoch-making discoveries being over is based on the observation that none of the modifications and extension of the old theories offered by Freud and Jung have had a comparable impact. Although it is too early to say, I doubt whether evidence from the couch and chair alone will take analysis as a therapy any further, although methods of direct observation, for instance of infants, may influence existing analytic theories. Also improvements in reviewing and communicating analytic methods, such as I suggested at the end of the previous chapter, may yet lead to discoveries which persons outside the dyad can appreciate.

WHAT DISSENSIONS?

William James used 'pluralism' in his *Varieties of Religious Experience* in contradistinction to monism (James, 1902). Wallerstein in his presidential address to the International Psychoanalytic Association, 'One psychoanalysis or many?', applied pluralism to the present situation when many and divergent theories concerning mental functioning, development and illness have become the rule rather than the exception (Wallerstein, 1988). By sanctioning two newcomers, 'the present unconscious' and George Klein's 'clinical theory', Wallerstein attempts to rally the supporters of the 'One' psychoanalysis (Sandler, 1984, Klein, 1976). Positively, he restates Freud's 'cornerstones' of 1914: analysis of the transference and of the resistance, of unconscious fantasy and of conflict, and allows all those who practise accordingly to stay within the fold.

While acknowledging that the Jungian movement has endured worldwide as an alternative psychotherapeutic system, Wallerstein regrets that these analysts have appropriated the title 'psychoanalyst'. For a negative, excluding criterion he relies on a paper written by a Jungian analyst concerning Jung's first patient, mentioned in Jung's thesis, published in 1902, which clearly shows neglect of transference as well as emphasis on the complex (rather than the conflict). After specifically disclaiming any political motive and acknowledging his relative ignorance of the Jungian developments, he nevertheless proceeds with what I can only call the excommunication (Wallerstein, ibid.). But that was not the end of the affair. As it turned out, the excommunication became an unimportant side-issue compared with the problems that had been raised and became evident in the choice of the theme of the next International Psychoanalytic Congress, Rome, 1990, namely 'The common ground'. The search was led by Wallerstein as president. Three speakers had been invited as representatives of as many major directions within psychoanalysis (Wallerstein, 1990). In essence, Wallerstein repeated his impassioned plea for 'our overarching theoretical structure or diversity of structures (as at present) [which] is not yet adequate either to those common clinical understandings or to our deep needs as a discipline and as a science of the mind.' A closer look at 'common clinical understandings' reveals that despite avowed theoretical differences, the analytical method evokes comparable observational material. This does not satisfy a science of the mind. Ideologically, as Schafer in his reply observed, the theme of the Congress as such implied a conservative value system and expresses the hope that the regrettable differences can eventually be counteracted by a single master text (Schafer, 1990). Clearly, the search for common ground represents a gallant rearguard action.

The true line-up which becomes evident is between 'observable data in our consulting rooms' and thereby the reconstruction of causes, historical truth on the one hand and, on the other, the humanistic stance that combines narrative truth with a hermeneutical discipline. The latter implies the interpretation of *the meaning* of a text, originally the Bible, and the acceptance of 'a congenial and satisfying story-line or accounting of the clinical interactions of the consulting room' as Wallerstein pejoratively calls it (Wallerstein, 1990). The, for him, undesirable shift is to 'a psychology that is based only on reasons, the "why" of human behaviour and not at all like a science which is based on causes, the "how" of human behaviour' (Wallerstein, 1988).

Here we encounter indeed an important and possibly unbridgeable difference in analytic attitude, although historical and narrative truth may occasionally coincide, as when a description given in analysis of the patient's maltreatment as a child is borne out by documentary evidence or coincides with facts provided from other sources. But this does not mean that narrative and historical truth do generally and precisely coincide. It is quite true that the neglect of a 'scientific' explanation of a complaint can do harm if interpretations that are based on motives and meaning (hermeneutic) are insisted on. In my experience this is exceptional and I find myself close to the attitude and clinical approach that Wallerstein brands as unscientific. Yet I cannot agree with the ultimate division of analysts into scientists (*pace* Wallerstein) and hermeneutic heretics because of the all-important role that the imagination, or fantasy, plays in linking causes and meanings within the context of the analytic setting.

Schafer in his view of Wallerstein's address comes closest to what does seem to be truly common ground on the methodological level when he states that we *create* common ground inasmuch as we establish and understand analytic content by the making, breaking and remaking of *contexts*: that analytic understanding comes about as the result of dialogue between analyst and patient; and that this *dialogue*, spoken and unspoken, *shapes the observational data* of analysis (emphases added). Whether the way this is done – Wallerstein's science-seeking 'how' – can be recorded by present methods of communicating about the work is an open question about which I shall have more to say in Part III.

Schafer further draws attention to linguistic considerations which are of direct relevance when common ground is looked for in order to minimize dissensions and assertions threaten to usurp the place of reasoned argument (ibid.). The words (technical terms) used by various analysts may be the same, yet they mean something rather different. The first example he gives is 'trans-ference'. It is a good example, because having been present at more than one discussion among Jungian analysts from various institutes, I can say that all maintained they analysed the transference. On going into detail however, it soon transpired that the term was used differently and the method of analysing the transference varied considerably and this was not just a matter of personal style.

What can be learned from the discussion? The attempt to conserve common ground seems futile; looking carefully into small, well-defined areas of dissensions may bear fruit. Here the 'how' that Wallerstein stresses would come into its own, a point to which I shall pay attention when we come to the non-existence of a separate Jungian metapsychology (see p. 47). Turning from the detail to the wide vista of analysis, we must agree with Ellenberger who compares the case of Freud with that of Darwin and comes to the conclusion that the historic significance of an idea is not limited to the area that was in the originator's mind (Ellenberger, 1970). He goes on to say that the extensions, additions, interpretations and distortions of the theory may result in others built on totally different basic principles. Yet all were in reaction to Freud's psychoanalysis (op. cit.). The situation seems to me comparable to the 'big bang' theory of the origin of the universe. That is to say, we are witnessing in the various consequences of psychoanalysis a natural phenomenon. But here again, the theory that is formulated or preferred by the individual analyst depends much on the kind of person on whom the seed falls. Therefore, although in the case of analysis we are dealing with an 'expanding universe', the time for significant extensions within the field of analysis as a therapy appears to be over.

Of course it will remain convenient to sail under old flags with well-established reputations. Also analytic institutions are, like all others, subject to inertia. But ancestors can be honoured without being worshipped, and discoveries, even rediscoveries, are more important than old loyalties. Cremerius (op. cit.) takes a more realistic view of the situation than Wallerstein when he writes, 'The roof many times extended – still stands; the cornerstones have nearly all been replaced by others' (author's translation). Cremerius then gives specific examples to substantiate his architectural metaphor of the state of analysis, as indeed he does when he writes about the history of the splits. To his mind, the latter originate rather more from psychopathological than from scientific or theoretical causes. In my view, scientific convictions cannot be separated from 'psychopathology'. Interestingly enough Cremerius makes out a case against Freud, writing that he repeated in an affect-laden and thoughtless way the repudiation of people who were in disagreement with him; an experi-ence to which Freud himself had been exposed for many years (ibid.). It does not seem as if we always learned from experience.

WHAT ARE CONTEXTS MADE OF?

The dissensions among analysts which bring about splits and highlight the pluralism of theories are not the only reason why the analysing of analysis is a complex undertaking. The provision of contexts in which Schafer can find common methodological ground is therefore welcome and important enough to deserve detailed consideration; without this, 'context' would be in danger of becoming another global term about which specious agreement can be reached but no real clarification of the intricacies would have been achieved.

Causes, meanings, aims

There exists a close connection between the aim of a therapy and the concept of the cause for which it is sought. When matters are as straightforward as the broken leg of a healthy person as the result of a fall, questions of diagnosis, treatment and prognosis don't tax our ingenuity. The cause is clear and the aim is simple, that is restitution of function. But if accidents occur repeatedly, questions will be asked about 'accident proneness' or, dependent on the culture, about malign influences or insulted deities. Gone is the simple explanation: gone also is the simple criterion of cure. Of course, the leg will have to be immobilized anyway. No psychological theory is required for that.

However, other remedies will be resorted to additionally, depending on the belief of causation. Psychotherapy of some sort is likely to be used in our culture, just as exorcism or placatory rituals are appropriate to others. Let us assume that these are the context to the 'text', that is the complaint, in this case the broken leg.

My naïve example is intended to serve as introduction to the complex subject of therapeutic aims in relation to psychological causes. Is it possible to analyze without an aim? How do we link the presenting complaint (symptom) with the cause on the one hand and the outcome of our intervention, analysis, on the other? What happens when the outcome differs from the aim? Here analytic literature does not abound with references and what one can find is scattered. I should like to attempt brief answers before going into details.

Clearly, it is not possible to analyse without an aim. Analysis is based on concepts and theories such as the unconscious mind and repressed motives. So to analyse must mean to bring light into these areas. To apply a theory is to have an aim, and an aim to have a hope, if not actually a desire to see it fulfilled. Therefore Bion contradicts himself when he says that the analyst should be free from desire on the one hand and to be blind to anything that does not belong to his 'vertex'. The sharply focused psychoanalytic point is an aim in itself and implies others. (See also, below, p. 48 and Chapter 14.)

As patients we also have an aim which is commonly referred to as 'getting better', meaning to get rid of obstacles (symptoms) that prevent us from leading a 'normal' or fulfilled life. But the modesty of this aim hides the enormous curiosity that we humans have about ourselves coupled with, if not the hope of immortality, then certainly the Utopian myth of infinite improvability. Add to this aim the further illusion that it can be achieved with the help of a charismatic person and you have sufficient common ground on which analyst and patient can meet. A successful analysis therefore implies a balance between disillusionment and a modicum of satisfaction that is 'reality', alias the human condition.

Freud's trauma theory was based on strict 'causal-determinism' which made the aim of analysis a foregone conclusion: full recognition of the cause would be followed by restitution of function and unimpeded enjoyment of reality. The theory demanded that there had been defences, notably repression, that served patients to cope with the trauma without having to face it. On the other hand, they paid for the avoidance of open conflict by the compromise solution expressed in symptom formation.

The state of the ego, say, its immaturity or weakness at the time of the trauma and the possible repetition of the latter was important, as was the individual disposition to be 'traumatized' or to regress (give up ego-control). When it was not just a matter of recovery by means of catharsis, as might have been sufficient in cases of 'shell-shock', but of a psychological trauma in childhood developing into a fully fledged neurosis, a detailed understanding of the psychodynamics and psychopathology was required of the analyst. To make it effective the analyst had to be equipped, i.e. he had to understand and master the technique of analysis.

Among the first technical terms that Freud had used was 'overdetermination', signifying that a symptom could have more than one meaning or that more than one cause had contributed (*SE 4*: p. 135). Again, the symptom might have been reinforced on several levels of the personality (Rycroft, 1968). It supports my initial argument that the term found parallel usage five years later in Freud's 'Interpretation of Dreams' (op. cit.).

What had happened between 'Hypnosis' and 'Studies on Hysteria' was that intrapsychic causes had been recognized as interacting to a significant extent with the external sources of trauma (op. cit.). The importance of this to the present theme is that the intrapsychic causes, e.g. elaborations as by dreams and fantasy, contributed their own message and meanings. The latter are open to much wider and varied interpretations, because meaning, as we shall see in discussing the specific Jungian outlook, has purposive and future implications and therefore opens the door to speculative aims of a 'global' kind (see below p. 53).

When the defences against traumatization had been recognized, the state of the ego assessed and the specific psychopathology diagnosed, the analyst would be in a position to interpret the a-verbal and unconscious language of symptoms into everyday language that allowed assimilation of the trauma into consciousness. The idea was that the insight so gained, both on the intellectual and emotional plane, would make further repression and hence symptoms unnecessary. Energy previously required to keep up defences would thus be freed and the patient would get on with life. Or so it was hoped. As this did not always eventuate, the theory had to be overhauled and the technical equipment changed or added to.

I shall continue with my historical outline in order to demonstrate only some of the landmarks that point to 'additions'. The analytic theory of infantile sexuality, also known as the instinctual drive or 'libido' theory was called topographic to indicate the locality and phases of sexuality from oral and anal to genital; it was followed by the structural theory, emphasizing the intrapsychic struggles between *id, ego* and *superego*. Then Ego-psychology and object relations theory followed and later still came Kohut's self psychology. Each stage in theory building had a curious air of finality about it. At the time of its inception it seems totally convincing, as Jung pointed out (*CW 16*: para. 154). Here was the equipment to make previously untreatable patients analysable. The obstacle that had previously blocked the road to success could be removed. Although the earlier theory had not been altogether useless, it had certainly been incomplete. (Naturally, this would in due course apply to the newcomer as well.) Thus each addition to analytic knowledge made the relation of the existing parts to each other more complex.

Therefore, a special branch was set up and called *metapsychology* with duties to survey the hypothetical 'psychic apparatus' and to be responsible for energy distribution among the dynamic, structural, genetic, developmental and adaptational aspects of theories. The hope was that eventually metapsychology would result in a 'general theory' as understood in natural science; see also Freud's 'The Project' intended to create a psychobiology. Freud called metapsychology 'the witch'. Jung, who did not distinguish between metapsychology and theory, called the latter 'the very devil'. (I shall discuss the consequences of this lack of differentiation, using 'the opposites' as example; see p. 121.)

Metapsychology may be useful to distinguish between observations during and discussions after the event, when, in the absence of the patient, various concepts and theories are invoked to help in understanding the events. Theories which are close to the clinical observations can be thus distinguished from others which are more abstruse. Perhaps the separating out of metapsychology from observations and theories also helps one to notice when the whole system ('psychic apparatus') is threatening to 'take over', i.e. begins to outweigh other considerations of a practical kind, going off on its speculative own. As I see it, the 'psychic apparatus' represents, in essence, an extension and refinement of the methods of detection that had made the 'Interpretation of Dreams' possible (op. cit.). It was a fiction intended to fill the gap, i.e. before there were sufficient well-analysed cases from which general conclusions could be drawn (*SE 17*: p. 105). Yet this 'fiction' had a way of acting as if it were the much wanted scientific explanation. If, therefore, the analytic aim directed toward research is given priority, this too can become 'global', i.e. all-encompassing at the expense of the therapeutic aim, although an excuse can be made by saying that in principle all research must, in the long run, benefit the patient.

A way out of these entanglements and a new perspective on causes and meanings was offered by Bion (1960). His 'desiderata' that analysts should proceed 'without memory or desire' at the beginning of each session and simply observe transformations of mental processes seemed designed to prevent the analyst's repetition compulsion. Inasmuch as 'desire' expresses the hope to be therapeutic this must not, of course, be discouraged. However, Bion pointed out the value of making short-term observations from the 'psycho-analytic vertex'. This could reduce the analyst's compulsion to think of causes and to be preoccupied with the complex steps leading up to a successful ending of analysis. Unintentionally (I think) Bion also included the possibility of becoming less spellbound by Freud's (1914) 'cornerstones' of analysis: the analysis of transference and resistance which have for so long held undisputed sway.

Various explanations aimed at cure

The distinction between causes and aims is in some ways artificial, as is also the distinction between 'efficient' and 'final' causes. If we take the (hypothetical) sexual instinct, we are inclined to consider its root in biology as the cause and its fulfilment, as by orgasm and/or propagation. In either case the instinct is seen both as the effective and the final cause of much of our behaviour. Or, again, we may think of the death instinct as the efficient cause of destructive activity; in its aim it is final. (Very!) The moment we have psychological concepts which presuppose a 'psychic apparatus' – or, as I prefer to call it, 'system', designed to explain how things happen now and what preceded the present event as well as its likely consequences, its cause and aim can no longer be sharply differentiated.

But this wish to make sense and to explain may be regarded as the primary driving force of analysis. We meet it as the 'epistemophilic instinct' (Klein) which is, as we saw, also present in the form of the patient's creation of 'context' (p. 45, above). I regard this wish as the dominant aim of Freud's psychology and consider that 'causal determination' is a manifestation of this wish. The saying 'You cannot interpret too much!' (where interpretation is regarded as a kind of explanation given to or by the patient) is based on the assumption that everything that happens in analysis must have an (unconscious) cause. This should be rendered explicable and hence interpreted. The technique of constant interpretation that stems from it can be regarded as an example of a 'dominant' aim. (For definition see also Midgeley, 1988.) The single-minded attitude that goes with it can, for a time, achieve a great deal. In the long run it spells, in my view, poverty, of the kind that can be seen in the miser or addict.

I am bringing some philosophical thoughts into my historical sketch of causes and aims because I want to point out a dual danger inherent in analysis. If in the following I refer to the one as 'Freudian' and the other as 'Jungian', this is not to be taken literally, but rather as a device for referring to contrasting approaches to analytic understanding of phenomena and, therefore, also to techniques of analysing.

Freud's causal determinism was linked to an attitude that Thomä and Kächele call 'materialistic monism', meaning that his model remained under the guidance of the body–mind unity which stemmed from his neurophysiological training and manifested itself in the 'Project for a scientific psychology' (about 1879) (Thomä and Kächele, 1987). (It should be remembered that Freud later abandoned the idea of combining neurophysiological and analytic findings.) But in his view on causes and consequently therapeutic aims he never went beyond explanations within a rigorously cohesive but increasingly complex system of theories etc. These were to make sense of clinical observations but also, one feels, to explain failures as for example by the 'negative therapeutic reaction' (see Rycroft, 1968).

Jung, on the other hand, started off in psychiatry and his early experimental studies were psychologically oriented, e.g. the association test. Against the monistic view of the Christian church, as he saw it in St Augustine's teaching, 'evil is nothing but the privation of good', he took up a dualistic standpoint which was also reflected in his analytic work: all entities were known by their opposites, e.g. good and evil (see p. 122, below) (*CW 9, II*: para. 89). He called his chief analytic method 'amplification', meaning that he enlarged the unconscious material, say of a dream, by means of adding around it analogous themes gathered from a wide range of the humanities: learning, art, literature, religion etc. Characteristically, the analytic material was not systematically retraced to infancy or childhood nor treated as being due to a trauma in the patient's past. The main features of a patient's history were grouped together as 'archetypal constellations' and 'complexes'. Therapeutic success would then be seen in terms of a *reorientation* of the patient towards him/herself, and his/her background and environment, resulting in an enrichment of the psyche. The aim and method was thus seen as a synthesis rather than analysis. The cause of the neurosis, although by no means irrelevant, was less important for the curing of it than the (inferred) aim. In other words, the explanation of causes was along purpose- and meaning-determined lines within a comparatively elastic system. The teleological explanation depended for confirmation on the analyst's knowledge of a health- (=wholeness) seeking, non-pathological current in the patient's psyche. According to Jung's notion of illness, the patient would be suffering from something like a lack of vitamins rather than a trauma. The origin of the condition would then be seen arising in the socio-cultural sphere, only secondarily affecting the individual's psychology: 'Modern Man' had lost his roots and connectedness with the symbolic life. A new synthesis rather than analysis would be the therapeutic aim and method (*CW 16*: para. 365 and *CW 9,2*: para. 390n). It should be added that he also recognized 'psychic infection' as a cause of illness to which analysts were particularly exposed. This too has a collective aspect in that whole populations might succumb to it. (An obvious reference to Nazi Germany.) We can see from the examples that teleological explanations of causes have values attached to them.

Progress toward the analytic aim in terms of a Freudian model can be viewed as a linear progression, e.g. ego strength would be increased by the end of analysis. It was further expected that patients would be able to withstand the onslaught of both the id and the superego. In ordinary terms, they could cope with the demands of their instincts as well as of their conscience by means of an unanxious and balanced judgement. If all had gone according to precept, every part of the patient's story as it unravelled would articulate, via the 'psychic apparatus', with explanatory analytic concepts. And all this had been brought about by what was called 'standard analytical technique'. Questions after causes might then have been answered according to the following over-simplified schema, Table 1:

Table 1   Causes and explanations

Questions of cause	*Analytic explanations*
1 What was the origin of the ailment?	Diagnosis: Hysteria, due to trauma
2 How had this caused illness?	Repression, due to ego weakness
3 Why was this the cause of suffering?	Patient preferred symptoms to conscious conflict and suffering

The schema shows that the traditional fourth question after the final cause, also called the 'teleological explanation', need not be asked; the patient is suffering as the result of not wanting to suffer. All that would be required to bring about a *cure*, would be a simple reversal of the situation described in answer to the third question, that is the *transformation* that Freud had written about as early as 1895, from hysterical misery into ordinary unhappiness. The notion of cure was also contained in the last sentence of the 1895 paper (as revised in 1925: the patient would be better equipped to cope with ordinary unhappiness because of his *recovered psychic life* (emphasis added) (*SE 2*: p. 305). But the first of the twin dangers to which I referred above was that patients refused to see that the exchange offered was a reasonable bargain from which they would benefit: some remained unreasonable.

Let us return now to Jung's model of causes and aims. Cure did not so much depend, as I said, on the tracing of a definite cause to its earliest beginning, although connections and contexts, say in the form of a characteristic family pattern or a religious background, were taken into consideration; so was the diagnosis, at least in distinguishing between neurosis and psychosis. (The latter was not, however, regarded automatically as untreatable.) On the other hand, the final cause of the ailment and its symptoms, in the form of a teleological explanation, was now so dominant that it would not be too much to say that the second and third cause, see the above schema, became correspondingly unimportant. And what was the central aim or telos of this spirally (not as in the first model, linear) progression towards the centre? Well, it was known by different names, e.g. integration, self-realization, individuation and the like (see Table 2). The 'meaning' of the presenting symptoms could already be seen as pointing to the central aim. According to this model, the analyst, with his knowledge of mythology, fairy tales, anthropology, alchemical symbolism etc. was equipped to point out parallels with the patient's dreams, spontaneous paintings and other unconscious material.

By means of the educational factor more or less implicit in all analyses, some patients could be helped to appreciate the symbolic value of their symptoms. But, as with Freud's model, the ability to suffer was regarded as a precondition to reaching the aim, 'cure' or as good as, because of becoming more whole. Although this could never be completely achieved, progress in that direction, by a 'circumambulation' would bring one closer. The journey would take the form of a spiral (see 'spiral' and 'labyrinth' p. 233 below). There is a close connection in both models between the assumed causes and explanations and the therapeutic aims (see Table 2, p. 53). However varied and difficult the obstacles on the road, the name of the road itself was 'transformation' or, simply, change, namely change in the relation of psychic structures or 'apparatus', change in the distribution of psychic energy (libido), change in attitude and symptomatology. At all events, 'change'. Here then are the relevant differences and danger inherent in the two models summarized: in the first, patients were seen as recovering their psychic life, whereas in the second the hope is that they will discover it.

If the danger with the Freudian model was, as we saw, that patients would not see what they were being offered as a bargain, the danger with Jung's was that they would accept it. For who would not be pleased to discover that they had riches, dreamed-of riches, within themselves that made the experiences of the past tolerable, traumas and all, and those of the present exciting? Perhaps they could face the present and look to the future with greater confidence than before?

If I have exaggerated the danger inherent in the second model, it could be for a personal reason: I once escaped from it. But there is, I think, a genuine and objective danger in the neglect of detailed investigation of the question 'how'. The 'causa finalis', like the other causes, may only work by the grace of God (Jung's 'deo concedente') but it would be irresponsible to leave all the work to Him. If recovery of health were the aim of analysis, the analytic model would be close to the medical notion of restitution of normal function. If health were to be discovered, by means of understanding the manifestations of the unconscious psyche, e.g. the symbolism of dreams, the model could be called heuristic. This makes it into something close to a revelation in which the elements of re- and dis-covery, as well as of efficient and final causes, are inextricably interwoven.

I cannot leave this statement about the link between causes and aims and their connection with concepts of 'cure' without giving another thought to the doubtful role of the Freudian 'psychic apparatus'.

Whether analysts regret or enjoy the existence of this contrivance is not as important as that it had apparently to be invented in order to account for and control the obstacles that were cropping up all the time in the form of new 'resistance' to the application of theories designed to uncover and understand causal networks which, when unravelled, would lead to a logical conclusion. Did the apparatus, in the service of causal determinism and rigorously applied by conscientious analysts, possibly also reinforce resistance? Differently put, could the analyst's wish to control the analytic process and to see his/her theory confirmed by favourable results be the cause of a secondary trauma against which the patient defended him/herself? Whatever the answer, it seems more than likely that the apparatus lends itself to intellectual games. It can fascinate by the power to work out a solution to intricate problems as well as vindicate its existence by curing the patient. The excitement of the chase can become the *analyst's repetition compulsion*. Here is an illustration of some of the points mentioned.

A patient came regularly a few minutes late to his analytic sessions which he left of his own accord just as early. The conscious message of this behaviour seemed to be: 'I don't want to be a nuisance.' As he had expressed himself similarly in so many words, the question was, why did he continue to enact the message as well? Of course, the timing device had another aim which I understood as a self-assertion, a declaration of his independence from my fixing the time and duration of his sessions. Realizing the compulsive nature of his behaviour, I had tried to interpret it on several levels, e.g. developmentally, bringing in the persons to whom it related then as it did to me now, his justified anxiety about being dependent and so on. Of course, the patient realized that I felt provoked by the persistence of his behaviour and my frustrated hope that the right interpretation of the cause would change the timing pattern. However, it recurred after a brief interval during which he tried to please me by coming too early and by waiting politely until I told him to leave. I had plenty of evidence of the hidden aggressive component which seemed to surface in this and other ways, but my attempts to make it overt only seemed to make matters worse. I then realized that the patient had no option but to repeat the pattern as he had done over a very long time. I said I knew that he had to behave in this particular way and that I could bear it, which was true. There was no immediate change, but he forgot about the time for leaving and then became more relaxed about the time of his arrival too.

I quote this trifle as I think it shows how, in practice, one occasionally gets on better without the psychic apparatus, defences and all; and without interpretations too. My words formulated what I had empathically felt. 'Something understood.' Not explained. Which brings us to some of the large issues mentioned.

GLOBAL AIMS

I refer to a series of aims of analysis, whether implicit or clearly known by special terms, as 'global' because of their all-encompassing nature. The latter makes these aims harder to define than to describe. Even when descriptions are supported by illustrations these may not speak to readers unless their own experience and imagination permits them to identify some known element. One could, for example, say that the global aim of analysis is to make the unconscious conscious; or, in terms of the person, to bring about a transformation from a less to a more healthy (whole) state of mind. But such a formula may not convey anything even when illustrated with the help of myth, fairy-tale or parable.

On the other hand, '*global*' can apply to small issues as well as large. At the end of the previous section I illustrated a small step in an analysis as an example of the general principle of not persevering with an interpretation, no matter how correct, when interpretations as such had shown themselves to be counterproductive. This was a detail and insignificant as such, if it had not embodied both a general observation and a therapeutic aim, that is to free the patient of his compulsion. I allowed it to override my larger aim of using interpretations to make the unconscious conscious. In contrast to the therapeutic aim the latter constitutes the analyst's global aim. One hopes, of course, that the division does not have to be invoked too frequently and that analysts will more often than not find Blake's 'holiness in the minute particular'. However, 'global' generally conjures up a comprehensive, large image and analytic aims are usually set in such frames.

Here I have grouped together some representative examples of global aims. Some of the references in the table below seem outdated. But it must be borne in mind that no drastic change seems to have taken place over the years in the case of stated analytic aims.

Comments and reflections on Table 2

The table shows that Jung repeatedly expressed the aims of analysis in conceptual and global terms. In his 'Problems of Modern Psychotherapy' (1931) he had written that he had also divided both aims and results into four stages (*CW 16*: para. 114f). Aims and results in large terms may truly reflect how the psyche operates, but as such they are not conducive to making detailed observations. 'Wholeness' is an especially frequently recurring term. Lacking space within the table does not permit me to distinguish, as Jung did, between a primary, undifferentiated wholeness and its reconstituted wholeness. Nor is there room

Table 2 Examples of global aims

General	To make unconscious contents of the psyche conscious
	To be able to love and to work (attrib. to Freud)
Transformations	– of the libido and in mental processes (Freud, Jung, Bion)
	– symbols of, Jung (1912, *CW 5*, title)
	– as fourth stage of analysis Jung (1931, in *CW 16*: para. 122)
	– change from learning to growth, Bion (1965, title)
Transmuting	– internalizations, to fill defects of the self Kohut (1984)
Wholeness	– sense of Jung (1913, *CW 4*: para. 556)
	– as a result of intrapsychic processes depending on the relation of individuals to each other Jung (1946, *CW 16*: para. 454n)
	– incest as symbolism of instinct for Jung (1946, ibid., para. 471)
Lifelines	– provision of
	– Jung (1916, *CW 7*: para. 500f)
Integration	– Jung (1912, *CW 5*: para. 459)
Individuation	– definition
	– Jung (1921, *CW 6*: para. 757f)
	– Fordham (1985)
	– also Samuels et al. (1985)
Self-realization	– Jung (1945, *CW 7*: para. 171)
Rebirth	– as transforming symbol Jung (1931, *CW 16*: para. 363)
	– the psychology of Jung (1950, *CW 9, I*, Ch. 3)
Development of the personality	– Jung (1934, *CW 17*, title)
The maturational processes	– Winnicott (1965, title)
'New Beginning'	– Balint (1965)
Ordinary suffering	– hysterical miseries transformed into Freud (1895, *SE 2*)
	– 'Where id was, there shall ego be'
	– Freud (1933, *SE 22, 80*) also Klauber (1987)
Ego-functions	– analysis should create the most favourable conditions for Freud (1937, *SE 23*, 250f)

to mention the outstanding function that is allotted to the symbol in Jung's psychology. It is the major transformer from an unconscious to a more conscious state of mind. If the terms Jung uses to describe the aims were taken at face value, they would be idealistic, i.e. unfulfillable. In fact they are not intended to do more than indicate the direction of psychic development.

Most noticeable among the terms Jung and others use are those referring to transformation. This term is ultimately based on that fundamental division of the mind into conscious and unconscious, where consciousness is regarded as the end product of transformation. The assumption is that this transformation will coincide with the transformation of the person. Were it not for the fundamental division, there would, logically, be nothing left to transform. Strachey's 'mutative' interpretations which have remained for many analysts the chief instrument of transformation would be left without their raw material (Strachey, 1934), unless, of course, the emphasis had shifted from the division mentioned to developmental concepts such as maturational processes, ego development, self-realization and the like, expressed as movements within or between such psychic structures as conceived. This shift of emphasis has been in progress for quite some time and is reflected further by greater attention now being paid to self concepts than to ego functions. Being nearer to that part of the psyche we call 'conscious', ego functions are apparently more definable and therefore *seem* less in danger of becoming a global aim of analysis. But developments within the direction of analysis called ego-psychology, particu- larly well represented by Anna Freud and followers in North America, showed that this was not the case: as the psychic apparatus became more and more intricate the duration of the analysis became, if anything, longer. The results of analysis did not noticeably change. If we take any item of the mechanism, such as projection, identification and 'projective identification' we can notice that in practice, instead of doing their *ad hoc* explanatory job between obser- vations and theory the 'mechanisms' themselves, instead of doing the job, take on global importance or, as I called it earlier, make a takeover bid for the whole works.

This tendency stems, to my mind, from a fact that Freud had commented upon when he summarized the case of the Wolf Man and its unsolved problems (p. 56). The origin of the symptoms, Freud wrote, could be explained, whereas the psychic mechanisms and instinctual processes which one encounters on the way could only be described. To arrive at general laws about either of these would, according to Freud, require many cases that had been as well and deeply analysed. And what would be the alternative? Speculations, Freud answered, were under the patronage of some philosophical school. And that, he wrote, would certainly be inadequate for the requirements of science.

What had happened to analysis in search of science? In order to draw a conclusion, let us see whether Table 2 makes any sense when taken together with Freud's remarks.

Whether we look at aims from the global point of view, or consider these on an apparently more down to earth scale as steps towards getting there ('mechanism' and techniques), something escapes our ability to explain. We shall see this confirmed in the utterly ingenious and detailed explanation of the symptoms of an *'infantile neurosis'*, described by Freud with enviable clarity (see p. 77 below). The long division sum could not be solved without a remainder, not even when daily usage had made us as familiar with the handling of projections and the like, as a workman is with his tools. Moreover, our results do not justify that we should hide our ignorance concerning the operations of the psyche behind the usefulness of our insights. The gap between the aspirations raised by the ideal of global aims, whether in the form of causal explanations or, as in the case of Jung, meaning-seeking, teleological explanations and the results remain formidable. All the hopes raised by global aims and theories come up against the infinite variety that in reality constitutes human nature.

As one of the best researched and documented cases, the 'Wolf Man' can be quoted as evidence that only minor transformations may be expected of analysis in the long term. The success was that the patient had remained well for twelve years after four and a half years' analysis with Freud. He then returned in a sad state of hypochondriasis with paranoid features according to Mack Brunswick to whom, after a few months, Freud referred the patient for a second analysis. On reading her report I cannot avoid the conclusion that the second analyst being a woman was the essential factor in the eventual (but partial) recovery of this latently homosexual man. How else could this be explained if, as she wrote, no new 'unconscious' material was brought to light? It shows that none of the global aims, even when applied in the detailed step-by-step technique, were as relevant a therapeutic factor as the sex of the analyst was in this case. On the other hand, we may assume that the second analysis could have got as far as it did, because the patient had had the first. Details of this case will be of further interest when it comes to a discussion of suggestion (below, p. 69).

A convenient way out of the dilemma posed by a joint consideration of aims and results would be to declare: 'The way is the aim'. This somewhat cryptic statement implies that the analytic work and process as such are worth all the effort invested: that 'To travel hopefully is a better thing than to arrive, and the true success is to labour' (Stevenson, *El Dorado*).

At this point the reader may well ask why, in one form or another, global aims continue to fascinate analysts and attract patients. My preliminary answer is that the archetypal longing for the panacea and for salvation continually finds new modes of expression (see also notes on mysticism and Utopia, p. 310f, below). But the trend from the specific to the general remedy is not confined to analysis. The same tendency is noticeable in the field of general medicine. 'Holistic medicine' emphasizes that the whole person rather than the affected part be treated. Ever more therapies appear on the 'fringe' of medicine and some of these have become recognized by medical practitioners. Numerous diets and psychosomatically orientated techniques indicate that the striving for improved general health is gaining adherents, even devotees. And that is not all. Doctors, health services and insurance companies, aware of the ever-increasing number of the population who depend on the pharmaceutical industry, are also promoting the idea of general health in order to reduce drug dependency. This is particularly noticeable in the treatment of a variety of painful conditions. A pamphlet issued by one of the largest German insurance companies (A.O.K., 1988, Brochure 28) stresses the importance of general flexibility of the organism and offers guidelines to healthy living which will promote well-being and thereby increase pain tolerances, a striking parallel to the analytic notion of equipping the patient so as to enable him to cope with life's miseries.

This is also the point to register my agreement with the disillusionary view Blomeyer takes of 'The School of Individuation' (Blomeyer, 1982). But I disagree that a sober ego and practical aims-restricted view could be the alternative. Although insurance companies will pay for the bread we know that man cannot live by bread alone whereby bread becomes equated with non-psychic or 'external' reality. But if psychic reality is to mean what it says, global aims, however Utopic they may be, have to be accommodated. Because the alternative, hedonism, offers no substitute for ideals and illusions.

As the heading of this chapter demands an answer, I would reply that if 'analysed' means taking a critical view of some major aims and issues, the answer is in the affirmative. If, on the other hand, 'analysed' meant we can know in the case of a particular patient what precisely it was that affected a cure or, at least, a favourable outcome, the answer would be, no. Finally, one would be right to suspect that analysis as a discipline aspiring to academic status is not yet in a state which makes communication with non-analysed people meaningful.

Chapter 4

Concerning results

In the previous chapter the aims of analysis occupied our attention. Although analysts try to dismiss all aims and preconceptions from their minds when working with a patient this in itself is also an aim. While it is one worth having, it is, in my view, an ideal, impossible to fulfil. What is more I hold that aims are related to results. The link between the two may be complex, but I do not doubt that there is one and that suggestion plays an important role in it. Therefore several pages have been devoted to the way the subject of suggestion has been regarded by analysts.

Although much of what is written in this chapter is well known to analysts, it nevertheless may be worth repeating because familiarity breeds contempt and the significance of the familiar could escape attention. For instance, the narrow focus required for our daily work can make us disregard how its outcome is to be assessed. But any attempt to understand what analysis as a therapy is about must be concerned with both, the aim as well as the outcome. To what extent can the aim actually be achieved? Can the outcome be satisfactory even though the aim has not been accomplished? Before coming to the difficult problem of assessment other fundamental questions have to be faced, notably those of selection. Therefore:

- *Analysis for what conditions?*
- *Analysis for whom?*

Important as both questions are, they cannot be answered without prior thought concerning their origin. What are the preconceptions underlying such questions? Rather than go into the philosophical and social aspects, we shall have to limit ourselves to some practical pointers.

In analytic literature references to diagnostic categories have been largely derived from psychiatric classifications. Thus we have neurotic, psychotic and, more particularly, borderline and narcissistic disorders. But the usefulness of such classifications is often determined by administrative purposes (e.g. insurance). In addition, the severity of a condition in terms of a psychiatric diagnosis which may have been missed at diagnostic interview is also sometimes stated when it seems desirable to account for a failure, or, conversely, to underline the brilliance of a success. Exceptionally, quantitative differences in the psychodynamic mechanisms are observed, for example, the amount of projective identification and the near absence of symbolization which is associated with some psychotic conditions and severe personality disorders.

By now the questions asked are beginning to merge into one. That is to say, the typical diagnostic procedure includes the criteria of selection because the patient's personality contributes directly to the diagnoses. These can be understood as the sum total of the patient's reactions to a particular doctor at a particular moment in a particular setting (Balint and Balint, 1961). So now we have to add to 'for what condition?' and 'for whom?' also *under what circumstances?* The resultant model rightly gives pride of place to the therapeutic prospects as seen in terms of the analyst–patient relationship. But it is also built on the shifting sands of psychodynamics which cannot be cast into the firm mould of such diagnostic entities such as medical insurance companies are accustomed to (as pointed out elsewhere, see p. 61, below). In psychiatry it is easier to ignore or separate dynamic analytic criteria. The introduction to the classification of the Diagnostic and Statistical Manual III (DSM-III) lists as its first goal 'clinical usefulness for making treatment and management decisions in varied clinical settings: reliability of diagnostic categories', as quoted by Kernberg in *Severe Personality Disorders* (Kernberg, 1984). But in analysis the emphasis is more on the individual than on the disorder.

The major difficulties of assessing the outcome of analysis arise from the highly personalized working model of the diagnostic-therapeutic interview. This places analysis outside the ken of the experimental sciences with measurements, repeatability, predictability and therefore statistical probability of results.

In a rough and ready way, the heuristic (after 'eureka' – I have found it!) art of discovery has remained the principal means of collecting and organizing relevant information in analysis as stated by Thomä and Kächele (op. cit.). As the heuristic principle is of no use in the assessment of the results, what do analysts themselves think about the outcome of their work?

Faced with the complexity of assessing results analysts and patients alike are tempted to resort to simplicity. Thus patients could be said to have got 'better', if not in all, then at least in some respects which are not always obvious to the layperson. Patients, on the other hand, are either satisfied or dissatisfied with the outcome. Obviously, such simple criteria will not do, for many analysts who like to think of their work in terms of research and hope that each completed case will constitute a discovery or rediscovery which increases not only the fund of their personal knowledge but will also become an integral part of their very being. In this respect failures, as Jung wrote as long ago as 1930, are more valuable than successes (*CW 16*: para. 73). An additional complication was that 'success' according to straightforward criteria such as the cure of a symptom did not prove the validity of a theory. There were far too many variables involved to make the assessment of either success or failure an unambiguous matter. A fresh start would be needed. A network or multi-dimensional grid for preliminary orientation concerning the type of ailment, person, theme and conceptual framework under consideration might do for a start. Here is how such subjects could be divided into categories or guidelines which are likely to have a bearing on the outcome:

(a) by using a specific criterion like a diagnostic category, e.g. borderline states, delinquency, frigidity/impotence, schizoid or paranoid personality, manic defence/depression, narcissistic disorders. The large number of entities mostly corresponds with a psychiatric classification;

(b) alternatively, an analytic concept or theme is chosen as a selective criterion, e.g. symbol formation, regression, projective identification, splitting, acting out; the ego, the self, the superego, transference and countertransference, transitional objects or archetypal themes, such as the trickster, the hero or heroine, the wounded healer and the like, again an almost unlimited number of motifs or themes.

And, of course, any combination of (a) and (b) may be presented in order to demonstrate the validity of a theory, the usefulness of a technique and the beneficial outcome achieved in different circumstances by different analysts. A third somewhat neglected group can be added, consisting of

(c) Gender- or culture-specific factors as well as psychic development, ranging from infancy to old age.

This rough classification is sufficient to indicate that the combinations and permutations are so numerous as to make every case and – what is more – every person who comes to analysis too unique to be a suitable case for statistics. At the same time some grouping of patients according to common characteristics is required for descriptive purposes even if it does not help in predicting results. Jung's typology of 1921, of which the division of persons into extra- and introverts is best known, is a case in point: more and more subdivisions had to be made in order to group persons into a category and yet do justice to them as individuals. However, without some selective criteria, analysts could not make informed guesses (prognoses) about the suitability of patients, nor, which is practically the same, exclude certain categories, for example addictions and, usually, psychoses. This apparent contradiction between uniqueness and grouping can be overcome by compromise, e.g. by showing that enough psychodynamic or psychopathological features are shared by patients of one kind to allow of more precise observation and description, and yet not enough to make statistical analysis of the results meaningful. So, statistics were unsuitable for an assessment of results. Both Freud and Jung were agreed on this as are nearly all analysts to this day (*SE 16*: p. 469) (*CW 10*: para. 494). But I would question whether small and definable parts of analysis could not eventually be statistically analysed. It should, for instance, be possible for analysts to state when they have observed that a barely psychic content, assumed to exist in an imageless, indefinable state – Jung's psychoid level, Bion's beta-element – has become transformed into a discernable image, dream or myth. The reason for my wanting to keep an open mind on this possibility is that we have at present too many theories in need of verification by persons other than the reporting analyst to make any further advances possible.

But for as long as analysts are trying to orientate themselves with the help of a psychiatric classification on the one hand and the analyst–patient relationship with its psychodynamics on the other, it is not surprising that selection procedures and individual characteristics, such as the therapist's personality, should make each patient and each dyad so unique that the results must escape the statistic dragnet.

None of this means that we can neglect to keep a wary eye on the relationship between the deliberate aims and their actual, in contrast to their expected, achievement. So once again we ask the following.

WHAT ABOUT RESULTS?

General comment

There exists to my knowledge only *one* large statistical study concerning the outcome of 'analytical psychotherapy' in clinical terms, which is by Dührssen (1972). Earlier follow-up studies, e.g. Denker (1946) either applied to hospitalized patients or to psychotherapy given by general practitioners. Denker's criterion had been comparable with Dührssen's. Her study, carried out on just over one thousand patients and using sophisticated statistics, showed that in a significant number of cases analytically based therapy had been of prophylactic value: persons so treated were afterwards less frequently ill than persons in the control group. Patients who had been left on the waiting list showed no such improvement.

Eysenck's findings in the matter had been to the contrary (Eysenck, 1965). But Farrell in 'The effectiveness of psychoanalytic therapy' criticized Eysenck on the grounds that the assessments he had made contributed to an optimistic figure for spontaneous recovery and a pessimistic figure for psychoanalytic therapy (Farrell, 1981).

Welcome as Dührssen's results have been it must be admitted that analysts do not usually think of the effectiveness of their work in this way. Indeed, statistics are a different sort of dream-life.

As a consequence of Dührssen's work the health insurance companies in Germany (everybody has to be insured) drew up certain rules and directives which enabled anyone deemed suitable, regardless of their financial circumstances, to undergo analytic therapy. As I said earlier, the latter cannot, on formal grounds, be distinguished from analysis. But analysis in such circumstances can and has been objected to on the grounds that it differs from 'classical analysis', because of the presence of a third, anonymous agency, the insurance companies. Cremerius, under the title 'The presence of the third', defends this analytical psychotherapy against the charge that the contract is not exclusively between patient and analyst, and that these analyses have to be of limited duration (Cremerius, 1984). The time allowed, as indeed the commencement and possible extensions of treatment, are dependent on the assessment of approved medically qualified analysts who do not see the patient but go by the report which the treating analyst has to submit and which patients who want to may see.

Viewed from the standpoint of 'classical analysis', these are considerable disadvantages which are, however, in some measure offset by the much greater availability of analytic treatment to the whole population instead of only to those who are able to afford private analysis or pass the selection test as suitable for 'analysis by analysts in training'. In this way the social circumstances are bound to be reflected in the results but, again, no detailed study of these effects on the outcome of analysis exists. We do not know for certain whether the level of the patient's intelligence and education plays any part in the outcome of analysis.

Whatever else one may think of this situation, it is clear that the insurers expect that the beneficial effect that Dührssen reported will continue to be repeated. For that reason too the policy of the insurance companies (Krankenkassen) must be approved of by the Ministry of Health. Because the taxpayer contributes to it the result has to be warranted on financial, medical and social grounds.

This shows that when the material circumstances demand it *statistical evidence* of the efficacy of analysis *can be produced*. But the difference in contract, including the pressure to demonstrate socially and medically acceptable results, must inevitably affect both the spirit and method of analysis. Another point is the *absence of any evidence whatever, statistical or otherwise, to show that analysis practised according to one theory or 'school' produces 'better' results than another*; at least, not if time is allowed for any initial enthusiasm to wear off. Nor is there any convincing proof that 'analytical psychotherapy' is more efficacious than various other forms of psychotherapy, e.g. behaviour, Gestalt, group, family. It could be maintained that the indications, aims and, therefore, results are somehow different. Although there is likely to be some truth in this, *proof* is an altogether different matter.

There are further *intrinsic rather than administrative reasons* which account for the difficulty of assessing analytic results. I shall discuss these intrinsic reasons in a general way now before going into detail later (see p. 63).

To begin with, it would probably be better to speak of the 'outcome' or effectiveness of analysis, because 'result' implies something definite and measurable. With that proviso, I shall continue to refer to 'results', and bear the following questions in mind.

Results:
1 Judged on what premisses, by what criteria?
2 assessed by whom?
3 considered when, at what point in time?

As these questions are intertwined, we can only adhere to the sequence given above to a limited extent in the discussion that follows.

Obviously, the first question is the most difficult to answer. It would not arise if the analytic procedure were, in reality, comparable to a surgical intervention – as Freud's analogy had it. The surgical analogy occurs no fewer than half a dozen times in the Standard Edition between 1885 and 1919. This is not surprising, as in those days analysts had to struggle to establish their work as a discipline, comparable, at least, to neurology and psychiatry. Criteria had to be 'incisive'. Today the image analysts have of themselves no longer borrows sharpness from the surgeon's steel.

The difficulty about trying to tease out any comprehensive statement concerning the results of analysis is that references to the subject are not only scattered, but also have to be found under such various headings as 'termination', 'cure', 'aims', etc. In the not very rare case of persons who have had more than one analysis one would further have to ask: *which analysis*? and also, who, *what kind of person* was the analyst, was she or he of the same or opposite sex as the patient, older or younger, and so forth.

Another relevant consideration is that *people come to analysis for a variety of reasons* only some of which may coincide with the categories given earlier (see also p. 313 below). In any case, categories give no indication as to the strength of personal motivation, and the ability and stamina required to cooperate. Less obvious, but equally important for the outcome and its assessment, are the basic assumptions and more or less unknown expectations with which a person comes to analysis. For instance, do they expect to be cured without hard work and a certain amount of anguish? Or, again, are patients coming to be cured of an isolated complaint without the rest of their outlook and personality being affected? Do they want this form of therapy for their own sake or in order to please somebody else who also had an analysis; or, perhaps, to regain the love of a spouse or to get out of a marriage? These examples are practical, and not just given in order to indicate that the degree of personal suffering on the one hand and the reality of expectations on the other are decisive factors. They are mentioned here in order to remind us that the criterion by which the result is assessed must take the original expectations and aims of both patients and analysts into account in order to arrive at a reasonable conclusion.

On the other hand we find that the analysts' aims are in themselves divided. Analysts would like to help their distressed patient, to be therapeutic, avoid illusions yet also find their theories to some extent confirmed. It is only when these aims and, by now, modified expectations merge at the end of analysis with those of the patient that an all-round acceptable result can occur. I think Ticho's finding is important enough to paraphrase here: *a congruence between the patient's and the analyst's conceptions of their goals is a precondition to a satisfactory outcome* (Ticho, 1971). This involves recognizing the limitations of analysis by both sides. Therefore, any criterion of eventual outcome would have to include the acceptability of compromise. I want to demonstrate this point by introducing two patients. Both were men in their thirties who suffered from impotence. They had been the favourite sons of their mothers and their fathers were described as ineffectual by others. Also, both had brothers who had satisfactory heterosexual relations which my patients were unable to establish. Toward the end of their analyses one of these men entered into a stable homosexual partnership. The other had married in the hope that this would cure his impotence, expecting that his analysis with me would play a supporting role. I gave him to understand that this was beyond my competence and had indeed warned him that marriage would not be a cure. All this time his voyeurism gained a compulsive strength and included a homosexual identification which was reflected in the transference. His anxiety about becoming the passive partner in a homosexual relationship was such that the analysis broke down. What I want to stress by quoting my failure in this case is that there are patients with complaints that are so crippling to their hope of cure by normalization that no deviation from that expectation, no alternative, no symbolic equivalent of their situation and relationships is acceptable. The 'immobility of libidinal cathexes' (Freud's term) is not always due to faulty technique, the rigidity seems at times to be in-built. Are these indications for a change in the assessment of analytic efficacy?

When the trauma theory of hysteria had been predominant matters were simple: an unacceptably painful event had been coped with by 'repression' and 'dissociation' and resulted in a compromise between the conscious denial of the trauma and some way of expressing it symptomatically, e.g. by a paralysis, vomiting or fits. By lifting the repression, the trauma could be relived in a modified form ('catharsis') and with the help of the therapist the painful reality could be faced. Energy previously required for repression was now released and at the disposal of the patient again. Clearly, the result, disappearance of the symptoms, was regarded as proof of the theory and satisfactory to both parties. And although this happy state of affairs has not lasted and only seems to apply in quite exceptional circumstances, it was still true enough when Freud wrote that only when the case is predominantly traumatic will analysis succeed in doing what it is superlatively able to do (*SE 23*: p. 220). This leads me to suspect that the 'results' in many cases in terms of aims and expectations have been disappointing, despite very considerable additions to and modifications of theory and corresponding extensions of duration from a few weeks or months to several years.

Differently put, there is now an ever-widening gulf between analytic theories and aims and results that are satisfactory to patient and analyst alike. Nor does there seem to be any prospect of improving the method of application (technique) in such a way that the treatment could be shortened without modifying the clinical theory and standard practice. Freud had expressed such hopes in connection with the Wolf Man (*SE 17*: p. 10f). But the experience gained after long labour with one patient has not shortened the duration of treatment in the next case of equally serious illness as had been hoped. Nor can we complain, as Freud could, that the failures of analysis during its early years were due to unfavourable (external) conditions, viz. resistance in the general climate of opinion (*SE 16*: lecture 28). Not only did Freud warn against being overambitious regarding results, but he also extended the conditions for termination (op. cit.). The first aim was, as before, the disappearance of symptoms attributed by the analysts to anxiety and undue inhibitions; the second the establishment of a state in which patients need not fear the repetition of the pathological process from which they suffered. I take this to mean that it was hoped the former patient would be equipped at the end of analysis to face adversities. The endless self analysis to which analysts themselves are committed prepares the ground for the third question: *when are results to be assessed*?

If termination of analysis is not the best, and certainly not the only time, and if analysis is endless, as I think it is in most successful cases and not only for analysts, the answer could well be toward the end of life or even posthumously. After all, the value of many a person's life cannot be assessed earlier. To be particular: Klauber goes so far as to say that a process such as the synthesis of illusion and reality 'begins more than it ends with the analysis' (Klauber, 1987). Such a view would be in keeping with modern thinking about the aims of analysis which has all but replaced the simple aim of 'cure'.

It is also necessary to recall that for quite some time now the trend has been towards greater emphasis on the analyst's personality, spontaneity and fallibility. Personality has been regarded as a major factor in the therapeutic outcome. As early as 1929 Jung wrote about the analyst as a fellow participant in the dialectical process and referred to the surgical analogy in a way totally different from Freud's: the analyst who suffered from a running abscess was not fit to perform a surgical operation. On the other hand, the emphasis on the human relationship between analyst and patient has made the answer to my questions more complicated. For example, Hobson calls psychotherapy a friendship of a very special sort (Hobson, 1985). If despite this marked restriction ('special'), friendship, however 'asymmetrical' it may be, is to retain the sense of equality, it is difficult to see how the analyst can judge the result *without the independent judgement of the other, friend and patient*. Alternatively, and despite there existing, as I said, no agreed differentiation between analysis and analytically orientated psychotherapy, the kind of friendship that Hobson has in mind may constitute the criterion that has for so long eluded people who tried to define that boundary. Certainly this 'friendship' can increase the illusory aspect of the therapeutic alliance. However that may be, even the well-known term 'therapeutic alliance' makes it questionable whether one partner of the analyst–patient dyad can judge the result without the other, no matter how different the language by which they express themselves (see also 'The patient speaks', p. 76).

We note in parenthesis that the change in the model of collaboration and with that also the criteria of results has been accompanied by a change in the philosophical frame of analysis from the causal-deterministic to the purposeful (teleological); that would seem to be in keeping with our regarding analysis today primarily as a 'creative' process. *The hermeneutic* (interpretative) element, capable of attributing many meanings to an event, which may or may not coalesce into one, has increased beyond the expectations one could have had at the time when the trauma theory held sway. The thin end of the wedge that brought about this dramatic ideological change seems to have come about when Freud wrote 'Constructions in Analysis' in 1937 and allowed imaginative constructions to take, when necessary, the place of the familiar reconstructions intended to explain present conditions on the basis of (repressed) past events (*SE 23*: p. 255). It must be added that this way of thinking about the primacy of psychic events in terms of assumed rather than factual causes, and thereby of meaning and purpose, had come quite naturally to Jung in 1924 or earlier (*CW 5*: para. 90). All of this makes it necessary to reconsider the questions, how are we to judge and when and who is to judge results?

As it happens, very few descriptions by ex-patients have been published that clearly demonstrate the connection between the detailed course of the analysis and its outcome. In the next chapter I shall examine some of these in detail. This is in marked contrast to thousands of case histories, narratives, case illustrations or vignettes, linked directly or by inference, with the result and published by analysts. Obviously, analysts have a vested interest in publishing successful outcomes. But I doubt whether this is the only reason for the disparity.

THE NEGATIVE TRANSFERENCE; AT WHAT POINT IN TIME?

Most analysts would probably agree that a satisfactory outcome is accompanied by not hearing from their patients again. This does not, of course, apply to any news reaching the analyst fortuitously, because, while remaining naturally interested, analysts are also careful not to rearouse the emotional links that existed before the work ended. Their hope is that former patients will have been able to use the 'libido' formerly invested in analysis in real relationships and integration of the analytic work. This is in fact the view to which I have myself subscribed until fairly recently. But I believe it is no longer tenable. Whether this is as the result of administrative pressures brought about by agencies such as insurance companies or national health services, or because of the view repeatedly expressed in this book that cognition has to be systematically brought to bear on analytic phenomena, I cannot say.

It is certainly understandable that in such different centres as Pittsburgh and Heidelberg analysts' – as well as psychotherapists' – initiated post-termination contact with former patients is being systematically investigated. The researchers are not unmindful of the potentially harmful effect of their studies but so far have not found any evidence of it. This does not seem surprising but it is surely too early to be certain. At any rate, investigations of this kind will continue. At the moment of writing such different papers as Schachter's 'Post-termination patient–analyst contact' (1990) and 'Research in success and therapy in psychoanalytic treatment' by Bräutigam, von Rad and Engel (1984) give a good overview of the work in progress.

It is now time to return to the beginning of the realization that a negative transference can be of positive value in analysis. The climate of opinion about negative transference as leading to the end of analysis was summed up by Ferenczi in 'Problems of termination of analysis', when he wrote about it being desirable for (former) patients slowly to overcome their mourning over the discovery that in terms of external reality the analysis had yielded nothing (Ferenczi, 1927). Therefore patients would look around for real sources of satisfaction. Obviously, analysts must deny themselves the pleasure of having grateful patients and I think this is true to this day. However, in my view, the meaning of what 'reality' is in analytic terms has again become open to question (see also p. 319, below). Certainly, ideas regarding the desirability of follow-up studies is gradually changing from being strongly against, for the reasons just given, to being cautiously accepting. This at least is the case in countries where analysis depends for administration and funding on sources such as insurance companies whose assessors have the last word on the duration of analysis according to results hitherto reported. Although we are here concerned with intrinsic aspects of results, the administrative factor remains relevant to my general thesis of the 'periphery' or setting of analysis influencing the central events and the outcome to an unknown and hitherto unacknowledged extent.

Problems of termination which are closely connected with the assessment of results are well surveyed by Thomä and Kächele in their textbook (op. cit.). As the chapter on 'Means, Ways and Goals' demonstrates, the goals are hardest of all to define and to distinguish from the outcome. What emerges from the authors' review of the literature is that the 'evidence from the couch', meaning here evidence based on the analytic point of view ('vertex') does not only confirm the aims and hopes with which the analyst sets out, but also the criteria by which analysts judge and describe the outcome. Of course as analysts we require enthusiasm as well as perseverance for our work. But that is not to say that we become blind to our patients' frustrations and disappointments when hopes in terms of ordinary reality remain unfulfilled or if the state of mind should be worse when analysis ends than when it began. It is therefore all the more regrettable when the former 'therapeutic alliance' leads to an outcome that is not, in due course, assessed by both partners. As mentioned above, whether and how, in practice, this can be done without the risk of doing harm is debatable. But when it seems desirable to both, there is no real reason for the abstention. Admittedly, the analyst-partner knows more about the work, its theory and practice, as well as from his or her own experience of having been a patient. In addition, analysts have learned how to verbalize their findings.

For reasons such as these, analysts cannot ignore the danger that they will find what they are looking for and that patients will bear them out (see above p. 64, and 'Suggestion' p. 69, below). The internal consistency of the various components of analysis, including the very real knowledge of unconscious processes that form the basis of the analyst's equipment, offers no protection against this possibility. It would be very strange indeed, if the analytic view-point were not conveyed, in the fullness of time, to patients and would not influence them to see the world through the analyst's 'eyes'. And although I think that the analytic vertex does reveal important and valuable truths about human nature, I am, like many analysts, aware of the *discrepancy between our findings and their explicatory force on the one hand and the therapeutic effect on the other.*

This being the case, it is not surprising that analysts have had to find explanations for the failure of patients to respond. A negative transference, so-called, is perhaps the best known of these; others would be 'resistance' and, more elaborately, the 'negative therapeutic reaction'. None of these are as insidious and deceptive as far as the ultimate outcome is concerned as the opposite, that is the patient who in a state of compliance may appear to respond very well, having apparently taken in all formulations the analyst offered. What has happened, as becomes evident later on, is that the patients are left in a state of 'positive transference', or worse, in a state of identification with the analyst. In that case much work will have to be done before autonomy can be acquired or regained. Balint's paper 'Analytical training and training analysis' is relevant in this context. He refers to Freud's opposition to Ferenczi, see above, who had accused his master of not having paid enough attention to the *negative transference.* Balint adds that for once psychoanalysis subsequently developed in opposition to Freud (Balint, 1954). Jung had considered that a negative transference in the case of an infantile/obedient type of patient could be a step forward in 1913 (*CW 4*: para. 659). Later he seems not have regarded it as a hindrance, inasmuch as it endows the other person (analyst) with too much importance and puts every conceivable obstacle in the way of a positive transference. When this happens the symbolism which leads to the desirable synthesis of opposites cannot develop. Obviously, the matter was full of complexities (*CW 16*: p. 165n).

My view on the history of the 'negative transference' is that, in fact, neither of the pioneers tolerated opposition very well, whether it came from the side of patients or pupils. Nor have subsequent generations found the passion of the patients' negative feelings easier to manage than its positive counterpart.

Only in retrospect does it become apparent that the separating consequences of hatred can, if tolerated, be of greatest value to the patient's development. This comforting knowledge does not necessarily help in the heat of the moment as analysts and parents of adolescents will appreciate. No analyst in our day would be satisfied if that state of affairs were the ultimate outcome, not even if the patients appear to have lost all their complaints. But it took some time before analysts could discover the potential value of the 'negative' transference for the psychic development of the patient and therefore for the outcome of analysis.

RESULTS RELATED TO SUGGESTION

Suggestion can be briefly defined as the action of prompting to a particular action; or the putting in mind of an idea (abstract from *Shorter Oxford English Dictionary*). In hypnotism, see below, it meant the insinuation of a belief or impulse in accordance with which the subject is expected to behave.

In early use it also meant the prompting or incitement to evil. Although now obsolete, some of this sinister implication still adheres to suggestion: the word still strikes a deprecatory note, see 'defences against suggestion'.

By retracing the outlines of suggestion in analysis, I shall try to arrive at the changes within the dyadic model, starting with the traditional idea of the doctor–patient relationship (see p. 85, below).

We have seen how crucial it is for any kind of success to be eventually experienced as such by both partners. The work done should become a mutual enterprise and be remembered as such, a joint journey of exploration and discovery. A precondition for the undertaking is the patient's trust in the analyst. To a degree this is trust in the patient's creation because the analyst seen as a person has to a greater or lesser extent become amalgamated with the analyst as a projection. Such trust will therefore be subject to fluctuations, but some ability to trust is a 'must' for imaginative processes to be shared and tested. (See also 'Imagination in the process of discovery', Plaut 1979.)

Analysts must have established sufficient trust in their theories and techniques so as to be able to abandon both should this become necessary. The judgement required depends on a fundamental paradox: a line of exploration should be pursued without expecting the patient to confirm it (see note on Bion's injunction, p. 306 below). The explorer-analyst need not take it as evidence of having gone in the wrong direction, if such confirmation is not forthcoming; perhaps the approach or the timing was inappropriate. On the other hand, the absence of a response, or a vehement denial, does not necessarily and of itself indicate that the patient is 'resisting' the interpretation or has developed a negative transference. Even the light of past experience offers no guarantee that it will show the way in the present circumstances. Given all these imponderables, what is it then that constitutes 'confirmation'?

Certainly, a patient's too ready agreement with an interpretation could arouse the analyst's suspicion: the patient might be consenting in order to cover up unwittingly a more disagreeable (and important) event. The only confirmation with which Freud would have felt happy was a recovery from 'infantile amnesia', the recollection of hitherto repressed data and associated fantasies. For Jung confirmation could have consisted of a series of dreams in which an archetypal theme developed and coincided with the patient's 'symbolic realization'. So here was a situation in which the pioneers required patients to confirm their theories without, however, wanting to use suggestion as a *direct* means of bringing this about. There were both outer as well as inner pressures that drove them to defend themselves against the charge of suggestion.

Recriminations

What happens when the results do not confirm the theory and suggestion fails?

Practical experience suggests that the analytic partnership has something in common with all other partnerships, that is, in the face of disappointments each side tends to blame the other. But while the allotment of blame, in whatever terms it may be expressed, brings about, at best, some short-lived relief from the sense of failure, it is totally inadequate for the professionals who must start afresh and question their basic assumptions. My attempt to set about this task exposes two Achilles' heels of analysis.

The first has to do with its historical roots in religion and philosophy, or, more broadly speaking, in a 'Weltanschauung'. The strongly eschatological (=science of last things) flavour of some global aims (see p. 53 above) indicates that there is a link which I shall take up in detail in the last chapter.

The second concerns us immediately as it is connected with the origin of analysis in hypnosis and therefore related to suggestion. Both vulnerable spots have in common that for analysis to be established as a discipline in its own right, such kinship has to be repeatedly played down or disowned by drawing and redrawing the lines of demarcation which sceptics never tire to attack. Both Freud and Jung as well as subsequent generations of analysts have had to defend their positions against the accusation that they suggested their own fantasies to the patients. In the case of Freud it was, as mentioned earlier, imperative that he should clearly distinguish his early practice of hypnosis from the later science of psychoanalysis. It therefore comes as no surprise that he should have repeatedly referred to the differences, as I shall presently show. But although analysis has been pretty well cleared of the allegation of hypnosis, whether this can be done in respect of suggestion remains a moot point to this day. Here is an example: Freud, in the preface to the Wolf Man, wrote that it required a long *education* (emphasis added) in order to move the patient to take his own share of the work (*SE 17*: p. 10, op. cit.). Fifty-five years later the famous ex-patient, now aged eighty-seven, was giving interviews to a Viennese journalist (Obholzer, 1982). The former law student was still arguing with the intelligence that Freud had called 'unimpeachable'. He declared that he found a contradiction in Freud when he, on the one hand, maintained that if analysis had clarified everything the patient should be healthy; on the other, he demanded that the patient must want to get well. If not, the analyst, as Freud had said, had provided him with the train ticket which would remain unused. The Wolf Man's summing up was as follows: either everything is determined, in which case I do not have to do anything other than help in the archaeological dig, or, there is free will and hence no need to rely on excavating the past. Whatever the force of his argument, I would conclude that the Wolf Man's initial wish to remain in a position of dependency appeared to have undergone little noticeable change. It would have suited the patient's books to manoeuvre the analyst into a position where *he* would have to appeal for help by pleading with the patient to make proper use of the train ticket.

Generally speaking the patient's motivation and ability to collaborate in the joint venture is as important nowadays as it was in those far-off days as a decisive factor from start to finish. But collaboration is not compliance. If it goes wrong, the wish to get well can become secondary to the substitute-gratification of either making the analysts feel they are right or of putting them in the wrong. Too much pressure, however indirect, will in some patients be counterproductive (see the example of the man who came late and left early, p. 52 above). But whatever the rights or wrongs of the argument the unused train ticket reflects a sad state of affairs.

We have looked at the situation concerning suggestion as part of the changed working model of collaboration mainly from the analyst's point of view. In the next chapter we shall let the patient speak. In the mean time, *is the defence against suggestion really necessary?*

As analysts well know there exists an increasing scale of sinister words, all indicating that the patient may be exposed to undue influence. They are: (Suggestibility) – Suggestion – Persuasion – (Re-)education – Manipulation – Conditioning ('Brainwashing'). Accordingly an analyst who apparently does not suggest anything values this capacity on the analytic scene more highly than the activity of colleagues who unashamedly do so. The resultant scale of values could be sent up by conjugating the verb 'to interpret' as follows:

- I facilitate the process or 'hold' the patient
- You make interpretations/interventions
- He or she manipulates the patient.

It is understandable that the sense of awe regarding the wisdom of the unconscious is the greatest when it seems to work without being prompted. It then looks as if the unconscious had revealed itself.

What are the facts?

As there are many references to the contentious subject in the works of both

Freud and Jung which differ interestingly, I have chosen some representative examples.

In his twenty-seventh and twenty-eighth lectures on the 'General Theory of Neurosis', Freud refers to his teacher in hypnosis, Bernheim, who regarded suggestion as the essence of hypnosis (*SE 16*: p. 446f). For Bernheim, suggestion was a fundamental fact that needed no further explanation. Similarly, he regarded 'suggestibility' as a universal tendency. Freud adds that suggestibility is nothing other than the transference disposition except that it leaves no room for the negative transference. Nevertheless, suggestion and transference obviously remained for Freud close relations as the following quotation shows: 'It is perfectly true that psychoanalysis, like other psychotherapeutic methods, employs suggestion (or transference)' (*SE 20*: p. 42). It is strange that in the Gesammelte Werke the juxtaposition reads 'suggestion or transference' (trl.) which makes the equation stronger than in the Standard Edition where brackets are used around 'transference' as a *cordon sanitaire* to keep the transference uncontaminated.

Freud then continues here, as elsewhere, to explain the fundamental differences: suggestion is used in analysis to induce the patient to perform a piece of psychical work, and to overcome transference-resistances. Analysis may make use of suggestion in order to make patients conscious by *convincing* (emphasis added) them that their transference behaviour revives feeling reactions originating from earliest object relations during a (subsequently) repressed period of childhood.

It is relevant that we should form a correct impression of the kind of collaboration expected of patients, as described in the quotation from which three points emerge (*SE 16*: p. 450).

1   The analyst is trying to convince the patient.
2   There is difficult work to be done *by the analyst as well as by the patient* (emphasis added) in order to overcome the resistances.
3   The essential achievement of the analytic 'cure' was, according to Freud, something the patient had to perform. The analyst can only enable him so to do and does so with the help of suggestions that act as a kind of *education*. It can, therefore, be truly said, wrote Freud, that psychoanalytic treatment is a kind of further education.

What transpires from these observations is, first, the existence of a delicate balance between the use of suggestion as the analyst's instrument with the aim of assisting the patient, on the one hand, and on the other the work that the patient has to do alone.

Second, in 1916–17 a model of analyst–patient cooperation (both had work to do in their joint interest) emerged, the like of which had not been acknowledged before. True, Freud had spoken early on about the patient's collaboration but this had been in rather paternalistic tones at a time when the comparison with the analyst as surgeon (see above) was still to the fore (*SE 2*:

p. 301). By declaring their attitude to suggestion the pioneers incidentally showed what kind of model of cooperation they had had in mind.

Suggestion as a regrettable factor in analysis also receives recognition in Jung's work. This is more noticeable in earlier writings and for the same reason as it was with Freud, that is the dreaded kinship with hypnosis. Again, I shall confine myself to a few selected writings.

Jung's justification of the use of suggestion was similar to Freud's. He wrote as early as 1916 that his constructive method of giving insight into the meaning and purpose of unconscious phenomena rather than their historical causes was simply 'suggestion', adding however, 'A suggestion that is accepted for any length of time always presupposes a marked psychological readiness which is merely brought into play by the so-called suggestion' (*CW 8*: paras 147–50). The final reply to the charge of suggestion was that the patient's own associations pointed out the symbol to which Jung had referred.

While we cannot be certain that the patient's associations were uninfluenced by suggestion, a further defensive reply cannot be doubted on clinical grounds. If suggestion had the magical powers with which it was sometimes credited it would be an enormously effective therapy – which it was not (ibid.). In sum, while Jung would like to avoid suggestion, he also admits that unconscious suggestion is inevitable (*CW 16*: paras 315 and 359n).

Once suggestion was no longer anathema a change in the general model of working with the patient became explicit. In 1916 we still note the moralizing tones in which Jung wrote about the neurotic's refusal to take himself or the world seriously, going from one doctor to another, seeking to be cured without any serious cooperation on his own part (*CW 7*: para. 479f). Whoever was incapable of moral resolution, he wrote, would never be relieved of his neurosis. Analysis by itself was insufficient to dispel neurosis. Jung said it as clearly as Freud and at about the same time: the doctor can only enable the patient to do the work that he alone can do.

What remains true to this day is the importance of motivation as a determinant of the outcome. I think that it too is part of the 'transference disposition' and cannot distinguish the latter from Bernheim's 'suggestibility'. By whatever name it is known, the preparedness awaits harnessing by the analyst's knowledge and skill.

Of course, a certain amount of direct suggestion of the kind, 'If you want to get well you'd better remember', was used by Freud at the very beginning when he tried to bring memories back by pressure on the patient's forehead, a practice that has long fallen into disuse. But less tangible pressures such as setting a date for the termination of analysis (in order to overcome resistances) and also the rule that sessions cancelled by the patient have to be paid for are still standard practice. Although the rationale is not to encourage resistances, the practice comes close to being a 'manoeuvre', see above.

The analyst's dread of suggestion has receded because he recognizes it as an inevitable factor in analysis, as indeed in every human situation and so no longer banishes it. As members of the 'consumer society', for instance, we are inundated by suggestions in the form of advertisements which rely on our suggestibility. The pressure of suggestion in this case may seem so obvious that we believe we can shrug them off. The advertising experts obviously believe they know better.

It seems that suggestion gained a new importance when Freud in his 'Construction in analysis' opened up the possibility that the analyst's constructions could, if necessary, take the place of the hitherto imperative reconstructions of memories (op. cit.). As the chasing up of repressed memories right back to earliest infancy ceased to be the absolute priority, so the pressure of suggestion on patients to do their psychical work and overcome their resistance and amnesia began to ease up. (For Jung the pressure of suggestion for this particular purpose had never been an essential requirement of analysis. When he employed suggestion incidentally by offering his constructions, he seemed to have been aware of doing so.) In fact, the whole interaction between analyst and patient now tended towards a non-authoritarian 'equality', although not sameness. Admission of suggestion as mutual influence has removed its accusatory sting (see also 'mutual transference' p. 25).

Were it not for the sinister implications of suggestion as indicated at the beginning of this section, its possible harmful effect on the outcome of analysis would not have created a stir! As things are, the bad repute has probably been intensified owing to the misuse made of suggestion by totalitarian regimes in our time.

The positive use of suggestion in *education* was well known to both Jung and Freud. So it is largely an ethical question whether what is indirectly taught or constructed in the process of analysis and with the incidental aid of suggestion does exert a beneficial influence on the individual.

Summarizing, we note two aspects concerning the results of analysis which, although by no means unknown are neither aimed at nor frequently referred to in professional discussions and publications. The first is that ordinary human interaction including mutual influences and suggestion play a larger part in determining the result than is generally acknowledged. Differently put, the techniques of analysis unaided by the 'human touch' cannot bring about a satisfactory therapeutic result. Second, in considering results we concentrate on what appears to be the demonstrable and immediate effect. But by so doing we may underestimate the educational aspect which in turn influences the cultural climate in which analysis is practised. At the moment such influences can only be surmised. Whether analysis can be analysed will depend on the formulation and design of research projects.

Chapter 5

The patient speaks: analytic comments

What can we learn from the accounts patients have given of their analyses? It is true that all analysts alive today have been patients in the course of their training and hence could also speak as patients. But can we presume that their recollections are still vivid and clearly in their minds when they write 'case' reports from where they stand today? I would not wish to depend on it.

A look at some of the books written or published by ex-patients during the last twenty years suggests that a primary distinction should be made between those written by persons who have 'turned professional' – that is have become analysts themselves – and those who have not. Obviously, the former are unlikely to offer any severe criticism of analysis, even if one analyst or one kind of analysis is compared unfavourably with another. A further distinction has to be made between the writings of patients and analysts in that patients address themselves to the public and more or less obviously to their former analysts. The latter, on the other hand, write mainly for their colleagues but also hope to be read by the public including potential patients. Of course, the possibility of narcissistic pleasure in self-revelation cannot be ruled out, especially in cases where the analyst (or the patient) has become famous. But it would be more charitable to assume that analysts who write about their analyses have managed to overcome their natural reluctance to reveal personal data in order to contribute to our knowledge about the analytic process and experience.

What attempts have been made to remedy the one-sidedness of the present situation? In their well-conceived exploratory study called *The Client Speaks; Working-class Impressions of Case-work* authors Mayer and Timms recorded interviews held fairly shortly after the cases were closed and 'memories had not yet faded or become indistinct' (Mayer and Timms, 1970). It is quite true that their clients, sixty-five of them, spoke, but it was the authors who initiated, recorded and edited the interviews. They also had decided from the outset to subdivide their clients into two groups, 'satisfied' or 'dissatisfied'. Rough and ready as these criteria were, the method directly reflects the view of the 'consumer' in contrast to reports by analysts which were entirely written by and for the practitioners. The authors referred to their method as 'client-orientated'. This certainly was correct, but the aim, context and setting of the investigation were chosen by the authors. Although comparable follow-up studies of analytic patients have been made, for instance by Bräutigam (1983) with statistics in mind, no study of this kind can have the same status as a voluntary report unprompted by any interviewer. This applies when the aim of recorded interviews is to demonstrate a particular method and model of psychotherapy. For example, Hobson, in his *Forms of Feeling* introduces the 'Conversational Model' (Hobson, 1985). Here the patient's words and manner form part of the vivid exchange with the therapist. But the reader is introduced to it by the author whose comments are essential to convey the message. In this, as well as in instances where direct speech has been used to illustrate psychotherapeutic or analytic sessions, *the patient did indeed speak, but it was the therapist-author who had the say.* I am not aware of any publication in which the patient was invited to introduce, edit and comment on tape-recorded interviews.

But one may well ask why anybody should want to speak or write about their analysis. Indeed, it would be easier to understand, if people were particularly reluctant to publicize their having had analysis, seeing that it is widely known that analysis involves the sharing of their most intimate lives, usually regarded as strictly private. And further, 'having had an analysis' arouses curiosity about what the person must have been like before, much in the way as having undergone cosmetic surgery does. Furthermore, in parts of the world where analysis is not widely practised, a person who makes it known that they have undergone analysis risks being regarded as eccentric by the others, that is by the majority of the population.

So what could it be that prompts some ex-patients to write about their analysis while others keep silent? Indeed, why do some people write about any personal experience at all? The first answer must be that some like writing and are able to express themselves well, while for others the opposite is the case, just as some people like to attract interest while others are naturally reticent or shy.

Next we have to consider that the emotional residue of the analysis will be rearoused and with it the relation to the former analyst. This, as we saw, is the very reason why analysts refrain from contacting former patients to find out about the long-term effect of their work (see 'results', p. 67, above). However, when patients themselves feel prompted to write a letter it may well help them to assimilate such residues. A new perspective on the territory that had been traversed may be gained in this way, just as it is by a geographical survey. But for every manuscript that gets into print there must be thousands of unpublished documents, letters, entries in journals and suchlike that never see the light of day. Such books as have been published tell us at least as much about the writer as they do about the analyst. In some instances the books may have been intended as a contribution to our knowledge, but more often condemnation or praise, revenge or gratitude are transparently the prime motives. The analyst's motive for writing is based on a wider experience of analysis and less obviously linked with their person. Where two or more accounts are available as in the case of the 'Wolf Man' readers have to decide, not who is right but rather *which combination of reported facts makes the best sense. However, we may be sure that there are no accounts without ulterior motives*, neither by patients nor by analysts nor by commentators. In addition to the categories which divide former patients into those who have or have not become analysts themselves, there is also the vanity of the writer and the possibility of a commercially successful book which act as additional spurs to writing. In view of all these circumstances criteria such as 'satisfied–dissatisfied' are obviously not differentiated enough to examine what can be gained from the accounts.

With these general considerations in mind let us turn to the patient about whom so much has been written that I have to ask the reader's special indulgence to look at his case once more with the present context in mind. Is there anything to be learnt by comparing different statements about events in and around analysis?

THE WOLF MAN AGAIN

The story of the man who became known by this title is summarized by Gardiner in *The Wolf-Man by The Wolf-Man. Sigmund Freud's Most Famous Case* (Gardiner, 1982).[1] The patient wrote his reminiscences during the twelve years, 1958 to 1970, finishing nine years before his death in Vienna, at the age of ninety-two. Freud's translator, James Strachey, declared that the patient, about whom Freud had written 'From the History of an Infantile Neurosis' (1918) was 'without a doubt the most important of all Freud's case histories' (*SE 18*: p. 125f). Yet Mahony, at the end of his *Cries of the Wolf Man*, exclaims 'what a bizarre development that Freud should have presented as the show-piece of clinical psychoanalysis an incurable case that continued to be followed up for another half century!' (Mahony, 1984). It would be no exaggeration to call the Russian emigrant of aristocratic birth a 'professional patient'. I mean that much of his mental and physical life, including part of his income, was determined by the role he had played in Freud's analysis. His pseudonym was lifted for the first time by Gardiner (ibid.). It had been derived from *a dream of white wolves in a tree* which he had had repeatedly from the age of four years. The dream was closely connected with the onset of phobic symptoms which in one form or another recurred most of his life, especially at critical times. Before letting the patient speak, it is essential for the sake of non-analyst readers to sketch in some of the most relevant background features.

In addition to his first analysis with Freud, which lasted for four years, and a second one lasting one year, he had had analyses and/or analytically-orientated interviews during a period extending over fifty years and longer, if one includes psychotherapeutic and neurological contacts he had before meeting Freud. He was then twenty-four; the year was 1910. (A precise chronology is listed by Mahony (op.cit.).) The chronicity alone suggests the psychiatric diagnosis of 'obsessional neurosis'. The basic incurability does not mean that the unravelling of the complex strands and connections, in terms of causes and meanings, which Freud had reproduced by the admirable medium of his 'poly-phonic' (Mahony's term) and persuasive prose had been ineffectual. If nothing else, being listened to with intense interest and being regarded by Freud, his senior by thirty years, *less as a patient than a collaborator* (in the patient's own words) in the exploration of only recently discovered new territory obviously made an important and beneficial difference to him. In the first paragraph of his *Recollections of Sigmund Freud*, Serge Pankejeff, to give him his real name, recalls the hopeless (the German term 'trostlos', literally means 'desolate', 'bleak') situation that neurotics were in before there was psychoanalysis. The patient's recollections have been edited by Gardiner and are contained in the first 150 pages her book. Other contributions are by Freud himself as well as Brunswick, his second analyst, and by Gardiner as analytic observer and editor (op. cit.).

When I write here, as in other places (see p. 62), about the gap there is between analytic insights, both deeply felt as well as intellectually grasped, and analytic efficacy in terms of symptom removal, I do so in order to highlight the vast area of our ignorance concerning what in general – not just in 'obsessional neurosis' – is changeable and what remains constant in the psyche and its pathology (see also 'The psychopathology of individuation', p.145ff). At any rate, most analysts have met the type of obsessional patient whose symptoms are accompanied by episodic hypochondriasis. I am not aware of any reports of a complete and lasting 'cure' of such patients by analysis or any other form of therapy. Freud's famous patient turned out to be no exception. We do not know whether Freud fully appreciated the prognosis when he, according to the patient, told him at their first meeting that his case was suitable for psychoanalytic treatment (Gardiner, 1982). (The German word *Kur* does not mean 'cure' but therapy.) It can however be claimed that analysis had a beneficial effect on the completely dependent and spoilt young man, who later on was to lose his fortune as the result of the Russian revolution. Gardiner enumerates: a good marriage lasting for over twenty years, thirty years of satisfactory work, friendship, happy holidays, painting and later writing.

To evaluate the balance sheet of what analysis could and could not achieve we have to add that 'heredity' probably also played a part in the unchangeable aspect. That is to say the patient's father suffered from depressions and died probably by his own hand at the age of forty-nine when the patient was twenty-one. The patient's sister had committed suicide two years earlier. There further appears to have been a paranoid cousin on the maternal side. Other adverse influences on the patient's mental health were: the impact of Freud's first operation for cancer and, possibly, the loss of fortune already referred to. Later, when the patient was fifty-one, his wife committed suicide. We can say that in the circumstances the patient adjusted remarkably well to life but whether this was due to the specific effect of the analytic investigations and interventions seems impossible to determine in this as well as in many other cases. Opinions are emphatically divided on this point. Without being able to go into detail here, I would refer to Anna Freud's letter to Gardiner of 4 November 1970, who had written regarding the progress the patient had made in the ways just mentioned. In her reply she wrote 'usually one does not know in detail how analytic successes came about, the failures are more obvious' (op. cit.). If 'in detail' had been omitted, the statement would, in my view, still be true. Let us see what the famous patient had to say on this point.

His general impression of Freud and analysis

After summarizing how he came to consult Freud, the patient described his appearance and how impressed he was by Freud as an outstanding personality. He then fills in the details and recalls 'as if it were today' the environment and how it made him feel removed from the hustle of modern life and safe from daily cares. Although he does not go into particulars about the phases of his analysis and their 'collaboration', one gathers that it must have been fairly early on that Freud was so pleased with the patient that he told him it would be good if all his pupils would grasp the essence of his teaching as well as he did, adding, however, that some patients with an 'unimpeacheable intelligence' were often cut off from their instinctual drives (this sentence agrees almost exactly with Freud's account of the patient (*SE 17*: p. 11)). It is clear that Freud was referring here to this patient and that he knew it. The patient also tells us further that Freud often mentioned the struggle for recognition that psychoanalysis was confronted with in those days, but spoke only 'very rarely' about his family situation. At this point, the patient observes that in view of the transference situation, this reticence was understandable. He nevertheless lets us know that he was quite well informed on this matter. Not as well, of course, as he shows himself to have been regarding Freud's taste in literature. It becomes quite evident that their discussions concerning world literature must have taken up some of the analytic sessions.

Clearly, in those days analysis took place in a much more relaxed, almost homely atmosphere, than it does in most places today. At that time, Freud certainly did not act in keeping with his own injunction of 1912 that the analyst should be nothing other than a mirror for the patient, that is to show nothing more of himself than what he was shown (*SE 12*: p. 118). Subsequent generations of analysts have tried to follow Freud's advice to the letter. What we realize when reading the patient's reminiscences is that analytic technique as taught and largely practised today has become more stringent. (Analytical psychologists, 'Jungians', are in many centres more easygoing about giving information regarding themselves than their Freudian colleagues are.)

The patient also learned from Freud that Jung 'about whom he had always spoken with the highest praise' had separated and gone his own way. As regards the transference the Wolf Man writes how Freud discussed it with him towards the end of the analysis and suggested that a present would reduce his gratitude and dependence. To us this may seem a manipulative technique; similarly when Freud deferred by a year the reunion with Teresa, the patient's future wife, 'by dictate', as Mahony calls it (Mahony, 1984). But the ambience of a joint exploration and the value of a symbolic action may also arouse in us a nostalgic feeling for the pristine days of analytic discovery. Clearly, Freud did not then believe that interpretations combined with the patient's thinking ('secondary mental process') would by themselves have the desired effect. Whether this or any other form of technical progress would, in this case, have resulted in a different outcome is, to say the least, doubtful. Anna Freud, from whose letter I quoted earlier, also voices her doubt on this question when she writes 'I have never believed in analytical omnipotence' (ibid.). I would go further and question the analytic potency in terms of curing neurotic symptoms and changing individuals by means of interpretations that link past causes with present symptoms and future personality development. This still applies after both the transference and the patient's resistances have been worked through with great care.

Discrepancies: their likely explanation

(a) General

There is a marked difference between the laudatory note which characterizes the patient's reminiscences of Freud and his analysis and the scepticism which pervades his replies in the interviews with Karin Obholzer published as *Gespräche mit dem Wolfsman* (Trl. 'Conversations with the Wolf Man') (Obholzer, 1980). How are we to understand this?

In her supplement, Gardiner gives a well-balanced assessment of Obholzer's book, with the German subtitle *A psychoanalysis and its consequences*. She is remarkably fair and perspicacious in her assessment when she draws attention to the provocative word 'consequences' which leaves the readers to decide for themselves what sort of consequences are meant (Gardiner, G. ed.). 'Consequences' were omitted from the English edition entitled *The Wolf-Man, Sixty Years Later* (Obholzer, 1982). Obholzer, in her journalistic professionalism, might claim to have given an objective view; after all, it is the famous patient who speaks, while she apparently does no more than give him the opportunity. So the pre-existing doubts with which he approaches questions of the value of analysis remain hidden behind the mask of her neutrality. But this does not mean that the human relationship that developed between the woman interviewer and the aged Wolf Man had been worthless. And Gardiner generously concedes this. For reasons such as these I feel that to call Obholzer's book a 'vituperative frontal attack on psychoanalysis' as Masson in his review did, shows an oversensitive one-sided reaction (Masson, 1982).

Gardiner, who knew the patient as well as anybody and over a longer period, redresses the balance particularly when she writes that the patient would automatically show negative feelings towards people who had been kind to him and whom he liked or loved. This strikes me as a psychologically correct view for which evidence is scattered throughout the interviews. The highly ambivalent and indissoluble relationship of some twenty years' standing between the patient and the woman called Louise is an outstanding example of what Gardiner is referring to. But Obholzer doesn't seem to have taken this characteristic feature into account even though the former patient complained to her at length about the complexity of his relationship. In view of his persistent ambivalence we are not surprised that the patient expressed his negative feelings about Obholzer later on to both Eissler and Gardiner. I do not think that the Wolf Man of the Obholzer interviews had undergone a character change due to senility as Mahony suggests (op. cit.). Despite a fair number of repetitions and a few contradictions, the patient who speaks here is patently the same person that Gardiner describes. Brunswick had also mentioned a character change in the patient whom she saw when he was in his later thirties. It was the time of the preoccupation with his nose. She also noticed the patient's minor dishonesties of which he was totally unaware. He seemed much more inaccessible than he had been during his first analysis with Freud. The supposed character change was summed up in the psychiatric diagnosis 'hypochondriacal type of paranoia'. To my mind Brunswick was right to see in the severe hypochondriasis a cloak for persecutory ideas (Gardiner). But here too I believe that no character change needs to be stipulated in order to contrast the patient with the obsessive–compulsive neurotic Freud had treated. These changes are, in my limited experience, compatible with phases in the natural history of the illness by whatever name it be known. Throughout all the accounts given of him the patient as a person appears to me all of a piece. At any rate, Brunswick's diagnosis seems to have enraged the patient. If his remarks during the Obholzer interview are anything to go by, the wrong diagnosis had helped him when nothing before had. He gathered all his strength together, stopped looking into the mirror, and overcame the ideas that had been troubling him and within a few days it was all gone. It was, he said, his greatest achievement (Obholzer).

We are once again forced to the conclusion that the interviewer's slant, whether he or she be a journalist or analyst, influences an interviewee's or patient's statement to a greater or lesser extent and also the diagnosis that is derived from it. The position is that Gardiner as an analyst has to emphasize the overall benefits of the Wolf Man's analysis, Obholzer on the other hand has to throw doubt on analysis in general and, above all, write a sensational book. And the Wolf Man had to please whoever he was speaking to which usually implied discrediting others.

Instances in which patients could hold their own ground are therefore all the more remarkable. Here are some examples.

In an early interview, Obholzer says she has read that Freud at the beginning of an analysis invited patients home for a meal. Our patient denies this emphatically. She modifies: but it is said that he asked for refreshments to be brought in. Again the patient twice replies 'No' (Obholzer).

On the occasion of a later interview Obholzer wants to go into sexual details. Referring to Freud's case report she intimates that his preference is from behind. The patient denies this, adding, if she really wants to know, the first intercourse with his wife took place with her sitting on top of him. Suddenly, an association seems to strike him. Linking the past with the present as a good student of psychoanalysis should, he is able to take the initiative in the interview and say, 'I have asked myself the following: *are we sitting* here in judgement of psychoanalysis?' (emphasis added). He laughs, knowing that this time the joke is at her expense. But the rebuke seems lost and a few lines lower down, he is in character again when he flatters the interviewer: she understands him better than his present analysts do. She feels forced to reply modestly that she is not a psychoanalyst, as if he could have forgotten. He then gives her the line she seems to have been waiting for: 'We see that they can't help either.' He makes a brief attempt to return to the present by adding that she herself said that at least the sister complex should have disappeared – which evidently it has not! (ibid.).

I have gone into fragments of the dialogue here in order to demonstrate that a few lines of unrehearsed direct speech can tell us more about the participants and their interaction than many pages of psychodynamic description. But without having read and compared the latter I could not have selected the snippets.

On the next page the patient tells Obholzer that Gardiner had written about him in her book as a 'showpiece', to demonstrate how serious a case psychoanalysis could cure. Earlier on he had admitted that he had really worshipped Freud, adding that analysis had certainly helped him (ibid.). But then he immediately launches into a long diatribe to the effect that his was a 'transference cure' and with that he makes up to Obholzer by telling her about his feeling more critical of psychoanalysis today. Does she feel more positive about it? he asks guilefully. But she neatly avoids the trap with: 'Your story does not precisely encourage me' (ibid.).

If we sum up the general impression with which the patient's accounts left us, both the glowing reminiscences he handed to Gardiner and the sceptical interviews, and further compare both with Freud's classical case reports as well as with Gardiner's summary of analytic interviews and events over some fifty years, I think it is fair to conclude that the limits of what analysis could achieve in this case are more striking than its achievements. The original analysis with Freud, followed by the massive support, material, analytic and emotional, certainly kept this colourful personality going to a ripe old age. But what in detail the connection between analytic understanding and the clinical conditions was remains far from clear.

(b) Specific discrepancies

The most striking of these is Freud's cornerstone of the case, the wolf dream. It figures as the most important single piece of evidence in Freud's theory of infantile sexuality and its development.

To do justice to Freud's interpreting the dream by a serious of ingenious steps as the boy's memory of parental intercourse ('primal scene') we have to bear two points in mind. First, Freud was professionally in desperate need at the time to refute Adler and Jung by establishing the fundamental importance of infantile sexuality with the help of the primal scene (see Mahony, op. cit.). Second, Freud did not insist on the child having witnessed and remembered the scene, but leaves it open how much was recollection and how much fantasy, or, whether indeed the child may have witnessed animals at intercourse and then deduced that his parents did the same (Gardiner, op. cit.). By whatever route children were supposed to arrive at a dream image of the primal scene, Freud presents us with the conclusion that patients become gradually convinced of its reality. He tells us that the conviction is then no less strong than it would have been if it were based on actually remembering (SE 17: p. 51). Here we enter an area of uncertainty in Freud which he was more than reluctant to admit. After much twisting and turning he moved in the end very close to Jung's position when he had to allow for an inherited phylogenetic component to the child's observation of parental intercourse (SE 17: p. 97). Mahony, quoting Rycroft, comments that this move makes the famous quarrel appear to us like a storm in a teacup (op. cit.). At any rate the question went on nagging in Freud's mind which we can appreciate better when we consider what the patient in Freud had to do with the Wolf Man (see p. 85, below).

But let us first return to what the Wolf Man had to say. It is hardly surprising that in his reminiscences of Freud he forgoes mentioning the crucial dream. But when he speaks to Obholzer we find that he flatly contradicts Freud's assumption, namely that patients would by one route or another become convinced of the reality of the primal scene. In fact, the patient declares that he does not think much of dream interpretation in general and of Freud's interpretation of the wolf dream as relating to the primal scene in particular. It is all dragged in, he says. He remembers the dream and had thought that perhaps the memory of the primal scene would come, but it had not. And finally: 'He maintains that I saw it, but who will guarantee that it is so. Is it not a fantasy of his?' (Obholzer).

The travel ticket and the threat of termination

In the context of discussing analytic results (p. 58ff), we saw the patient's conflict clearly emerging over Freud's analogy between analysis and the travel ticket. Freud had no doubt correctly assessed not only the patient's wish to remain dependent and passive but also the fear that the fulfilment of the wish would arouse in the patient's fantasy; to adopt the female sexual role would be equivalent to castration. A kind of compromise between wish and fear was for the patient to remain dependent on Freud as a father figure, and yet bide his time to emasculate him. The secret way of solving the conflict would be not to make use of the treatment; the more openly aggressive way would have been to criticize the analyst to his face. But the Wolf Man did not even voice his criticism of Freud towards either Brunswick or Gardiner, both successors of Freud's. In keeping with his character he responded to Freud's analogy with the argument referred to earlier. To summarize it here: analysis may make the repressed conscious but this does not automatically cure. It merely puts the patient in the position to make use of his increased knowledge and energy. It is like a ticket that enables one to travel but is no substitute for the journey (Obholzer). Even in his laudatory reminiscences, the Wolf Man had ventured to question what this will to get well really was and what in detail determined it (Gardiner, op. cit.). To which to this day we have not got the answer. However, in the Obholzer interviews the Wolf Man questioned the logic of Freud's analogy much more vehemently than he had done years ago.

Freud's threat to terminate the analysis when the patient's resistance became apparently insuperable was an innovation in analytic technique which has been criticized. By adopting the role of the overpowering father, Freud may inadvertently have strengthened the patient's resistance to becoming more independent and active. In the long run, Freud's intervention probably had the opposite effect from the one he had intended. The threat may even have contributed to the residual father transference (Mahony, op. cit.). The patient had not written about the unusual measure during his analysis with Freud. But the suspicion that the intervention was ultimately detrimental seems justified when we read what he had to say on the matter to Obholzer. To appreciate the discrepancy and its likely significance fully, we shall first have to summarize Freud's account in his introductory remarks.

The patient in his reluctance to lead an independent existence clung to his illness. Therefore Freud waited until the attachment to him had grown strong enough. Taking 'other reliable signs' into consideration, he then chose an appropriate moment to set a date by which he was determined to end the treatment. 'Under the inexorable pressure of this fixed limit his resistance and his fixation to his illness gave way, and now in a disproportionately short time the analysis produced all the material which made it possible to clear up his inhibitions and to remove his symptoms.' During this period of work when the resistance *temporarily* disappeared Freud could obtain the information which enabled him to understand the infantile neurosis (emphasis added). And further 'the patient gave an impression of lucidity which is usually attainable only in hypnosis' (*SE 17*: p. 11). We recognize the mark that the practice of hypnosis had left on Freud. 'Temporarily' was certainly right as we can see when we read the following snippet from an interview with Obholzer.

Wolf Man: 'But he wrote that things moved along afterwards. He set that date and then it went all right, allegedly.' Obholzer points out that the treatment must have stagnated for Freud to have resorted to this measure. The patient replies that he cannot judge that. He had always talked about something, but Freud did not find what he was after, whatever that was. 'All those constructs must be questioned', he says and explains that he means the scene in the dream of the white wolves: 'those are the parents and coitus, and that is how it is all supposed to have started'. He then makes a characteristic move which forces her to give the obvious answer when he asks: 'Do you believe that?'.

(Obholzer)

The Wolf Man's resistance to Freud's dream interpretation seems to have returned with a vengeance. It can of course be argued that the significance of the dream had at one time been realized by the patient, only to be repressed again later on. But even if this unlikely explanation were true, we would still be unable to tell for how long the realization was effective.

Freud as patient

In his reminiscences the patient described what could be regarded as two contradictory sides of Freud. On the one hand he never flinched from revising a theory, if it was not borne out by observation and experience. Freud pointed out that this was justified by the way that exact sciences like physics proceeded. 'If one of his hypotheses was not confirmed by the associations and dreams of the patient, he dropped it immediately.' So the Wolf Man wrote and added that Freud was convinced that psychoanalysis would take its due place in medicine and other fields (Gardiner). I think that the patient here expresses correctly the scientific model which Freud had aspired to follow. But what are we to make of his comment?

In spite of his forbearance and tolerance of his adversaries personally, he made no concessions or compromises about questions to which he believed he had found the true answer. To search for the truth was for Freud the first principle.

(ibid.)

Would it were so simple! We now know that this ideal stemming from the natural sciences is infinitely harder to approximate, and impossible to reach, because of the complexities that beset our field of exploration. In retrospect we can see why something like a holy war in the pursuit of truth turned out to be a 'storm in a teacup' (compare also the power of thought, p. 308). In such wars the opponents get wounded but they also tend to become unreasonable and obstinate to the point of sickness once they begin to suspect that the other side may have got hold of an equally large slice of the truth.

Likewise, a long drawn-out battle may go on in a submerged way when relevant similarities between analyst and patient remain unrecognized. (Compare my example in the 'mutual transference', p. 25.) Something of the kind appears to have happened in Freud's first analysis of the Wolf Man as the following account shows.

The patient's reference to Freud's fantasy and construction mentioned above (p. 83) strikes a highly sensitive spot. Freud's rhetoric, although admirable as such, is unusually involved at this point. For example, he first attempts to neutralize the reader's doubts before he introduces his interpretation of the wolf dream by writing that he has now come to the point when he fears he will lose the reader's credulity. Having interpreted the dream he quotes an imaginary opponent as saying that the interpretation is based on the fantasy of the doctor and not that of the patient. But the analyst, continues Freud, is quite unshaken because he knows that his constructions and conclusions are based on a synthesis that is quite independent of what he may have said or even had in his mind. Lastly Freud returns to the earlier tactic of disarming his opponent. He knows that even this plea will be lost on all those who have not themselves undergone analysis (*SE 17*: pp. 35, 52). Mahony refers to the exceptional maze of argumentation about the material reality of a child's primal scene and thinks that Freud was ultimately unconvinced by his own arguments. He suggests that *it all began in the bedroom which Freud shared with his parents* up to the age of three (Mahony, op. cit.).

There were, according to Mahony, other similarities between Freud and the Wolf Man, who became his favourite patient. He draws a parallel between Freud's intimate friendship with Fliess who had played an important part in Freud's formation of a theory of bisexuality. Their friendship ended in a quarrel. Freud had undergone nasal operations at the hands of Fliess. And an acute hypochondriacal episode centring on the Wolf Man's nose is described in Mack Brunswick's analysis of the patient. Mahony implies that not the least of the similarities between Freud and the Wolf Man was their repressed homosexuality. But Freud was insistent, not to say penetrating, whereas the patient was apparently cooperative, 'obliging' and compliant. Another similarity was that both were capable of tireless perseverance (Mahony, op. cit.). Brunswick described this feature well: 'granted the basic tenets, he (the Wolf Man) could with his logical obsessional intelligence make the most improbable notions plausible' (Gardiner, op. cit.). In this respect too the patient seems to have resembled Freud.

We observe that in the Wolf Man's case the apparent compliance and admiration lasted much longer than these traits did during the seven years of friendship between Freud and Fliess. The Wolf Man was well aware of his admiring father transference. But the negative side of it only became obvious when Obholzer provided the ideal climate in the form of her interviews.

Summary

The case of the Wolf Man offers a unique opportunity to compare a variety of reports, his own as well as Freud's and others' who had known him over the exceptionally long period of nearly seventy years.

To review the reports we have to bear some of the history of psychoanalysis in mind. Discoveries of the relatively new territory were still being made, even if they were based on little more than 'travellers' tales'. The metaphor is elaborated in Part II. That is to say the precise conditions which would be most conducive to accurate reports were, and still are, regarded as negligible. No wonder that apparently contradictory accounts resulted when the emotional climate and the viewing angle changed. The quarrels that broke out among the explorers about how to understand and interpret what they had seen are, in retrospect, of little consequence. For the pioneer-analysts it was a matter of survival to get support from their followers and patients against the objections of an originally hostile profession and public. It is against this background that we must judge Freud's analytic practice and the loyalty he inspired among his followers. Similar considerations still apply to all reports. Although with the passage of time analysis has become established as a phenomenon in our culture that still arouses wonderment, curiosity and antagonism, it is also true to say that the practice of analysis and its ramifications have become widely appreciated. Despite much criticism there is still a continuing demand. New ideas, directions and techniques are still sprouting and on the whole members of the profession feel less insecure than the pioneers.

An important influence of this increased security on analytic practice has been that aggressive–destructive emotions towards the analyst are more readily accepted as an essential part of every thorough analysis, as indeed they are of every human being and in every relationship. But in the early days their appearance must have been a threat which the analysts suppressed because it looked like the end of the badly needed analytic relationship. We now see in such negative transference feelings a signal of developing independence. Without bearing this change in climate in mind, Freud's handling of the Wolf Man's analysis is bound to be judged with unhistoric harshness and his generosity as well as that of his successors towards the patient would appear as a spoiling of the case.

What is more, the reports on the Wolf Man's case force us to reconsider the relation between the specificity of an analytic theory and the therapeutic outcome. Briefly put: would the beneficial effect of analysis on the life and well-being of the Wolf Man have been the same as those described by Gardiner (see above p. 78) without specific reference to the primal scene and the vicissitudes surrounding it? Nobody can be certain but my guess is that the omission would have had no direct effect on the result. In that case all the arguments and strife surrounding the wolf dream and its interpretation and consequences are even less than a 'storm in a teacup', they are almost irrelevant.

Almost, but not quite. Although I shall go into detail in the appended section, I want to anticipate the reason for my reservation about the specificity of analytic interpretations and their effect without delay.

It seems that the explorer–analysts need the passion of their convictions concerning their vision in order to go on with their work which is the understanding of the phenomena observed in the patient. For this purpose they need to be engaged in perpetual exploration, including self-analysis. Whether it be of immediate or even long-term benefit to the patient does not seem as important *at the time* as the pursuit of psychological 'truth'. Although the criterion of truth, meaning something that is impossible to disprove, applies only to the physical sciences and cannot be applied to analysis, the seductive sound of absoluteness which surrounds 'truth' has been quietly adopted and used like a banner by our explorers. The finding of hitherto undiscovered truths remained the glittering prize. Here the explorers' enthusiasm exceeded their faith in the theoretical vision that had enabled them to see further than the eye could see. They appear to have hoped that the gratification of curiosity by discovering *the* truth would effect the patient's cure. At least that was the assumption in the early days. Later a cautious note crept into the writings of Freud and other analysts. This brings us back to the relative importance of theories and interpretations *versus* non-specific factors in analysis. As the subject is relevant to every patient's statement and to every case report, it deserves special attention, see below. But first let analysts as patients and other patients speak.

ANALYSTS AS PATIENTS

My Analysis With Freud is the title of the book by which Kardiner, a practising analyst in New York, published his reminiscences some fifty-five years after he had been Freud's patient in 1921–2 (Kardiner, 1977). The dates are important because they almost coincide with the end of the Wolf Man's second analysis with Freud in 1920.

Kardiner's professional appreciation and criticism of analysis can therefore be compared with those of the nearly contemporary patient who was destined to become famous. In order to do this we have to bear in mind that their meeting Freud was and remained a peak experience in both their lives. However, the background of the poor, first-generation American Jew was in marked contrast to that of the son of wealthy Russian landowners. Also, their personalities and ailments were, as far as one can see, quite dissimilar. Nevertheless, Freud's psychodynamic understanding of their cases seems to have been much the same. What is more, Kardiner, who had compared notes with his contemporaries, found that Freud had interpreted their neuroses in the same routine way (Kardiner). Also, Kardiner's professional criticism on this point corresponds very closely to the Wolf Man's retrospective sceptical comments. Therefore we can conclude that the patients' opposition to Freud's theory and interpretations was due to 'resistance' which would mean that Freud could not have been mistaken. Alternatively, we can hold, as I do, that Freud had been preoccupied with his theory which stipulated that unconscious passive homosexuality was at the root of a variety of ills. It was a theory, incidentally, which Freud had already applied when he established the link between unconscious homosexuality and paranoia in his observations on Schreber's autobiographical case description in 1911 (*SE 12*: p. 1f). Add to this the link that Mahony made between Freud's intimate friendship with Fliess (see above, p.85) and it seems justified to conclude that Freud had a vested personal as well as professional interest to collect confirmatory evidence for his theory. But even if the theory had become, like the Oedipus complex, the cause of all troubles, we need not assume that Freud was wrong, but rather that, as Kardiner put it, 'as a therapeutic tool this concept of unconscious homosexuality is misleading'. He further reasons that it turns the patient's attention to a non-existent problem, away from the present and increases his helplessness, thereby confirming his anxiety that he cannot direct his own life (ibid.).

A tragic note is struck by Kardiner's reflections which are in agreement with the Wolf Man's argument about the travel ticket. It concerns Freud's concept of 'working through,' which meant at the time that *the patient* should make the link between his childhood neurotic manifestations with his current life. Kardiner's reply to Freud was 'I thought that was your job'. So we could say that the accusation of wanting to be passive was a game that could be played by two. Anyway the argument left Kardiner bewildered and he observes 'from this point on the analysis drifted' (op. cit.).

The sense of tragedy is heightened when we read about Freud's remarkably sincere self-assessment or 'insight'. Kardiner had asked him what he thought of himself as analyst. 'I have no great interest in therapeutic problems, I am much too impatient now', came the answer. Significantly, Freud added that he was occupied with theoretical interests and that he was too much the father and, further, that he wanted to spread his influence (ibid.).

Much as we must admire Kardiner for his cheek and Freud for his self-knowledge, nothing seems to have changed for either of them. Freud remained the despotic father whom Kardiner had feared like he had feared his own father when he was a child. He also gives an example of what happened when one incurred Freud's wrath (ibid.). As for Kardiner, we cannot really blame him if he decided that discretion was the better part of valour. In his own words: 'I would repress my self-assertion with Freud in order to maintain his favour and support. The central fact in the transference situation was overlooked by the man who had discovered the very process of transference in itself' (ibid.). It is a tribute to Kardiner as it is to some post-Freudians and post-Jungians that such exasperating weaknesses in their spiritual ancestors did not prevent them from recognizing their greatness as well as by improving the techniques and applying these to the wider field of psychotherapy and beyond. However the sense of tragedy about unchangeable aspects in our psychic make-up remains the more so as we become aware of it. One practical outcome of this realization has been that several institutes of training have acknowledged the unalterable father authority vested in training analysts by prohibiting their having any executive share in the procedure governing admission.

In fairness to Freud and his self-description 'too much of a father' and to Kardiner's impression of his despotic power, I must add that my own impression of Jung, only partly based on apocryphal stories by some of his first-generation followers is much the same. All sincere denials of wanting to wield father-authority to the contrary, Jung's image in that respect became no different from Freud's, which proves the irresistible power of an archetypal constellation.

We cannot take a book like *Contact with Jung* to which some forty analysts contributed in support of my statement. Some of these had been in analysis with Jung (Fordham ed., 1963). But the book in question was published shortly after his death. So it is hardly surprising that no critical voice was raised. However, since then no Jungian accounts comparable to that of the Wolf Man or Kardiner's *My Analysis with Freud* have been published by people who continued to stay in the fold.

Years of Apprenticeship on the Couch

This is the title of Tilmann Moser's book (Moser, 1974). In contrast to Kardiner's reminiscences, it was written shortly after Moser had finished his training analysis. His analyst is not mentioned by name and we can be certain that Moser was not cashing in on his fame. The author tells us about the difficulties he had to overcome to publish so much self-revelatory material under his real name and in the face of being accused of exhibitionism. He nevertheless managed to write a book, sub-titled 'Fragments of my analysis' that was widely read, not least of all because of its rollicking style. Although he did not intend to add to already existing biographical literature which is illuminated by psychoanalytic snippets and to describe instead the experience and technique of the process, the craft of analysis and how it works, the book is nevertheless mainly autobiographical. The experiential parts, details of the author's sexual life included, outweigh by far the fragments of professional interest. In saying this I do not wish to minimize the book's value as a human document. The spirit of the enterprise is after all the same as that which gave rise to analysis itself.

Among Moser's observations which deserve more attention than is at present given to them are remarks about the 'analytic family' or 'couch-brothers-and-sisters' which Moser, like Kardiner, refers to as having played a part in his analysis. Analysts know, of course, about this 'family' and use the patient's comments as grist to the analytic mill by interpreting it as incestuous fantasies. But this is rarely the end of the 'projected' matter. Besides, by referring to one of the roots of this curiosity another, which is equally relevant in our time, is receiving short shrift. I am thinking of the search for a group identity (see also p. 108).

Moser's account is largely focused on interactions. Interpersonal events, with the exception of dreams, are neglected. This is hardly surprising because, as Moser rightly says, the patient in analysis is in no position to make self-observations. It is much easier to write about one's own analysis as if it were a play on the stage, a matter of dialogue and interactions. Dreams lend themselves to dramatization, but silences and intrapsychic processes that go on much like digestion, do not. Nor do depressions which Moser also reports, but words spoken or written with the reader in mind cannot convey the depressive feelings. So the style he adopts takes priority over what he wants to convey about the analytic process. That is to say the book gives the appearance of an entertainment for the general reader. But if Moser does not do justice to the intentions with which he set out, this need not prevent us from taking note of some points which are relevant to our theme. For example, he as well as Kardiner are in agreement about the social factor in the genesis of psychopathology which is usually neglected (Moser). Both these patients who became analysts seem to know from their own childhood what they are talking about. Also both had lost their mothers in childhood. Equally striking is their great difficulty in gaining trust and in being able to commit themselves to a loving relationship. Perhaps their early disappointments account for their need to de-idealize analysis. In a postscript to his 'apprenticeship' Moser tells us that he had a severe depressive relapse one year after the supposed end of his analysis. He adds that in order to cope with his disappointment he wrote another small book.

Observations about the analyst as a person and the author's reactions to him fill most of the pages. As with most patients, Moser's need to discover the person behind the analytic technique and behind the couch is compulsive. He tells us that he could only speak freely about his own failures after his analyst had shown some of his real feelings about him. These had been anger as well as sadness about the parting towards the end of the analysis. Wanting to know about what the analyst 'really' thinks and feels is common enough in all patients. Analysts as patients are no exceptions to this. It makes no difference at all if their analyses were known as training analyses.

No less personal and revealing about herself as well as about her analyst (Winnicott) is Little's *Psychotic Anxieties and Containment* (Little, 1990). This autobiographical case description is in a class of its own. It is moving to read about the depth of communication between the two. Both were inspired by the value of regression to infantile dependence. Their oneness or identity was of delusive strength. The experiences recorded date back to the 1960s when the model of the analyst–mother with the infant–patient in partly enacted non-verbal communication seemed extremely convincing. It is beyond doubt that the intensity of this analytic relationship left its mark on patient and analyst alike. Winnicott probably acknowledged his indebtedness to this former patient. Certainly for Little, who has written about her analysis before (for example, on the value of regression to dependence, *Free Associations*, October 1987), it was the beginning and centre of a new life. But it seems to me that Winnicott's gift and vision of the analyst's mothering function were a unique interpretation, attracting however less gifted imitators as the next autobiographical description by a non-analyst patient shows .

OTHER PATIENTS

What happens when a guiding idea becomes a theory but also develops into an article of faith in the analyst's mind is well borne out by Ferguson's *A Guard Within* (1973). It was written from the clinic where she stayed after her analyst's death.

To appreciate the background, the reader has to be aware of the theory which was widely applied by analysts during the 1960s in London and elsewhere. It is summed up in the term 'therapeutic regression'. Without going into the origin and details, the theory's relevance to Ferguson's description of her analysis is that with greater experience it became necessary to distinguish between 'benign' and 'malignant' forms of regression. This is a useful distinction but it is very hard, at the outset, to predict which kind of regression will occur (cf. Balint, 1968). Regression was thought of as touching 'deeper and deeper' levels and this was equated with 'earlier and earlier' states of development. The implication was that the analyst should respond with appropriate *behaviour* to these deeper levels rather than by verbal interpretations (cf. Winnicott, 1965). It frequently happened, as it did in Ferguson's form of regression, that an extreme state of dependence on the analyst developed. He would then attempt to respond to it as if he were a 'holding' mother always on call to the patient. The idea was that the patient could avail herself of the chance to make up for the lack of emotional warmth and starvation which she had endured during childhood. But despite all the devotion that was lavished on her, the patient remained unable to accept the offer which was to help her in finding trust and to be able to express gratitude.

Looking back one can see that the more was done to meet her demands, the more she feared the loss of her analyst and to be left abandoned again. She was frequently in a state of rebellion, even rage. But this she turned against herself in the end and not, as was hoped, into some viable form of self-assertion.

The Guard Within did not yield in this case. She could not respond to the analyst's offer during his lifetime nor afterwards to others. That is to say she did not develop an independent life of her own. The book represents her attempt to make amends. However, in the writing of it she developed a remarkable skill, justifying, I think, the word 'creative'. It is marred by sentimentality as when she addresses her late analyst as if he were a ghostly lover. The prejudices and imprint of her social class remained her guide which she used as a shield behind which to hide her most defenceless self. 'I do not like people with bad manners.' This she wrote after breaking up her room at the clinic (ibid.). And also 'I was not, I am not, and never will be, a patient. I am a proper ordinary person. I told you a hundred times.'

There could hardly be a better contrast to *A Guard Within* than Cardinal's *The Words to Say It* (1977). The contrast is the more striking as there are also certain similarities. Among these is the powerful imprint of the French ruling class in Algeria before it became independent. However, seen from an analytic perspective, it was the patient's mother, a woman as cold as she was rigid and desperately clinging to her daughter with whom she lived alone during the patient's childhood and adolescence. It seems that the patient was not allowed to express her separate self by any other means than by psychosomatic symptoms. In this respect, her emotional starvation was comparable to that of Ferguson's and so was her intense isolation. But what a difference in personality! Here is a dimension that determines the outcome of analysis to a much greater extent than is acknowledged in analytic reports. Jung's 'Psychological Types' concern 'attitudes' and 'functions' (*CW 6*). Other analytic theories acknowledge differences in 'the strength of drives'. But none do justice to the combination of traits that go to make up the individual personality. The probable reason is because it is neither pathological nor subject to change.

It becomes obvious when reading her book that Cardinal is a fighter, fully involved, where Ferguson is a schizoid observer with outbursts of uncontrollable temper. Cardinal makes full use of her analysis, which one gathers is of the traditional Freudian kind. Of course, her book is autobiographical too. But for the duration, seven years, her analysis was the pivot of her life. From having been disgusted with her mother and her own sex, she became sexually alive.

She observes that most people can only talk about their analysis if it has been unsuccessful and further that the analytic process as such cannot be described. If one tried, it would become an enormous book, full of everything and with nothing in it. She herself could only write what she calls the present novel after she had completed her analysis. After one really dramatic session she felt that the analyst had just helped her to give birth to herself. From then on her body was her own. Her analyst remained as impassive as ever, but after this session she tells us she felt sure that when she left she could see a sparkle of pleasure in his eyes.

From our point of view the description of her analyst, his conduct and her relationship to him is of particular interest. The patient's own words bring it out best. For example, although she describes the above session as one in which *she* gave birth to herself while the analyst stood by, the book is dedicated to 'the doctor who helped me to get born'. Yet she frequently mocks the little man for his unfailingly correct and humourless attitude of neutrality. Their divided roles are well described by the following fragment: 'What does it make you think of?' He could transform everything provided I said what the "that"

in fact was.' The most important of all the discoveries she had made while she
learnt to pay attention to the signals coming day and night from her unconscious was that it was she who was in possession of the discoveries. No analysis
could change that. And to make use of it she tells us the analyst's consulting
room would hardly be big enough. We can hear a note of defiance. Clearly in
her case 'the damned little man' had been right to keep up 'his mask' up to the
very end. This does not seem to have been unduly frustrating and certainly
worked the way it was intended. That is, in the course of her analysis which
she started at the age of thirty she lived out the considerable energies which
had been gradually set free. Her life unfolded. She used the travel ticket, no
question.

Summary

What have we learnt from comparing Ferguson's with Cardinal's account? Is
it different analysts for different patients? Or, is the situation, as I believe, that
some patients can get what they are looking for from most analysts, while
others would need analysts whose originality makes them specially suited for
their case perhaps because they are prepared to learn from the patient? There
remain a small number of patients who ask for analysis but turn out to be
unsuitable for the method; the same holds good for persons practising analysis.
To make matters more complicated, states of unsuitability may be temporary
or permanent.

But Cardinal and Ferguson are also opposites in what they are looking for.
Cardinal is searching for a healthy body which can serve her natural vitality
and talents. After she wrote the book about her analysis she continued with
her writing. Ferguson was too fragile to be viable. She was looking for a shell
or even a host within which she might have discovered that there is also a world
outside which is not completely hostile. The host must know his way about
in that world and also prove indestructible by her attacks. Alas, such conditions could not be found.

Yet another kind of patient comes to mind, who is well described in
Dinnage's *One to One*, where she quotes from the journal of the Swiss
philosopher Amiel written when Freud was fifteen (Dinnage, 1988). Such
patients are curious about their personal existence and its multiple aspects
constituting a *cosmos*. Living without on the surface and without an inward
orientation, the environment feels to them like a prison. They have to take
possession of their inwardness. This is the kind of patient whom Jung was most
interested in and closest to.

A NOTE ON THE EFFECTS OF INTERPRETATIONS COMPARED WITH NON-SPECIFIC FACTORS

I do not wish to imply that theories are 'mere fantasy' in the derogatory sense
pointed out earlier. On the contrary, I view the imagery of the psyche and the

patterns of infinite variety that it weaves as part of our psychological heritage which requires constant cultivation. Like food, it is necessary for survival. But it does not follow that a theory that helps us to make an unconscious content conscious with the help of 'mutative' interpretations will bring about so-called 'structural' and relatively permanent changes followed by curative or, at least, therapeutic results.

Is there anything about the origin of analytic interpretations other than the factors already mentioned that would account for such high hopes? We recall that there were *the analyst's vision, the pursuit of truth and the ever-present hunger for spiritual nourishment* which is shared by analyst and patient alike. But a fourth or balancing ingredient is crucial. Although insufficient of itself, without *the analyst's empathic assessment* of what the patient is able to digest interpretations must sooner or later be rejected.

But my assumption that 'making conscious', 'empathy' and 'interpretation' are self-explanatory terms proves to be unwarranted. If, for example, at the beginning of a session I say to a patient that she is having difficulty in breathing, I am not adding anything to what she is already aware of. We had noticed the symptom before. Sometimes she has remarked on it, today she does not. Let us assume that the reason why I want to voice my observations is to show my willingness to share the distress and whatever the underlying cause may be; I show empathy. But the patient cannot make any use of my comment until her feelings have determined whether my communication was based on anxiety and impatience ('still no better!') or curiosity (prying) or, as I hoped, on selfless empathy. Whatever the outcome, I must accept the patient's judgement before I go further.

So far, I made two assumptions, namely that I could increase her self-aware-ness by making reference to the symptom which she did not mention on the day, and secondly, that empathy is invariably at my disposal. But when I spoke, I also acted on the underlying assumption that with goodwill on both sides we could discover the cause of the symptom and so 'explain it away'. All three assumptions, that is self-awareness, empathy and curative effect are naïve oversimplifications. But the example may still be of some use in demonstrating that the apparently non-specific factor 'empathy' and any interpretations based on it must fail in the long run, unless it is supported by a new intuitive insight which connects me with the situation I observe. How can this come about?

A present trend, set probably by Bion, is to rely on intuitive flashes which are the more likely to occur as the analyst is able to empty their mind of all knowledge, memory and desire (Bion, op. cit., see also p. 48 above and p. 306 below). Agreeing with these desiderata Fordham was able to write about 'my method of not knowing' (Fordham, 1991). But desirable as the freedom from preconceptions is, and illuminating and gratifying as intuitive flashes are, it seems more than probable – nobody can be sure – that such flashes are based on previous knowledge. Knowledge about the patient and other patients that has become integrated with the analyst's reading and self-analysis. All these have shaped the current theoretical orientation which sees flashes arising, apparently out of the blue.

Whatever the constituents of an interpretation, it is clear that in order to be effective the mixture must be adapted to the recipient's current capacity.

This in turn depends not a little on the state of the 'transference'. It seems that in the case of the Wolf Man Freud's vision and intuition outstripped his empathy. The patient seemed compliant. Freud knew about his transference as well as about the resistance to it, yet he tried to insist and force the pace. The patient, full of admiration for him, delivered just the kind of material that Freud needed. And the 'cure' based on this transference apparently lasted for twelve years. But then the indigestible contents, Freud's 'transference remnants', had to come out. The Wolf Man's later ambivalent and even hostile remarks about his various analysts do, at least in part, account for his apparently ungrateful behaviour and unchanged neurosis.

Now let us return to the question regarding the effect of analytic interpretations which are apparently accepted by the patient and expected to have a transforming effect. The sequence was to be: first, an element of the unconscious is raised to the level of consciousness; second, this change is accompanied or followed by a 'structural' change in the patient's psyche with therapeutically beneficial results. *What if it does not happen?*

The interpretation had been arrived at by a gradual synthesis of observations each of which fitted or enlarged the analyst's theoretical orientation and past experience. Let us further assume that the 'blend' of the interpretation was perfect, it got home, was 'on target' and really had an illuminating effect: it clicked. Yet no lasting change occurred. A case of 'repetition compulsion'? Or of a 'negative therapeutic reaction'? Or is it as I think our unwarranted assumption, namely that the first change must be followed by a second, the transformation?

To find an explanation let us return to slips of the tongue and the like, the so-called 'parapraxes' which Freud described in 1901 in 'The Psychopathology of Everyday Life' (*SE 6*). With very little tuition we can uncover, or make 'conscious', the motivation behind such significant mistakes. Their becoming conscious is usually greeted with a smile of recognition. A trivial example perhaps, but the model is the same as the one which is applied in analysis where our interpretations are aimed at bringing to light much more deeply buried and complex causes, meanings and aims behind the patient's ailment. But no one would expect that a person's recognition of the significance of a parapraxis would be followed by a change, a transformation of his or her personality. We know that in one way or another we shall repeat such 'mistakes' and are not too worried about it. Of course, in addition to the greater complexity and gravity of the analytic situation there is also the importance of the relationship to the analyst including the transference which complicates the issue. But I would maintain that *the greatest single obstacle to change can be the expecta-*

tion of change which affects both patient and analyst. This is another reason why I hold that the non-specific, supportive factor in analysis does contribute to the long-term therapeutic effect to a greater extent than the highly sophisticated techniques of interpretation would suggest. And the strongest non-specific factor, supportive or destructive or both, is found in the undissolved and probably insoluble transference, as the case of the Wolf Man clearly shows.

Lastly, my contention concerning the relatively greater importance of non-specific factors seems to be borne out by Wallerstein's investigation. After an unusually thorough follow-up study of forty-two patients the author comes to the conclusion that the results of classical psychoanalysis, analytic psychotherapy and supportive treatment were more comparable than the research team had expected. All the therapies, classical analysis included, contained more supportive elements than expected. Wallerstein's team concluded that the supportive aspects of every psychotherapy, particularly of psychoanalysis, must receive more attention than has hitherto been the case. Interestingly enough, 'structural changes' could also be demonstrated in *all* three forms of psychotherapy (Wallerstein, 1986).

Therefore the long-term effect of interpretations on the outcome of analysis remains questionable. They represent the analyst's most spectacular instrument, not least, I think, because the words in which they are clad are easily reproduced. But that does not mean that all, or even the most important, part of the interpretation is verbal. The tone of voice, the grunt, the gesture and facial expression, all these can speak louder than words.

Analysts vary in their preference: some hold that one cannot interpret too much; others again feel happier to let patients make their own discoveries. My own view is based on my recollections of having been a patient and on what I have gathered from other patients who have had long analyses. That is to say, in the long run it is not the single or even many illuminating and convincing interpretations that make a lasting impression. *What matters is the cumulative effect of learning from the analyst that it is possible to make links with hitherto unknown parts of one's self.* Although analytic techniques have changed a great deal since the days of the Wolf Man, the sobering lesson for analysts remains how not to become fascinated by *any* theory, nor too pleased with a clever and apparently well-received interpretation. But in this area it is not always possible to distinguish between enthusiasm and faith (cf. p. 15).

However it does not follow that the theories on which interpretations are based are as such worthless and that it does not matter what exactly the analyst believes or has faith in. I would argue that the value of analytic theory cannot be measured by whatever the outcome seems to be, because it is always a product of specific interpretations and non-specific factors. Important as the latter are, nobody can, in my view, be supportive over a long time and in an intensive way without a *specific orientation*, an internal map representing the road network and an image of the destination. The sense of exploration and a possibility of enduring discoveries are the sustenance without which analytic work would deteriorate into chat. The hope of helping the patient is of itself insufficient because it would soon give way to despair, if it were not rewarded by the patient 'getting better'.

We further have to take into account that patients in the course of a long analysis become very good at spotting what the analyst is looking for. Yet not to expect anything seems to me humanly impossible. Even a clear, uncluttered field of vision is still a theoretical expectation. The situation is that analyst and patient share a stretch of their lives during which they try to make sense of what happens under the laboratory conditions of analysis while their separate lives proceed outside. Occasionally they make real contact of a kind that is unique because of the professional limitations and rituals involved that hold all the elements together. Sometimes concurrent events tend to confirm the benefit of the analytic process, at other times the opposite seems to be the case. At all times the theories offer the distilled vision of a cosmos with a potential space for each person. Without this analysis would become a lifeless set of rules. Therefore the analytic vision and the specific interpretations based on it must continue as the nourishment on which therapy feeds.

NOTE

1 This is the title of the American edition, Basic Books, 1971. I found additional material in two chapters: 'The Last Years of the Wolf Man' and 'Supplement' (trl.) in the German edition, Fischer Taschenbuch Verlag, 1982. Neither appear in the English edition of *The Wolf Man* by Muriel Gardiner, published 1972, reprinted H. Karnac Books 1989. The Supplement is particularly important since it contains Gardiner's reply to Obholzer. Where reference is made to the German edition this is indicated.

Part II

Learning from experience

INTRODUCTION

As mentioned earlier, Freud referred to metapsychology as the witch, and Jung commented similarly on theories as being the very devil (see p. 47). What is it that gives these thought products such uncanny power? I should like to defer my answer until the last chapter, particularly to the note on mysticism (see p. 310, below).

Nevertheless the question is relevant as an opening to the second part of the book where I am trying to show how I learned not to put too much trust in theories which – if left unquestioned – arrogate a dominant position in our work and disturb the altogether essential working alliance with the patient. However, without a theoretical viewpoint we cannot analyse. For practical purposes the power of concepts and theories can, I think, be reduced, if we are prepared to deliberately suspend our belief in the 'proof' that case material so persuasively offers and focus instead on what does not fit in with our theories and techniques and could perhaps be more adequately understood in some other way such as the patient's inborn dispositions. Better still, we can make allowance for ignorance, admitting that we simply don't know the answer and start again.

Chapter 6 describes yet another way to sobriety, which is to pay attention to the neglected non-specific aspect of analysis as a form of long-term psychotherapy. By non-specific I do not mean the helpful empathic human relationship which analysis also is, but rather the effect of a ritual which offers a safe container to people whose culture is lacking in living rituals and at the same time puts enormous emphasis on individual attainment; hence the name of the chapter, 'The Autonomous Ritual'. Autonomy here means that the ritual as such, regardless of the detailed content, acts as a container that offers concentration in the midst of turmoil. This can effect a change in the rhythm of people's lives. Those who experience it may change their outlook in several respects, discover new meanings, thereby finding they themselves have undergone a change.

The aim of the paper on which Chapter 7 was based is expressed in a slightly mocking style which has not been changed. At the end of the chapter I criticize all analytic ideals and recipes in general and the opposites as a primary conceptual principle in Jung's work from which psychic energy as well as the 'union of opposites' as a healing-whole-making phenomenon with all its attending symbolism is derived. What is more, the ultimate and highest aim of analytical psychology, individuation is based on this union as a *sine qua non*. But as it is so rarely, if ever, seen in practice, I suggest that as an alternative to persons becoming themselves via 'the union of opposites' another way may be open to people who do not 'change'. I therefore question Jung's dominant concept of 'the opposites' as well as the corresponding developmental psycho-analytic concepts which I brought together under 'object-constancy' in the comprehensive sense given at the beginning of Chapter 8 (see p. 135, below).

Chapter 8 contains what I have learned most of all which is to appreciate the unchanging parts of the personality. The emphasis on change or transfor-mation that is expected to occur in the course of analysis makes us blind to the unchanging aspects, possibly because they are regarded as failures. It is this that drives analysts of all persuasions to dwell almost exclusively on demon-strating the changes that have occurred, assuming always that these changes are for the 'better' and will last. Of course, changes do come about both as improvements in symptomatology and in personality structure. The appeal for help and the healing power attributed to and implicitly accepted by analysts as members of a 'helping profession' often combine and result in an early feeling of improvement which does not mean that such changes, even if they were to last, prove the specific analytic theory.

Yet a personality development does occur inasmuch as people seemingly become more and more 'themselves'. It is apparently centred on what I refer to as a 'constant object'. Even so, a permanent defect can often be noted in such persons inasmuch as they fail to form intimate and enduring relationships. That failure is, however, so common in our society, that it would hardly do as a diagnostic criterion for this category.

In Chapter 9 two non-clinical examples of the alternative road to individ-uation are given. Although it is no coincidence that in both cases religious faith plays a part, I think that it could equally well have been some other kind, for instance faith in another person or a scientific theory which becomes the centre of the person's life. In this sense the constant object plays a part in the lives of all kinds of pioneers. The theme is taken further in Chapter 14 in conjunction with the power which emanates from certain thoughts and theories.

Chapter 6

The autonomous ritual

We have already met the significance attached to '*Changes*' brought about by analysis in general and particularly by interpretations (see p. 53, above). Like 'change', so the word 'transformation' plays an extremely important role in Jung's psychology. But he is well aware that transformations do also come about without analysis. Even if they are observed in and attributed to analysis they may, at least in part, still be due to the ritualistic aspect. Furthermore, the difficulty I mention at the beginning of the next chapter, namely to convey to a lay person what analysts actually do, is usually connected with that person's unfamiliarity with the region referred to as 'unconscious'. If the ritualistic part of analysis were used as example, it could indeed be pointed out how a person's frame of mind can, at least temporarily, be influenced by participation in a ritual, a funeral or a procession for instance. Yet that person would not be able to explain why 'Our intellect alone is absolutely incapable of understanding these things' as Jung wrote in 'The Symbolic Life' (*CW 18*, para. 617).

But to set about rituals and their connection with the transformation observed in analysis in a systematic way, we have to go back to 1911 when Jung was thirty-six and began to work on the epoch-making book that was first translated as 'Psychology of the Unconscious' (1916) and is known to us in English as 'Symbols of Transformation' (*CW 5*, 1956). As a concept 'transformation' is bound up with that of psychic energy, which, like its physical counterpart, has to do with dynamics and movement. Jung devoted much interest to physical and other analogies of psychological transformations and their whole-making potentialities. He also found parallels in anthropological, religious and, above all, alchemical texts. The particular aspects I shall be concerned with are the transformations intended to be therapeutic and accompanied by certain rituals, more often implicit than explicit.

In 'Concerning Rebirth' Jung mentions that by witnessing of, or participation in, some rites of transformation, such as the Mass or pagan mysteries, the individual is promised immortality (*CW 9, I*: paras 199–258). Jung then turns to the psychology of rebirth and mentions a number of possibilities among which there are: diminution of the personality as well as states of 'possession' and of identification with ancestors, for example, or with cult heroes or, again, with groups. Positively he mentions enlargement and enrichment of the personality and individuation.

Jung also comments on spectators at a ritual who may become involved for a time yet without undergoing any lasting change. Although impressed, they can remain 'outside' and treat the ritual performed by others as an agreeable aesthetic experience (*CW 9, I*: para. 211). In contrast to this there are therapies like analysis which can have a transforming effect, if they are syntonic with the cultural background of the participant who is willing to be taken out of his routine life and into a dimension of time and space which forms the container for possible changes.

It is sometimes overlooked that Jung in his listing includes more negative than positive outcomes. Neglected too is his observation that transformations play a considerable part in psychopathology in general, that is not just in individuation. Provided there is no pressure of time and expected aims, the ritualistic aspect of long-term analysis creates its own context and containing function. By this I do not mean that everything should remain stable, but rather that the containing frame of analysis provides the opportunity for some gradual psychic growth to occur. It seems, however, that even ritualized and stereotyped actions as such – divorced from underlying symbols and myths – may help to maintain a balance of mind. We shall return to this point at the end of the chapter (see p. 111). At this stage some definitions are needed.

Rituals pertain to rites and can be of a religious or secular kind. Dictionary definitions stipulate a formal procedure, custom or solemn observance which is characteristic of a culture, people or class of persons. Ceremony, or ceremonial, refers more to the outward trappings; for instance the precise observance of conventional forms of deference or respect. These need not detain us here, except to mention in passing the hollow or fossilized meaningless façades of rites which may be kept up for purposes other than those intended at the inception, such as pomp, pageantry, protocol, advertising and political expediences. We also note that social changes are capable of bringing such deteriorations about; what was a solemn observance at one time may end up as a stereotyped performance. But it is surely of psychological significance that we are reluctant to abandon a rite even after it has become a formality, a mere going through the motions for the sake of appearances, perhaps because of some superstitious awe, possibly without any obvious motive, a mere habit. If a royal wedding is enjoyed by millions of television viewers all over the world the need for such pageantry may be a direct indication of the loss of significance of the marriage rite in ordinary circumstances. At any rate, I doubt whether the temporarily moving, watching and witnessing of this ritual will significantly increase the number of church weddings or reduce the divorce rate.

My general aim, then, must be to indicate why a society and the individuals who constitute it cannot survive in a state devoid of rites and ceremonies which carry a vital, symbolic message. In order to do this I shall postulate that every rite is accompanied by implicit or explicit instructions as to what must *not* be done in the pursuance of the rite, in other words a prohibition or taboo. We shall come back to the psychological reasons for wanting to break taboos.

As I am not qualified to speak about religious and sacramental aspects of rites as such, I shall have to restrict myself to some clinical observations made in a society which doubts every dogma but is not prepared to pay the price of uncertainty (see p. 106f below). A time also, when theories regarded temporarily as sacrosanct (because 'scientific') are subject to frequent revisions or radical changes.

It is relevant to recall that according to Jung, Freud placed the stamp of dogmatism on his theory of infantile sexuality, thereby hoping to prevent schisms (*CW 4*: para. 746) (see also p. 42 above, 'dissensions'). He was then expressing his criticism of Freud's attitude. Yet, in 'Psychology and Religion' he acknowledged the value of religious dogmas as 'immediate experiences', which are both extremely eloquent and last longer than a scientific theory. On the other hand Jung writes that the existence of dogmatism can also act as an efficient defence against further immediate experiences (*CW 11*: para. 75).

I think the answer to this paradox must depend on how slavishly one feels forced to adhere to a religious or secular dogma and its rituals which are *intended* to keep the symbolism of vital events alive. It is true that within our practice of analysis the emphasis may shift from one dogma to another, for example from awe-inspired observations of 'archetypal material' to veneration of the transference and countertransference or of the mothering analyst 'holding' the infant–patient. What matters more than these changing emphases is the careful cultivation of meetings involving 'abstinence' and designed to facilitate a stable frame in which transformations can occur. (Jung recognized and compared it with the sacred precinct of Greek temples, the *temenos*.) Analytic sessions can therefore also be regarded as rituals within the definition given. However, the transformations achieved often turn out to be more limited than the high expectations.

RITUALS IN SEARCH OF A CONTAINER

Of course, neither the efforts of Freud, nor of the Church prevented schisms and the proliferation of dogmas in the long run, although both have functioned as strong containers of a diversity of human beings who followed the teaching. The reason why organized religions have managed to fulfil their function for so much longer than short-lived theories can be found in the relation to an immortal Godhead, the presence of a third which holds together any two or more loyal believers and worshippers. In the past, elaborate rituals perceived and appreciated by the senses within the safety of a permanent institution took care of the individual's hope of salvation, a readily available symbolization of life everlasting for every believer. The container of a personality-centred cult is but a weak vessel, requiring, like other status and identity-bestowing institutions, ever more stringent initiation rites; the younger generation of analysts has to have qualifications and undergo tests which some of their elders did not possess or would not have passed. When such methods put more and more stress on the external ceremonial aspect, the more symbolic value of the ritual is forgotten. One could even postulate that the greater the repressed doubt in the value of the institutionalized dogma becomes, the more emphasis will be placed on appearances, such as selection and admission procedures and protocol. I would further regard the rise and fall of institutions as part of natural history, learned societies included. But while initiation rituals stabilize and maintain institutions and their 'establishments' in *power*, the question remains: *Why should we need rituals at all?*

Ethologists have demonstrated that rituals are not confined to human beings; elaborate ceremonies function as social regulators among animals. Jung, as always interested in instinctual patterns, points out the direct powerful impact of religious rituals on the irrational aspect of our minds. He stresses the numinous archetypal effect communicated by rituals rather than by reason. Rituals then seem the executive agency by which communication and even communion is achieved, sometimes in elaborate premeditated ways, at other times by simple but repeated actions. These may vary from stereotyped facial expressions or gestures which constitute a sign language such as standing together in silence betokening mourning. Although speech is not a prerequisite for this kind of ritualistic communion, were man bereft of speech, the 'no-speak' of such a silence could not have attained ritualistic significance.

It would further appear that we have an inner need to cut through false appearances, hypocrisies by speech and, specifically, by jargon: a need to rebel against hierarchies, establishments, political systems, churches or other social institutions. But I can think of at least two additional incentives for breaking taboos which, as I said, are regular accompaniments of rites; one is the *'stolen-fruits-are-sweetest'* motif which brings about an immediate feeling of freedom that accompanies the breaking of a taboo. Iconoclastic excitement too runs highest where, before, worship by elaborate and stringent ceremony and unquestioning obedience had been the rule. There can be little doubt that the fashion for non-verbal encounter groups owes much of its existence to the stringency of purely verbal communication, the non-touch technique of psycho-analytic doctrine. The other incentive I should like to refer to is the *'forbidden room motif'* alluding, of course, to folklore and fairy-tales. Here, too, the driving force is transgression of what is prohibited in the name of established order. But unlike the stolen fruit motif, the temptation by means of sensuality is less marked than, for example, in the story of the Fall as commonly portrayed with all its moralizing overtones. I suggest that such transgressions take place because of the singularly human curiosity to learn the secrets of our own nature and the world around us. Such knowledge had been tabooed as being the privilege of the gods. Hence the development of science and technology and the secularization of knowledge untrammelled by religious dogma, yet also constantly developing its own traditions and dogmas; thought containers which become in due course codified and broken again in turn by new ideas and observations – a process, we note, that has gathered momentum during the last 500 years and is now also exerting its influence on the evolution of psychotherapies that constitute a multitude of paths all seemingly leading to self-discovery, the road to salvation, as it were.

In the setting up of new methods of psychotherapy there is both the stolen-fruit and the forbidden-room motif: sensuality as well as curiosity are evident driving forces. In 1928 Jung wrote in 'The Spiritual Problem of Modern Man' that there had been a rapid and worldwide growth of interest in psychology over the last twenty years (*CW 10*: para. 167). Certainly, the momentum has not decreased since.

Whenever a new school or method of psychotherapy has been given birth to, its proponents, as likely as not, create a personality-centred cult and, as regularly, new dogmas and rituals. The mixed communal bath in the nude under a starry sky may at first be an uplifting experience in which the breaking of a taboo has its share. But soon that bath becomes a pseudo-initiation rite. To appear in a bathing costume would then be an offence, like the breaking of the taboo had been before. The annual celebration of its birthday is likely to be the first sign that the new institution has gained formal status. The auditing of accounts, committees, annual general meetings, international congresses etc. all bear witness to its having become established. And so, gradually, the wheel turns full circle.

But during the brief interval before hierarchies and organization take over, there is likely to be a vacuum, experienced as liberation by many and as the yawning gap of chaos by a few. Chaos, in the form of instinctual rioting, seems to be lying in wait at all times. When violence follows in the wake of any man-made or natural catastrophe anywhere in the world it is callous to sing in praise of Dionysus.

So far, then, my conclusions are negative in that we cannot foretell whether, or when, rituals are strong enough to fulfil their containing channelling function without becoming so rigid as to be suffocating. In order to clarify the issue let us turn to some direct observations in the psychotherapeutic setting.

CLINICAL CONSIDERATIONS AND ILLUSTRATIONS

So far, I have attempted to show that rituals and taboos belong together and have assumed that this is the case both in religious and secular practice. I have also indicated that there has been a secularization of religion in our time. For example, Jung pointed out in his 'Principles of Practical Psychotherapy' how a formerly religious rite, the securing of absolution after confession, had become a group experience. He was then referring to the Oxford Group movement in England in 1935. In 'Problems of Modern Psychotherapy' (*CW 16*: para. 21) he had already classified four stages of psychotherapy of which confession was the first, followed by elucidation, education and transformation. The development of many forms of psychotherapy since then points in the same direction, namely that various methods may be practised in which the relations *between* persons is of primary importance, the relation between a person and the deity seems to receive less attention. In contrast to such methods analysis proper still cultivates the relation between a person and an unattainable goal, a 'third' or virtual point known by different names such as integration of the personality, resolution of the transference, individuation and self-realization or Bion's 'O' (see under 'global aims', p. 53). Of course the two methods are not mutually exclusive, but the new dogma of healing by interpersonal relations has, in my opinion, resulted in a progressive secularization as well as in a proliferation of psychotherapies in which various types of group, encounter and family therapies play an important part. The emphasis on interpersonal relationships has accelerated the cycle of broken prohibitions but has not been attended by new rituals. Lacking further the background of a traditional hierarchy, one wonders whether the *emphasis on interpersonal relations* is *also* responsible for the apparent *increase in incest*. It looks, however, as if the pendulum has begun to swing in the opposite direction in that at the intrapsychic end of the psychotherapeutic spectrum, meditative practices with intensive ritualistic patterns are now being cultivated but, again, without roots in home-grown traditions. Although social diagnoses are not within the analyst's competence, he nevertheless must pay attention to the social milieu. Having already postulated that there is an inherent and influential element of ritual in analysis, at least as much if not more so, than in other forms of psychotherapy, I shall concentrate mainly on the question of *what constitutes a transformation and how we diagnose degrees of transformation.*

Illustrations

The case of a woman in her early twenties comes to mind, whose parents came from a strictly puritanical background which had left its mark despite the liberal views which they adopted later in life. The girl was talented but became a university 'drop-out', behaving in ways which could not have been better designed to provoke her parents' anger and anxiety. When I saw her she had adopted a Buddhist cult and behaved in bizarre ways according to the rituals she thought that cult expected of her. Symptoms of a disintegrated personality were breaking through this ritualization and she was becoming paranoid. The adoption or, rather, imitation of eastern cults and rituals is not uncommon among the young in our society and one has learned to be wary of the religiosity which accompanies not only spiritual crises but serious breakdowns: rituals grown overnight in a hothouse cannot function as containers for long enough to stabilize and foster natural psychic growth.

A hidden alternative to rebellion against empty rituals and the violation of accompanying taboos is the obsessional practice and over-zealous observation of rituals, often compulsive and accompanied by ruminations. *A young man* whom I first saw as a patient twenty years ago had good reason to be afraid of his incestuous desires, which were acknowledged and yet only partly conscious. His major phobia was that he might persuade people that poisonous substances were actually harmless. By indirectly persuading them to eat poison he would become responsible for their deaths. The substances were associated in analysis with oral taboos in his childhood. This history so far corresponded to Freud's formulation in 'Totem and taboo': 'It is a law of neurotic illness that these obsessive acts fall more and more under the sway of the instinct and approach nearer and nearer to the activity which was originally prohibited' (*SE 13*, p. 30). Jung expresses himself on the same topic, but with a characteristic difference, as follows: 'The rules of the ritual must be scrupulously observed, if it is to have its intended magical effect. Generally the rite has a prophylactic, apotropaic significance, and when incorrectly performed or used may conjure up the very danger it was intended to avert' (*CW 5*: para. 248). However, insight had no effect in this case (it rarely does) but coming regularly to unburden himself alleviated the patient's anxiety. It was of interest to me that his phobia about doing harm to people had changed only in unimportant details, but that he had for the moment found some relief in the practice of an eastern religious cult. When I saw him again a few years later he had abandoned that cult at the insistence of his wife. Consulting me twice a year for the last ten years seemed sufficient to keep him from becoming disabled by his obsessions and ruminations.

A further example of the relativity of transformation as an analytic event is provided by the case of a *middle-aged man*. He had already undergone a thorough psychoanalysis a few years before he came to me. His symptoms were manifold, but the common denominator was his lack of decisiveness, an inability to commit himself on the one hand and what he called 'the need to become defined' on the other. In order to achieve this he went in for certain eccentric practices in a ritualistic way. Some were deliberately contrived by him, others were recurrent involuntary habits. The latter did affect his life in detrimental ways; I shall only mention two. Whenever he embarked on making something with his hands, which he was very good at, or engaged in a competitive sport, or went on holiday, he first had to spoil something which could and sometimes did ruin that particular activity. He realized with my help that he was practising a kind of apotropaic magic designed to avert greater evil, but the habit continued. He needed my help mainly to be reminded of his limited capacity to become and stay 'defined'. This part of the patient's ritual was practised unconsciously and there was little or no transformation in the direction of further development of his personality during the time that I analysed him. In fact the analysis, including the transference, was used by him in a magical, evil-averting way. Nevertheless, he made some progress in his social and emotional life during the time that I saw him. In that limited sense some enlargement of the personality took place.

Another striking example of relative non-transformation or non-development was seen in the case of *a youngish man* who had also had two shots at psychotherapy before I saw him. I considered him to be a latent psychotic. He spoke no more than for approximately ten minutes on the average during each session. Most of the time he sat silently and motionless. Yet he continued to come for many years and was very reluctant to give up the so-called analysis which consisted in the main of reporting some events, airing his grievances and very rarely recounting a dream in the interpretation of which he was not interested. He also showed little interest in what I had to say and regarded my words as an intrusion which sometimes made him angry. Frequently he was absorbed in his fantasies during sessions, which occasionally he allowed me to share. My comments on these occasions were again of no particular interest to him and seemed quickly forgotten. But the fact that I commented at all seemed important. It was a sign that I cared. When I said so, he agreed with me. The point is that he valued this 'analysis', got on better with his life than before and seemed a little happier. (Countertransference-wise I might mention that despite the very long and frequent silences I never felt bored.) I cannot say that any development of his personality took place which I could attribute to the analysis, although some creditable social adaptations occurred and he survived some hard knocks. (With reference to what I wrote regarding the mutual transference (see p. 27), I suppose that his capacity to survive had endeared him to me.)

Finally, take the case of *a girl aged eight* who was referred to me on account of very destructive and spiteful behaviour. She required a lot of 'holding' both in the literal and metaphorical sense of the word, and paper witches had to be ritualistically burnt at the end of every session for many months on end. Also every session started with my having to find her when she was hiding. In fact we never got any further because of her mother's breakdown. (Seven years later, however, I heard that she no longer presented behaviour problems or other obvious symptoms.)

Conclusions

I hope these thumbnail sketches will help us to take a closer look at the transforming function of rituals. The university drop-out girl was rather desperately looking for a creed which would fulfil the function of establishing her identity. For this it would have to be as different from her parents as possible. What is more, the patient used her ritualistic observances to establish a kind of group identity with like-minded contemporaries. This helped her not to feel helpless when faced with a 'shrink' like myself. It would have been unbearable to her because she felt indebted to her parents who had bestowed so much care on her and had brought her to me. We can regard the over-emphasis on ritualistic practices as a futile attempt to reconcile her rebellion and guilt. But the confession of her new creed was half-hearted and she could not bear the burden of guilt and separateness. It was therefore not surprising that without some intermediate steps her short cut to transformation did not succeed. Transformation in her case would have meant from child to adult or a 'rebirth' symbolically conveyed by initiation rites. As it happened her own half-conscious doubts about the validity of the alien rituals had led to paranoid projections and a breakdown requiring a spell of hospitalization and later analysis.

The second patient, with his phobia of killing people by poison, also demonstrates the need for a container, which was eventually found in biannual consultations and confessions with gradual attempts at elucidation. In this way his life became bearable and he could be said to have become a useful member of society. Although the transformation, such as it is, has taken over twenty years so far, there may still be some potentialities for the realization of which the analyst's survival as an externalized control point is desirable.

The third patient was the man who had to spoil things involuntarily before he could risk success and who also practised some rituals which he had invented in order to get himself 'defined'. The role he ascribed to me was to help by being firm. He tested me by playing various 'games' such as coming late and then arguing the inevitability of these events, or by staying away or by delaying payment of his bill so that I would have to insist on payment.

By being firm without entering into arguments I managed to replace the rituals he had previously enacted outside his first analysis and, as he said, without the analyst's knowledge. When I did not yield to coaxing and arguments he would try abuse. To his relief this did not change my attitude, which helped in his search for 'definition'. I had guessed that his belief in his own magic had to come up against my reality, as shown by the need for regularity of sessions, punctuality and payments. However, I failed to stop his involuntary spoiling of success and enjoyments. Although I felt certain that I knew the infantile dependent roots of this complex, my interpretations did nothing to change matters. I thought that in this way he was keeping his option open to enter a tabooed area, namely to have power over a mother who only seemed to have had time and love for him whenever illness or misfortune befell him.

The outstanding feature of the silent patient's analysis was that he did not accept interpretations in the form of reconstructions of his infancy and childhood, nor of transference projections. Whatever had happened in the past or was happening in the present were to him circumstances to which he could only passively react. He never permitted the idea of his having made a contribution to the events. In Jung's terminology, 'the shadow' was disowned as it has to be in narcissistic conditions. It was only with the help of occasional humorous confrontations that he could at least see his own mood-swings and thus a certain continuity of being himself, of being a unique person, was established. But his vulnerability to anything that could be construed as criticism remained at a point of almost total intolerance.

I had gathered from his account of previous analyses as well as from the content of some fantasies which he *did* share with me, that there was an unusually large reservoir of unresolved aggression and destructiveness in his psyche against which he had created a barrier, a 'reaction formation' in the form of being on the side of the underdog and social justice. This defence and his militant atheism had to be left intact. Only on one occasion did he thank his 'lucky stars' for something he had not undertaken, thereby giving me the opportunity to draw his attention to the magical-superstitious faith he had in unseen and uncontrollable forces. I should not be surprised if at some future date he were to undergo a religious conversion experience or a paranoid psychotic breakdown. At least he knows now that his motivations are not dictated by sweet reason and a praiseworthy sense of social justice. But I do not expect this realization to last or to be powerful enough to contain the violent taboo breaking forces in the deeper layer of his psyche which I did not reach.

It will be remembered that the last case was that of the eight-year-old girl whose mother had a breakdown. She usually brought the girl to sessions when she was well enough and my 'finding' the girl herself constituted a *rite d'entrée* which established her separate identity, while the ritualistic burning of the witch at the end of the session was meant to render the dangerous aspects of her relation to her mother harmless. Interpretations did nothing to lessen the need for these ritualistic, repetitive activities. On the other hand she never burnt witches or set anything else alight outside the sessions. My presence and participation in this ritual seemed to be required. Perhaps we practised a kind of exorcism together.

The autonomous ritual

The title of the chapter implies that rituals acquire a certain autonomy, that they can 'go places' of their own accord or, alternatively, change their appearances but stay what they are and become mere habits which do not transform, that is do not bring about any change in the psyche. Indeed it is probable that they offer *protection against catastrophic changes*. Sometimes it seems impossible to predict whether a person is stuck with a habit or just marking time until a favourable moment for discarding it occurs and retrospective accounts do not help us with other cases. The witch-burning girl, for example, looked to me completely stuck at the time when I stopped seeing her. Had I known the compulsively spoiling man at the time of his first analysis, I would probably have despaired at his ever getting beyond his ritualistic practices with his then girlfriend. There may be a positive prognostic point in that both patients required a specific partner for their ritual; it was not practised in solitude nor indiscriminately.

One could stipulate that once this specific imprinting or, as the ethologist Lorenz later called it, object-fixation, occurs there exists opportunity for wider emotional relations to grow between the partners which may make the ritualistic habit irrelevant (Lorenz, 1966). But I do not wish to sound unduly optimistic and am far from underestimating what Freud called the 'repetition-compulsion', or the force of habit whether in or between individuals and society, 'the solidified, that is to say institutionalized, system of social norms and rites which function very much like a supporting skeleton in human cultures', to borrow a phrase from Lorenz (ibid.)

In my use of case illustrations I particularly selected situations in which one could observe *formes frustes*, abortive or at least incomplete attempts at transformations or personality development by means of ritualistic activity. On the contrary, the rituals including obsessive ruminations and repetitive compulsive acts served mainly to preserve the *status quo*, to stabilize persons threatened by disintegration. In my selection I emphasized a non-specific aspect of analysis because containment by ritualized meetings would also apply to other forms of psychotherapy. Frequency of sessions is relatively unimportant from the ritualistic point of view when compared with regular availability. The same applies to religious rituals like confession. Within this framework, or container, transformations may and do occur more or less spontaneously, without, or regardless of, our attempts at active intervention. However this may be, none of the patients I referred to was in a strong enough position to break the taboos or, what amounts to the same thing, stop self-imposed rituals in exchange for the transformation that analytic interpretations offered. By stating this I have arrived at the point where it becomes necessary to clarify what rituals in general recapitulate and what their aim is. We can then compare this with the personal, often compulsive, ritualistic activities described above.

One way of doing this may be a classification. I am well aware that this is an area in which many disciplines such as anthropology, theology and ethology have a vested interest. But the psychological significance which Jung attributed to this area and the changes which I believe are taking place in our society in general and in psychotherapies in particular make a brief addition to the dictionary definition I gave inevitable.

I shall put the *rites de passage* first, because they contain an essential criterion of all rites as dramatic events, that is the relationship to time. Every event has a before and an after. Ritual enactment of transformations such as initiation is needed in order to underline, to impress on consciousness, that the after is irreversibly different from the before. Events like birth and death occur, one might say, quite unceremoniously. Yet everywhere rites are established to mark the passage from one state of being to another. Their significance stems from the human animal's special preoccupation with time and immortality. These rites then underscore and help us to integrate events in nature, and in the life cycle of man.

A second category of transforming rituals is somewhat different in that they show an added specifically human characteristic. Baptism, or its equivalents, initiation, weddings and periodic renewals of spiritual life, belong here. Such rites serve as vehicles for the communication of symbols required for the survival of the culture in which they are rooted. The rites in this category are often geared to a predictable time scale like the seasons of the year, physical maturation, other phases of life, or a calendar which prescribes rituals and celebrations according to the life of religious and cultural myths.

A third category consists of the *ad hoc* rites, especially invented for the purpose of driving out or averting evil and restoring health. Exorcisms and propitiation of deities, pilgrimages and other special acts are akin to the apotropaic magic which some of my patients practised in involuntary and compulsive ways. It is in the nature of illness and accidents, states of 'possession' and other misfortunes that they cannot be geared to any predictable time scale. But humans do not like unpredictability: it causes anxiety. Small wonder that at different times oracles and astrologers, priests, doctors, analysts and other assorted experts have to be consulted. The widespread use of sooth-saying procedures is a case in point. Not a few Jungian analysts consult the *I-Ching* which has a respectable ancestry in Chinese philosophy and 'consulting the unconscious' makes it doubly respectable.

What matters here is that for many patients, at least to begin with, the ritual aspect of analysis or other psychotherapies belong to this third category. Some newer therapies may offer what amounts to a cure by ritual. This is cheaper and quicker to obtain than a favourable analytic result. Analysis has by now acquired a patina of tradition. When it was new, satisfactory results were apparently quickly obtained. Also, taboo breaking is made easy in this area since disaffection with one form of psychotherapy virtually guarantees a welcoming reception by another and so the new ritual begins with an unspoken promise of a happier future just around the corner.

There is, however, a positive aspect to what I call the relative autonomy of rituals. On what Balint calls 'the creation level' there is no external object and man's main concern is to produce something out of him/herself (Balint, 1958). Readers of *Dreams, Memories and Reflections* may remember the manikin Jung carved as a child and the ritualistic purpose it served (Jung, 1967). But no out-of-the way act is needed. We can perform our daily tasks in a ritualistic way. Whether it is clearing a desk, cleaning the house or eating a meal, each step in the action can be carried out in a ritualistic, devout manner. Clock-time is in abeyance, competition irrelevant, in fact the value of the ritualistic action in utilitarian terms is nil.

In this state of mind any ordinary action can be unifying ritual: in its performance there is a sense of being united with all of oneself and 'together' in this sense as well as joined with mankind and the non-human environment or, if you like, the cosmos. But easy as it may sound, it requires discipline to introduce a ritualistic attitude to one's daily life. Deliberate, non-compulsive, ritualistic actions are, therefore, totally different from being stuck in a rut like a routine consisting of nothing more than repetitions.

Analysis, too, has a ritualistic aspect and rituals have a tendency to become autonomous, 'to go it alone'. Therefore there is always a danger that analysis may deteriorate into a habit rather than an ongoing process which leads to independence. It is hard to tell when the dividing line has been reached, and most analysts know of this difficulty. They certainly know that analytic work is habit-forming and not only for the patient.

THE PROLIFERATION OF PSYCHOTHERAPIES

It is against the general background of rituals without a cultural context that the proliferation of psychotherapies in our time has to be considered. Add to this the everlasting hope of a panacea, the cure for all ills, a belief which has surely found new impetus from the technological achievements of the twentieth century, the hope of immortality being within sight and the Utopia that man's natural estate is one in which there is 'no problem' and you have all the prerequisites for a proliferation of psychotherapies. This is the modern myth on which many short cuts to happiness are based.

One could, of course, argue that various methods or techniques are mutually complementary and what suits one person does not suit another. But I think that blunderbuss methods and emphasis on differences between individuals, cannot replace the virtue of a clear orientation as long as one safeguards oneself against the blinkers of a mind-closing doctrine. Within the context of this chapter and the question it poses concerning the state of psychotherapies, the short answer must be that therapeutic rituals are proliferating all over the place. Transformations by analysis are in reality not only slower but also more limited than theory and the romantic vision lead one to expect. Such transformations as do occur are, in part, due to the ritualistic aspects.

RITUALS IN ANALYSIS VS THERAPY AS A RITUAL

I had started with the hypothesis that the ritualistic setting of analysis favoured the aim of providing a suitable climate in which a therapeutic transformation process could be set in motion. However, the five illustrations I had chosen as being specially suitable to demonstrate the ritualistic aspects all came from cases in which that process never got under way, the *'formes frustes'*. On the one hand my interventions made no difference, on the other it could be said that the non-specific, containing and concentrating function of regular sessions gave the natural healing and developing processes the breathing space required.

The focal point seemed to consist of a person who listened and tried to tune in without making even an unspoken demand on the patient to 'get better'. Is this humanly possible? The short answer is that analysts strive for it while other therapists, notably behaviour therapists and some family therapists, do not even try. Some invent *new rituals to counteract the patient's old*. Maybe analysis does something like that too. But the 'paradoxical injunctions' used by some family therapists seem crude counter-games or rituals. In his *The Language of Change* Watzlawick, while appreciating Jung's recognition of the psychotherapeutic importance of rituals as well as my chapter on rituals, took me to task for not recommending planned active intervention by means of creatively invented rituals as therapy (Watzlawick, 1978). He is quite right when he says that anything of the kind would be regarded as contrary to the analytic attitude and be called 'manipulative' by analysts, a word that is anathema. However, the distinction between an open-ended and a directive form of psychotherapy cannot only be made on the grounds that the one is restricted to verbal interpretations while the other intervenes by prescribing actions. The distinction seems to depend rather on the pressure exerted by therapists of whatever kind on their patients to respond by 'getting better'. Denials notwithstanding, 'better' implies all too easily, better in terms of the therapist's expectation. The pressure is further increased, if therapists feel impelled to demonstrate the success of their method and thereby their own worth. All this points to the existence of a dilemma which could be abbreviated as follows.

As long as rituals in analysis could be seen as the motorial counterpart or executive organ of symbols of *transformation, transformers* of psychic energy, there was no difficulty for Jung and others to accept ritualistic aspects of dreams and the like in analysis. The ideational basis of this attitude is that rituals have a purpose, a goal. The teleological attribute is emphasized by others, like Henderson who sees the symbolism of the self which prepares the way to individuation by three stages of initiation as in tribal rituals, that is submission, containment (incubation) and liberation (Henderson, 1967).

But the dilemma cannot be solved by a division of therapies into those that take the ritualistic aspect as part and parcel of the procedure and others that use rituals deliberately. Analysis for example can make sense of rituals but does not explicitly use them. On the other hand, behaviour therapy does not look for the symbolic meaning of dreams and behaviour but can institute procedures which strike one as ritualistic.

The dilemma can be reconsidered by asking what constitutes a ritual. Clearly the hoped-for transforming function of analysis like that of other therapies does not always materialize. How can this be explained? We know quite a bit about rites and their origins as well as about their threshold-negotiating usage. A neglected factor of ritualistic behaviour is the physiological root. For example, some patients submit fairly easily to pressures of the kind mentioned and respond positively to demands, while in others pressure creates counter-pressure despite their also wanting to be cured of energy-wasting and depressing habits. We also know that some persons can be easily 'conditioned', yet others only with difficulty, or not at all. It would make sense to link such findings with Jung's distinction between adaptive 'society-syntonic' behaviour and the more rugged type of individuality up to the point of 'individuation'.

However, my purpose is not to take this and other possible dichotomies any further, but to draw attention to the innate physiological rather than the psychologically determined origin of ritualistic activity. This is necessary because of the non-specific aspect of analysis as a ritual and also because actions speak louder than words, meaning here that the motoric activity accompanying rituals suggests their being deeply implanted in our minds. In his anthropological studies, Jung drew attention to the rhythm that accompanies ritual preparations or transformations of instinctual energy for which rhythmic chanting and dancing seem to be indispensable. Whether we think of the sucking reflex of infants, the heartbeat or sexual activity, all organisms are subject to bi-phasic, repetitive rhythms. It does not seem too farfetched therefore to consider this as the innate contribution to rituals whatever the spiritual or transforming function they may serve. Seen in that light the repetitious and perseverating activities which are devoid of any psychological meaning and purpose become understandable as does also the tenaciousness of habits and addictions. The innate physiological component can continue of its own accord, in which case the activity may appear 'ritualistic', yet nothing is transformed, psychic energy can be explained yet no change occurs.

In this connection Freud's observation in 'Inhibition, Symptom and Anxiety' is of interest. Here he described a number of recurrent symptoms which showed ceremonial characteristics. These surround some routines which should be automatic, such as going to sleep, washing, getting dressed, locomotion and time-consuming repetitions (*SE 20*: p. 75f). Although Freud refers here to serious disturbances, the tendency to such ritualization is a widespread phenomenon. Tennis stars at critical moments can be seen to blow several times rapidly on their fingernails; other people may feel the need to light a cigarette or make a cup of tea or coffee. Actions of this kind punctuate the working routine and whether deliberate or not, they seem to serve the purpose of lessening anxiety, to give a breathing space or to propitiate fate.

To sum up the problems surrounding the ritualistic aspect of analysis: analysis with its own conventions and setting shares with other ritualistically performed actions that it functions as a stabilizing influence. As a regular rhythmic activity it serves at once as a bulwark against a sea of unpredictable chaos and a beacon in the fog of meaningless, monotonous daily routines. But the unchanging conditions which strengthen the container-crucible required for transformations can at the same time promote stagnation, repetition and sterility. The safety of a prison wards off the fear of catastrophic freedom and the insecurity of unpredictable change. That this fear is extremely powerful becomes evident when both partners of the dyad cling to the unchanging ritual despite their increasing awareness of and even rage against the stranglehold, hence my plea for a ritualistic form of ending analysis, a *rite de sortie* (see also p. 192).

SUMMARY AND CONCLUSIONS

It seems justified to draw a parallel between the way rituals and taboos are treated by contemporary society and by various psychotherapeutic methods. By conducting the argument from general social observations to particular analytic case illustrations, I arrived at what seems to me a common denominator, that is the relative autonomy of rituals and their capability to perseverate although divorced from myths and symbolic meaning. In short, we have to be aware of the formation and strength of rituals as habits.

Rituals are useful as stabilizers and containers both in the social and psychotherapeutic sense. By the same token they can also hold up progress and development. Similarly, with prohibitions and taboos which commonly act in support of various rituals: by their very existence they may also incite destruction of the ritual, particularly when it has become threadbare, no longer serving as a vehicle for symbols. In that case, the breaking of a taboo as the dark side of the ritual fulfils a scavenger-like function.

What I said applies especially to the *ad hoc* health-giving and evil-averting rituals according to the classification provided. These are particularly prone to proliferate indiscriminately. The hope of finding panaceas has not disappeared and the increasing secularization of knowledge by science and technological achievements has added to the illusion that there must be a solution to every human problem; hence the proliferation of psychotherapies, with disillusionments following illusions in endless procession. Some new theories and techniques as well as the alleged results would glitter less brightly if the enduring ritualistic aspects of every psychotherapy were borne in mind.

The implication is that although inter-personal and intrapsychic relations are useful bases for psychotherapies, there seems a special need and a particular value attached to the conscious practice of performing activities in a ritualistic way, whether these be ordinary daily tasks, special religious or psychotherapeutic practices or participation in traditional festivals. All these can form useful aids to self-synthesis, 'becoming centred' as my patient called it. In our society we are much more frequently on the move in physical space than previous generations. Yet the limit of mental moves and changes that really matter has not changed. How are we to negotiate the discrepancy without appropriate rites of passage that remind us of the end of the journeying and the finality of existence? The deliberate cultivation of ritualistic observances and actions holds out advantages over mere habit formations and repetition compulsions which take possession of us, both individually and collectively.

Finally, we live much closer to the magical, ritualistic layer of the psyche than we care to admit. This does not mean, however, that we know more about the phenomena which emerge when we give them a name, nor that we have been able to discover satisfactory methods of investigation which would allow us to dispense with a myth of our time, namely that systematic, scientific investigation will lead to a better understanding of the effects and value of rituals. I hope to have shown why I regard it as our duty not to lose sight of the power of rituals and their whereabouts both in analysis and our daily lives.

Chapter 7

'What do you actually do?'

My first reaction to the question, 'What do you actually do?' varies according to the person who asks the question. Sometimes I feel embarrassed because I know that whatever I am going to say cannot do justice to the intricacies of the analyst's job, nor will it satisfy some questioners who even after lengthy conversation may remain puzzled. He or she may even become a little indignant because the reply cannot be grasped by intellect alone. It is therefore liable to be called 'vague'.

If, on the other hand, the question is put to me by a colleague, my answer is likely to depend on the emotional climate between us. But however favourable that may be, a defensive factor will colour it: not because I have done something dreadfully unethical, nor because I fear that my reply will reveal that I am 'not an analyst', but because a little voice (I am deliberately avoiding technical terms) tells me that I do not know, or at least do not know very well, what I actually do. Therefore, before I have time to formulate my reply, my affective reaction to the colleague's question could be 'Why do you want to know?'

The circumstances which make a colleague ask this question are, of course, that I have given him/her good reason to believe that I have deviated from some standard, e.g. 'Classical Analytical Technique'. In addition to frequency of session (four or five per week) and use of the couch, the outstanding characteristics of CAT in psychoanalysis are that the analyst:

1 eschews all giving of advice, prescribing of drugs and management of his patients' lives;
2 confines his utterance to interpretations;
3 instructs his patients to obey the fundamental rule of free association (Rycroft, 1968).

Whether we agree with Rycroft's criteria or not I think we must admit that, although Jung's interpretations of his patients' imagery appear to be easily grasped on a poetic level, it remains uncertain whether and to what extent Jung interpreted such material verbally. Where, you may go on to ask, are the detailed dynamics of analyst–patient interaction, that he himself called 'dialectical process'? In his writings one finds many case illustrations but no long, dialectical case history from which one could gather how he worked. We know about the importance he put on the analyst as a person but by comparison with Freud, Jung published nothing about the way he dealt with long analyses.

WHAT ANALYSTS CANNOT BE

Rycroft's summary is a classical example of an ideal that is unrealizable in practice. But even if it were, it seems doubtful whether an analyst who is still recognizable to the patient as a human being, could act as if he or she were *nothing but an implement of theories*, and as such unacceptable to the patient. (See also 'The patient speaks', p. 75f.) Jung's reminder that analysis requires the whole person is liable to lead to a misinterpretation which introduces the opposite kind of error (*CW 16*: para. 198). The illusion of palliness is easily induced by an archetypal theme that affects both partners. In the example given in Chapter 2 (p. 28), I showed how by *not* telling the patient about my own separation anxiety of which I had become acutely conscious again, I managed to avoid this pitfall. Considerations of this kind point once more to the 'being' that in the long run becomes more important than the alternatives of 'doing', that is interpreting, or not doing. This statement is more specific than saying that in analysis it matters not so much what you know, but who you are. The 'being' particularly involves the capacity to be totally and unanxiously present and – alone. There can be no pretence, no cheating: at least not on the conscious level. This has to be added, because it has often struck me that such *desiderata* and other points of emphasis, although strongly advocated and publicized, are rarely carried out by the proposers. Recognizing this truism leads to the following considerations.

Whether imaginary questioners are colleagues or laypersons, they are asking the question now, but I have not got a standard reply ready. Whatever it may be it relies on my abstractions of events that have become 'case illustrations' dating back to the past. Looking back is a kind of stocktaking, that is, the writer's present attempt to take account of *what* and *how* he had learned from experience. All past failures may be regarded as milestones in the analyst's evolution, but it must remain open to doubt whether something has indeed been learned and therefore changed or whether the writer is merely being hopeful. The crunch comes under stress when the old mistakes are likely to be repeated.

So the answer to what I actually do must include what *I believe* to have learned from experience. Being the fallible human instruments of their theories and observations, analysts have to become acquainted with the built-in flaws and peculiarities which are as permanent as the 'personal equation' implies. This refers to a factor that had to be taken into account when in the eighteenth century differences in the observations made by different astronomers yielded different results. It had caused a lot of trouble before electrical instruments took care of such apparent inaccuracies. Jung's 'psychological types' are another systematic attempt to make allowances for our peculiarities (cf. *CW* 6). But no single dimension is adequate for the determination of genetically, culturally and socially determined factors which in the aggregate determine *the personal premiss*, that is those biases and prejudices which are relatively permanent and influence to a varying extent the individual transference problematic. Although I am merely reformulating a statement of Jung's to the same effect (*CW* 9, *I*: para. 150), it is worth repeating here because individual transference situations occupy much mental space in our daily work and the permanent premiss and its often decisive influence on analysis are often left out. Therefore it has to be recognized anew in each case. In theory this is easily agreed, in practice, if analytic literature is anything to go by, this kind of learning from the experience of one's personal premisses receives little or no attention. The probable reason for this omission is a combination of not wanting to expose one's weaknesses and to emulate the natural scientist's objectivity instead.

The personal premiss, like the personal equation of old, can only be recognized by making comparisons with the experience of colleagues and even then one cannot get beyond probabilities. Redfearn, for example, collected enough material to publish a paper entitled *Dreams of Nuclear Warfare* (Redfearn, 1989). None of my patients has ever reported a dream referring to the subject. In the absence of any research into the possible causes of the discrepancy, one may conjecture that it is due to our starting from dissimilar personal premisses.

A different kind of learning comes about by paying attention to one's bodily responses. As analysts we are very used to making observations about the patient's words and averbal behaviour, forgetting at times that the patient, although at a disadvantage, can also make astute observations about the analyst. This applies, as mentioned both earlier and again later, most particularly to the *tone of voice* (see p. 97, above and p. 334, below). I have found it worth listening from time to time to my own voice and to take note of my breathing and the tension of my abdominal muscles. Of course, this is hard to do during the cut and thrust of a session. But the heat of the spontaneous exchanges does not abate immediately and it is possible to monitor such expressions and reactions shortly after the event. This too is a way of learning from experience which includes the possibility that even if patients have misconstrued the analyst's interpretation, they may have heard correctly what he or she probably did *not* say but may have felt or thought.

For example, a patient who had been in analysis for a long time, and had established a trusting analytic relationship, got into a critical situation over the weekend. He reported this on Monday and said that he had thought of phoning me but then decided not to, adding that he did phone a friend. I asked 'Why did you not phone me?' in what I thought was an even voice. Later in the session it transpired that my question had come across to the patient as meaning: 'You should have phoned me!' From a conscious point of view the question was meant to elicit the reasons for phoning the friend rather than me. Someone might say that a proper analyst does not ask such questions, and I would agree. The thought did in fact pass through my mind, and the next moment I realized that the patient had a good point: I *had* minded not being used and that someone else had been used instead. Nevertheless, it was also true that I was curious about the patient's motivation and especially about his reason for reporting the incident and for taking me up on the way I had spoken. All this could not have been analysed without raising the emotional temperature to a 'who is right' argument, had I not realized in time how the misunderstanding could be changed into a better understanding.

The patient had probably noticed something in my voice before I became aware of it. My realization, however, had come about by thinking of an imaginary rival. This goes to show that in analytic work there is more than one way of learning from experience: neither the understanding of dreams and fantasies nor bodily reactions, including the tone and pitch of one's voice are the only way. No more are intuitions, deep empathy or knowledge of mythology, fairy-tales and the like.

LEARNING TO AVOID BLUEPRINTS: JUNG'S OPPOSITES

Another mode of learning from experience about analysis is to be on the look-out for attractive generalizations, such as those known as '*the opposites*' which figure so prominently in Jung's theory and the writings of post-Jungians; for a summary see Edinger (1972), Samuels (1985), also Redfearn who describes how by facing the intrapsychic clash of opposites we may avert nuclear warfare (op. cit.). The opposites are closely associated with symbols of the self in which the opposites are joined as in the '*conjunctio oppositorum*'. 'The opposites are the ineradicable and indispensable preconditions of all psychic life' wrote Jung in his last great work, the 'Mysterium Conjunctionis' in 1954 (*CW 14*: para. 206). The concept has a respectable philosophical ancestry from Herodotus to Hegel by whom Jung was no doubt influenced. Alchemical texts and the 'Yin-Yang' doctrine of classical Chinese philosophy are also quoted evidence that 'the opposites' are an archetypal concept. But there seems to be a difference between the observation that such symbols do appear in dreams and that symbols of the union of opposites act as a transforming influence on personality development on the one hand, and the portmanteau citation of 'The Opposites' on the other. What is required is differentiation into categories of opposites for the term to have a consistent meaning. And further, each half of the pair needs to be studied in its own right when it may turn out that it already contains some characteristics of the other, as is the case in the study of chaos in which a measure of order has been discovered. Without categorization and differentiating, the 'union of opposites' makes no sense. For example, Jung's definition of a symbol as uniting the opposites, such as a symbol of the self, must *include* the domain we call conscious. On the other hand a person's cultural background is assumed to be partly *both*, conscious and unconscious. No matter how much the personal dispositions and background are analysed, such data are *not* subject to change: no more than one's I.Q. Therefore, of what practical value can the 'union of opposites' be, if *either* each moiety already contains some qualities of the other *or* is unchangeable anyway? Because of the important bearing this point has on Jungian theory, I shall return to it in Chapters 8 and 14 (see pp. 136 and 312, below). With considerations such as these in mind, let us take a closer look at the paired (bipolar) opposites.

PAIRED (BIPOLAR) OPPOSITES

The reader may find it convenient to refer to the table for the discussion that follows.

Table 3   Paired (bipolar) opposites

Category	Reason for pairing
1 Nouns and adjectival pairs	Physical and emotional experience
2 Concepts, e.g. conscious–unconscious	(a) Division for the purpose of study, mainly of 'unconscious' processes (b) Synthesis for symbol formation and healing (c) 'Psychological types'
3 Analytic techniques and attitudes	(a) Interpretations (verbal–averbal/none) (b) Attitudes (related to psychological types and/or classic versus romantic)

1. Nouns and adjectival pairs of experience

It is probably for the sake of an internal economy that we divide and order our daily perceptual and emotional impressions according to their contrasting qualities. This categorization is so easy that it appears to be nature-given. Adjectival pairs such as white–black, pleasurable–painful, would not be worth enumerating, were it not for their associative and frequently metaphoric link with perceptible natural phenomena such as day–night, birth–death, health–sickness, satiety–hunger, whereby the first of the adjectives and nouns mentioned becomes linked with 'good', the second with 'bad'. Once these associative links are established it is only a small step to the metaphor that – like poetry – evokes as it creates a vivid image that speaks to us and is best understood without explanation.

However, the poetic appeal of a nearly imperceptible transition from well-known things and qualities to fresh images and meanings has its beguiling aspect. It stops us from enquiring further into the nature of the apparent oppositeness of the original perceptions and their associated *experiential* quality. When for example the 'good–bad' qualities that are easily attached to phenomena become amalgamated both emotionally and conceptually with modes of feeling and thinking, further enquiry and differentiation is lost. It is as if an aura of familiarity had surrounded certain archetypal images like that of the parents. This pre-empts and stops any further thoughts and discovery. *When we speak of transference as 'positive' or 'negative', we know that we have become prey to the simplifying power of paired opposites.* If one nevertheless took the liberty of asking what outside the field of immediate sensory or intuitive perception each half of the apparent opposites of light–dark, warm–cold, good–bad, really signified, the arbitrariness and generalization inherent in such rudimentary polarizations would soon become evident. Their fleeting relevance to a situation depends on an all-too-easy and deceptive agreement about feeling tones like loving–hating between partners, such as patient and analyst. If the questioner went further and enquired about the lasting value that such easy agreements have for the partners, he or she would very likely be criticized for disassociating or 'splitting,' or of underestimating the 'unconscious' as the source of all relevant information. This is understandable because such questioning undermines the existing conceptual and practical framework of expecting to unite the opposites psychologically by interpretative 'working through' and/or waiting for the self to act as, or produce a symbol that will heal the 'split' opposites.

Finally, are the paired opposites really treated as equals or are analysts so fascinated by the 'unconscious' moiety that the other is left out?

An alternative to the exclusively analytic approach which aims to make unconscious data conscious and facilitate a new synthesis, is to supplement the traditional analytic framework by a cognitive and even frankly, rather than – as at present – implicitly, educational procedure, for example, explaining a figure of speech or a local custom to a patient who may be a foreigner, thereby encouraging the patient to do the same for the analyst. But such an alternative or supplementary attempts to enlarge the horizon other than by freeing a person from the bonds of unconscious motivations and lack of uniting symbols, that is to say by aiding consciousness directly by cognitive methods, is liable to be regarded as unanalytic.

2. Conceptual opposites

The intent to use mapping as a means of recording and facilitating discovery will show up dangers and flaws surrounding concepts in general and analytic concepts and theoretical models in particular. For details see Part III. It is as if we could not hold on to a pure concept for very long. Let the first danger we meet be called 'reification' (and personification), and the second 'syncretism'.

Here is an example of the first danger. Winnicott's 'transitional objects' being a concept cannot as such be seen. It can however be inferred once the concept has been adopted. The danger of destroying a concept by personification was demonstrated to me when someone mentioned that the patient treated her present boyfriend as a 'transitional object'. What was meant was that the young man had been regarded as a makeshift arrangement between the person from whom she had parted and a permanent relationship for which she hoped. Something similar happens in analytical psychology when a person is said to be someone's 'shadow' or 'anima'. What is meant is that the person in question has become the carrier of the projected archetypal image. This slipshod way of talking would not be worth mentioning, were it not an example of our laziness of mind which dehumanizes people by confusing concepts with observable phenomena.

Analytical psychology is full of conceptual dualities or paired opposites used as technical terms which unlike the natural events to which they make reference (see 'nouns', above, p. 122) have been invented, discovered or revealed depending on the attitude of the person who uses the verb. All have in common that one of the opposites is unthinkable without the other yet each pair represents no more than a rudimentary way of ordering natural phenomena. Graphic devices which have been repeatedly used to this end are centring, layering and polarizing both in the making of world images as well as in the case of early analytic structuring of the psyche (see also p. 47, above).

Again, conceptual dualities become reified and thereby 'un-thought', when, for example, a person asserts that Jerusalem or Rome is the centre of the world or that the aim of Jungian analysis is individuation, without any doubt or qualification. The proposed construction of a map showing where analysis stands in Chapter 14 makes me repeat the *caveat*, namely that few attributes make a concept as liable to reification as allocating a definite place to it as if on a geographical map. We know that there is no such place or location or thing as 'the unconscious'. Yet Freud's first purely psychological theory of mind was called topographical. If the intention had been to destroy the *concept* of the unconscious, the adjective could hardly have been better chosen. His second, 'structural' theory had the great advantage of emphasizing the relation of hypothetical agencies or structures to each other and on several levels. Similarly with the Jungian pantheon of archetypes and their relation to the ego and the self. Indeed Jung, in 'The Structure and Dynamics of the Self' did use a series of diagrams to demonstrate various psychological and gnostic configurations in their relation to each other (*CW 9, II*: paras. 347–429). While the object was to demonstrate that a variety of psychological phenomena could be understood with the help of the invariant concept 'archetype', the unifying parallelism derived from different disciplines was threatening to create not a synthesis, a 'unus mundus', but a syncretism. Events in nature, or models chosen from physical sciences cannot be linked with categories of human perception and emotional experience without running this risk. For there are disciplines of knowledge which for the purpose of study and advancement beyond a certain rudimentary point are *not* opposites to be united by a common archetypal denominator. We shall see this in the case of the *mappa mundi* which had represented a united world image, a syncretism of geographical and religious elements. It may have symbolized unity but contributed nothing to discovery. The implicate static order may even have prevented it.

As long as the concept of opposites holds undisputed sway, unification, synthesis, must be the desired objective. That is to say the acknowledgement of an irreconcilable diversity between the reality-principle of 'asymmetrical logic' (to use Matte Blanco's term) as a means of discovery is not part of a frame of reference that strives for symmetry and synthesis (Matte Blanco, 1975).

3. Opposed attitudes and techniques

The difference between the classic and the romantic attitude of analysts was discussed earlier (see p. 33), when the connection between the classicists' preference for verbal interpretations and the romanticists' expectant attitude was taken up. It is mentioned here as an example showing how analytic technique and the analyst's personality are or become so interwoven that even analysts who officially belong to the same school or discipline and are treating similar patients can have irreconcilable differences. This also applies when they are treating the same type of patient. (The controversy between two 'Jungians', Fordham and Schwartz-Salant using Bionic language and both treating so-called 'borderline personalities', clearly demonstrates this point.) Classicists would hold that the correct technique can be taught and is not dependent on the personality of the analyst, just as science subjects can be taught up to a point to pupils of sufficient intelligence. Bion, for example, leaves us in no doubt about his classical attitude when he regards any interpretation that is dependent on the analyst's *personal knowledge*, experience and character as analytically worthless (Bion, 1970). However much Bion and Jung are opposed on the value of personal knowledge as well as on the use of images and interpretations, we shall see that there is an essential similarity when it comes to the mystical element in their vertices.

The existence of the controversy is all that matters for the present purpose which is to show that the attitude-tehnique bond is a relatively invariant factor not allowing of any meeting place or union of opposites. This can be represented by an axis, the angle of which can vary according to the particular criterion chosen whereas the individual analyst's proclivity (see personal premiss) seems constant. This will make analytical psychologists think of Jung's 'Psychological Types' (*CW* 6). A further differentiation can be introduced by saying that it depends on the type and clinical condition of the patient. The subject will be taken up in Part III, Chapter 14 (see p. 310, below).

For the present we note that while attitudes can be endlessly argued about, technique is the more reliable guide to the way analysts feel and set about their work. Here the details such as chair or couch, frequency of sessions per week, verbal interpretations or silent participation, give a clear indication about their basic attitude derived in part from their training and background. Frequent sessions and verbal interpretations would point to the classical attitude and the analyst being without a doubt in charge of the situation (see also Chapter 13, p. 299, below). Less frequent sessions and the chair leave much of the work to the patient while both partners observe 'what the unconscious has in mind'. (I cannot describe this particular attitude without exaggerating the implicit personification of the concept 'unconscious' in analytical psychology.)

The literature on techniques, let alone classical techniques, in analytical psychology is scanty when compared with psychoanalysis. The reason for this is to be found, first in Jung's emphasis on the guiding role of the 'unconscious' which, given the opportunity, will become manifest in archetypal images and configurations such as the 'shadow'. The complexes of the individual and the conflicts aroused by the meeting between ego and archetype will then determine the analytic process. Second, there is the emphasis, as already mentioned on the analyst's personality on the one hand and the clinical outcome which is expected to follow the symbolic union of opposites. So there can be hardly any room for a 'standard' or 'classical' technique. Analysis is seen rather as a progressive series of archetypally determined encounters culminating, if all goes well, in a synthesis of the personality. In the romantic view in which personality development is the aim, the question 'What do you actually do?' should therefore be rephrased by *How do you think it (the process) actually works?* Also according to the same view the role of the analyst is hardly more than that of a privileged witness or, at most, a guide. The answer he or she gives would have to be illustrated by a series of images such as occur in dreams or actually pictures illustrating the synthesizing autonomous process. The technique according to that view of Jungian analysis consists of not doing anything that could interfere and to tolerate being deeply affected by the process observed.

But that is not the only view and, in any case, many patients who come to analysis do not fall into the category outlined. Therefore, I shall return by way of an example to the more run-of-the-mill situations which require something like the classical analytical technique in which interpretations are the mainstay.

'CLASSICAL ANALYTICAL TECHNIQUE' AND DISTORTIONS

In his *The Basic Fault*, Balint shows how psychoanalysts are divided into defenders of and offenders against classical analytical technique, 'CAT' for short (Balint, 1968). He leaves the reader in no doubt that he does not have much time for the defenders. In this I join him and will take it as read that classical analytical technique is an ideal and will be looked upon and treated as such by many analytical psychologists, meaning that it is always more or less unrealizable even when dealing with so-called ordinary neurotic adults.

We need not concern ourselves with the ideal of a standard technique any longer, but go straight on to the *intentional* modifications more or less recognized by analysts in order to meet the needs of particular classes of patients. The range of acceptance of such planned modifications by analysts varies from total in the case of children to rather less in the case of adolescents to even less in the case of psychotics. The attitude of psychoanalysts towards the class of patient I have chosen as case illustration (the patient was a compulsive drinker) is as divided as it is about psychotics. In any case, neither the defenders of nor the offenders against classical analytic technique can claim great success with alcoholics or other addicts. So I may assume that a questioning colleague would like to know more about any intentional modification of technique which I may have adopted.

But before I can attempt to satisfy their perfectly justified curiosity, I have to make a few generalizations which have to be borne in mind concerning the communication of analytic events to colleagues. The generalizations are based both on my reading and on my own observations. The latter are derived from differences I noted between statements meant for publication in contrast to what is said privately between colleagues who are also friends, or else in discussion groups and the like.

Let us deal first with the involuntary distortions which enter any narrative which purports to be a factual account of what happens in a session. It is, as Bion says, absurd to behave as if our accounts were somehow exempt from the psychoanalytic finding of unconscious motives which distort our memories and, I would add, the process of making a written or spoken account of what we remember (Bion, 1967).

Then there are the voluntary distortions made for reasons of discretion – discretion, that is to say, about the patient's identity. All manner of data have to be omitted or deliberately falsified in order to prevent identification. We may decide that such distortion of detail has no bearing on the modification of technique which we want to communicate. But I hold that this can be an illusion – we may be kidding ourselves that details do not matter. One way around the difficulty of preventing identification is to ask the patient's consent by letting him/her read and agree the account to be published. I know of one case in which this was done and the psychoanalyst in question later told me that it had had unpleasant consequences for the patient although analysis had officially ended before publication. Yet not to publish what you actually do or did until the patient in question has died is, or was, the policy of some analysts. It seems to limit published accounts rather severely.

As to discretion towards oneself – this is not often publicly admitted as a reason for curtailing or deliberately distorting accounts of modified techniques, and I do not propose to go into the manifold possibilities here beyond stating that discretion towards the patient and towards oneself as the analyst may coincide. On the whole, analysts in their publications are understandably discreet about their failures. In small and friendly groups I have found that colleagues are inclined to deter one from declaring a faulty procedure and what one regards as a disastrous failure. On the other hand, their doubting of and probing into what one may feel to be a useful acquisition of knowledge, technique or success redresses the balance.

Distortions are used deliberately in three ways.

1   As a special method or technique of communication: the slanted, elongated or foreshortened view in the visual arts and the pictorial language of poets are analogies. Much of language contains ideographs, and skilful agglomerations of figures of speech can achieve more by way of striking chords in an audience than the articulate elements of language and the strict adherence to grammatical rules. While one could not become an analyst without being alive to such ideographs, metaphors and overtones, these are at the same time extremely open to misconstruction when taken out of context, and downright unreliable as a means of communication of analytic techniques, especially to persons unfamiliar with our conventions.

The moment the emotional climate in which communications take place changes, reception becomes disturbed by various cross-currents. Skilful narrative and artistic means of relating what the analyst said and did and what actually happened may appear to come very close to the actual events. But it can also mislead the recipient in the direction intended by the author who relies on memories and/or notes and recordings (cf. on memory, p. 23, above).

2   The opposite kind of distortion is based on a deliberate search for essential elements in the many events and interventions which take place. It is a selection of data according to a preconception, in a state of mind adapted to receive a restricted range of phenomena. The common elements or bare bones and their particular usage in a given analytic situation can be pieced together with the help of a grid such as Bion has described (Bion, 1963). By allocating the content and function of an analytic happening according to certain *categories* of mental evolution, the transformation of such events can be observed without the disadvantages of a bewildering variety of images or other 'sensa'. Or so it was hoped.

In practice, however, analysis always contains elements derived from non-analytic sources, which can influence considerably what the analyst actually does but is likely to omit from any public communication about the technique and its theoretical foundations. The example of insurance companies was given in 'The presence of the third' (see p. 39). Furthermore, if I were able to describe what I select and what I leave out according to whether it is either essential to my thesis or irrelevant, I could probably not continue writing. What I actually do (say) or do not do is not the same as the technical procedure which I describe and sincerely believe I adhere to.

3   The conventions of presentation and style of a paper are another reason for a 'credibility gap', meaning: 'I don't believe that is how it actually was'.

Next I want to draw attention to the danger of imitation in the hope of acquiring technical competence. Many analysts know about Winnicott's joined squiggles as part of the therapeutic–diagnostic interviews with children. When Frieda Fordham gave a paper entitled 'Several views on individuation', she referred to adult patients doing finger paintings during sessions (Fordham, 1969). In the discussion which followed, this activity and the paintings became the focal point of interest. It became apparent that the integration of an analytic technique is a very different matter from a gadget which can be bought or a procedure which one can copy. No wonder that in response to the 'what-do-you-actually-do?' question I would sometimes like to answer: 'What *precisely* do you want to know?', fearing that not only do I not know the answer myself but also that it cannot be communicated even when I believe I know.

But the reason for my exceptional ignorance in the matter is worth pursuing. I sense that a better way of formulating the question would be if, addressing it to myself, I asked: 'What actually is it that what you do is based on?' The standard reply is likely to be: 'Certain theories and techniques.' But it has become rather more than less difficult in recent times to be satisfied with that kind of overall reply, and the likely reason is that both theories and techniques have lost their unquestionable status among all the analytic disciplines. This makes it urgent to find a better answer. As a preliminary step I have drawn up a map for Chapter 14, 'Where does analysis stand?' (see p. 306).

Although I have given up individual case reports in support of any theory or concept, I shall quote snippets from a long analysis which will show something I learned from experience. The example has been supplemented by bits of theory and technique which were not included in the original paper.

AN EXAMPLE

There are two unspectacular selected events which occurred in the eleventh year of this analysis. I shall report the last one first. During my three weeks' vacation at Christmas the patient sent me voluminous hand-written notes, fifty-two closely written pages, which came in three lots. In the accompanying typed letter she told me that the writing had been compulsive and that the notes had all been written in bed. Other remarks, such as that she was sorry she had to break into my holiday, she hoped I was having a good holiday and so on, were apologetic and polite. I read the covering letters and after glancing at the first page of the notes decided not to read the rest. I did not throw the notes away. *Neither the patient nor I referred to the notes and letters when we resumed.*

The following facts were brought to light by a group of colleagues who had read the manuscript, 'On transference phenomena in alcoholism' (Plaut, 1969). In this paper I had made a general technical point with this patient and two other compulsive drinkers in mind: 'Transference interpretations which make the patient aware of his dependence can trigger off the well-known vicious circle.' I linked this observation with another, couched this time in theoretical language, namely that the patient had not had adequate experience of the 'first not-me possession' (meaning Winnicott's transitional object).

From this concept was derived the hypothesis that before this stage had been reached verbal interpretation would underline the 'not-me' aspect at the expense of the 'possession' part which was still essential to the patient in her archaic ego state (as I called it). I am now adding for clarification that the boundary experience of 'I–you' inherent in spoken interpretation and the ability to communicate across this boundary were not yet established. In the paper I also emphasized the importance of the analyst's vulnerability and the use the patient can make of the analyst's letting him/herself be experienced as a 'not-me' possession. This was a clear reference to a principle of technique, leaving out all details.

Let us see whether any part of the event I reported links with the paper from which I quoted. My decision not to read her notes was based on previous experience of a similar kind. I knew that as long as the patient kept on writing and posting notes and letters to me she was not drinking. A quick glance at her notes convinced me that everything had been said before, in one way or another, that is the content was not on the level at which the important non-verbal communications had taken place. There was no point in reading, but a lot of point in her writing and my receiving and keeping the notes. In ordinary language the patient was keeping in touch with me. I would touch the paper she had written on. By not referring to the communication I did not question her right to regard my silent acceptance as a kind of consent. That is I colluded with her pretending that I existed in her inner world, as her object. However, the covering letter and the posting which the patient had to do herself, was her acknowledgement of my existence outside herself, the 'not-me' part. The writing and the posting when taken together constituted a compromise between my being her object *and* having my separate existence. As such it was a transitional phenomenon between my being myself *and* her invention. Many comparable notes and letters never reach the addressee and remain 'private' and unacknowledged.

As regards the compulsive writing in bed, the patient and I knew that this was related to her anxiety over defecating and the magical and dangerous attributes which faeces had had in her childhood: there was also the terror of incontinence which had been instilled by her upbringing, when the faeces had been referred to as 'no-no'. By receiving the incontinence of her compulsive note-writing I also accepted her ambivalent feelings about me and said (silently) 'yes' to their existence. I had omitted from my paper as well as from the group discussions, that on previous occasions my reference to letters received during holidays had had the same negative results as other verbal interpretations. No matter how accurate, the interpretations were given to a person who could not yet distinguish between 'I' and 'you'. She reacted like to a foreign body. Reading my paper it looked as if I had not had to learn the hard way, that is by 'trial and error'. Out of discretion towards myself I did not refer to the fact that the patient's token incontinence of faeces (the compulsive writing in bed and posting it to me) was infinitely preferable to my being burdened with her literal oral incontinence (the compulsive drinking) which felt like my being annihilated.

So far as discretion towards the patient was concerned this was more important than usual in determining the form of my public statement. I knew beforehand that the patient would read the paper and asked her about it, which had apparently no adverse effect. At least she raised no objection. I should have known that words made little or no real impact. At least, not in the form of interpretations to which she reacted with apparent compliance. She coped quite efficiently with ordinary matters by means of a 'false self' in contrast to relationships with people to whom she wanted to be close. Then the false self was worse than useless.

Most of what I learned from this patient is contained in Balint's *The Basic Fault: Therapeutic Aspects of Regression*, particularly in the chapter called 'The Unobtrusive Analyst'. It deals with the difficulty of communicating with a regressed patient when the level of the earliest love-object relationship is reached (Balint, 1968). The obtrusiveness of language is then responded to either by conforming – as the patient tried by writing notes – or, by storing up all the analyst's interpretations as if they were unfair, or worse still fair accusations.

The major indication for the modified technique was based on the patient's total inability to take in and digest my interpretations although she was trying hard to memorize and repeat the words. I just could not put anything to her that really got through, try as I might. *My words as such were resented as an intrusion.* Her inability was quite different from what one usually understands by defences, repression and all the rest. It amounted to a lack of 'fit' and indicated to me after many futile attempts at interpretation that she could only be reached on the level of an archaic ego-object relationship, which I previously expressed as 'zonal' excitation that is not linked with the 'nuclear ego' to which we ascribe the function of providing experiences with a sense of continuity and meaning (cf. 'object constancy', p. 135) (Plaut, 1959).

I learned that the creation of the right atmosphere, or emotional climate, reaching the patient on the relevant level, must take precedence over our pride and joy, the technique which interprets everything, especially the transference (cf. p. 334). In some of her post-alcoholic, dependent states the patient helped me to realize this. In order to show that I am no stickler for 'consistency in technique', but rather believe technique to be a tool to be adjusted to the level on which we meet the patient, I shall reproduce the relevant part of my note (unedited except for the omission of identifying details).

> I saw her today for the first time since giving my paper on alcoholism at a meeting which she attended. I think it is clear that she did so in a counter-phobic way.

(Further omission here for the sake of discretion towards the patient, yet influencing the method and content of this presentation.) Note continues:

> She wanted to overcome the whole of the emotional difficulty which she had experienced by using a few things which I had said in a self-accusatory way. This was to be expected and I had actually said so in my paper. I pointed this out to her adding why I thought she was trying not even to acknowledge that she and I had been in an unusual setting together. The implication was that she felt guilty about it, as if she had broken a taboo. Eventually I got from her that she 'must have been' very disturbed. She had come to the lecture accompanied by her friend and when they got home they talked about it and had coffee and then she could not go to bed. In fact it was quite clear how disturbed she was because she walked to the post office at 3 a.m., met a policeman, talked to him, etc. But all this would not have come out, if I had not interpreted her avoidance of speaking about the lecture.

Then follow the contents of my interpretation which would bring in a lot of detail, presumably not to the point. As usual in my experience of note-taking, the important and repressed (by me) material is in the postscript. The latter shows, I think, that on the level of the 'false self' the patient's conforming was quite uninfluenced by my paper. Her true ego reaction had been mobilized during the events of the night when she was alone. The postscript reads:

> It is important that after my paper in which I had said that this kind of alcohol addicted patient never dared to put a foot wrong, she came and paid her bill, which had been the subject of discussion during the previous sessions. That was the first thing she did on entering the room. Compliance again.

The second event then shows how instead of keeping silent I interpreted her behaviour which, as I knew from previous experience, was indicative of a dangerous not-wanting-to-know how much her 'true' self or 'archaic ego', as I had called it, had suffered. My interpretation took care of this self-destructive inclination for the time being. I did not interpret – presumably because I was not quick enough to notice – the significance of the post office and the policeman. I could have been excused had I not known about the significance of posting the earlier letter. As it was, a colleague with whom I discussed the case drew my attention to it. From the therapeutic point of view I am glad I omitted to make use of this interpretation: it would have been taken as a further sign of my omniscience which was intolerable to the regressed patient .

Case summary

Several years after the analysis had ended she let me know by letter that she was leading a sober and satisfactory life. The letter read like a balance sheet of what had and had not happened. I thanked her in writing. It seems as if the patient had forgiven my blunders. I do not think that I 'cured' her. Although our working through some anxious times together seemed to have helped, I do not consider that analysis is the treatment of choice in alcohol addiction. But I don't know of any that is.

The example shows that I was in doubt about interpreting on three occasions. I did interpret the patient's keeping silent about her having been at my lecture and did not collude with her. On the other hand I kept silent at a time when my having any words at all aroused anger because it made her feel that I was able to control everything, while she was incontinent. In particular, I did not refer to the notes she had sent to me. I thought that she would feel slapped down for something she was ashamed of as an incontinence; possibly also guilty for the intrusion into my private life. It would have been like the 'no-no' experience of her childhood. Instead I made allowance for her aggression.

I am not sure whether it would have been right to interpret the post office and the policeman. The post office was a sign of her acknowledging my existence outside being her object. The policeman I thought of as her conscience (superego) which she tried to placate by talking to him at 3 a.m. The superego had been overactive at other hours as well.

CONCLUSION

In reply to the question 'What do you actually do?', I hope to have demonstrated some differences between the following.

1   What I do at one time and not at another.
2   What I think I do and can remember about it, and what I may be doing or not doing without knowing it and therefore leave out of my account. Discussion with colleagues can help in elucidating these differences.
3   As regards the differences between any acknowledged technique and the actual events in analysis: the events can only to a limited extent be regarded as consequence of our technique. Indeed, some events outside the analyst's control necessitate modifications of technique. It is true that some of these may be regarded as enactments of the past in the present and that they can be true reflections of patterns which were established before speech developed, at least in the way we use it in adult language. But in any case the atmosphere and 'feel' of a meeting between two people, especially during

states of regression, cannot be expressed in words alone. Our means of communicating to outsiders about the content of a session rely heavily on the images in the language and also on the 'climate' in which we anticipate it will be received. Therefore we cannot be satisfied to regard all non-comprehension of what analysts do, or say, as being due to 'resistance' or ignorance. Much of what happens is beyond verbal description and I doubt whether audio-visual aids can change that.

The search for a widely acceptable connotation of the elements which make up ineffable analytic situations must go on. As Part III shows, I believe that it may become possible to record subjective interpersonal experiences by cognitive, that is ego based, methods. With his concept of the archetype and archetypal images, Jung laid the foundation for expressing the bipolarity of affective reactions such as 'good' and 'bad'. But while it is easy to see that an archetypal pattern can affect both analyst and patient to varying degrees, the techniques with which such situations can be met and communicated require a more precise terminology than 'the opposites' or 'the transcendent function' imply. In order to help us study phenomena such as regression and progression more systematically, Jungian analysis requires an outline of detailed steps.

A specific example of what analysts do is that they react by interpreting verbally what they observe in their patients and very sparingly in themselves. In any case, patients develop very acute hearing in the course of an analysis. So what the analyst says and how he/she says it, or indeed reacts bodily by gestures and looks, may at times be more important than the argument whether or in what circumstances to interpret. To keep silent is certainly not the same as doing nothing. Again, silences vary; some may indicate the decision not to say anything irrelevant, others are a passive receptive response such as waiting. In view of these complexities, the question whether it is right or wrong to interpret in specific circumstances cannot be settled by arguments between the protagonists and the examples they adduce. What I referred to as the 'personal premiss' may exert a decisive influence on what different analysts do about interpreting. Even when clinical conditions seem similar enough to make comparisons possible no rule can be laid down.

Chapter 8

Object constancy or constant object?

Psychoanalytic theories of child development employ the useful concept of object constancy, which forms a milestone in the relations between the developing ego and its images, technically referred to as objects. Strictly speaking the term (object constancy) refers to the stage where no substitute for the mother representing the child's (inner) object is accepted. However, I am using it here to include: (1) the acceptance of love and hatred as stemming from the same source (ambivalence); (2) the change from a part-object-(nipple) to a whole object (mother)-relationship; (3) Klein's depressive position which begins between the fourth and sixth month and implies that the child feels anxiety and guilt and wants to repair (imaginary) damage done. It must however be recalled that the depressive position is not a once and for all transformation and achievement.

When for one reason or another this milestone, which is also a formidable hurdle, has not been passed, the crucial question arises whether the person can nevertheless make progress towards a viable mode of living, including stable relations with others. Some of the differences between psychoanalytic theory and analytical psychology may be semantic rather than fundamental: when it comes to the application and aims of therapy, the similarities may occasionally outweigh the differences and incompatibilities of theory. Therefore a mutually acceptable model of child development may still emerge.

There is however one aspect in which analytical psychology may claim a uniquely different orientation inasmuch as 'objects' and their symbolic representations are granted a certain autonomy. This opens the road to an alternative mode of development. I shall refer to it as the 'constant object', in contrast to object constancy.

For the newly-born a need-satisfying union is established between mouth and nipple (or teat of feeding bottle). To this must be added a number of other perceptions, such as warmth, skin contact, smell, surrounding arms and gazing eyes, all of which create a secure situation required for satisfactory nourishment and growth. An object-less phase of fusion has been postulated to begin with, but some measure of differentiation soon occurs. For example, the infant will notice that not every feed and contact is equally satisfying, and he begins to distinguish between good and bad experiences, which become internalized (introjected) and charged with corresponding affect.

It is assumed that in the earliest stages the emerging ego is unable to link good and bad experiences, to maintain a continuity between opposite affects and also to associate these with one and the same organ, the nipple, which is the first part object *from the adult's point of view*. Later on, when the manifold sensory impressions have coalesced, it is possible for the infant not only to focus on the nipple, but to become aware of its connection with a whole body, a person and a specific person: his mother. But, for the time being, good and bad are *experienced* as totally disparate qualities without continuity, functioning on an all-or-nothing principle, even if the oscillations from one extreme to the other can occur quite rapidly. It is not difficult to understand that such a division into opposite qualities and affects comes naturally to the immature ego and that it requires effort to link the two which is often painful. When for some reason the growing infant or child cannot make this connection, we say that an ego defence, splitting, has been called into operation. It looks then – and this can happen right throughout life – as if opposite experiences could not possibly stem from the same source. If the source is thus perceived as divided, the 'I' which responds affectively is divided too. No division of objects, without division of ego. Or, as Hartmann wrote, 'Satisfactory object relations can only be assessed if we also consider what it means in terms of ego development' (Hartmann, 1964).

The next developmental step comes about with the help of our increasing capacity – given favourable environmental conditions – to create continuity out of memories, which leads to a dawning awareness of the inseparability (and relative unpredictability) of good and bad feelings within ourselves and in relation to objects. Thus a precariously balanced state of *constancy* is established in the relation between ourselves and our objects. The acceptance of this state of affairs presents a harsh reality because it requires the surrender of a comforting illusion whereby every experience could be made into a good one, and all pain and frustration counteracted and avoided by means of splitting. The time of the first giving up of this illusion in return for object constancy coincides with the Kleinian 'depressive position' during which ambivalence and despair change into the ability to feel sad. The reward, if one may so call it, for the sacrificed illusion of an only good (idealized) object is a reduction of anxiety. For while the bad object was repressed it also became persecutory in the unconscious, and, conversely, the ego retaliated with punishing sadistic fantasies and subsequently expected similar treatment from the split-off, bad object. Once object constancy has been achieved, the good and bad aspects of one and the same object are no longer denied. A degree of fusion of characteristics has come about and with it 'object constancy'. In that respect Jung's 'conjunction of opposites' bears a *functional* similarity. Although based on his psychological interpretation of alchemy, the common denominator is the combination of contrasting elements (of experience) which on the face of it are incompatible. (But see my discussion of 'paradox', p. 143.)

It cannot be over-emphasized that this developmental attainment is slow and remains permanently threatened by the impact of extremely good or bad experiences at any age: regression to splitting remains a lasting human propensity both in individuals and in human groups. Jung recognized this when writing about the dissociability of the psyche (*CW 8*: paras 365–6) and the child's struggle for an ego (*CW 8*: paras 771–3). Within the present frame of reference object constancy is seen as the prerequisite of all human relations which are based on 'reality' rather than on idealizations and projections. It results from the ability to reconcile opposite qualities both within ourselves and in others.

The burden of this constant struggle is rewarded when the outcome is 'the establishment of lasting emotional relationships' (Jacobson, 1965). But there exists an additional aid in the form of an intermediate area in which the boundaries may be blurred and where play, experiments and illusions have their rightful place: it is the area which Winnicott referred to as transitional-phenomena and objects to which we have recourse throughout life (Winnicott, 1958). Art and religion are, from the psychological point of view, the grown-up counterpart of the child at play, a situation in which he is partly inside and partly outside himself. (Here one can see an obvious parallel with Jung's transcendent function and the technique of active imagination, see p. 292.)

Let us suppose that despite varying terminologies and vested interests in theories, the above represents a widely acceptable although incomplete outline of intrapsychic development leading to desirable and satisfying relationships. The question remains whether object constancy could also be attained in a different way, and could indeed have a different meaning. *Could a part object, in the absence of a steady enough environment but given suitable cultural conditions, find symbolical expression and thus act as a focal point of reference and meeting place for people of a similar cast of mind?* And, if so, could this part-object-become-cult-object lead to lasting relations between people, not primarily because of the balance of good and bad feelings in each individual and between them, nor because of a stabilizing social structure, like the family, but because of shared celebrations of a cult or religion based, for example, on the mythical elaboration of phenomena in nature, events in history and revelations received by visionaries.

The answer to such questions could have far-reaching consequences on the future of psychotherapy as it had in the past on religion. But it cannot be given in a sweeping way. In order to reach a point of view let us consider some illustrations of part objects in Jung's work. Differently put, the question is whether the development of object constancy is the only valid stepping-stone to personal relations and individual development or whether there are indications that alternatives have existed in all cultures which are (in various guises) still with us today.

Among the illustrations in Jung's *Symbole der Wandlung*, fourth and final edition (1950), which have been omitted from its English translation as 'Symbols of Transformation' (*CW 5*), there are two in particular which I reproduce here as being relevant to my theme.

Fig. 8.1 appears in the text of the general chapter heading, 'The hymn of creation'. Jung's footnote, which gives a reference to the phallus worship here depicted, is affixed to a sentence in which he states that religious experience in antiquity was frequently conceived as a bodily union with the deity (1950, p. 113).

Figure 8.1   Worship of the phallus, being illustration No. 28 in 1952 edition of Jung's *Symbole der Wandlung*, Rascher Verlag, Zurich

Fig. 8.2 appears in the introduction to the second part of the volume. Here Jung speaks of the creative deity and refers the reader back to fig. 1. (As both pictures have been omitted from *CW*, the cross-reference cannot, of course, appear either.) He adds that the phallus was thought of as independent, 'an idea that is found not only in antiquity, but in the drawings of children and artists of our own day'. This independence with which we are sufficiently familiar through *graffiti and pornography* could simply be regarded as express-

Figure 8.2 Phallic amulet found in London 1842, being illustration No. 71 in 1952 edition of Jung's *Symbole der Wandlung*, Rascher Verlag, Zurich

ions of infantile sexuality, were it not for the wings, which are a striking feature of both illustrations.

Just as light is a standard symbolic device for depicting awareness, so wings, when attached to a human or animal shape (other than birds), are widely used to indicate the divine or demonic nature of a creature. (Interestingly enough, our first illustration is meant to convey worship, while the second is an amulet or charm worn to avert evil.) Of course, light, especially in the form of a shaft of lightning or a halo *and* wings, often appears in combination, as we know from numerous mythological or religious paintings that symbolize impregnation by a divinity as in paintings of the Annunciation.

The difference is that the wings in our illustrations are attached not to a whole human figure, but to a part. Nevertheless the reader familiar with Jung's interest in transformation of the libido from lower instinctual to higher spiritual levels will also remember the picture series that Jung used to illustrate his 'Psychology of the Transference' (*CW 16*). Fig. 5 of that series shows the king and queen having intercourse underneath the water. In fig. 5a entitled 'Fermentatio', the alchemical analogy of a psychological process, the queen is preventing intercourse, and both she and the king are now bewinged, indicating that a 'higher' development is expected than mere carnal sex. Jung's series ends in the winged hermaphrodite, the new composite and perfect being. (This is fig. 10 of the Rosarium in the 'Psychology of the Transference' and Jung attaches significance to the *denarius* as the perfect number (*CW 16*: para. 525)). In his chapter 'Archetypal Foundations of Protective Identification' Schwartz-Salant used as his illustration picture 11 of his series, the same as Jung did in his 'Psychology of the Transference', where it is numbered 5a (Schwartz-Salant, 1988). In either case it refers to 'Fermentation'. Furthermore, the figure is followed by the hermaphroditic denarius, symbol of new birth and wholeness. All are winged indicating their spiritual aspect. But winged figures, it should be noted, can also indicate evil spirits as the figure of a Lamia, a nightmare phantom, in Jung's 'Symbols of Transformation' shows (*CW 5*: fig. 38a). Her breast is pointed towards the baby which she is carrying away.

I have previously drawn attention to the extraordinary intensity with which part objects such as breast and penis are experienced, and therefore suggested that they are comparable to Jung's 'luminosities' (Plaut, 1974). Although we know that their brilliance and fascinating quality, like that of the 'cats' eyes' used on roads, stems from reflected light (projections which become introjected), the part object is nevertheless perfect to the beholder. Such perfection does not vary: it is constant, admirable or demonic but in any case as compelling to the devotee as to the addict. It differs markedly from the completeness which, according to Jung, is an attribute of the self archetype imposing surrender of omnipotence when object constancy is realized. But whether he responds to the luminosity of an apparently perfect object or to the demands for tolerating the reality of complete rather than ideal relationships, the individual's ego has to find an appropriate attitude towards the 'master' whom he is going to serve. In either case he/she is forced to abandon the illusion of *mastery* over the objects.

In the paper referred to I pointed out that although according to Klein the breast-penis is the first part object, if no object constancy (in the sense described above) develops, other objects will take the place of earlier ones with the same compulsive effect. Thus the miser is more or less possessed by his money, the alcoholic by the bottle, the addict by the drug, the artist by the muse and the medium in which he works, and the religionist by the deity he worships.

In the winged phallic images reproduced here we are, no doubt, dealing with idolatry. Omnipotence has been surrendered but is, in the form of endless creative power, attributed to the part object. This is magic and from the theological point of view, heresy. But as psychologists we have to admit that in practice the boundary between it and superstition on the one hand and the worship of religious objects on the other is hard to define.

Wings and light are not the only symbolic devices by which the unvarying (constant) power for good inherent in an object can be portrayed. Several others spring to mind. Within the field of visual representation we find other images of part objects in abstract form, such as the Lingam and Yoni statues of India which are garlanded and worshipped. There is also the ritualization of sex in the stylized and elaborate forms and techniques of Tantra art. *The power of the object appears to be constant*: thus sexual organs are depicted in constant tumescence, god and goddess in constant copulation. The power is always for the good (but *not* good in the sense of pleasurable; see Kali as slayer of man), but for good in terms of renewal of the life cycle, an affirmative, creative power.

The idea that the sexual act as such can be sacral is by no means dead in our civilization, as the following quotation from an important writer, Heinrich Böll, a Catholic, shows:

> It is impossible for me to despise what is erroneously called physical love; it is the substance of a sacrament...there is no such thing as purely physical or purely spiritual love, both contain an element of the other, even if only a small one.
>
> (Böll, 1962, tr. F.P.)

If for physical love we were to read union of sexual parts, regardless of the personalities involved, we could not avoid the image of a part object relationship. Such pre-object constancy (promiscuous) encounters which do not lead to the development of personal relationships are nevertheless credited by Böll with spiritual potentialities. Jung refers to the frank eroticism of the coitus pictures and almost apologizes to the reader, whom he reminds that the pictures were drawn for medieval eyes and that the analogy of this illustration is 'a little too obvious for modern taste, so that it almost fails of its object' (*CW 16*: para. 460). Since he wrote these words forty years ago, pornography has spread, and 'modern taste' is used to even strong meat. But one wonders whether the capacity for understanding sexual symbolism, without which, as Jung says, the sphere of the instinct becomes overloaded, has grown at all. (The omission of figs 1 and 2 from the *Collected Works* edition and subsequently from the *Gesammelte Werke* could indicate that the editors not only wanted to reduce costs but also had little confidence in the readers' comprehension of symbolism in this form.)

Be that as it may, the perfection with which part objects (incomplete by definition) can be endowed seems characteristic of specific life styles. Thus we find people who with single-mindedness devote their lives to a deity, a muse or an ideology. We may therefore come to the conclusion that they have elected to serve a constantly good object. But the persons concerned may prefer to describe the situation as having resulted from a call, a vocation. At this juncture one could ask whether what I called the constant object is identical with the Kleinian 'good internal object' which 'forms the core of the ego and the infant's internal world' (see Segal, 1964). This question cannot be answered by theorizing, but two practical points arise from the comparison: if the ego-core with its 'good internal object' were resilient enough, there would be no reason why object constancy with all its subsequent socializing benefits should not be attained via committed personal relationships. Secondly, because 'good' means a great deal better than 'perfect' or 'idealized', are we able to supply such goodness and bring about a fundamental change by means of analytic endeavours which had not occured at a critical phase of development? The answer to such questions is of practical interest but must remain open. For while it is all too easy for us to attach pathological labels to people whose life is ruled by a constant object but who have not achieved object constancy, observation makes me wonder whether analysts do not idealize object constancy just as much as the devotee or worshipper idealizes his/her constant object. In both instances the idea of something '*constant*' = permanent, contains an illusory element.

Whether we look at the relationships of individuals or the state of our civilization, there must surely be some doubt as to our enduring capacity to combine 'good' and 'bad' feelings towards one and the same object. The suffering involved seems as commonly expressed in disease and violence as is the suffering that constant objects exact. Therefore, one may question whether 'good' relations and the stability of our family-based society can lay claim to being the standard model of mental health. So what is 'pathological'?

Jung writes in 'The Stages of Life': 'The meaning and purpose of a problem seem to lie not in its solution but in our working at it incessantly' (*CW 8*: para. 771). What really matters is whether analysts can keep an open mind towards patients whose capacity to develop along the path of object constancy is severely limited. If, on the other hand, such patients have a talent for expressing their devotion to a constant object, they may still lead satisfying lives even if the constancy is more apparent than real. For them the alternative here called the constant object may be 'therapeutic', as I outlined in an earlier paper, 'Part-objects and Jung's luminosities' under the subheading, 'Devotion versus addiction' (Plaut, 1974).

Does this mean that individuation is out for such persons? In order to arrive at an answer we have to consider briefly by what psychodynamic changes we move towards individuation. If the answer is that without object constancy there can be no ego constancy, and that without a sufficiently coherent ego the 'completeness' required in personal relationships cannot come about, the conclusion is obviously negative. If, on the other hand, we hold that acts of devotion to an apparently perfect object – in whatever form it may appear – are in themselves arduous and demand the surrender of immediate ambitions for the sake of a common or ultimate good, then even a divided (pre-constant) ego may be held together by the apparently perfect part and cult object. A life led under such auspices can potentially be rich and fulfilling, as we can see in the lives of some artists whose personal relationships were defective and inconstant.

It is likely that this alternative path of personality development where there is very little ego cohesion is just as charged with the dangers of inflation, paranoia and depression as Jung's classical mode of individuation. Yet it is of practical importance to make allowance for this alternative path rather than to insist that without object constancy there can be no *ego-integration* of the personality and hence no progress towards individuation.

Analysts will probably agree that combinations, compromises and diurnal fluctuations between object constancy and constant objects are more commonly found in practice than the word 'or' in the title suggests. However, a theoretical standpoint is best stated in extremes. Clinical examples have been omitted here, and considerable detail would be required to give flesh and blood to the present outline. (An attempt to fill in the gap is made in Chapter 9.) Jung's terms 'perfection', 'completion' and 'wholeness' used in the context of individuation are large counters, and the small change of clinical and/or biographical examples is required to illustrate their meaning.

But then again, the question which this chapter poses constitutes only one aspect of the still more fundamental problem facing analysis: *to what extent and by what means can we supply or make substitution for what was lacking or went awry in the history of an individual's life?* Being somewhat less tied to a psychogenic theory of neuroses and personality disorders than psychoanalysis is, analytical psychology is in a favourable position to study other means by which the problem could be broken down into smaller questions to which a person's discovery of a constant object may provide one of the possible answers.

Differently put: object constancy implies the ego's ability to combine and tolerate opposite qualities and affects in one single object. Conceptually this does not seem difficult. In practice, however, the demands thus made on the unfolding and even on the developed ego are so exacting that it is regarded as impossible to fulfil the desiderata of object constancy at all times and in all circumstances. Perhaps we should take our limitations to heart. Practically speaking a constant object, even if it is derived from, and bears the hallmarks of a part- as well as cult-object, is a valuable concentrating point for a personality that would otherwise be in danger of disintegrating. Provided only that the ego does not become totally absorbed by it, the constant object offers the person a viable chance to integrate around it, in which case its function can be regarded as an alternative to object constancy. The constant object becomes a central point of reference in daily life. As such it is neither 'good' nor 'bad' like the Kleinian breast, it simply *is*. Its appearance may be fascinating or awe-inspiring, hence numinous. Always there, its 'faces' depend on the condition and viewpoint of the beholder. Janus-like the constant object faces in opposite directions indicating peace or war, idealization or demonization and so on. *But the quality of constancy or permanence supersedes the others.* Janus represents the paradoxical unity, to which I previously drew attention (Plaut, 1986). But does that make him a symbol of the conjunction about which Jung wrote: 'Naturally the conjunctio can only be understood as a paradox, since a union of opposites can only be thought of as their annihilation' (*CW 9, II*: para. 124)? I think the answer must be in the negative because unification implies a prior division. Janus represents a constancy in unity which is there from the beginning of time; the first month of the year is called after the god who represents a paradoxical unity the realization of which makes a 'conjunctio' superfluous.

It could be argued that the constant object represents the primordial or gnostic unity which Jung castigates (CW 11: paras 445-6, CW 13: para. 456). But there seems nothing 'primordial' about the division of time into a calender year. Furthermore, Janus had arisen out of chaos (his former name) so he cannot be a combination of the opposites in uncombined form as the 'prima materia' as Jung suggests in the context of the arcane substance and the philosopher's stone (CW 14: para. 36).

Certainly, we *experience* by means of contrasting qualities. Peace cannot mean much without knowing about war and vice versa. Our experience separates these states of affairs as pointed out, see the opposites as paired experiences (p. 122, above). Of course, I do not recommend an atavistic return to idolatry. But mankind's need for household gods continues unabated. I therefore agree with Meltzer who wrote that every person has to have a 'religion' in which the gods, like parental figures, perform functions. This is the sense in which Jung used *religio* ('linking back' but the etymology is uncertain) (CW 9, I: para. 271). Meltzer adds that if a person does not put trust in internal gods, that person must live in a state that Kierkegaard described as 'despair' (Meltzer, 1984). It follows that if an object is numinous and constant or permanent it is thereby 'good', regardless of whether it is experienced as pleasant or unpleasant, good or bad.

Chapter 9

The psychopathology of individuation

I GORDON'S PARADISE

Individuation is a key concept in Jung's contribution to personality development. It means a person's becoming him/herself, whole, indivisible and distinct from other people or collective psychology, although also in relation to all of these.

The concept is closely related to that of the self and the process of self realization or the person becoming unified, whole. Jung acknowledged the difficulty he encountered in getting across that the self had to be distinguished from the ego. The latter's relation to *integration, consciousness* and *social adaptation* was comparable to the role the self plays in the process of *individuation*. It is a distinction of much more than theoretical interest as references to the consequences of confusing the one with the other and to the psychopathology of individuation show (*CW 8*: para. 432 and *9, I*: paras 290 and 495f). (See also *A Critical Dictionary of Jungian Analysis*, op. cit.)

Rather than go into details of definition I have chosen to illustrate conceptual differences and problems of psychopathology with the help of two examples. One, Gordon, is based on biographies, the other, Celia, is derived in the main from fiction. Elsewhere, I have given my reasons for not using so-called 'case material' or vignettes (see p. 27). In my 'General Gordon's Map of Paradise', I drew mainly on an illustrated essay by Gordon then in my hands (Plaut, 1982). The present 'Gordon' is an analytic construct because the personal data available from childhood are precious few. Also, analysts like to know something about a person's dreams. Sadly, so far as I know, none have been recorded. Yet Gordon who was in many ways a highly practical person, could, as we shall see, in other respects be called a dreamer. I shall presently go into details about this and other apparent contradictions. Trying to reconcile and make sense of the many puzzling features of Gordon's character has involved filling the gaps in the already slender documentation with analytic speculations. Such speculations as I have ventured are, nevertheless, deduced from my wider analytic knowledge of persons with comparable characteristics who I got to know as patients or in a social context and from biographies.

As analysts we are used to attaching a great deal of importance to the developmental history and are forever on the alert for clues which could help us to work out the psychodynamics and psychopathology of a case. As early clues are scarce here, it is likely that I have given undue weight to the relatively few pointers to Gordon's personality and character development. But I am of the opinion that a person's character and actions are ordinarily not as much due to environmental circumstances as the strict determinism of early psychoanalysis would have us believe. The individual's 'constitution' determines what a person makes of the environment because of their being what they are and influences the finished product to a significant extent. As it happens, we know more about 'Gordon of Khartoum' than we know of Charlie Gordon. Although far from being wholly fictitious, I must stress that my Gordon has nevertheless been constructed with the psychopathology of individuation in mind. But then most 'case reports' are also the outcome of similar constructions.

Another difficulty arises out of the different meanings of 'wholeness'. 'Whole, 'healing' and 'health' share the same etymology. So it comes about that wholeness, health and the self, form a cluster of associations from which the advertised image of a healthy human being is derived. Whatever else that collective image conveys in our day, it is not that of a suffering person. And yet in his 'A Psychological Approach to the Trinity' Jung describes individuation as 'an heroic and often tragic task, the most difficult of all, it involves suffering, a passion of the ego...' (Jung, *CW 11*: para. 233). Jung's 'empirical man' feels robbed of his fancied freedom of will and 'suffers, so to speak, from the violence done to him by the self'. We note that at this point the self is experienced by the person's sense of 'I' or ego as if it were an external agency. As such it is easily projected on to the deity. Jung further considers that through the Christ symbol man can get to know the real meaning of suffering; he is then on the way to realizing his wholeness. The cause of the suffering on the human level would then appear to be 'individuation' (ibid.). As previously pointed out (see p. 67), both Freud and Jung as well as subsequent generations of analysts recognized the necessity of the patient being able to tolerate frustration and a certain willingness to suffer the effects of self knowledge as an absolute precondition to successful analysis.

In order to describe the suffering of an otherwise healthy individual, Jung uses the example of a vigorous Jacob struggling at the ford with the angel. This is in marked contrast to our image of Christ's agony and death at the cross. Although Jung was writing here within the context of a specifically Christian theme, namely the holy Trinity, there can be little doubt that he combined this with Dorn's *unio mentalis*, out of which he fashioned his concept of individuation as an outline of personality development (*CW 14*: para. 670). It had been formulated as a virtual but never completed end of the analytic transformation process. Jung found the observational basis in the dreams and drawings of people, notably in the form of mandalas symbolizing wholeness. He specifi-

cally recognized a psychopathology of individuation including physical illnesses, depression or the opposite, inflation. He also gave a psychodynamic
explanation of these twin dangers. And yet the criteria by which to distinguish
abortive or psychopathological forms from the genuine individuation process
remain uncertain. In view of the issues raised in the previous chapter this is not
surprising. There I suggested that the demands of object constancy might
sometimes have to be reduced and replaced by a constant, perfect or idealized
object. This alternative route to a unified personality makes different though
no less formidable demands depending, as we shall see, on the ways in which
they are met. The dangers of individuation to which Jung referred as psychopathology exist in either case. This makes us pause and consider the meanings
of the term.

Taken literally it means the study of the suffering, or the passions of the
soul. Jung uses it in this sense when he writes about individuation and admits
that such suffering can show itself at times in the unmistakable form of mental
or physical disease. But in ordinary usage psychopathology means primarily
the study of mental disease as it is recognized by psychiatry and, to a lesser
extent, by analysis.

This is the sense in which I shall consider the psychopathology of Gordon
and later of Celia in the ordinary sense, implying mental anguish. Let us assume
that this was due to minds that could not adjust to reality. As Gordon could
not accept authority, so Celia, as we shall see, could not mourn her loss.
Neither would have thought of themselves as peculiar and still less as ill,
although others did. Therefore the question arises to what extent we can
tolerate symptoms based on psychopathology and yet remain patient and keep
an open mind about there also being psychopathology of the other kind that
expresses the suffering of the soul on its way to self realization (individuation).
There are essentially two possibilities. We can either say that their lives ended
as they did in violent deaths because they failed to accept and integrate reality.
In analytic terms, they split their objects into ideally good and correspondingly
bad objects and therefore did not achieve object constancy; consequently the
ego continued to project both instead of integrating the good and bad. Or we
could use Kleinian terms and say that Gordon and Celia, instead of reaching
the depressive position, remained stuck in the paranoid–schizoid position. A
different alternative is to allot the highest value to the potential goal of
individuation and look upon the ensuing psychopathology involving the death
of the persons concerned as a sad but inevitable accompaniment. Both judgements would have been arrived at by analytic hindsight and, in our example,
without the benefit of direct analytic dialogue. But I would argue that the cases
in point are sufficiently well defined to make inferences. Furthermore, the
analytic viewpoint alone is inadequate to arrive at any judgement unless the
historical and cultural background be taken into account. What is more, I have
come to the conclusion that when Jung's concept of individuation is applied
to individual persons the criteria by which we judge both individuation as well

as its specific psychopathology are bound up with metapsychological, philosophical and even religious considerations. It is for reasons such as these that it would be futile to ask whether the fate of Gordon and Celia would have turned out differently had analysis been available to them.

GENERAL GORDON'S PARADISE

I shall now illustrate what in the previous chapter was called the constant object. The psychopathology of individuation frequently opens up with the pursuit of an object so persistent and constant in a person's life that they are liable to be called eccentrics and worse. As analysts we are used to linking psychopathology with events that happened during infancy and childhood. In both my 'cases' these data are not available. Nevertheless we can deduce a lot about the possible or even likely origins from the later history. There exist no doubt biographies which are much more firmly based on early history, but few show so clearly that psychopathology is no obstacle to fame and admiration.

Not many generals can have gone to paradise, for their profession involves slaughter on a large scale. And though some of them might deny that they killed with gusto, pleading that they acted in defence of the rest of us, I think General Gordon would have been honest enough to admit the charge. It would, however, be necessary to add that he had a truly kind heart, was assailed by terrible remorse, and was, by all accounts of the day, a Christian. But whatever the outcome at the Last Judgement, it is certain that Charles George Gordon (born Woolwich 1833, slain at Khartoum 1885) is the only general in history who proved to his entire satisfaction where the terrestrial paradise, the Garden of Eden, was located.

When the haze of hero worship which followed his death had dispersed, there remained an unusual and, in many ways, admirable as well as complex character.

He had started his brilliant military career as 'Chinese' Gordon (because of the outstanding part he played during the Taiping rebellion) and ended it as 'Gordon of Khartoum' (the city he refused to surrender). When he was sent to evacuate Khartoum, it was clear to those who knew him that the decision would end in combat, and sure enough, not only was the city besieged, but a tragedy unfolded as the *dramatis personae* confronted each other. The Mahdi was no less a convinced Moslem than Gordon was a Christian: and both, in their way, were noble warriors. Impulsive and hasty activity by Gordon was opposed by delay in organizing an expeditionary force to raise the siege. On 28 January 1885 (it would have been his fifty-second birthday) the relief column arrived. Gordon had been killed and subsequently decapitated two days earlier.

Is it as a hero who chose death rather than surrender his Christian faith or abandon his post that Gordon remains an impressive and fascinating figure?

Certainly this interpretation was current at the time (twenty-five books were written about him in the first eighteen months after his death), and it strikes a sufficiently archetypal note to account for the nationwide mourning and worship that followed. But Gordon had courted death, and his behaviour at Khartoum was perfectly in keeping with his personality.

A man of remarkable integrity and fearlessness, Gordon was often very awkward to deal with, and was widely regarded as 'eccentric', even a little crazy. One biographer, Nutting, entitled his book: *Gordon: Martyr and Misfit* (Nutting, 1966). Gordon constantly quarrelled with authority, to the point of disobeying orders, and his tendency towards asceticism was certainly not shared by his Victorian contemporaries. Who else would have slashed his own salary, as governor-general of the Sudan, from £10,000 to £2,000? 'I am', he wrote, 'like Moses who despised the riches of Egypt...' The Chinese, too, became decidedly anxious when he refused to take their bribes.

He suffered furious outbursts of temper, often followed by complete withdrawal – cutting off all contact, reading the Bible, and drinking cognac. Yet he was never seen to be the worse for wear. His tendency to self-criticism and remorse was considerable: when he emerged from his self-imposed isolation he was at pains to make amends to those he had hurt or punished. Indifferent to physical hardship, he could also long to lie in bed until eleven every day and eat oysters ('not a dozen but four dozen'). More than once he gave up alcohol and tobacco: it was a running battle between making a pledge and yielding to temptation. Yet, despite his unpredictable moods, all descriptions of him agree that he appeared to have been happy most of the time, good-humoured, and full of energy.

Quite the most important aspects of his character are his version of religion and his sexual orientation. What do we know?

Gordon, in accordance with the ideal of the times, but unlike most Victorians of his class, lived simply and gave generously to those in need. Abstinence was a virtue and death the ultimate triumph of the spirit over the flesh: the dichotomy between the flesh and the spirit was for him absolute. Death was devoutly to be wished for, yet to hasten it would be sinful, for God had given us work to do – was this the reason why he was fearless in the face of physical danger?

As to Gordon's sexuality, it seems well attested that he was more homo- than heterosexual. He avoided opportunities to meet eligible ladies, said that marriage was not for him, befriended young boys. It is improbable that he was ever a practising homosexual; in a man who lived so much in the public eye and had many enemies, this could hardly have escaped notice. The public view of his time was that a man could do without sex or amuse himself from time to time with those ladies whose profession it was. But, of course, there is no evidence to that effect either. No doubt, he suffered. At the age of fifty, in a letter to a friend, the Reverend R. H. Barnes, he wrote, '*I wished I was a eunuch at 14...*'

In his family history, there are no more than a few pointers to Gordon's development other than his having been a mischievous boy, remarkable also for his 'high spirits and pluck' as one biographer (Lytton Strachey) had remarked. A later biographer referred to these characteristics as 'naughty, ruthless and resourceful' by another (Charles Chenevix Trench). Charlie was sent to boarding school (Taunton) at the age of nine where he did not distinguish himself except for his skill in drawing maps. His father was of Highland and military descent and had risen to the rank of lieutenant-general, Royal Artillery, a rank which our Gordon never achieved. His mother came from a family of merchants, well known for their sea voyages. Charlie was the fourth son of eleven children and had been destined for the Royal Artillery. But owing to an act of uncontrolled temper and near-insubordination there was a delay in the officer-cadet being commissioned and so he went into the Royal Engineers. What data we have are from his adult life, when he found his mother demanding and possessive after his father's death. This occurred in 1865, when Gordon was thirty-one, and he dated his religious conversion to that year. Earlier, however, a mild dose of smallpox in China had made him reflect on things eternal: '*I am glad to say*', he wrote to his sister Augusta (a formidable spinster with whom he shared his theological theories in a long and voluminous correspondence), '*that the disease has brought me back to my Saviour.*' Although Gordon had shown no religious inclinations as a boy, and never joined any church nor become confirmed, he seems to have come under the Evangelist and Salvationist influence of a Captain Drew when he was staying at Pembroke where he took the first sacrament at Easter 1854 when he was twenty-one. He also began to study the Bible, examining every passage minutely to discover the true meaning with results that seemed extraordinary to other people. We note that Gordon dates his conversion back to the year his father died. Actually the conversion seems to have taken place some ten years earlier after he had met Drew. Later we shall refer to the special purifying significance that communion had in Gordon's religious view.

Although Gordon passionately believed that what distinguished Christianity from all other religions was God's in-dwelling in man, a condition was attached: belief in Jesus as God the Son. In his twenties, he printed and distributed his own religious tracts, embarrassing complete strangers with queries as to the state of their faith; and his constant Bible-reading led him to speculation far beyond what would be regarded as normal for a Christian living in the Victorian era. He determined where Satan would finally be imprisoned – in the centre of the earth, having been sucked down through the Dead Sea. Similarly, he decided where Our Lord now was. 'Being a Man He must be in some definite place' (*Reflections in Palestine*, 1884). He concluded that Christ was hovering just over Jerusalem, above the Altar of the true Temple. 'All prayer (from whatever part of the globe) must pass by and through Him...' To a modern reader this might provoke comparison with a communications satellite, but for Gordon there was *no 'as if'* about this or anything else. If the

Lord and Satan were real, they must have HQs – and these had to be properly located.

The discovery of Eden

In 1881, languishing on leave in England (one of his periodic resignations from the Army having been refused), Gordon met a friend, Colonel Sir Howard Elphinstone, who lamented having been posted to Mauritius, a terrible backwater for a Royal Engineer. Gordon offered to take Elphinstone's place: this was accepted and he left England shortly afterwards. From a letter to 'My dear Elphin' we gather that Gordon may have regretted his generosity. However, once in Mauritius he took up his Bible studies again and also became interested in botany. The combination was important for what was to follow, for Gordon, receiving orders to look into the harbour installations on Mahé, the largest of the Seychelles, also visited the neighbouring island, Praslin, which he promptly identified as the site of the vanished Garden of Eden.

Praslin was the only place in the world where a palm tree grew which bore that strange fruit, the *coco de mer*. Gordon describes '*its fruit shaped in the husk like a heart, when opened like a belly with thighs*'. I am quoting from a manuscript in my possession entitled 'Eden and its Two Sacramental Trees' – it consists of eight folio pages in Gordon's writing, accompanied by two pages of maps in colour; it is signed by him and dated '26.2.82'.

Trench in a recent biography tells us that Gordon's theory was based on '*the remarkable similarity between the ripe fruit of the coco de mer, a gigantic palm tree, and Eve's pudenda.*' Delicately put ... and no one who sees the illustrations, including Gordon's photograph of the fruit, could mistake what he means. We know that his friend Gessi, possibly with reference to the photograph, wrote: 'Carlo has never seen what there is between a woman's legs' (MacGregor-Hastie, 1985). Certainly Gordon was in no doubt that this was the fruit from the Tree of Knowledge (fig. 9.1).

The *coco de mer (Lodoicea Seychellarum)* had occasionally been washed ashore in India and Africa. Before Praslin was discovered to be its original home, it was thought to grow at the bottom of the sea. Numerous legends surround it, including the not unlikely story that the Holy Roman Emperor, Rudolf II, had offered 4,000 florins for one of the fruits because it was reputed to be an antidote to poison. A tale survives to this day that the semi-transparent, glutinous pulp (which makes good eating either as a fruit or as a vegetable) has 'other invigorating qualities'.

Although it is called a double coconut this is, according to botanists, a misnomer. What matters, however, is that there is a male and a female tree – it is not difficult to distinguish between the two (fig. 9.2). One writer describes the male tree as being covered here and there with groups of phalli each about eighteen inches to two feet long, and three or four inches in diameter – it was said that these become erectile after sunset and remain so until sunrise!

In another remarkable palm tree (the breadfruit, *Artocarpus Incisa*), Gordon recognized the Tree of Life. So there were the trees, the climate was right and '*there was also a 3-foot-long serpent there*', Gordon added.

It is the second part of Gordon's essay that is devoted to the Sacramental trees, and the opening sentence of these pages reads:

> *God has used instruments at all ages, to manifest Himself to man, these instruments though nothing in themselves, were everything when connected with Him.*

(MS. p. 5)

Gordon gives a few examples showing that

> *when things are done with, they pass back, are relegated into ordinary things ... thus there is no reason why the two trees which were in the Garden of Eden should not exist to this day. They fulfilled their functions and are relegated back to their ordinary condition. The bread and wine in themselves are nothing yet they are Christ's flesh and blood.* (We note '*are*', not symbolize.)

Gordon's explanation for the dual nature or state of being is in keeping with *his dichotomy between the flesh and the spirit*, and these are accompanied by a more elementary one, between *male* and *female*. After the 'belly and thighs' comparison, he continues:

> *It is a magnificent tree, the Prince of trees in every way and full of types, its germination is extraordinary when taken with the words ye generation of serpents.*
>
> *O generation of vipers, who hath warned ye to flee from the wrath to come? Bring forth therefore fruits meet for repentence (Matt. 3: 7–8).*

The point here is that '*the tree of knowledge*' is *not hermaphroditic* like the coconut palm, but is divided into two sexes. Gordon's 'types' look as if they foreshadowed the 'Fall' by virtue of this sexual differentiation and germination – they represent the forbidden knowledge on a botanical level. Like the other objects which he enumerates as examples of ordinary things, the 'extraordinary' germination was apparently all right, since when 'God used them, they were most holy' (MS. p. 5). Yet Gordon never succeeded in accepting the union of opposite sexes, even as a necessity for the propagation of mankind, although the requisite parts were being, or could be regarded as being, used by God.

Trench quotes the correspondence between Gordon and W. Scott (superintendent of the Royal Botanical Garden at Pamplemousses) which includes anatomical sketches by Gordon of Eve's reproductive system. Gordon wanted to know whether the flower of the breadfruit (his Tree of Life) were male, female, or hermaphrodite. Would Scott put him in touch with the Liverpool doctor who had examined a pregnant man? Sexual confusion, sexual differentiation and union – and above all, the search for a way in which union could

Figure 9.1   Male and female *coco de mer (Lodoicea Seychellarum)*. Aquatint
    engraving by W. J. Hooker

Figure 9.2   Coco de mer fruit

be made comprehensible and therefore innocuous to the soul – seem to have been the mainspring behind Gordon's curiosity.

Gordon needed a reconciling symbol, and the illustrations make it understandable that the sight of the forbidden fruit of the *coco de mer* displaced the authenticity of the humble but traditional paradisical apple. When he had 'pretty well settled the site of Eden, of the Garden and the Trees of Knowledge and Life' (letter to Augusta), he rejoiced that '*Milton wonderfully works it into my idea*', and quotes from *Paradise Lost* (Book IV, 218):

> And all amid them stood the Tree of Life
> High eminent, blooming Ambrosial Fruit
> Of vegetable Gold ...

Milton (though not Gordon) continues the line as follows:

> ...and next to Life,
> Our Death, the Tree of Knowledge, grew fast by –
> Knowledge of Good, bought dear by knowing ill.

The omission is significant. Gordon never forgave Eve, or accepted the Fall as a necessary evil. He selected from Milton's poem only those lines which he regarded as confirmatory evidence for his topographical discovery. But Milton's description was poetic and symbolical, not to be used as a guide-book, as Gordon seems to do. He then expatiates on the sequence of events in the Garden:

> *Adam (and Eve) were perfectly free from any temptation except that of eating of the* Tree of Knowledge. *Luxury, power, etc, etc, which are temptations to man now could have no effect on these two, the only way they could be tempted was by their stomachs and by curiosity.*
>
> (MS. pp. 6–7)

> *They ate and they fell. Now I believe that neither had the very faintest idea of what would follow, that their act was one we commit every moment, as to say forgetting God and trusting self, heedlessness, greediness, forgetfulness. They were poisoned, and I must say that I think, if it is looked deeply into, there is a close analogy between the first eating and the second eating of Christ's Body and Blood. By the first eating we commune with Satan, by the second eating we commune with [illegible word in MS] Christ.*
>
> (MS. p. 7)

Here Gordon is travelling a well-worn path, reminiscent of his pamphlet, issued in earlier years, entitled 'Take Eat'. Christ's injunction 'Do this in remembrance of me' (the words accompanying the Communion) are then repeated, and the tone of the MS. becomes admonishing and preaching: '*We shall never get power over our bodies till we take the antidote of the poison we have in us, a child can understand you have eaten what does make you ill, eat this for your cure'* (MS. p. 8). A little later he castigates Eve (without excusing Adam or accusing Satan): *'What did Eve think, did she go and study the tree, no, she took and ate to see for herself, she wanted to gratify herself...'*

Obviously he saw no connection between Eve's lapse and his own insubordinations and episodic incontinence – his rages, drinking and excessive smoking. Although for secular occasions he relied on self-control or willpower (Richard Burton, the African explorer, noted Gordon's 'controul'), he could not escape his obsession. The flesh *must* be defeated by the spirit. The only antidote to the Tree of Knowledge, from which springs sexuality is the second eating, the Sacrament of the Communion. The bread and wine become the means or instruments by which we are purified of wilful disobedience.

There are a number of extraordinary contradictions in all this. First, Gordon's conflict – between wanting to do good and be abstemious on the one hand, and his inclination to contrariness on the other – finds its remedy in the Communion and, generally, in trying to follow Christ. He believes in that antidote *literally: not by transubstantiation, but as if it consisted of minute particles* descending from heaven. Similarly, he regards the attributes of evil as having been physically introduced into Eve's body: 'the fruit was the vehicle of *the virus of evil*' (and he does not use this phrase as a mere metaphor).

Second, while the Fall is brought about by temptation (via the stomach), it introduces sexual knowledge. And for Gordon there appears to be no Sacrament, such as marriage, which will counteract that poison. Eve cannot become 'the means' or instrument by which God works.

Gordon seems to have forgotten that Jesus, the son of Man, was thereby also a descendant of Eve, albeit with the addition of special purifications (the Immaculate Conception, the Virgin Birth). Milton summed it up by writing about the Messiah: 'So God with man unites...' Not for Gordon these glad tidings. Eve, and thereby Man, remains *unredeemed during her lifetime*, except for occasional dispensations by means of the antidote.

The manuscript ends on a note of modified pessimism (MS. p. 8):

> *The two trees are here now, and we eat daily sometimes of one, sometimes (less frequently) of the other the tree of life. In return, the tree of knowledge is dying out, men have eaten it nearly up, its effects are manifest, the tree of life shall exist more abundantly, but few eat of it, except the poor. The table of the Lord is contemptible not worth considering (Mal. 1: 7).*

The final statement contradicts the earlier assertion, namely the return to the ordinary state of things after God has made use of them. *Their instrumentality persists* in a negative way when Gordon requires it to serve as a dire warning, no doubt as much to himself as to those he wanted to address, and God's 'union with man' via Eve and the Virgin is denied. No reconciling symbol for Gordon.

Gordon had been stimulated by the sight of the 'forbidden fruit', the *coco de mer* – and his ideas, intuitions and rationalizations did the rest, finding expression in the manuscript and the accompanying maps. The major driving force for his extraordinary theories seems to be the return to a conflict-free state, prior to temptation – to be a eunuch at fourteen ... to be dead. His literal child-like comprehension of the Bible – and his apparent inability to grasp symbolic meanings – helps us to understand his longing to return to the Garden of Eden as it was before the Fall.

Gordon's map and the rivers of Eden

The opening sentence of 'Eden and its Two Sacramental Trees' reads 'God works by means and by natural laws.' (The phrase 'by means' – according to the *Shorter Oxford English Dictionary* – refers to the resources, but also to the *instrumentality*, of things or persons.) And so I have deliberately postponed discussion of the first part of Gordon's MS., because the inspiration for the search, the means or instrumentality, should come before 'the natural laws'.

Gordon used his knowledge of these laws in order to rationalize what he intuited after seeing the *coco de mer*. His geographical and geological arguments, if one can call them that, certainly strain credulity where he relies for supportive evidence on the Bible and on etymology. But when he proceeds to account for the four rivers of Eden, his knowledge as a Royal Engineer is harnessed in support of his thesis: and this is where we meet the working of his mind in its most original and ingenious, but also eccentric productivity. For the lengths to which he had to go to make the rivers flow to his location are nothing short of extraordinary.

The first logical step for anyone taking Genesis as his guide is to reconstruct the world as it was before the Flood – and Gordon makes us imagine, with the help of an illustration, the way the rivers flowed at that time. He stipulates a habitable zone or belt around the equator, towards which (before the earth was tilted on its axis) all rivers from the melting northern and southern icecaps flowed. When God's breath, in the form of fire, produced the Flood, it caused the toppling over by $23\frac{1}{2}°$ of the upper northern hemisphere (because of its greater land mass, it carried more ice than the lower hemisphere). Floods do not change the general features of land, but simply modify them by silting up rivers in low-lying land, or blocking up channels and causing rivers to change their course.

Gordon writes (MS. p. 2): '*To the Rev. Berry I owe the final thought on the subject of the site of Eden. I had already thought that the two trees were distinguishable at Seychelles.*' He now reverses the usual interpretation of Genesis – that a river flowing from Eden watered the Garden and then branched into four streams as 'the mass of men' falsely believe. But Gordon, with the help of the Revd. D. Berry, translates this not as 'four rivers' (or streams) but as 'four heads' (i.e. origins), which form one great antediluvian river basin: '*in no instance in this world do we find four rivers flowing out of one river, while there are many instances of four rivers flowing into one.*'

This is the geological basis from which Gordon launches a hypothesis which becomes more and more bizarre as he continues. He states that west of the Seychelles there is a deep basin in the Indian Ocean. (This is correct: it has a depth of 2,600 fathoms.) He mentions a cleft near Socotra which has two branches, one of which runs up the Persian Gulf, the other up the Red Sea. (I have not been able to trace these 'branches' from the information likely to have been available to Gordon: and modern oceanography does not confirm their existence.)

The Tigris, having been joined by the Euphrates, comes down the Persian Gulf and forms the eastern branch.

'*We have therefore two rivers – we want two more*', writes Gordon (MS. p. 3) clinging fast to elementary arithmetic.

The remaining two rivers are called 'Pison' and 'Gihon' in Genesis. While other reconstructions regard the Gihon as the Nile and the Pison as the Indus or Ganges, Gordon's, not surprisingly, does the opposite. He admits that we have no very clear clue to these two, but as Babylon and Nineveh, situated on the banks of the Euphrates and the Tigris, were opponents of Israel, '*so the other two rivers we want must have this peculiarity also.*'

Whatever the truth of the matter, it would be difficult to find a better example of *how misleading an argument by analogy can be*. By a variety of attributes, other than Egypt's enmity to Israel, Gordon proves to his satisfaction that the Pison is the Nile.

> *The Nile is considered by good authorities to have once discharged into the Red Sea and its changing its course after the Flood is not a very improbable thing as the land is low and much silt must have swept down with the melting glaciers.*

The Canal of Hero appears as a dotted line on Gordon's map – although not lettered as such, his brother H. W. Gordon in his biography makes this explicit. Hero was an Alexandrian mathematician and inventor who lived c.250BC: the canal connected the Nile north of Suez with Lake Timsah and hence the Red Sea. The anachronism of the antediluvian situation represented in Gordon's map is obvious, for the Flood predated the Canal.

'*The Gihon is the next river*', but its course proves even trickier than the Pison's. Gordon identifies the Gihon in the now dried-out riverbed or brook just south of Jerusalem which by a deep ravine falls via the Valley of Fire into the Dead Sea. As for the common denominator, the opponent of Israel, he writes: '*In Genesis [II. 13] Gihon is said to encompass the land of Cush. Cush was the son of Nimrod and Nimrod was of Assyria.*'

In the sentence which follows, Gordon finds a rather confused way of regarding geneology and hereditary enmity as more important than the historical geography which usually equates the land of Cush with Ethiopia. He simply reiterates. '*I therefore think the Gihon [in the vicinity of Jerusalem] is the Gihon of Eden.*'

There remains the difficulty of bringing Gordon's Gihon from the Dead

Sea into the Red Sea, but this is overcome (in the main) by means of an underground river.

The rest is plain sailing. The cleft coming from the Red Sea carries the waters of both Pison (Gordon's Nile) from Suez and Gihon from the Gulf of Akaba. It flows via Aden. '*Aden is Eden*', writes Gordon. What could be more obvious? For '*Eden was a district* [i.e. in what is now the Indian Ocean], *the Garden of Eden was a chosen spot*'. The antediluvian river-beds joined north-east of the Island of Socotra, and from there the great river flowed south-by-west to water the Garden of Eden. To make all this 'real' and thereby convincing, Gordon illustrates his thesis with skilfully drawn coloured maps.

Gordon among the paradise mappers

Gordon's talent for drawing maps had been noted at school: his letters are interspersed with elegant botanical or zoological sketches and illustrative maps. But it is chiefly Gordon's idiosyncrasies which give him a unique place among modern cartographical reconstructions, for although he may have been aware of other attempts in modern times to locate the site of Eden, there is no indication that he had the slightest idea that he was following in the footsteps of Christian cartographers going as far back as the sixth century AD. What are the reasons for this remarkable regress? Such is the complexity of historical and psychological factors that a classification, however rough, is required which will provide a perspective and a background against which Gordon's attempt to put the Garden of Eden on the map must be viewed.

The attempt to bring Gordon's map into the context of other mappers of paradise will bring a principle into focus which has received insufficient attention in analytic circles. Analysis being a specialist subject has, like other specialities, tacitly assumed that its findings are of equal importance in all parts of the world and at all times; or, alternatively, that archetypal patterns are invariant, only their mode of expression changes. I find this generalization too sweeping. It leaves out the cultural dimension as an important factor in the conduct as well as in the retrospective evaluation of a person's life. In Gordon's case this means the Victorian era, the height of the British empire and his having been a member of a distinct social class. The present example shows that what must be regarded as 'pathological', abnormal, eccentric or even psychotic in our time, would have been perfectly in keeping with the world view (*Weltanschauung*) of another age. One might well wonder whether Gordon, had he lived today, would have become the subject of as much hero-worship as he did in the Victorian era. As an eccentric character he was, no doubt, a nuisance to officialdom and treated accordingly. Dying as he did would have aroused sympathy at any time. But hero-worship at a time when the country was not at war? It seems more than doubtful save for the context.

My going into detail about Gordon's mapping of Eden is meant to demonstrate the relationship between the historical and cultural setting and the way an individual's action and character are psychologically assessed. In doing so I hope to make an addition to the criteria by which we may distinguish an abortive or pathological form of individuation from the virtual goal of personality development that Jung had proposed.

But to return to Gordon. Had he lived at the time of Cosmas Indico Pleustes, an Alexandrian monk who lived and travelled in the sixth century, his attempt to map Eden and other biblical localities would not have aroused the suspicion of his being cranky or worse. On the contrary, it would have earned him the approval of faithful souls who regarded biblical authority as the ultimate source of truth. Indeed he would have added to their faith the dimension which we in our time regard with equal confidence as unquestionable, namely scientific evidence. Gordon's arguments are for us pseudo-scientific and as absurd as Cosmas's who in his *Topographia Christiana* showed the world shaped in the form of the Tabernacle with Eden as a separate oblong part in the East beyond the ocean. Although Cosmas's successors deviated from his tenet by mapping the world in the shape of a disc, Cosmas's localization of Eden and its four rivers in the East remained the authoritative cartographical model.

With the advent of the Renaissance and the age of discoveries, the location of paradise on the map became doubtful and therefore mobile. That is to say, the existence of the cradle of mankind as a geographical place was not in doubt. But now there were rival theories regarding its exact whereabouts. 'In the East' was no longer precise enough. That it was a zone into which re-entry had been forbidden no longer deterred explorers from inventing rival theories. One of these, a sea-chart of the fifteenth century, places the Garden fairly close to Gordon's Seychelles, namely in East Africa. Gradually, however, Eden became extruded from the body of the map and was awarded an honourable place as a marginal decorative detail. The map-maker himself may have had doubts, but he played it safe and satisfied the customer.

A further stage in paradise mapping was reached in modern times when variously motivated persons reconstructed the site. Gordon was not the last person so to do. But his thesis is as bizarre as von Wendrin's who in 1924 resited paradise between northern German provinces. Gordon, being the person he was, reconstructed the site in an unusual place much further south than east of Jerusalem. In 1919 Sir William Willcocks, a British water-engineer, came to the conclusion that the Garden had been situated in Mesopotamia. A more plausible location, it is true, and one that was in keeping with Genesis and the Bible maps of the sixteenth to eighteenth centuries. But what is it that makes a person in modern times want to find a geographical site for a symbolic image at all? We shall have to return to the question, using what we know about Gordon in order to understand the phenomenon analytically (see 'Literalmindedness', p. 164, below).

Gordon in context

Placing Gordon among the mappers of paradise both ancient and modern gives the text an historical and cultural context, a dimension of which analysis takes insufficient notice. Whereas in past centuries the mapping of paradise was quite common and perfectly in keeping with the prevailing implicit faith in revealed biblical knowledge, reconstruction of the site of the Garden had become an anachronistic phenomenon requiring the particular outlook referred to in the text. More will have to be said below, see 'literal-mindedness'. Had he lived two hundred years earlier, Gordon's mapping of paradise would, as we saw, have been in keeping with the tradition of literal Bible interpretation. Only the spot he had chosen would have caused criticism. In a still earlier century, at the time of Calvin, he would have been accused of heresy with the usual dire consequences. Not that this would have deterred Gordon. In fact, it would have suited him quite well, as we shall presently see.

But taken by itself, literal-mindedness does not explain why a colonel of the Royal Engineers should in the course of his duties have linked a series of diverse and dubious facts in order to construe and actually map the site of the biblical place. Living in the post-Darwinian era most educated persons would have regarded Eden as a symbolical reference to mankind's origin. As part of a cosmogenic myth the location of paradise is irrelevant. To map it was an anachronism. The mapper's state of mind would therefore be in doubt; why should he wish to turn the clock back? Gordon did not see it that way.

From a biographer's point of view Gordon's affair with Eden was not an important milestone. Whether it was passed over with politeness or embarrassment, the 'discovery' seemed to have received no attention. But psychologically the illustrated essay epitomizes its author's repeated preoccupation with a combination of sexual and religious matters. What made Gordon's brand of religion highly idiosyncratic, was, as we saw, the mixture of literal-mindedness and salvationism. From our point of view Gordon's 'constant object' was his God (see above, p. 135f). Unlike Job, however, Gordon never questioned but idealized God, just as he demonized Satan and his instruments, foremost the 'flesh' in the form of Eve.

But let us first turn to the social and cultural milieu without which no one can be understood. There were eleven siblings in all, of which Charlie was the fourth son. Nothing unusual seems to have occurred during his mother's pregnancy nor at birth. The circumstances as well as the exposure to daily Bible readings from an early age were perfectly standard features considering the family's social background and the Victorian era. We also know that his family had moved house about half a dozen times before he was nine when he was sent to boarding school.

We can assume that with so many on her hands Elizabeth Gordon managed to give enough care to all her children so that none of them died, as frequently happened in those days. Whether each of them received the special personal attention that from today's point of view they required is improbable. The parents did not neglect their marital and social duties on account of the large household in which Bible readings were supplemented by the large collection of religious tracts in Elizabeth Gordon's hands. Nothing suggests that fairy-tales were ever read to the children. Nor did poetry or music figure in the home. One can be fairly sure that their conscience was more frequently catered for than their imagination. All this appears quite up to the standard accepted for the bringing up of children at the time. We must therefore question whether whatever it was that made Gordon the highly unique person he was, as well as an 'eminent Victorian', was due to specific environmental influences. A question which is all the more cogent when we know of no unusual or exceptional features in his ten siblings. It seems more likely that his constitution including gifts, sensitivity and homosexual leaning led to a specific reaction to or against a 'normal' family life. This it was, more than anything else, that made him an individual and caused his suffering. Officialdom did the rest.

Gordon's constant object: psychopathology and individuation

When Jung wrote about Christ as a symbol of the self, he distinguished between the image of the perfect man and the archetype of the self which denotes wholeness or completeness. The crucifixion of the perfect man symbolizes that perfection has been sacrificed for completeness (*CW 9,2*: paras 123–5). An imperfection is needed for life to round itself out into completeness (*CW 12*: para. 208). If it were not a paradox, Jung could have referred to Christ's shadow although he did not mean the Anti-Christ.

This statement of the classical view became the model of individuation in analytical psychology. I am using it here as a preamble to my bringing other analytic views on the subject together and if possible to simplify the matter. The object which I call constant here is Gordon's 'God'. It demands constancy or persistence of the believer's faith in his object. If he falters, he sins. In psychoanalytic terms such inflexibility indicates psychopathology and would lead to 'repetition compulsion', meaning the tendency *not to change* or even to revert to earlier states of mind. The tendency is regarded as innate. Therefore the term can only *describe* a psychic condition but does not explain it psycho-dynamically. It is nevertheless used as if it were an explanation resistant to therapeutic change (see Rycroft, op. cit.). In analysis repetition compulsion is something that the patient is expected to 'give up'.

'*Reality*' is a similarly convincing psychoanalytic description, only this time it is something the patient is expected to accept in contrast to his illusions which he must give up in order to 'change' and so get better (see also p. 102). This is not quite fair because psychoanalysis distinguishes between inner or psychic reality and objective or outer reality. But the psychoanalytic concept of 'reality' originated as a biological concept like 'instinct'. It is a notion that has persisted to some extent. If we take objective facts like birth and death as criteria of reality, the definition obviously makes sense. If we go beyond that and look at the individual ways in which people conduct their lives, we must conclude that reality varies to such an extent that no matter how we further qualify or subdivide 'reality' it remains inadequate, 'psychoanalytic reality' included.

Considerations such as these have an immediate bearing on individuation. In Jung's original view, individuation was a process that belonged to the second half of life. Was it the biological factor again that made individuation into a terminal phenomenon best judged after a person's death? We shall see.

Meanwhile, Fordham in his later work extended the concept to include childhood. His observations of children forced him to relativize the sharp distinction that Jung had made, first between ego and self, second between first and second half of life. Anyway, he came to regard individuation as a special case of ego development (Fordham, 1985). Up to a point, Fordham's view is compatible with Sandler's who as a psychoanalyst was not hampered by Jung's specific distinction between ego and self. He too sees individuation as going on throughout life and as a progressive personality development. On the other hand he regards the task of individuation as *adaptation* to life situations. When Sandler lists university entrance as one of these, he includes a social situation; the same holds good for marriage. But psychologically there remains the necessity to relinquish not only earlier modes of drive satisfaction, but also previously satisfying or secure states of the self which have to be given up in the service of adaptation (Sandler, 1987). More to the point, Sandler distinguishes 'theoretically optimal individuation as a relatively painless, depression-free process', but admits that 'in reality it is never seen without some degree of pain' (ibid.). Here is a distinction to which I shall presently return.

Both of Sandler's formulations, that is 'adaptation' and 'relatively painless', are in direct opposition to Jung's concept nor do they fit the cases I have chosen. For Sandler the giving up of earlier ideals, the 'working through' or 'mourning' is the correct intrapsychic response to the individuation process and the accompanying separation from previous states of being so that a step can be taken forward. The steps are required for ego development and include 'object constancy', a condition without which no individuation is supposed to be possible – a theoretical assumption which I contested in the previous chapter.

Despite these discrepancies everyone is agreed that individuation is not without dangers. Fordham writes that there is a danger that the ego may disintegrate catastrophically (ibid.). Sandler states that it can fail for many reasons and may be followed by 'maldevelopment or a depressive response which represents a capitulation in the face of pain'. The phrasing is reminiscent of the admonitions that neither Freud nor Jung could dispense with (see also p. 71 where suggestion is discussed).

When Sandler differentiates between optimal relatively painless individuation and the reality in which it is never seen without some degree of pain, he makes a very helpful point. By 'in reality' Sandler must mean 'what really happens in analytic practice' and presumably also in 'real life' or the way people really live, in contrast to what is theoretically expected. Bearing Sandler's differentiation in mind we are ready to return to Gordon's psychopathology, using the term in the ordinary sense (see above, p. 162).

It would be true to say that my account of Gordon's essay, the core of our text, bristles with clues to his psychopathology. Therefore we must ask what the most outstanding clues are that when taken together enable us to reconsider by what criteria we judge his psychopathology and what is its relation to individuation (see also p. 145, above).

Literal-mindedness

As I have referred to this phenomenon already (p. 161), only a short amplification will be required in order to bring this key feature of Gordon's views on everything into analytic context. The apparent absence of fantasy divided his cosmos into a black or white world. The absence of shades and colours of meaning made Gordon an uncompromising, difficult person. Not that he was unable to revert his decisions; quite on the contrary. He would, for instance, hand in his resignation one day and take it back the next. But for the moment each impulsive decision was final. There are several analytic ways of looking at the absence of nuances in the white or black world of a literal-minded person like Gordon. We know for instance about Jung's transcendent function which negotiates between real and imaginary data, 'thus bridging the yawning gulf between conscious and unconscious' (*CW* 7: para. 121). A related concept is Winnicott's 'transitional phenomena', which are based on observations of child development. But neither seems to operate here. The situation is rather as when a person regresses to or is stuck in the black or white world of Melanie Klein's paranoid-schizoid position. In his *Transformations* Bion notes that psychotic patients are unable to think or imagine a situation but have to wait for the thing to appear in external reality (Bion, 1965). Again, in 'Reflections on not being able to imagine' I mention that the imagination of psychotic or borderline patients is restricted on account of their hardly being able to distinguish between what is going on inside and outside themselves, nor between reality and fantasy (Plaut, 1966). These are the dynamic descriptions of circumstances in which there can be no symbolic appreciation, and something of the kind appears to have at work in Gordon. There could be no better example than his reference to the Communion as the antidote to having eaten the poison of the forbidden fruit. Gordon's 'a child can understand' indicates that both literal and magical thinking operate instead of symbolic appreciation.

His fundamentalist view of the Bible fitted in well with 'a child's understanding'. If this mode of thinking appears atavistic to us, we have to remind ourselves that symbolic thinking is probably a recent acquisition in our evolution. It is a feebly established function and therefore the first to disappear when, not at our best, we regress to the alternative, a mixture of literal and magical thinking. In Gordon's case this led to a permanent confusion, particularly in areas where for different reasons the senses could not be used to verify his intuitions. This applied particularly to sex and religion. When Gordon nevertheless tried to counteract his confusion by reasoning as he did in his essay on Eden, a fantastic concoction resulted. *It shows how an otherwise sane person can contain psychotic areas* where imagination is not available as a bridge between the physical and the symbolic mode of appreciation. Unbridled fantasy then floods the area and confuses both. When Gordon was working as an engineer he could use his imagination and was inventive. But when it came to sexuality he not only controlled but very nearly stifled his fantasies, presumably because he intuited that they would lead to actions which would bring shame and dishonour upon his head. Homosexual seduction of minors could easily have been his greatest fear. Yet there were safe enough outlets for his creative imagination. Among these was his ingenuity as a military leader which he proved outstandingly when as a young man he had been in command of the Chinese army. Then there was mapping and sketching where he showed talent as a draughtsman. But this too had to be tethered to realistic drawings from nature or photographs.

What I have called literal-mindedness and the inability to imagine and to appreciate symbols has an obvious bearing on object relationships, as the passage in the text clearly showed. There he seems to regard it as something of a miracle that ordinary things can become holy in the hands of God and then revert to ordinary again. Instead of seeing these changes as symbolic transformations it looked to Gordon like it might have to an alchemist who looked upon the transmutation of metals as a realistic possibility.

Religion

'*I hope my dear father and mother think of eternal things ... Dearest Augusta, pray for me, I beg you*' (from a letter quoted by both Trench and MacGregor-Hastie). These words were written to his sister four years older than himself and from an early age Gordon's lifelong confidante especially in religious matters. Gordon was stationed at the time at Pembroke. He was about twenty and spent much time in the company of Captain Drew whose evangelical outlook influenced Gordon. He published religious pamphlets which enabled him to approach strangers and enquire after the state of their souls. One wonders however whether he had committed any 'sin' for which he asked Augusta to intercede on his behalf, or whether he just regarded her as a pure enough spinster who loved him and could therefore be expected to drop a good word for her brother into God's ear. Anyway, Gordon found a special friend in the divinity and person of Jesus. There can be no doubt that Jesus' sacrificing himself *and* wanting to be incorporated by being eaten became the prototype of Gordon's own aspirations. *Jesus certainly was the constant object* that he worshipped and tried to follow. He was the one authority to which Gordon was ready to submit. No doubt too that Gordon's interpretation of the crucifixion suited his own death-wish to which I referred in the text. To be dead meant not only to be free from further temptations of the flesh once the soul freed from the body could rejoin its maker. It also meant a state in which a person 'knew all things' thus having become omniscient like the deity itself. As one reads his journals one becomes aware that Gordon positively envied the dead. As analysts we have to ask whether with all his widely acknowledged humility Gordon projected omniscience and omnipotence on to the deity and longed for the moment when he could become identical with it, just as God the Father and the Son had become reunited. However this may be, his special relation to Jesus and his attitude to death cannot be looked at separately. On the phenomenal level, the wish to be dead showed itself, in my view, as fearlessness which impressed everybody who knew him (see p.149, above). It may have shown itself already when, at the age of nine, he was staying with his family at Corfu. Although unable to swim, he jumped into deep water and then waited patiently to be rescued. It is also testified that he personally led all critical assaults 'unarmed, except for a light cane and smoking a cigar', as one newspaper reported. While governor of the Sudan he once rode on a camel again unarmed into the enemy's camp. Thinking that only a madman or a saint would do such a thing, they must have decided that he was the latter. Anyway, the chief's son who was in command kissed his foot and surrender followed. On another occasion while engaged in the suppression of the slave trade, he said that he would stop the raids, even if it cost him his life. Everyone knew that he meant it. Finally there was Khartoum which Gordon had been ordered to evacuate but did not. One biographer, MacGregor-Hastie, asks the pertinent question whether Gordon really wanted to be rescued and adds 'Is it not possible that he wanted to die, as he did, in a sort of Holy War?'

Whatever the connection with his death-wish, Gordon's fearlessness was an inspiration to those who served under him. Whatever the analytic interpretation of his fearlessness, I think that being the person he was, it took more courage for Gordon to live than to die.

Other features of Gordon's 'religion' must be mentioned. One that bears repeating was the love and personal attention he gave to the underprivileged, the sick and the poor. Did he see his own emotional and sexual deprivation in their plight? Quite likely. Another was that he interspersed his private letters with 'D.V.' (deus volens, God willing). Although this was not uncommon in his day, Gordon seems to have sprinkled the D.V. about rather excessively. It was no empty phrase nor just meant as a propitiation of the deity but also, I think, as an expression of his wish to truly submit himself.

Submission seems a strange word to use in connection with Gordon whose rebelliousness was widely known and disliked. It had clearly shown itself when he was an officer-cadet and perhaps earlier than that in the form of 'mischievousness'. As an analyst one cannot help asking about a man who was in constant trouble with authority what his relationship to his father had been. We have no direct evidence but a number of clues which when put together give us intimations. What are they?

1   His father recalled that he did not bawl after birth, but fixed him with bright eyes which had an almost adult expression (MacGregor-Hastie). We don't know what it means, except that his father had noticed it as peculiar.
2   We recall that Gordon's near insubordinations were the direct cause of his not entering his father's regiment. Also, he made his reputation when serving foreign governments, thus becoming 'a soldier of fortune', a title which his father would have particularly disliked (op. cit.).
3   Gordon never joined a church, although religious matters were a major preoccupation. He corresponded with clergymen to draw on their knowledge, but in other ways preferred a direct relationship with God. Did he avoid the intermediary of clerical authority? It would seem in character.
4   Romolo Gessi, Gordon's close friend for over twenty-five years was an extroverted Italian, who according to Gordon knew him so well that it sometimes frightened him (see also Gessi's comments on the *coco de mer* (p. 151, above)).
    Why should Gordon have had a foreigner as his friend, someone who was not only different from himself but also from his father? H. W. Gordon had disliked foreigners and was highly esteemed at the War Office, an establishment figure. *One may ask whether our Gordon secretly longed for an intimate relationship with his father*, free from all ambivalence as his relationship with God, who was his constantly good and male object. His brothers apparently had no difficulty in conforming and following in their earthly father's footsteps.
5   Analytic curiosity is further aroused by his father's death closely coinciding with Gordon's illness which, as he wrote, brought him back to his Saviour. Did he, instead of mourning, project what he may have secretly admired about his father into the heavenly Father with whom he hoped to be united?

Although each of these clues may seem highly speculative, when taken together with Gordon's marked and continuous problem with authority, they present presumptive evidence in favour of Gordon's compulsive search for the constantly good Father in heaven. It was a search that contributed not a little to his dying the way he did.

Sexuality

Although I have already referred to it in several contexts, the absence of overtly sexual behaviour remains something which arouses curiosity and speculation. Gordon's case demonstrates very clearly that analytically speaking it is much more enlightening to consider a person's sexuality in the context of all other traits than to see in it the cause and origin of all troubles. When these are taken together the picture of a whole person begins to emerge. In our case this means that we have to consider Gordon in relation to his appetites on the one hand and to the search for the constant good object on the other. Both must be looked at against the background of his permanent handicap, his literal-mindedness.

The appetite that needs to be given priority because it must have been the first, is his orality. We remember the wild fantasy about four dozen oysters and the periodic withdrawals accompanied by 'B. & S.', Gordon's abbreviation for brandy and soda. Next we have to ask why the paradisaical apple did not simply cease to exist after it had served Satan as the instrument of temptation. Apparently it became transmuted into the *coco de mer*, alias Eve's pudenda, alias evil. We conclude that the quality of *Satan's instruments* remained *constant*, that is permanently evil, by contrast with God whose objects as we saw went through cyclical changes, from ordinary to holy and back. As Gordon had no capacity to appreciate events as symbolic, *God's ability to change*, or, at any rate, temporarily neutralize the poison that had been introduced by oral seduction could only be called *miraculous*. Gordon does not use the word but it becomes evident that it is this what his 'by means', the instrumentality as I called it, signifies. 'Miracle' would have brought Gordon too close to Rome. By 'unknown means' would have meant a contradiction in terms, an intolerable paradox to his literal mind. *Satan's evil ways* were by contrast *explicable*. Like human nature itself, Satan was also irredeemably sinful. Evil could not change as long as the soul remained in the body, that is during one's lifetime. Satan could use tricks of course and change appearances; the unchanging quality of the poison in the paradisaical apple might *seem* harmless enough, but would be revealed by one look at the *coco de mer*. That was no miracle, merely deception. But the Evil One could not trick Gordon who kept his appetites under strict control. We have seen that this applied to oral and genital appetites. His refusal to take money had also shown itself early on. Analytically this is interpreted as anal inhibition.

What might have happened, had he allowed himself fantasies in the realm of instinctual drives, does not bear imagining. The Gordon we know could not have lived with himself for an instant.

Conclusion

With this account of Gordon's constant object and psychopathology in mind we are now better equipped to return to the criteria by which we judge whether the individuation process was pointing in the direction of success or failure.

There can be no doubt about Gordon's constant devotion to the object that could not fail. His faith in it held him together despite all the splitting that made this world black and the world to come white. By being true to the object,

Gordon was true to himself as an individual. But was this individuation? Although the theoretical precondition of object constancy remained unfulfilled, I think that it was because by suffering his psychopathology the sufferer became more and more himself, unique and different from his fellows whose sympathy he nevertheless aroused. Nor were there any signs of his having become either narcissistically inflated or unduly depressed in the wake of the process, the twin dangers to which Jung had drawn attention. On the other hand, Gordon did not 'change' or become different in any way other than becoming more and more himself. It is a moot point whether or not we allow this to be one of the ways in which an individual may change. It is a change in the direction of the 'perfection' that according to Jung has to be sacrificed. What about completeness? Gordon managed to contain his psychotic area. He did not let his constant object become a preoccupation which would have interfered with his duties and even less a monomanic obsession which would have incurred the label of 'psychotic'. I suggest that such containment is equivalent to 'completeness'. Although it is not in line with the analyst's therapeutic aim, this way of self-realization and, as I hold, *individuation is a common phenomenon* in or out of analysis. But in Gordon's case, the self-realization resulted in the fulfilment of the death-wish. Whether we regard this as the absolute criterion of a failed individuation is a question beyond the realm of psychology and again involves moral and cultural factors.

Putting it like that means challenging the analyst's shibboleth, namely that the patient should change in the course of, or better still, as the demonstrable result of analysis. What is more, the change should be in keeping with his professional ethic which is not questioned when it is in keeping with the prevailing medical and social code. The patient may even be said to have 'completely' changed. The emphasis is meant as a compliment to the analyst's prowess, and must not be taken literally because that would mean changed beyond recognition and nobody wants to become unrecognizable. On the contrary, we usually mean it as a favourable reaction when we can say of persons that they are 'just like themselves'. This often means like their lovable, infuriating or even hateful selves. In any case, the statement indicates that we are pleased to know where we are with someone. Conversely, the reactions of the person so accepted may be agreeable, or they may feel themselves underestimated, even wronged but at least included and recognized as being part of the human race. By contrast, the person who has undergone a 'complete change' may well be admired but not necessarily loved, even made to feel like a stranger, left out in the cold. In the case of Gordon the reactions were mostly of the former kind and he won a considerable amount of admiration as well.

What about the two kinds of psychopathology to which I referred earlier in relation to individuation? In Gordon's case there was so much of the ordinary kind that the specific sort remains almost unnoticed, perhaps even doubtful. What there was of inflation in the form of omniscience and omnipotence was projected on to the good object, the deity. With his periodic bouts of depression he was, like everybody else, alone. They were unspectacular, and what solace he permitted himself was of the 'spiritual kind', in both senses of the word. It is therefore doubtful whether the distinction I drew on earlier between two kinds of psychopathology can be maintained in Gordon's case (see also p. 147, above). In so far as the sufferer or patient is concerned there is in any event only one kind of psychopathology, the theoretical differentiation makes no difference to the pain.

Lastly what about the severed head that was displayed and mocked in the Mahdi's camp? It is conceivable that analysts would see in it a symbolic confirmation of the split between the controlling superego and the instinctual drives that was one of our hero's characteristics. But if they did, they would be shutting their eyes to an act of barbarism which was in itself the consequence of blind psychotic literal-mindedness. To interpret the decapitation symbolically would, in our cultural epoch, be the symptom of a split and of psychopathology more dangerous than Gordon's.

It seems ironical that Gordon's design of a crest for the Seychelles after he had 'discovered' Eden could have been a fitting epitaph to his own life. It shows a palm tree as a central feature but we cannot say whether it is meant to portray one or other of the sacramental trees to which the essay refers. The tortoise is not only a natural inhabitant but is also, according to Jung, primitive and cold-blooded and 'symbolizes the instinctual side of the unconscious' (*CW 13*: para. 203). The inscription reads 'Finis coronat opus', the end crowns the work, and requires no comment.

Was Gordon mad? A discussion

The Chiron Conference 1991 had as its theme 'Mad parts of sane people in analysis'. My contribution had been called 'General Gordon's constant object'. The respondent was Ronald Kledzik for whose brilliant discussion I am grateful (Kledzik, 1991). It was particularly addressed to theoretical problems arising out of my having postulated the constant object as an alternative path to self-realization. However, I want to restrict my reply here to answering the practical questions Kledzik had put to me, starting with 'Where in our society do people who take the path of the constant object gravitate to today, if we exclude organized religion?' And 'Had I seen many in therapy?'

I have seen relatively few and some of these were among the nine patients I grouped together in the second part of this chapter. The reason why I have not seen many more is probably because some had had one form of psychotherapy or another already but had left it, realizing perhaps that they could not change in the way that their analysts expected. (Yes, analysts do expect *some* change, statements to the contrary notwithstanding.) I mean 'could not change', not 'did not want to'. But the patients must have wanted something to come to analysis at all. Looking back, I think they may have looked for what in chapter fourteen I refer to as the 'unitive state' as mystics do. I think the longing for it is more widespread than is generally realized and that there is no obvious outlet in our society, especially not if, as Kledzik stipulated, one excludes organized religion. However, he approaches the same point by a different route when he mentions the numinosity of the constant object and takes the conversion of Saul on the road to Damascus as example. Kledzik assumes that Saul was a well-integrated Roman citizen possessing the trappings of object constancy. Along comes the numinous experience. 'Did Saul have to sacrifice object constancy in order to become Paul?' he asks.

Linking his question to the theme of the conference, Kledzik continues: 'Do mad parts come as part of the deal, or does the constant object offer a way to deal with already present mad parts?' The question presupposes that we have a generally valid definition of madness which is independent of what a given society will tolerate. Gordon is a good case in point. Kledzik refers to examples I quoted of Gordon's actions and his handling of Khartoum which he calls 'stupid as well as insane'. All we can say is that his actions may look like that from today's point of view. Kledzik himself might have thought otherwise had he been a contemporary of Gordon's living in Britain. All the same, even at that time there were people who, knowing Gordon, were of the opinion that he had 'a wee bee in his bonnet'. Gordon's death-wish is now evident to us. But if we take the sexual problems and his religious ideas into consideration, must we interpret his death-wish as mad? I think our judgement depends on how much we feel in sympathy with Gordon.

Returning to the sudden conversion of Saul, how are we to tell with any degree of certainty what was hidden in the depths of his psyche before the event which apparently changed the person in an unforeseeable way? Again, a sudden break in a person's life may look to us as if he/she had taken leave of

Figure 9.3   Gordon's Crest of the Seychelles

their senses. But I am afraid our judgement depends a lot on what happens after the event. If the break with the past is successful, we speak of a rebirth or, at least, a new start. If not, the unfortunate person is said to have gone off his/her head. Therefore, if the analytically desirable object constancy with which Kledzik credits Saul, the solid citizen, implies that he had been an all-rounder before, who after his numinous experience became Paul, the single-minded missionary and successful saint, then – yes – we must assume that the conversion changed him in that the constant object took the place of object constancy. From a Christian point of view, it looks like a change for the better, just as from the art world's point of view, Paul Gauguin, the banker, did well to leave home for Tahiti. Whether the wives and family of the two Pauls thought so too, I am less sure of.

Let us return now to Kledzik's questions as to where constant object people gravitate to and had I seen many in therapy? Not a few analysts belong to this group and can privately admit that they have not changed and that they feel relieved that the constant object path to individuation which I outlined validates their unchanging way of life. The way includes analysing others who may or may not be able to undergo changes and become 'solid citizens' while they, the analysts, remain unchanged. As Balint put it: the patients must change, the analyst continues with his repetition compulsion (personal communication).

II   CELIA'S CROSS

In the case of Gordon, see Part I of this chapter, biography and a manuscript supplied the clues for an analytic reconstruction on which I based the thesis that there can be more than one kind of individuation. Reasons were given why the analytic setting had been replaced by the method of reconstructing and constructing the psychological development of a person along analytic lines. I am well aware that a review of biography and a play are not the same as making direct observations in analysis. But any report that is based on such direct observations, unique though it is, is also unavoidably coloured by the analyst–reporter's theoretical spectacles and personal involvement. It is true that a biographical portrait leading up to the hero's death is like the unfolding of the drama on the stage. Although it demands our participation, our sense of personal responsibility is limited; what there is of it comes to us afterwards, mostly on reflection. But then, the less involved observer of psychological phenomena has the onlooker's advantage of seeing most of the game in which he nevertheless participates.

Hitherto the assumption has been that individuation could not proceed unless certain preconditions were fulfiled. The concept had, as discussed earlier, been widened by both post-Jungians and psychoanalysts. Nevertheless, analysts have continued to assume that a certain state of ego development must necessarily precede individuation. That state is variously conceptualized as 'integration', 'object constancy', 'symbolic appreciation' or 'union of opposites' and 'the depressive position'. I am now going to argue that individuation can develop not only in relation to but actually through a person's ordinary and unchanging psychopathology. The latter is seen as part of the self. The outcome of the individuation process must be judged by analytic as well as socio-cultural criteria. *This thesis was introduced in Part I of the chapter and will receive further support by reviewing the case of Celia, the heroine of Eliot's drama* The Cocktail Party *whom several patients resembled* (Eliot, 1950).

To make use of a figure which is a fictitious construct originating in the mind of an author requires to be looked at with even more circumspection than was needed in Gordon's case where reconstruction was based on data. Celia had never been a definite person; she came to life because Eliot needed her. Yet, it seems more than likely that his invention was based on observations of one or more people that he had known. Therefore, we would really require a thorough knowledge of the author, his psychology and circumstances to do her justice. Even if I were able to do so, any attempt to analyse the author through his characters would take us too far from the present issue. We shall therefore have to content ourselves with a brief account of the play and its message. Here we find that a recurrent social problem is dramatized in an overtly psychological fashion. Moreover Eliot intervenes in the role of a psychiatrist, or rather, analytical psychotherapist. I therefore feel justified in evaluating the author's message analytically, having first added my comments on patients who resembled 'Celia'. She now becomes a composite figure based partly on Eliot's, partly on my own construction.

Eliot's Celia

Celia is the heroine of the play. As the drama unfolds we discover that she had been in love with a married man, Edward, who has returned to his wife. Celia is in a state of despair because she does not know how to continue living when she is taken to see an unusually enlightened psychotherapist, Reilly. He outlines two possible ways out of her dilemma and it is she who has to decide which one to choose. Towards the end of the play we learn that her decision has led to a gruesome death: having joined a religious order Celia was sent to a plague-stricken village on an eastern island to nurse the sick whom she did not abandon when a rebellion broke out among the heathen half of the population. She was crucified 'very near an ant-hill'.

Before returning to the play, I shall give my clinical impression of patients whose character structure seemed to me related to Eliot's Celia.

The patients

There were nine patients in all, six of them female. Their ages ranged from thirty to forty-five. Four of these had been or were married, unlike Eliot's Celia and some had had more than one marriage, love affairs and children. Yet these events did not seem to have changed their essentially uncommitted, 'virginal' nature. They had had what we would regard as inadequate mothering but gave a comparatively positive report on the care they had from their fathers. This seemed to account for their attachments to older men. The 'Celia' patient also tried to follow in father's footsteps in the choice of an occupation or profession. She did not get on too well with women, but felt drawn towards men who were homosexually inclined or invalids. If her efforts to make the men potent and to further their careers succeeded, her interest in them declined. She, as well as the three male patients who had comparable character structures, was always trying to gain mastery over circumstances and other people yet curiously enough also seemed to sabotage these efforts. It looked as if there were an unconscious tendency which worked in the opposite direction, a wish to succumb, to be used and, ultimately, to be annihilated. This could take on a variety of manifestations like trying to find surgeons who would cut out bits of or otherwise operate on their anatomy. Such operations eventually turned out to have been unnecessary or useless. Despite being anxious 'Celia' seemed to seek opportunities to be exposed to danger and had fantasies of being rendered helpless, crushed, dismembered or devoured. This feature was shared by all the patients under review.

In the males who showed what I shall refer to as the *Celia syndrome*, the predominant fantasies were about going bankrupt, imprisonment, being tied up and/or raped, in short, about circumstances in which they were rendered helpless. In some cases the fantasies were enacted. The women on the other hand had fantasies about having to become servants, even slaves. One of these told me about a pornographic book which she said had a bearing on her fantasy. Here the heroine undergoes procedures of total submission by which she is forced into a series of sexual humiliations, performed by anonymous men, or else she was blindfolded. In this way, she could not distinguish between her lover and any other man who might want to use her sexually. The reduction to an object, being allowed only to function as a part of herself, seemed to me comparable to being devoured as Eliot's Celia was by a multitude of ants: an extreme example of being consumed as food and thus re-entering the life cycle. In my experience this fantasy is not rare. As a theme it finds expression in rituals such as the Brahmin burial, where the corpses are thrown to the vultures. We also recall that Gordon had been fascinated by the ritualistic eating and drinking of Christ's body and blood in the Holy Communion.

It would be in keeping with psychoanalytic theory to interpret Celia's choice which led to her death and the symptomatology of the patients who survived as being due to masochism and, ultimately, the death instinct. But in order to throw light on the relation between the constant object and the psychopathology that accompanies individuation it is more profitable to return to Reilly's consulting room. His, that is Eliot's, sympathy with Celia is as genuine as his implicit philosophy is relevant to our subject.

The consultation

Although Eliot on the title page calls *The Cocktail Party* a comedy we are aware that he uses his comic art not only to enliven the play but to heighten the sense of tragedy at the end. (See also Howarth, 1965.) For instance, we cannot help smiling when the 'unidentified guest' becomes known to us by his full name as 'Sir Henry Harcourt-Reilly'. This, as well as names of other actors, is no doubt meant as a send-up of Mayfair society. So is the staging and manipulation that goes on in the consulting scene. Reilly's manner and pronouncements correspond much more to the popularized version of a psychiatric consultation that was current in the 1950s than they ever were to reality. But even if all this and the poetry of the lines were entertainment, it helps us to absorb the message. And that is what matters.

When it is Celia's turn to be ushered in she speaks of her disillusionment with Edward with whom she had been in love, that is in a state of mutual identification. It felt as if they had both become one new person until she found that they were only strangers. She asks whether we can only love something created by our own imagination. If that were true, and lover and beloved unreal then, Celia concludes, we are truly alone. Her conclusion seems commonplace enough for a person in a state of disillusionment. Celia is not bitter. What really bothers her is neither guilt about adultery, nor having made a fool of herself. In fact, it is not anything she has done, but her sense of emptiness and failure that troubles her. Of this she wants to be cured. She craves for something, a treasure she has gone out to find and is ashamed of not having found. She feels she must *atone* and seems quite surprised at having used that word. Reilly assures her that the condition is curable and makes us look at the alternatives between which Celia has to choose.

He describes the way of moderation in terms of the daily routine by which people maintain themselves. They may remember the vision they once had, but cease to regret not having followed it. Celia wonders whether that is the best life. Reilly tells her that in a rotten world it is a good life.

Howarth thinks that Eliot really means it and championed both the 'household life', as the Buddha called the life that he renounced, as well as that of the self-sacrificing martyr which Celia then incarnates (op. cit.). But my reading of the text is different. A note of boredom, if not of veiled contempt, runs through Eliot's lines when he describes the couple who meet at the beginning of the day and again in the evening, sitting by the fireside for a casual chat without understanding each other, breeding, as he says, children whom they do not understand and who will not understand them. Although Eliot makes Reilly say that neither way is better and both involve loneliness as well as communion, it leaves me unconvinced about his neutrality. I for one was not surprised when Celia said that the householder's way of life leaves her cold, *even if that is part of her illness*, she does not want to forget her vision of something unknown. She would be dishonest, if she were to try and make that sort of life with anybody. So we are not astonished that Celia should choose the second way which, like Jung's individuation, is the way of the few. It requires, we are told, both courage and faith.

The alternative of the 'terrifying journey' the destination of which cannot be described starts at Reilly's special sanatorium from which people do return '*physically*' yet changed in a profound way, although they very often lead active lives *in the world* afterwards (emphasis added). The description is mystifying. An air of predestination is added when later in the play we learn that Reilly had had a vision at the time when he first met Celia at a cocktail party which told him that she was under sentence of death. If further proof of Eliot's bias towards the way of the solitary journey into the unknown were needed, it becomes evident when, at the end, Reilly tells Celia that he charges no fee in cases like hers.

Religious elements

The 'household life' is only one of several pointers to the impression which three years of Indian studies at Harvard had left on Eliot's mind. Reilly is the vehicle for expressing a philosophy of salvation that comes very close to Jung's concept of individuation. The parting words addressed to Celia at the end of her consultation are:

Go in peace, my daughter
Work out your salvation with diligence.

Howarth points out that these are the words of the dying Buddha to his priests (op. cit.). Although psychotherapists do not speak like this and their advice is usually implicit or remains unspoken, it could ultimately amount to the same. What really matters is therefore how the counsel is applied. In theory there are the two ways between which Celia had to choose. In practice most people go in for more of a compromise than either Celia and Gordon or, for that matter, Edward who realizes that he is a 'householder' whose loneliness is less obvious than theirs.

A further religious element that would certainly not take place in any consulting room is a ritual in the form of a libation that is drunk by Reilly and his helpers after Celia has departed. It is accompanied by prayers for those that 'build the hearth' as well as for the others who 'go upon a journey'. At this point Eliot's beautiful lines catch, according to Howarth, some echo of Sanskrit poetry (ibid.).

'Diligence' no doubt demands concentration or, which is the same, the exclusion of tempting distractions. What are they? Eliot refers to a world of lunacy, violence, stupidity and greed which can be avoided by both ways, the household life and the journey into the unknown. Both ways also avoid what he calls the final desolation

Of solitude in the phantasmal world
Of imagination, shuffling memories and desires.

The woes of the world Reilly had enumerated are fundamentally the same as those represented by the three animals in the centre of a lamaistic mandala on which Jung comments (*CW 9, I*: para. 644). Here the cock, the snake and the pig represent lust, envy and unconsciousness. They are part of Kama Loka, the Buddhist world of desire. Now all kinds of analysis and many religions involve some kind of transformation of these desires with the help of interpretative techniques and/or rituals. 'Memories and desires' also remind analysts of Bion who demands that analysts should discard memory and desire as preparatory to a state of mind in which 'O' can evolve into knowledge, where 'O' stands for ultimate reality or absolute fact and is as such unknowable. This means that analysts should avoid recalling any memory, however relevant it may seem. Instead they should make use of a relevant 'constellation', which is observations that seem to belong together or are in 'constant conjunction', as Bion calls it (Bion, 1970). The analyst's desire to help the patient along any preconceived lines must likewise be discarded.

Although we do not know what kind of preparation Celia underwent at the sanatorium, we can be fairly certain that it was designed to exclude the 'phantasmal world', the illusory desirousness of the Buddhist *samsara*. Both, Bion's exclusion of sensa and the turning inwards and concentration on spontaneously appearing imagery which Jung observed as part of the individuation process bear a close resemblance to the conditions that Eliot is referring to. We would expect that quiet contemplation and an ascetic aim prevailed at Reilly's sanatorium. There is also Jung's comment on 'The Tibetan Book of the Great Liberation' and 'at-one-ment' as the state attained by withdrawal from the world of consciousness into one where there is freedom from tensions and conflicts (*CW. 11*: para. 799). Bion spells that word in the same way when he describes the state of mind that is desirable for analysts because it is conducive to the evolution of 'O' referred to earlier. We also remember that it was the word that Celia stumbled on when, not feeling sinful, she said she wanted to *atone* in order to get rid of her emptiness.

Earlier in the play Celia's former lover, Edward, explained why, by not leaving his wife he was true to himself and 'the indomitable spirit of mediocrity' that rules him. He sounds remarkably 'Jungian' when he explains that there are two kinds of self, one is the self that wants and wills. The other, the tougher self neither talks nor argues, but is the stronger partner to whom the former 'self', analysts would say the ego, has to submit in order to flourish.

The reader need not know much about Jung to recognize in this description a close paraphrase of a major theme, that is the changing relationship between the ego and the self during the individuation process which, according to Jung, usually starts with mid-life. From then on submission of the ego becomes the keynote in the play as it also does in the individuation process.

At the beginning of her disillusionment, Celia had chided Edward. The voice that formerly thrilled her is dry, meaningless, inhuman; like that of a grasshopper scraping his legs together. If she should tread on him nothing would come out except what comes out of a beetle. 'Do that if you like', says Edward, signifying mock-submission to the stronger partner. But Celia cannot continue the tirade because she realizes that the man she had seen in him before was only a projection of something she aspired to and now realizes does not exist. Where can she find it?

Celia's correct use of 'projection' removes any doubt about this being a psychological play. Other elements mentioned, that is the manifestations of the death instinct, the elimination of the phantasmal world and the conditions needed to undertake the terrifying journey in search of a goal that might replace the love in which she once believed, a goal to which she can submit without fear of disillusionment – all these show equally convincingly that the religious elements in Eliot's play are of the mystical variety.

The constant object: psychopathology and individuation

We see Celia go forth on her quest or, which is the same, in search of a constant object that will not disappoint or disillusion her, provided that she remains devoted to it. It costs her her life as it cost Gordon his life. Once set on this course, there seems to be nothing to deflect the sufferer who is also the hero. A bond appears to have taken place, a 'constant conjunction' between the person and the object which makes it look as if there was, if not actual predestination, then at least a certain degree of predictability about the further development. With hindsight we can say that neither Gordon's nor Celia's fate was really surprising. We do not know whether Gordon's difficulties were due to premature disillusionment. The disillusionment that precipitated Celia's crisis in adult life is clearly set out for us. The patients under review seemed to have suffered from early deprivations of a constant enough object, in theory the breast. Consequently they never gave up hope of finding it. Whether it was for this and/or other reasons, they did not acquire that tolerance of subsequent frustrations which is needed for the development of 'object constancy' (see above, Chapter 8). Important as the analytic understanding is in the formation of the substitute which I call the constant object, there are probably many people on whom the early disappointments did not have the same traumatic effect of having to search for something that is constant and can be idealized.

To assume that the condition of search for and attachment to a constant object is unalterable, runs contrary to the analyst's equally constant hope of being able to facilitate, if not actually bring about, a change in the direction that is theoretically desirable. When that hope is not fulfilled there remains, as pointed out earlier, the possibility of helping people to find a viable relation to the constant and other objects and to accept their limitations. Although the psychopathology is unchanged, in practice, *the result is the same and equally hard to assess as that brought about by the classical process of individuation.* (For criteria see below.)

The group of patients showing the Celia syndrome had come for help and that – as Freud realized long ago – contributes already fifty per cent to a possible cure. As for the work done, I think that the analytic relationship indirectly encouraged the patients to resume or take up relations to other persons ('objects') and so to shift from the narrow and isolating preoccupation with a constant object, including the pathology of their complaints, to the wider spectrum of relating to and valuing people and in this way to cultivate some trust.

At the start the patients' response to analysis was frequently to idealize me. This seemed favourable and necessary, if they were ever to increase the distance between themselves and the preoccupation with their constant object, be it a lover or other central person, or a habit or drug. For me these were images representing their constant object. To the patients the object was fascinatingly real most of the time. The crunch came when *my reality* by way of holidays, an illness or evidence of other people being around, began to intrude. If this turning point came with sudden intensity but the patients nevertheless managed to continue the analysis, there was hope. Hope that after my failure to come up to expectations had been brought home to me in ways that were often punitive, I could still be useful as a fundamentally reliable although sadly fallible container of their disappointments. As far as I could see the further course depended on whether and in what way the patients were able to tolerate the awareness of being alone with their longing for a better life and the inescapable solitude of the human condition that Eliot points out. This tolerance was never achieved to the degree that the analytically desirable 'object constancy' implies. When circumstances became disappointing, as they sooner or later had to, the suffering increased and with it the craving and so they would resume the search for a constant 'good' object, however illusory the patients frequently knew it would be.

So Celia is right: not risking to repeat the disillusionment of ordinary life and to search instead for 'the vision she once had' *is* part of her illness. She could not act otherwise, for solitude in the phantasmal world is desolation as Reilly says, and as such unbearable. Although Celia is as extraordinary in her persistence as Gordon had been, less extreme forms of the 'illness' are quite common. Therefore, when looking at the criteria of individuation and psychopathology we shall have to take into account *how* the hankering after constant objects is coped with ordinarily, outside analysis.

Analytic criteria

Celia's reaction to disillusionment seemed extreme to the point where we have to ask whether it was not also due to predisposing factors in her personality. Certainly, Reilly's premonitory vision suggests that her disillusionment was more of a precipitating factor than the explanation of her decision to undertake the fatal journey. We can further invoke a strong death-wish or instinct as I did in Gordon's case. But that is no more a satisfactory explanation than the analytic hypothesis of early trauma. Given that there is no ultimate explanation, I think it helps our understanding of the aim of the quest for a permanent union with the object (and *all* objects) if we quote, as Reilly did, the Zoroaster lines from Shelley's *Prometheus Unbound*. They refer to the world underneath the grave inhabited by

> *The Shadows of all forms that think and live*
> *Till death unite them and they part no more!*

At this point we also recall Gordon's constant interest in death and paradise which in his time was widely believed to be the place where reunions took place.

The use of poetry shows that the idea of being united with the object in death, the motif of *Liebestod* is in keeping with a collective image. As such it appeals to a wide readership or audience who can empathize much as they can with Shakespeare's Ophelia. It is true that this is the sentimentalized but ever popular version that covers up the suicide's aggression which is directed against the frustrating object as well as the self. Our sympathetic understanding for these extreme instances grows if we consider how labile 'object constancy' is in everybody, even in persons who have been fortunate enough to acquire that capacity and could therefore be expected to see both sides of a frustrating problem later on in life. Also, it is often assumed that those whose ego development has been favourable can discriminate between material or literal reality and situations requiring symbolic realization. This desirable state is known by a number of technical terms, some of which have been listed (see p. 53, above). However in the chapter on object constancy I pointed out that the acquisition of it corresponds to an analytic ideal. It is a point that I think bears repeating here because the ability of ordinary people, analysts most particularly included, *not to split* the object is decidedly more limited than theories of psychological maturation would encourage us to expect.

Theory is quite clear on this point: idealization of the object and the ego's illusory bond with it cannot be in keeping with the reality of any person nor a complete representation of any object. Therefore idealizations are bound to fail and turn into split objects either ideally good or correspondingly bad. Thereby the ego becomes itself split. Hence the patient needs to be helped to accept the object's dual nature. *In practice*, a unified view of opposites is rarely achieved and then only temporarily during analysis or when circumstances are relatively free from anxiety or, again, by exceptional individuals. Much more commonly we shuttle back and forth between our belief in a constantly good *or* bad object and moments of our being able to apply the unifying knowledge of the object being both 'bad' *and* 'good'. Here uniting symbols have little practical effect.

As regards Jung's concept of individuation, the whole-making effect of the self and the hypothesis that there can be no such development in the presence of splits, projection of the shadow and in the absence of symbolic unification, *my statement means that the premises of the concept have been idealized.* However, later modifications that allow for a shuttle between states such as Fordham's integration and de-integration (see p. 283), or Klein's paranoid–schizoid and depressive position (Ps↔D) are therefore closer to what is humanly possible.

It follows that if individuation is not to be regarded as a rare, élitist concept but rather as a common event, the psychopathology of the individual such as the consequences of a powerful death-wish and the hankering after a constant object, must be part of it. What remains attractive about individuation as a concept is the powerful concentrating or 'gathering in' that emanates from the self and frees the person from the many distracting and anxiety-arousing influences of the sensuous world.

The constant object does reflect self-qualities and therefore the persons who are in pursuit of it are liable to become identified with their self image and to fall, like Narcissus, in love with it. This is a classical danger which Jung had pointed out. Celia avoided it. She could not give up her vision and we must assume that she became identified with it in the form of her nursing mission. When her rival in the play tried to belittle her death, Reilly intervened; might not Celia's presence have made a difference to the dying natives? We further learn that to the survivors Celia became the equivalent of a saint, that is to say another constant object was apparently needed by the survivors. A problem for the bishop to sort out, Eliot quips.

We know that something similar happened when Gordon became a national hero. Neither his nor Celia's constant objects were projected on to themselves. Unlike Churchill who, as Storr writes, also possessed exceptional fearlessness, believing himself invulnerable. He also had been subject to idealizing persons (as objects) as well as to bouts of depression and became more and more the victim of self-admiration, in short, narcissism (Storr, 1989). Despite this, Churchill became, like Gordon, a national hero, the constant object of many. Whether we regard heroes as a desirable or a regrettable phenomenon is not as important as the apparent need of a large section of the population to idealize hero figures.

We have assumed that the concentrating process of individuation can get under way by means of the self and of psychopathology and despite the presence of a constant object, one that is not surrounded by acknowledged doubts and ambivalences. What are the analytic criteria by which we can judge the outcome? Two stand out.

The first depends on the nature of the constant object. If it and the self image coincide we have, as we saw, a narcissistic outcome. If, on the other hand, it is projected on to a divine figure or a cause, union with it may be tantamount to dying for it. Yet who can say that the individuation process ending in death is not also a way of self-realization? According to Jung this is what happened in the case of Christ.

The second depends on the way that the constant object is managed and related to other objects. For example, if the constant object becomes numinous, so does the split-off or excluded demonic part of it, 'the devil'. So much for the theory. But in the case of Gordon for whom the devil was as real as God we have seen a lifelong tolerance regarding people of different creed, nationality, race – and even sex, with the exception of 'Eve'. Although killing enemies was part of his job, there was no hint of viciousness in his character. Tolerance, then, becomes a crucially important criterion in the evaluation of the individuation process, whether it is based on object constancy or on a constant object. Without tolerance, the projection of the shadow engenders a paranoid development accompanied by an isolation quite different from the elected solitariness required for contemplation. In my view, Gordon was saved from this fate because of his tolerance and widely recognized humility. We do not know the origin of this virtue which is however linked with a devout attitude towards the object. In a paper on part-object relationships I contrasted devotion with addiction and showed how tenuous the boundary can be (Plaut, 1974). Our different moral and cultural evaluation of constant objects will, in turn, influence how the individual's relation to these objects is seen. If, for example, the constant object were represented by part-objects such as alcohol, drugs or sex it would be differently assessed and hence related to than is the case when family, work, art, politics or religion are central to a person's life. Gordon created a context for his religious belief and experiences by sharing them with his sister. His sharing examplifies how important it is for psychic health that the constant object be connected with other objects represented by persons.

Where does this leave Celia? In the scene referred to she certainly let out some venom against her former lover. But then she took her anger back much too quickly because she realized that Edward was only the vehicle of her projection and so asks his forgiveness. He is rightly astonished because her insight is much too quick. Perhaps Eliot's audience is moved by her apparent generosity, but to an analyst 'forgiveness' at this point sounds like a glib intellectual defence. She does not work anything out in the direction of object constancy but continues the search for the vision she once had, for her constant object. Here we note how Celia's psychopathology and her self becomes one and the same. We can call her self-destructive and most analysts have known patients who took Celia's way to individuation. But it is *her* way and we have no doubt that she will work it out 'with diligence'. We further recall that in Jung's concept of individuation 'perfection' has to give way to 'completion', or, which amounts to the same, the ego that wills has to submit to the self, the stronger partner that Eliot in *The Cocktail Party* also refers to as the *guardian*. I suggest that 'working out one's salvation with diligence' involves a degree of tolerance and humility that lessens the need to project the shadow. Whatever the details of that work may be, it becomes the saving grace in Gordon's and Celia's individuation. Integration instead of projection of the shadow combines with tolerance and humility to become the saving grace in their individuation. We recognized in these virtues the equivalents of the 'completion' that Jung stipulates. The common denominator is, in a word, 'submission' to something that is recognized to be more powerful than egoic desires and aspirations. In the habits of some of the patients mentioned, submission had, so to speak, gone off on its own and become manifest in perverted ways. In Celia's and Gordon's case, on the other hand, submission in the form of devotion to their cause became the guideline. Their journeys depended on the projection of omnipotence on to the highest possible authority. Their longing to come so close to the constant object as to be united with it proved fatal. Whether we therefore regard it as a negative criterion, excluding individuation depends on non-analytic criteria.

Socio-cultural criteria

If we now look at the values which matter most to our society, that is the society into which analysis was born and still flourishes, we must come to the sobering conclusion that, analytic insights notwithstanding, the wish for material possessions plays an immeasurably greater part than any symbolic realization. And further, the effect of object constancy, the supposed achievement of ego development and maturation and therefore the capacity to see both sides of a problem, is virtually nil as soon as vested material interests become involved. Having lived through the ideological splits in analytic societies and living through the continuing self-destruction by wars carried out in the name of deities and principles, that is to say constant objects, I can come to no other conclusion than that individuation by either path has remained an illusory aim.

Closely connected with this failure is the tremendous importance that our society attaches to the individual. Hence Jung needs to be emphatic when he states that *individualism* has nothing to do with individuation. However Elias, writing as a sociologist, points out that in western society we have virtually only an I-identity and no we- or group-identity (Elias, 1987). Group- or we-identity only reappears in times of collective anxiety, for example in wartime. At other times the 'success' of the individual is still measured in terms of personal, individual achievements for which the criteria are wealth and fame.

In comparison with this, the importance of self-realization as Jung envisioned it in the individuation process hardly counts.

The trend towards 'meritocracy', in the absence of a we-identity combined with 'equal opportunities' seem to reinforce the hypertrophy of the achieving ego and 'individualism'. In Gordon's time and social class there was, for better or worse, a we-identity. Even Celia, born, I imagine, a little less than a hundred years later and between two world wars was conscious of her class, which Eliot lampooned. This becomes evident in a way that is particularly relevant to the topic when Celia says that she was brought up to disbelieve in sin and goes on to mention the spoof values that replaced that criterion. Barely a century had elapsed since Gordon had been virtually reared on the belief in sin – this in the same country and roughly the same social class. The 'mistake' that made Celia feel sinful and for which she wanted to atone, was for something she had done towards herself. Here, of course, Celia speaks of the self that she knows. From our and Eliot's point of view she is referring to the self that in the play is called the stronger partner whom the ego wishes to but cannot oppose.

We note that the birth of analysis and in particular of concepts such as individuation and more recently Kohut's 'self-psychology' coincides with the lessening and virtual disappearance of the hitherto conventional criterion of sin. Once de-throned and replaced by concepts much more nebulous and harder to understand, the lonely individual without tradition becomes over-loaded with insecurity and responsibility of a kind as hard to define as it is to bear. For reasons such as these the analytic criteria of success or failure of Jung's individuation process are by themselves inadequate to judge the value of the concept and its outcome.

Summary and conclusions

I made use of Eliot's 'Celia', the heroine of *The Cocktail Party* and added observations on a number of patients who seemed to have in common both a marked degree of introversion and an attachment to constant objects as previously defined. The combination gave me a baseline from which to review the connection between individuation and psychopathology. The common assumption in analytical psychology is that integration, particularly of the shadow, is a precondition of individuation. It is an assumption that makes demands comparable with those of object constancy as a requirement for ego development. I have relativized the practical value of these concepts first by showing that even when the preconditions are not fulfilled the process of self-realization, synonymous with individuation, may still go ahead. Second, I postulated that a person's unmodified psychopathology can be the means by which he/she individuates. In such cases the psychopathology plays a role that determines the choice of a constant object. The latter can be a person, thing, cause or deity and becomes the centre of the person's life, although from the outsider's point of view they thereby become 'eccentric'. The constant object then mirrors the self, psychopathology included.

The existence of this object has a powerfully concentrating effect; it simplifies all decisions, determines priorities and therefore reduces anxiety. It gives a sense of direction to life. The concentration reduces the distracting effect of a multitude of sensuous images. There are, however, other effects ascribed to the numen surrounding such an object which vary from fascination to devotion. Here lies the parting of the ways which depends on whether or not certain old-fashioned virtues are available that can be practised. Courage, faith, humility and tolerance of one's own failings and those of others have already been mentioned. In practice then the *outcome of analysis depends much more on such conscious and moral factors than the weight given to unconscious motivation would lead one to believe* (see also p. 344).

Some analysts would regard virtues as mere reaction formation to the much more realistic destructive drives. However, I find myself in agreement with Jung who does not consider this to be the whole truth. He recognizes that human nature is also moral. If this were not a psychic fact, deeply embedded in us, our society could not have survived (*CW 7*: para. 30, and *18*: para. 1415). It follows that the life of the individual and with it individuation is more indissolubly interwoven with society than Jung's familiar statement contrasting social adaptation with individuation would suggest. His is indeed a markedly introverted point of view which accounts for the relative underestimation of the role that interpersonal relations play in individuation.

As regards introversion, Jung and Eliot are on the same side as becomes obvious in the course of *The Cocktail Party*. Jung's mandala material is largely based on the Tibetan Buddhistic prototype. We also see the influence of Buddhism on Eliot in his reference to the avoidance of the phantasmal world. Bion and the evolution of 'O', the ultimate fact, as well as his avoidance of memory and desire point in the same easterly direction. Whether Bion's having spent the first eight years of his life in India had anything to do with it is a matter of speculation. More to the point is that neither Bion nor Jung in their introverted psychologies take much notice of the pain involved in separation. The omission makes it seem as if all evolutions and developments were only intrapsychic. Were it otherwise, more attention would have been paid to individuation, meaning not only a separation from the preceding state of being but also separation from 'objects' as represented by persons.

Eliot refers repeatedly to loneliness. I think that much of the outcome of individuation depends on whether and how individuals can tolerate being alone yet deeply aware of their dependence on others.

Part III

Analysis mapped

INTRODUCTION

The general aim to communicate about analysis is further pursued as mapping as a medium is explored. In Chapter 10 Freud's travel metaphor is taken up along with the question whether the analytic journey could become more than a metaphor. It took a long time before world images could be replaced by world maps and accurate surveys of our planet. While objectively quantifiable data cannot be expected in the case of the analytic territory, the present state of our knowledge resembling world views is untenable. The method of supporting analytic theories by case reports is questionable. As a preliminary step to clarifying where analysis stands, mapping is presented here as a means of orientation which could also throw light on the way ahead. To start with, not one but a number of different kinds of maps by different analysts and possibly ex-patients too would introduce a new medium of communication about various dimensions and themes of analysis. Mapping gets away from the exclusive use of definitions by language on the one hand and the indefinable use of visual images on the other. Mathematics are not, or not yet, available for the purpose of conveying what analysis consists of. Other sensory modalities such as hearing lack the easy accessibility of sight. Between too much and too little definability mapping, according to the wide definition provided in the text, appears to be just the right medium.

Chapter 11 is intended to introduce the reader to the versatility of the map as a medium of communication and to the concept of spatiality. For this purpose a glossary is included right at the beginning in which four major types of cartographical maps are described and illustrated together with comments on their historical development. Inner maps and cosmological symbols are of special significance and are meant to prepare the reader for the project of mapping analysis. More than the usual attention has been given to the polyvalent symbol of the labyrinth in the hope of getting the reader 'into the swing' of designing his or her own maps by making use of kinaesthetic perception.

Chapter 12 should be regarded as a first attempt at applying – with due modifications – the four major types of maps described to analytic material. After that an *ad hoc* category, called the 'interactional map' is presented. It is designed to illustrate what in the mapper's view a pattern of an analytic relationship with focus on a recurrent theme looks like. The theme here also refers back to what in Chapter two was described as the 'mutual transference'.

Chapter 13, The Klein–Jungian hybrid, is thought to be of historical interest in its own right since it had first been presented as a spoken paper in 1962. The problem called 'hybridization' continues right up to the time of writing and I have reason to believe that my parent society, the Society of Analytical Psychology, London is not the only one to be affected by it. The chapter is placed in this part of the book interspersed with an updating commentary because it serves as a specific example to illustrate the nature and ambiguities which arise when disciplines of analysis are compared and contrasted. This is continued in the next chapter where an attempt is made to put the arising problematic on a map.

Chapter 14, 'Where Does Analysis Stand?' is divided into two parts. The first is designed as prelude to the overview map, figure 14.3. In Part I two crucial questions which had in one way or another been referred to throughout the book are focused on and brought together. These had been, what lends power to thought products and why people should still seek analysis. A note on the psychology of mysticism provides the key and is depicted on a map of which there are two versions, figures 14.1a and b which are thought of as alternative insert maps for the central portion of figure 14.3, of Part II.

A seventeenth-century celestial map was used as model, the various structures of which were transposed into the analytic cosmos. The content belongs to the realm of the intuitive, invisible 'things' of analysis. If they are given visual quality here, it is for the sake of better orientation and communication. Instead of axes and polarities a table is provided to establish the circumstances in which similar terms used by different analytic disciplines may or may not be interchangeable. Emphasis is placed on technique as the criterion that helps to distinguish between fundamentally different attitudes and theoretical assumptions. A reflection on the political and analytic significance of Utopia brings the chapter to a close.

Chapter 10

The map: metaphor and reality

THE TRAVEL METAPHOR REVISITED

When in the second chapter I made comparisons between dreaming and analysing, the intention had been to show that the dream as object of analytic study had made analysis itself into something as intangible and hard to delineate as dreams. Analysis may be convincing at its core, yet it has hazy outlines and resists an incontestable account. Eventually I came to the conclusion that 'the dreaming had to stop', meaning that a new phase in the development of analysis had started which aims to get harder data by direct observation, sometimes assembled by observers who are outside the involved dyad.

I further suggested that the historical development of analysis and the history of cartography showed certain common features. If these could be demonstrated, trends might emerge which would hold good for other branches of knowledge. In particular, a comparative survey could help practising analysts to orientate themselves in relation to their own history and to the wider world in which analysis plays a part. Should this succeed, it might become easier for analysts to let go of some theoretical assumptions that are no longer fertile and to explore instead new vistas that are opening up, waiting to be cultivated for the benefit of patients and analysts alike. Such considerations led me to regard Freud's (1913) reference to the analytic journey as a metaphor that is relevant to this day. He used it originally as an illustration of the 'fundamental rule' which was explained to the patient at the beginning of analysis (*SE 12*: p. 134). In order to appreciate the change that has occurred in the meaning of the travel metaphor let us first take a brief look at metaphors and other figures of speech in and about analysis. We recall that the patient was to consider himself as a traveller in a carriage who had to report everything he saw from the window to someone else inside the carriage. I still find the famous metaphor helpful, although it is not what it used to be near the time when the discoverer himself had been on a 'journey without maps'. The reason is that the two components, journey and analysis, are no longer far enough apart for the comparison to be regarded as truly metaphorical; anyone who has ever heard of analysis would consider the connection a bit vague perhaps, but quite a commonplace analogy. The metaphor has thus lost the poetic appeal of, for example, 'a sea of troubles'. Here the components are quite unlike each other yet the combination into a single image speaks its poetic language. Any explanation would be pedestrian and so reduce the joy of a daring leap across the dissimilarity to which the poet invites us.

In contrast to poetic expression, there appears to be a need to track the process of analysis by means of a network or grid such as maps use. Geographic maps refer to localities and spaces. An analytic map would have to facilitate movements such as Bion's grid was designed to convey. Although it was too far removed from the scene of the action to become a useful tool in our time, his grid nevertheless created a radical *precedent in the prosaic approach to analytic data* (Bion, 1963).

On a much less sophisticated level and closer to the phenomena observed are similarities and analogies that make comparisons possible so that links are established which lead to categories allowing of tentative classifications. Generic terms are then coined for an apparent interdisciplinary approach to various phenomena. Here are some examples: 'Topography' as in Freud's early topographical theory; 'School' as in 'school of thought'; 'Body' as in 'body of knowledge'; 'Family', borrowed to indicate kinship, in the case of botany or as applied in a family tree; 'Anatomy' points to the nitty-gritty or the bare bones, also the essentials, as in Burton's *Anatomy of Melancholy*. Between the metaphoric aptness and the catchy similes of captions and titles we find the following: 'Mundus imaginalis', the imaginal world of Corbin (1972) quoted by Hillman (1980) and Samuels (1989), and further: *The Dream and the Underworld* by Hillman (1979), 'Geography of phantasy', in the appendix of Meltzer's book *Sexual States of Mind* (1973), 'A mental atlas of the process of psychological birth' by Paul, in Grotstein's *Do I Dare Disturb the Universe?* (1981). Gay, in his biography of Freud, uses 'A map for sexuality' and 'Mapping the mind' (1988).

'Area of...' is used when no physical location can be determined. Metaphorical 'areas' are often implicit when, as in 'borderline personality', there is no physical border – and it cannot be precisely determined what the differences between 'borderline' patients and others are.

We recall that Freud used the travel metaphor in several ways and finally returned to it in a summarizing paper on psychoanalytic technique by using a related image. He wrote that the analyst would be quite satisfied with the role of a guide in difficult mountainous terrain, were it not that the patient projected figures from his childhood on to him (*SE 32*: p. 174). We know, of course, that these transference projections have been turned to good account in the exploration of the terrain, but Freud's first reaction sounds like regret about the complication. While Jung became very much aware of transference phenomena, he remained guarded about interpretations that would involve him personally (*CW 18*: para. 350) .

Bearing the 'transference complication' in mind helps me to enlarge on

Freud's original metaphor as follows: the analyst in the carriage is no longer the passive recipient of the report, nor is the patient at the window able to tell everything that passes by, or rather, through the landscape of his mind. The analyst is not the anonymous 'someone' who they perhaps would like to be and what they represent for the patient at any given moment will influence what they are told. This will happen despite the injunction to report everything without discrimination. The analyst in the carriage on their part seems to be aware of this handicap and also able to fill in some of the missing details. In fact, it looks to the reporting patient as if the listener had been there before. The comments coming from inside the carriage give rise to the conclusion that the listener must have a map on their knees with the help of which they can anticipate what they are told. Some features of the landscape would have passed the observer unnoticed if the person with the map had not pointed them out; at other times their comments clearly sounded as if based on some phantasmagoria of their own and correspondingly confusing. And so a gap or space developed between the person at the window and the 'someone' inside the carriage across which they dialogued until the time came when each had constructed a mental map or, rather, a series of maps of the places they had passed and the experiences they had had on their journey together. In the end they were also able to draw a pretty accurate picture of each other. And then it was time to part.

My expansion of Freud's metaphor has turned into a little allegory which will, I hope, help to introduce this part of the book for which the map is the first metaphor; later I shall assume that the metaphor-become-analogue can be mapped.

The position I have taken up here is derived from Jung. It allows me to compare the patient–analyst relationship with that of occupants of the same carriage, that is as *travel companions*. True, their knowledge about the potential aim of the journey, the territory to be traversed and possible dangers is unequal. Were it not so, there could be no starting point. Furthermore, the journey of discovery leads through a landscape which is essentially dream-like. This means that any maps prepared from a theoretical viewing point must allow for variations.

The space between the travellers in my story soon turned out to be not the void it was first thought to be. It came to be the medium of their human relationship which was, however, frequently overshadowed by transference projections. All communications were influenced by this medium (cf. 'the filter', p. 274 below), including associations, accompanying emotional reactions and feelings about each other. The space then, despite its fluctuating boundaries, came to occupy an essential portion of their maps. Each participant's map was valid without necessarily agreeing with the other. In theory, at least, patients were welcome to develop their own point of view. In practice the outcome often depends on its not deviating too much from that of the analyst. We have now reached the point where the travel metaphor and the analytic journey as an analogy have lost poetic aptness and appeal. *If I propose that the journey remains the metaphor on which analysis is based, but that the map should become a literal possibility of communication, I am well aware that such a project requires the sacrifice of something poetic about analysis which may cause a feeling of nostalgia.* However, some comfort is offered inasmuch as both metaphors, journey and map, can survive by becoming a model for analytic records (see p. 197f, below).

MAPPING ANALYSIS – A PRACTICAL POSSIBILITY?

Obviously, I would not be formulating the question, if I regarded the mapping of analysis as a mere metaphor, a figure of speech such as 'putting analysis on the map'. In this and subsequent chapters I shall advance reasons why I consider the mapping of analysis a literal possibility. I have already mentioned how the idea originated and now it is time to outline what possible benefits could be derived from it, without, however, omitting doubts and difficulties. It should be noted that even if the difficulties are found to be so great as to make the suggested method of recording impractical, not all would be lost: what matters is that a cognitive but not too abstract model of communicating observations and theories is presented. Should it turn out that another method of recording the analytic journey by 'mapping' – without necessarily using the types of maps I shall describe – should serve cognition better, my idea would still have been useful.

What prompted me to take up the matter in the first place was the clinical phenomenon of interminable analyses – a problem that Freud mentioned in one of his last (1937) papers and that is still with us today (*SE 23*: p. 209). Could it be that a cognitive approach to the end of a long analysis might prevent the unresolved dependency which not infrequently spoils the work that has been done? Following an analogy of the journey, not only the starting and finishing points but also the route taken should be marked on the map.

Doubts immediately arise about a radical departure from letting 'the un-conscious' (and chance events) determine the time of the last analytic session. Would it not constitute the kind of interference that goes by the pejorative term 'manipulation'? I cannot yet argue against this objection on experiential grounds but propose the procedure can function as a badly needed *rite de sortie*. As there are many implicit ritualistic aspects to analysis (see p. 101, above) *a debriefing ritual* at the end would not come amiss. After all, rituals arise from deeply unconscious sources – understood without explanation.

Although 'mental' maps have archetypal roots, as can be inferred from animal behaviour such as bird migration, *mapping* itself is an exclusively human activity. The idea in this context is that analytic maps can fulfil a practical function. Having served the purpose, such maps are of no further use.

Rationale of the project

The thought of communication by mapping will be less daunting to patients and analysts, if it is borne in mind that maps and written language have been around for the same length of time. Above all, preconceived ideas about what a map must be, can be dispelled, if the following definition is taken into account: 'Maps are graphic representations that facilitate a spatial under-standing *of things, concepts, conditions, processes or events in the human world.*' (Harley and Woodward, 1987) (emphasis added).

What is it then that distinguishes the map from written records such as tables, graphs, charts and diagrams and, on the other hand, pictorial repre-sentations? Analysts' diagrams and patients' pictures have frequently been employed in order to illustrate analytic theory or as 'products of the uncon-scious'. In published analytic diagrams, arrows are sometimes used to indicate changeability. Such diagrams are abstract and remote from the scene of the action. Within the diagram the location of the structures and therefore also the spaces between are fixed. And space, as mentioned, is a particularly important concept in analysis. Without wishing to extol the virtues of the map, I shall presently show that this medium of graphic presentation is capable of great variety and flexibility. Nor are maps an unusual method of communication; most people have at one time or another drawn a map with which to supple-ment verbal instructions, for example, how to get to their house. For present purposes no special skills at all would be required of potential map makers.

With these general considerations in mind, we are ready to identify some specific points that have a bearing on the adaptation of maps for the purpose of 'mapping analysis'.

Making something visible

If an unusual subject that is as hard to delineate as analysis is recorded in an unusual medium, it is possible that from time to time, features of that subject could emerge that would otherwise have remained invisible. Even the map I give to my visitor makes me aware of my own surroundings in a new way. As Robinson points out, mapping differs from other representational symbolism in that it depicts *a view that has not actually been seen* (Robinson, 1976). So when I hand the sketch of a itinerary map to my visitor, I also orientate myself quite differently in relation to my own house than I do when I look out from my bedroom window. What can now be made visible is a combined view, one from the outside, the other from inside the house. Two maps would be required to allow for the different perspectives.

A comparable synthesis may reasonably be expected, if analyst and patient were to make and later exchange maps. It could be argued that the dialectic of analysis should accomplish such an exchange, without having to resort to the perceptual reality of maps. But patients' reports have convinced me that this ideal rarely, if ever, occurs in practice, although the *feeling* of being in unison with the partner is not at all unknown. But then again the establishment of *an unanimous view* is not what is aimed at and *must be distinguished from the creation of a synthesis within each person*. Each partner needs the other's map for his/her own synthesis. It could therefore happen that the analyst changes his/her map having seen the patient's. In that case the situation in Freud's travel metaphor is reversed: the analyst may change his/her view as the result of the traveller's interpretation of the territory.

Actually, our visitor's synthesis starts already on the first journey to my house when he or she compares the abstract spatial relation of features outlined in my sketch map and fills it in with the actual landscape as it becomes visible and is experienced as part of the journey.

Differentiating something

We have seen that it is next to impossible to describe the fleeting experiential moment of analysis. Moreover, descriptions are inevitably fused with the point of view of the author. But mapping is a way of beginning to differentiate between expectation, journey and reproduction. Obviously, the expectations before and mapping afterwards differ markedly from the lived experience. Therefore the dream-like boundaries that divide analysis from everyday communicable reality would become firmer under the pressure of the cognitive processing which mapping requires.

Denoting something additional

Additional beacons

The act of mapping includes attention to details which are peripheral to the focus intended. For example, the map I draw for someone to find the way to my house will include landmarks that I think may be of additional help in telling the visitor 'where I live' although these may not be essential for finding the way. But eventually I have to stop filling in; visitors must also be permitted to lose their way.

Misconstructions and additions

However, the situation is different when the aim of the map is the reconstruction of an account, possibly of a hitherto unknown or unacknowledged event. The tracing of either may lead to a dead end or to treasure. Next, secondary elaborations are likely to be added, possibly in the nature of fantasies. A whole series of old geographical maps bear witness to misconstructions, some evidently owing their existence to wish-fulfilling fantasies. It is likely that some analytic theories which no longer determine practice are of this kind. In contrast to deliberate cartographical misconstructions there are analytic 'maps' which – although no longer in active use – have not been officially withdrawn. Are they to be kept for a rainy day, when analysts are at their wits' end?

Fantasy as a bridge to reality

Maps of dreams, fantasies, myths and fictions can be constructed and related or compared with each other and sorted according to themes. (See 'thematic maps' below, p. 213) Various kinds of fiction and cartoons make use of such pseudo cartographical maps which are given the verisimilitude of a geographical locality in order to lend credibility to the story. The kind of 'fantasy map' we know from *Gulliver's Travels* and *Treasure Island* and the accompanying story does not pretend to be anything other than fictitious. Although readers are invited to enter the make-believe map, they are free to do with it what they like; they may discard it, declaring it to be nonsense, or they may enjoy the humorous or satirical aspect finding a kernel of truth in it, if the story is allegorical. In short, we are now looking at *the map as a metaphorical bridge between dreams, fiction and everyday reality.*

Another kind of fantasy map is also an innovation that borrows actual geographical features in order to lend likelihood to the story and carry a concealed message. The type of fantasy map I am referring to is a conscious, or, better, deliberate projection of a configuration invested with symbolic content, such as a lion or a king, on to a geographical background. In Fig. 10.1, Europe is represented as a woman, but it may also portray the Emperor Charles V. Another famous example of an *allegorical map* would be the illustration of the low countries in the form of a lion. Other types of fantasy map make use of geographical features and outlines to superimpose caricatures of political figures for the purpose of propaganda designed to promote or damage an institution.

In all these instances the method is as deliberate as the message is transparent. The only fantasy to speak of is in the use of the map as a vehicle of non-geographical communication. But the content or message of such maps is a fantasy only in the pejorative sense of a deliberate distortion of reality and as such sterile.

The reverse is the case when mythological figures are projected into the sky and hypothetical lines drawn between the stars make the constellations visible. Such celestial maps are a bridge between myths and reality. The fact that the constellations are in themselves illusions and that the stars, being light years away, may no longer be shining does not alter the bridging function of the celestial map.

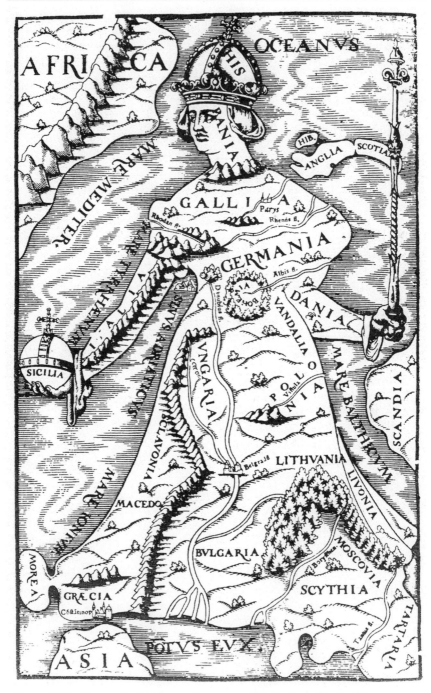

Figure 10.1 Europe in the shape of a woman (North is on the right)

THE VERSATILE MAP

An allegory

Let us assume that maps have fulfilled their function of representing the analytic territory traversed. The experience of journeying has been enriched by the persons who were in relation to each other during the undertaking. Despite or because of all the emotional upheavals they became travel companions, until at the end each returned home. They had done more than exchange addresses during the journey and thought of sending each other Christmas cards afterwards. But all went well and the hardships of the journey and the vicissitudes of their relationship sank into oblivion. And the metaphorical maps used on the journey and perhaps the maps used as a *rite de sortie* at the end were discarded, except by the research-minded analyst.

The model

According to Winnicott fantasy comes before reality and helps to deal with its frustrations. That is the developmental aspect. But fantasy is also needed for the creation of illusions throughout our lives. Were we deprived of these, say in the form of artistic and religious experiences we would be poor indeed (Winnicott, 1958). Illusions have been defined as false perceptions. However, they are often surrounded by an area of uncertainty; does not the illusion contain a grain of truth? Were it not for the admixture of this doubt, analysis would lose an essential instrument, that is the transference. Here I find myself in agreement with Klauber who regards transference as an illusion and the crucial question is, whether the patient can do both, submit to it *and* discard it again in the end after a new synthesis of reality (and illusion) has occurred (Klauber, 1987). Similar views are expressed by Milner who writes about the 'creative illusion that analysts call the transference' (Milner, 1955).

In order to use the map as a model for analytic purposes I have to make certain that the clarity with which we associate modern maps does not interfere with the paradoxical function of analysis which separates as well as synthesizes fantasy-illusions with the world of external events, called 'reality'. The map we know from geography lessons is obviously not the map to which the book-titles referred any more than a rainbow bridge is able to carry traffic. But between illusion and reality stands the metaphor. For those who can trust their fantasy without fear that it will run away with them, the metaphor, poetry and analysis can exercise the synthesizing function. However, the use of the map as model makes yet a different kind of demand. Users have to let go not only of the customary differentiation between fantasy and reality and of the allowance they have just made for the syntheses mentioned. They are further asked to let the synthesis be real enough to make use of its product (that is the map) as a guiding instrument during investigation and recording. As such the map must be different from the phenomena it is meant to investigate every bit as much as the map that *refers* to the territory remains in touch with it, yet retains its autonomy and hence versatility.

Making something cognitive

I am proposing that in addition to serving as an exchange of information, analytic maps can promote rites of transformation and of parting that might prevent analyses from getting stuck or interminably dragging on. Other types of analytic maps can further be designed to show 'where analysis stands' (see p. 306ff below). They can convey to interested parties, not only to analysts, something that is understandable on the cognitive level rather than by empathy alone. However inadequate, the attempt itself would signify that analysts do reflect on their work and are willing to share what they are doing.

While each attempt to map an individual analytic situation may be expected to assist the analyst in reviewing and, if necessary, revising their pre-existing map (theoretical views), they may also become interested to look at such maps in the aggregate and reflect on the psychological issues that led to their and their colleagues' and predecessors' discoveries or rediscoveries. In this respect too, the comparison with maps illustrating the history of discovery can be illuminating, as I hope to show (see below, p. 209). The evolutionary view provided thereby could lead to a fresh orientation which, by analogy with the above-mentioned tourist map, could tell us *where analysis has come from and which direction it might be taking next.*

Setting something in context

I started off with the assumption that the mental processes involved in exploration, discovery and recording are likely to be similar, regardless of the specific area for which they are deployed. But it is just as important to pay attention to the background and context: without consideration of the social structure, political system and the level of technical development and distribution of wealth, we cannot know where and how our special skills can be applied to best advantage. This cannot be discovered by the daily exercise of analysing individual patients, because *the narrow focus* and *high magnification the analytic microscope* requires tend to *make us analysts oblivious of the wider frame, the world map,* so to speak, which is the common background and framework of analysts and patients alike. The intrinsic interest in the job is such that the social conscience tends to be neglected. In the end that conscience becomes like the map for which the crew in Lewis Carroll's *The Hunting of the Snark* was thankful to their captain, namely 'a perfect and absolute blank'. In writing this I am not only prompted by unselfish reasons. The wider orientation is needed, if we are at all curious about the future of analysis.

The points just outlined for *the project of transforming metaphorical into literal maps* that could be used for representing analytic situations infer *no direct comparisons* between the history of discovery of the earth and the exploration of the psyche. Such similarities as there may be, are in the combination of the preconceptions and psychological processes involved in both kinds of exploration. The same applies whether the findings are recorded in writing or by mapping. What is more, the history of cartography shows that even wrong assumptions about the size of the earth and the distribution of land masses can, when duly mapped, lead to discovery, as everybody who has heard of Columbus's voyages knows. It is less well known that Columbus *after* his discovery of Haiti (Hispaniola) and South America believing it to be part of the Asiatic continent went on to defend the 'small world' theory stating that he had proved it *'experimentally'*. (Emphasis added because in our post-Renaissance world 'experimentally' means beyond all reasonable doubt (Fernandez-Armesto, 1991).) So it is better to have erroneous maps and wrongly interpreted discoveries than none at all.

Therefore our programme must be: first, can analytic maps be designed which might be useful in the manner indicated? Second, can the psychological processes involved in map-making and reading throw any light on the ways and stages by which analytic knowledge as a whole is arrived at? (That is, epistemology.)

But what kind of maps? In the next chapter, we shall look briefly at three types of maps, viz. world, thematic and fantasy. The map we imagined on the analyst–traveller's knees during the journey would be a fourth kind called an *itinerary* or route map; it resembles the sketch map I drew up for a visitor to find the way to my house. The map of my village, road and house is strictly speaking a *topographical* map, but it is grouped together with itinerary for present purposes and because of the large scale (showing a lot of detail in a relatively small area) used in both. I said during the journey, because before and after the analyst may well be using any other type of map without actually being aware of it or making clear distinctions. People are more or less familiar with the first three types of maps from their school atlases. But we may assume that neither analysts nor cartographers would recognize another kind as a map at all, because it makes reference to a state of disorientation. I am thinking of the maze or *labyrinth* which I consider to be an inner map. As such it is independent of geographical location. We shall see that the division between inner and outer maps has not always been as firm as it is today. (For greater detail, see glossary, p. 208 below.) The labyrinth then is of all the greater psychological interest as it strongly suggests centre-seeking and avoiding movements. And psychological movements and changes of direction are what analysts are concerned with and wish to make observations about. Therefore, even if cartographers cannot be expected to recognize the labyrinth as a map, analysts might be persuaded to. Besides, at least one historian of cartography, Delano-Smith, identifies the labyrinth as a cosmological map (Delano-Smith, 1987). Certainly, the origin of the labyrinth like that of maps goes back into prehistory. Because of its persistent fascination the labyrinth will require separate consideration (see p. 233, below).

The reason for mentioning some facts in the evolution of maps at this point is to show that it is essential to review the psychological and technological factors that enter into mapping and map-reading. For we have to remember that a whole host of other factors (historical, economic and technological) account for the finished cartographical product. All of these have played their part in bringing about the large variety of maps that bear witness to the general cultural development of mankind (for details see glossary).

The four types of cartographical maps plus 'inner maps' such as the labyrinth which will serve our purpose best will be described in greater detail in conjunction with their possible applicability to analytic material and situations (see also the interactional map, fig. 12.8, p. 271, below). What is needed first then is some 'map psychology' to facilitate the transition from the metaphorical to the actual mapping of analysis.

THE PSYCHOLOGY OF MAP-MAKING

The map as medium

In order to get from the map metaphor to the map proper two points have to be borne in mind. The first concerns the characteristics of the map as a medium of special psychological effectiveness that makes the customary distinction between metaphorical and literal meanings of the word questionable. The poetic ambience that surrounds words like 'sea', 'rose' and 'love' and makes them suitable for metaphoric usage (see p. 189f above) does not leave the word completely even when the context changes. Conversely, Samuels refers to Picasso's 'indelible mark' to illustrate that the original literalism, the 'raw material' that 'infects the metaphor', remains permanent (Samuels, 1989). The same applies to maps as an aesthetic medium. At least some map dealers and experts I met who handle maps as part of earning their living are not immune to their charm. When in the following pages I refer to types or categories of maps as classified by cartographers I am not leaving the aesthetic appeal out. For although the map is composed of elements in common with other forms of graphic recording such as the written word, tables, diagrams or schemata, the information conveyed by maps is multifaceted as compared with tables and the like. Even when mappers use measurements and coded symbols they still have some elbowroom left to choose the means by which to deliver their information. The element of selection is only partly determined by the purpose of the map. It is further combined with the techniques available at the time and the skills of the individual maker. The sum total represents the art and the craft of map-making. All of this applies particularly to the use made of empty spaces which we find on every map. And analysts, as mentioned, are particularly interested in space in which movement can occur unhampered by the focus of conscious intent, as for example free association and amplification. Space is also needed in order to conceive of distance or proximity between the person and his/her objects and between persons in relation to each other. But in cartography empty spaces on a map, used in former times to indicate unknown territories, no longer mean 'unknown'. Even the emptiness of the oceans could now be filled in with details about wind and weather, tides and currents, shipping lanes and magnetic deviations, to say nothing about the depths and nature of the ocean beds. Such is the flexibility of modern maps as medium that analysts tempted by fixed symbols and therefore associating blank spaces and blue oceans on maps as the correlates of 'the unconscious', or 'terra firma' as 'conscious', would be badly mistaken.

Maps to be made for a purpose

If analysts were to use this medium duly modified to meet the needs of the psychic 'territory' they would require multiple maps that could be superimposed and the layer or depth of focus would be determined by a clearly stated selectivity. In that way analytic maps could eventually become a medium of communication between all interested parties.

Mapping: the intrapsychic process, a hypothesis

I now want to return to the uniquely human ability to create visual arrangements in the form of maps. It is related to writing in words and ideograms on the one hand and to painting on the other. We can see it in the case of the analyst making notes and the patient painting pictures or, sometimes, *vice versa*; both methods have as referent the analytic process seen from different angles recorded after an event by different graphic methods. In contrast to the spontaneous drawings or 'squiggles' produced during an analytic session maps are deliberate acts of cognition. But the reconstructed material can stimulate contemplation as well as new ideas. Whatever the graphic method chosen, the common element is the *making visible* of something that was unrecognized before, private and uncommunicated. Whatever was stored, an essential step required before making visible seems to occur during the pause which the prefix 're'-, indicates, as in 're-collection' to be followed by 'reproduction'. We can assume that the sequence of psychological steps which leads to *map-making* is dependent on a feedback loop that other vertebrates lack and that for the inner vision to reach a certain degree of intensity, a contemplative pause is required. Although description makes it sound sequential, the steps which lead to the cave dweller's drawing, see below, are likely to have been simultaneous.

Divisions are an artefact, precluding simultaneity. Therefore, *is there an alternative way that could throw light on the psychology of mapping and allow us to link the findings with the psychological steps involved in analysing?*

Wollheim offers an art historian's explanatory myth to describe the development of what he calls 'Ur-Painting' meaning the prehistoric representation of, say, a bison on the wall of a cave (Wollheim, 1987). In his account he uses the term *twofoldness*, namely of seeing the marks someone has deposited on the wall's stained and cracked surface as well as the image of the bison. The two are joined in what he calls '*seeing-in*' – analysts would say 'projecting into' – the bison in the mind that guides the hand of the painter who at the same time uses the cracks of the surface on to which he makes his marks. The twofoldness Wollheim describes is familiar to everybody who looking at, say, a cloud sees into it fantastic images. Wollheim emphasizes that the awareness of both wall and image is a *single, simultaneous experience*, although the two components are *described* separately or as a sequence. The hand that marks the surface is guided by the simultaneous vision of bison and cracks. It is the single-minded concentration that leads to the emergence of a new image. Once the image has been definitely outlined and so made 'public', it is, according to Wollheim, up to the spectator to judge its correctness (Wollheim, op. cit.). It is like the patient's reactions which can confirm or invalidate the 'fit' of the analyst's interpretation, as long as he/she can keep an open mind. Later on the representation, its standard of correctness or incorrectness has to be determined by a spectator, or, better, by a group of spectators, whereas before the painters were free to 'see-in' whatever they fancied. It must be added, however, that the painters too fulfil to some extent the role of spectator when during the reflective pause they stand back and take a look at their handiwork.

Wollheim's account of 'making visible' (representation) differs from mine in that I stressed recollection before reproduction. Here I followed the traditional analytic concept that often divides psychological processes into opposites (in this case the temporal aspect of early or late, before or after). Now it seems to me that Wollheim's view is nearer to what really happened when I drew my route map on the back of an envelope: when I started by making a mark at an arbitrary distance from the edge of the paper I had decided on some kind of scale without being aware of it. After that there really was a pause during which I noticed that I had not left myself enough room and began to correct it. As I continue I discover that there are places of which I am not as sure as I had thought. I look at my sketch map and consider the user and add a few more signs hoping to make it clearer etc. The description sounds like a sequence of separate steps, but while I was drawing the map my experience of 'seeing-in' and of drawing was simultaneous. The corrections came later.

Before evaluating these alternative modes of understanding the psychological processes involved in the act of making visible, be it the bison on the wall, the way to my house or an analytic event, the question has to be faced whether the difference in subjects nevertheless justifies the activity as such to be the overriding psychological common denominator. Although differences in purpose, technique, surface etc. obviously play a part, I take the view that these are of secondary importance and shall pursue the possibility of mapping the –

mainly – invisible phenomena in and around analysis, as if the activity of mapping were a single or concurrent psychological process.

The question may be asked why the recording of all the complicated and complicating events of analysis cannot be left to modern technology such as video-tape? Afterwards, some neutral but experienced analysts who are not involved with the dyad could watch the recording and comment on it independently. Having done so, they could further comment on each other's interpretations. Streeck has in fact done this on an experimental basis (Streeck, 1986). But, in my view, this would require observers to have sufficient knowledge of the analyst and of the patient as well, so as to have a baseline from which to judge the finer nuances of their dialogue. If that were the case, would the observer(s) still be sufficiently uninvolved to be regarded as neutral? It could be argued that the bias or prejudice of each separate assessment can be further assessed and weighted accordingly. But that would involve a second set of assessors. In the end, still no 'objective' judgement is reached by compounding of evaluations.

It is clear that with the mapping of the analytic journey, a new set of complications is introduced, but I shall argue that this is also the potential strength of the method. The first complication has been alluded to already as Bion's objection to the usual method of case report with which I agree. He excluded the possibility altogether when he wrote that the photograph of the fountain of truth is the photograph after it has been muddied by the photographer and his apparatus (Bion, 1962). The falsification of the recording is the greater when it gives verisimilitude to what had already been falsified. This complication is reduced in the case of analytic mapping because it is quite openly an interpretation with no claim to objectivity. In fact, more than one visual interpretation by the mapper(s) is thought desirable and each reader of these maps is free to give further interpretations. Their subsequent discussion is likely to lead to new kinds of consent and dissent. These would lead to a clarification of viewpoints and private theories held. Retrospective maps that have been the subject of interpretations and debate are not, of course, to be used on subsequent journeys. But the ideas arising from the maps as a visual and spatial record can stimulate further thoughts and in that way influence analytic practice.

Like written and mechanical records, analytic maps (for example map fig. 12.8, p. 271 below) can also be enlarged upon or summarized but remain always subject to reinterpretation.

In conclusion: since mapping is for most people an unusual way of recording, the psychological processes involved have required special mention. Thus the relationship between mapper, map and map user is a subject which received attention in the chapter 'The map as a communication system' of Robinson and Petchenik's book *The Nature of Maps* (1976) and later in Hodgkiss's *Understanding Maps* (1976). It is relevant here that these authors differentiate on the one hand between the 'real world' and the cartographer's conception and the image he/she transmits by means of the map and, on the other, the image the user perceives and constructs. Allowance is made for *feedback* not only between the users' perceptions when they read the map before the journey and what they actually see when confronted with reality, but also – and this is particularly important – *between the user and the cartographer*. The best-known, if somewhat crude, example is Columbus whose discoveries not only changed the map he had at his disposal, but enlarged the whole globe – only not until reinterpreted after his death.

I am stressing this point in view of a possible exchange of maps between patient and analyst at the end of a long analysis. The view of each presented to the other would, quite likely, change both maps, provided that they can discuss their maps after the analysis. Without that the maps and, particularly, the importance of blank spaces on the maps would give rise to misgivings and misinterpretations.

Considerations of the psychological processes of the map maker and map user and how the two are linked together by the map as a means of communication and a bridge between illusions and reality can be taken as a paradigm of what is meant by intrapsychic and interpersonal processes.

Some special psychological properties of the map

Written instructions would perhaps have done just as well as a map in order to guide my visitor from the station to the house. But you cannot see as much and as quickly as you can when taking in at a glance. So the cave painter's *combined experience* of seeing in and making visible occurs in reverse when I read the map and actually use it on the journey. As I take in the features of the landscape and relate myself bodily to what the eyes, ears and nose perceive, I amalgamate my perceptions with the visible and tangible map that I carry with me. The map gradually becomes internalized while I learn from such repeated, simultaneous experiences. Although I can describe the experience as being the product of two separate parts, landscape and map, these merge and become my internal map on which I rely. Soon I can do without the actual map and feel that I could recognize the route 'with my eyes shut'. But should my inner map fade or the external landscape change making the old map outdated, I should have to repeat the initial procedure until I had achieved a new internalization.

However, the serious disadvantage of thinking of a map during an analytic session instead of taking in what is happening here and now is obvious: I would be like a driver whose attention is distracted by looking in the rear mirror or at a map when his/her eyes should be on the road ahead. But occasional glances are also necessary; otherwise what is behind, the past, would soon overtake the driver.

For the reader to whom mapping and map reading is not a daily occurrence, I should like to use an example of the advantage of *making tangible* in addition to making visible. It is what seems to happen to people who begin to use a computer for word processing. Although the text is perfectly visible on the screen and the editing of it is made technically easy, it is not a complete substitute for the printed sheet of paper with its tangible and easily portable quality; things that passed unnoticed on the screen stand out clearly on the print-out with which even practised writers would not like to dispense. The additional quality of tangibility makes the record psychologically more 'real'. In other words, the map that occupies physical space and represents a physical territory bears some *sensory similarity*, however remote, to the sight and feel of the water, grass, deserts, towns, roads etc. to which it refers. The conventional symbols for these places which by colour-printing and other techniques attempt to evoke a resemblance make it possible to look at the map as an artefact that attempts to simulate nature. The more technically accomplished the map (or the audio-visual recording), the greater the illusion that the map might, after all, *be* the territory. Or that watching the video, or even the actual session through a one-way screen, was as good as having been a participant. What has happened in the course of mapping the territory or recording the analytic session is a change in the physical substances and their properties, for example from a sphere to a flat surface, from water to blue paper. In this kind of 'transubstantiation' the demand on the map reader or watcher not to be taken in (or identify by means of projection) *is* very great. It is distinctly less so when the map has been designed to convey something that our unaided senses cannot grasp, say population statistics or magnetic variations. The same applies when an analytic report makes use of a medium such as a grid or a map which is of a completely different quality from the events or the 'territory' to which it refers.

More about the application and the possibilities of thematization in analytic maps in Chapter 12.

SUMMARY AND CONCLUSIONS

1 The map as metaphor and the map as reality share some subtle characteristics; spatial awareness, of which 'spatiality', and freedom of movement are the most important. Space is needed to make the relative location of a person's inner objects visible by mapping. Even crude maps differ from ordinary writing by the allocation of places on the sheet of paper that becomes a map. Although this rudimentary map has no scale, the map reader can gauge at a glance the distance by which these objects are removed from each other as seen through the mapper's eyes. Above or below, left or right, near the edge or near the centre of the paper are guides to distance, relations and orientation, forerunners of the concept of 'spatiality' as Piaget and others observed in the development of children (Piaget, 1955).

2 Even within the same category of map, e.g. one designed to show the emotional aura and intensity surrounding objects, a number of maps would

be required to indicate movements and changes during a given period of analysis. Changes in the same type of map indicate the historical or time factor in relation to space. The relative mobility or immobility of objects and their aura would point to the possibility of psychological transformation by analysis. (Freud's mobility of the 'cathexes' springs to mind.)

3   Reasons have been set out why the mapping of analysis is treated as a feasible project. The practical benefits are enumerated that could be derived from bringing a special cognitive medium and method, that is mapping, to bear on the narratives that are commonly used.

4   The act of creating a map as medium of communication is compared with prehistoric paintings in anticipation of a more detailed account in the next chapter. A hypothesis regarding the intrapsychic processes that lead to rudimentary map-making is offered. It is suggested that the psychological matrix may be the same as that from which discoveries and inventions in general are derived.

5   It seems probable that a step-by-step (sequential) process alternates with single-minded states, both during the act of painting and mapping, in short during *the act of creating while attempting to recreate an image.*

6   It is suggested that contact between analysis and other branches could be improved if analytic maps were to replace or supplement the prevailing methods of narration in support of theories. As an act of communication to non-analysts, it is hoped that a method that renders our observations visible would demystify analysis, and thus lessen the suspicion surrounding it.

7   Some special properties required of psychological maps are introduced. They have to be special because of the intangible nature of the 'territory'. The application of the principles outlined leading up to an analytic map will be discussed when detailed examples are given in subsequent chapters.

8   Mapping, it is hoped, can be an instrument of research into the syntax of analysis, the nuts and bolts ('logistics') that link the various theories with techniques and observations. Insofar as research into the ideas (preconceptions) out of which such theories and techniques are born and formulated is concerned, the project introduced is of an epistemological nature.

9   At the end of this opening chapter to Part III, it may bear repeating what the mapping of analysis is and is not intended to be.

   (a)   Mapping is an unusual system of notation applied to a subject that is in many ways dream-like, defying precise formulation. The primary intention is to bring cognition to bear on data, especially those that are traditionally classed as stemming from unconscious sources. Language, both ordinary and technical, is the usual way of doing this by means of 'secondary' (rational) mental processes including, however, figures of speech. But the spoken word and silent gesture and spaces of analysis differ from written accounts in the form of case illustrations, narratives and 'vignettes'. Nor can we be sure that the words recorded, played back and transcribed signify the same as when they were first spoken. If they appear to do so, it is because they have been brought back to life by the imagination of the reader which the author's skill had evoked. Similarly with mechanical recordings, selected and edited.

(b) By contrast with the writing of notes it becomes obvious that mapping is not only a system of notation used in an attempt to reconstruct what happened in the analytic territory. That territory appears to be the referent of the map and of the process of mapping which occurs after the analytic session(s): in that sense analytic maps must be 'meta'. (But we shall see that the 'territory' also exists before the event, that is in the head of the analyst.). By using various kinds of map the mapper becomes aware that he is not reconstructing a past situation but restructuring such situations and, conceivably, constructing new ones. The system of notation becomes one of data processing from which new ideas are likely to emerge.

(c) The reader versed in Freudian metapsychology may notice an apparent similarity between the map categories and metapsychological points of view such as the dynamic, structural, genetic and dynamic. The decisive differences are that *analytic maps are not based on a concept of psychic energy, but on variable spatial relations.* Such maps are visible interpretations of a territory and as such hermeneutic. The rules of interpretation are vested in the category of map selected.

In the next chapter we shall be concerned with the particulars and examples of this general outline.

10 Analytic maps have been considered for the following purposes.

(a) At the end of analysis, as a *rite de sortie* for patient and analyst.

(b) For the analyst: to make vertices and special features of the 'territory' traversed visible.

(c) In general: *not* to record where the journey took the participants, nor to recall it, like holiday snapshots. That is, not to cling to the illusion that the analytic *experience* can be kept on file.

(d) But as a reminder that we *can* travel into the depth of our beings, if we can entrust ourselves to visionary exploration rather than to what is already visible.

(e) If one function of analysis can be seen as an attempt to negotiate between external reality and its psychological interpretation, then mapping can be an aid to make the ineffable analytic experience into a visual, cognitive record. Lacking the technical means of multidimensional mapping, more than one type of map is needed for the purpose.

(f) The use of maps as a graphic record is just as much a cognitive ('conscious') method and as such alleged to be incompatible with unconscious processes as using a computer programmed to classify and collate archetypal dreams and symbols.

Chapter 11

Analytic maps: the tools

I will be outlining four basic cartographical categories or types of map. The specific use of each type is explained with the help of an illustrated glossary and examples are given. The intention is to introduce the reader to the tools available for the eventual construction of analytic maps, which will be discussed in the following chapter. Meanwhile it is hoped that the maps shown here will be of sufficient interest in themselves to draw the reader's attention to these products of human inventiveness.

Obviously the mapping of analysis will require a considerable transposition. Such maps can only be imaginative constructs, some of which will be in the form of schemata (cartograms), others again will be pictorial or any mixture of these. The common characteristic of analytic and cartographical maps is the particular distribution of space which makes, according to our definition (see p. 193 above), a graphic representation into a map. In order to emphasize it I have used 'spatiality'.

Imaginative as these constructs are, it is not imagination run riot, but ordered according to categories or types in cartographical use. Although the cartographical map categories I make use of are well established, the way I apply these is *not valid outside the present context*. Until we can proceed to mapping for analytic purposes it is well to remind ourselves that as a medium maps are not restricted to communicating geographical knowledge: indeed maps have been increasingly used as a medium of scientific communication and the momentum is still growing, as Wallis has shown (Wallis, 1973). In addition, the frequently metaphoric or symbolic nature of analytic communications (referred to in Chapter 10 above) as well as the ritual aspects of the analytic process called for a separate category. I have used '*inner maps*' to stress the cosmological significance.

GLOSSARY

1. Early world maps

Under this heading I have grouped together representations of the world and the cosmos, regardless of whether they are of prehistoric or of later origin. This abridgement is based on three common characteristics. *First*, they are largely imaginary from our point of view as well as comprehensive and epitomize the understanding of the cosmos at the time they were made (see 'Global aims', p. 53 above). *Second*, such geographical features as they do contain, were those close to the maker and correspondingly large and central, while those further away were merely named or else their small size or island status further underlined their insignificance. If celestial bodies are included, that indicates the relation between the mapper and the cosmos. *Third*, their scale was of necessity small since a vast area had to be covered within the limited space of the map.

These characteristics continued to be influential in medieval and early Renaissance maps. Whether schematic or in form of contours of the known continents, maps were encyclopedic rather than exclusively geographic. They described or depicted all manner of knowledge within a quasi-geographical frame. Some of this 'knowledge', or, more strictly, information represented myths, fables and legends while other parts were based on travellers' tales. The homeland of the mapper was given not only a disproportionally large but also a central position in the map. Sometimes this coincided with the religious centre, such as Delos, Jerusalem, Rome or the mythical Mount Sumeru as in Buddhist maps. The central belief of the mappers was mirrored in such maps and showed their cosmic relationship.

A reflection of this *ego-* and *deo-centricity* can be seen in the assumed geo- or earth-centredness of our planetary system. The nationalistic struggle for the site of the prime meridian in modern times is another extension of the wish to see the homeland as the hub of the universe. In the event, agreement was not finally reached until 1844 when Greenwich, England, was decided upon 'after a lengthy and animated debate'; the careful phrasing makes us suspect acrimony behind the scenes (Wallis and Robinson, 1987).

Of major relevance to the subject of analytic maps is the tendency towards centralization and schematization in many early world maps. Geometrical shapes and natural numbers, notably three and four are often the foundation of schematic diagrams, such as the 'mappa mundi' which appeared in illuminated manuscripts between AD 300 and 1500. The type known as the 'T in O' map is a world schema in which the O represents the circumfluent ocean and the T indicates two watersheds at right angles, the vertical being the Mediterranean, the horizontal an imaginary line connecting the Don with the Nile (fig. 11.1). The Christianized version (fig. 11.2) shows that the pagan schema admirably fitted Old Testament notions and allotted a central position to Jerusalem where the two lines of the T intersect. This 'oriented' the map, that is east and sometimes paradise was at the top. Africa is to the right (south) and Europe to the left (north) of the map: an apparently preordained division of the world shared out between the three sons of Noah. The (usually) round geometric shape of the *mappa mundi* must be distinguished from the later

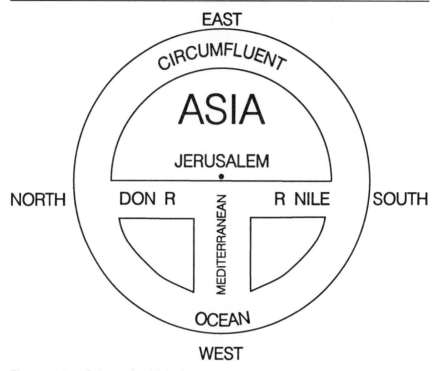

Figure 11.1a   Schematised T in O map

'planisphere', the roundness of which is *consciously constructed*, as by Ptolemy and his successors in modern times who try to get the spherical body of the earth projected on to a flat surface. In brief: *the undertaking and planning of a journey of discovery reflects both the cosmos and technology of the explorer.* The same can be said of the analytic journey undertaken with the patient lying down as for sleep which reproduces and reflects the link with the origin of psychoanalysis in hypnosis.

Schemata, whether geographical, religious or psychological lead to closed, static systems (see also Plaut, 1973). Freud's theories of the mind are both based on the number three; Jung's typology on four. Such simplifying orderly arrangements seem to spell security and satisfaction but are not conducive to questioning or making observations that lie outside the set framework. Like the prehistoric cosmological map, see example (fig. 11.3), the *mappa mundi* must be read within its social context (cf. Harley and Woodward, op. cit.). It is paradigmatic rather than representational in style. Only when combined with the charting of voyages of exploration could the world image of the *mappa mundi* gradually change, contain more geographical information, and be abandoned altogether.

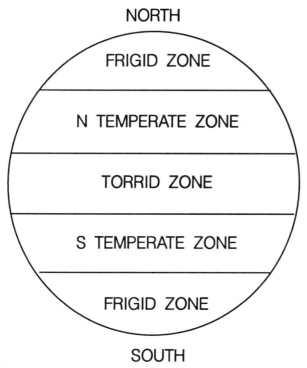

Figure 11.1b   Zonal map

2. Itinerary and topographical maps

I have grouped these categories together because of the large scale they have in common. This facilitates showing details but at the expense of the wider context. Reference has been made to the everyday use of such maps which everybody sketches occasionally (p.193). Itinerary maps are also called route maps and even referred to as 'tourist maps' by Wallis and Robinson (op. cit.). They are on a large scale in contrast to the small-scale early world maps. The itinerary map fills up the whole map with comparatively little territory and indicates how to get from A to B. It goes back in early history at least as far as early world maps, i.e. about 6000BC. The routes it shows certainly existed before there were roads.

Strictly purpose-designed maps, for example Roman route and medieval pilgrim's maps did not have to show more detail than turns of the path, distances, staging posts or fortifications. No example is necessary because the basic elements of mapping in this case have remained virtually the same from prehistoric to modern times. Thus we find dots, lines, circles and place names representing paths, towns, boundaries and junctions. Delano-Smith has

Figure 11.2 Isidore of Spain. Although this is the first printed map in the *Etymologiae* (Augsburg 1472), it might just as well have appeared in a manuscript of the twelfth century. It is a T in O map, Christianized by the division of the three continents between Noah's sons

demonstrated this by comparing a Bronze Age map with a modern topographical map (op. cit.). But she warns against the fixed meanings of symbols which could lead to confusion. Citing an ethnologist on a Sudanese tribe she quotes that a row of coloured triangles signifies mountains, uncoloured it means female breasts, and if two lines enclose the triangle, the design becomes non-representational! (op. cit.).

Topographical maps are also found on Egyptian coffins, about 1400BC, and were apparently meant as a guide and passport to the afterlife. Although topographical in their day, from our point of view they would probably be considered as mythical or even as 'fantasy' maps. However these maps tell us

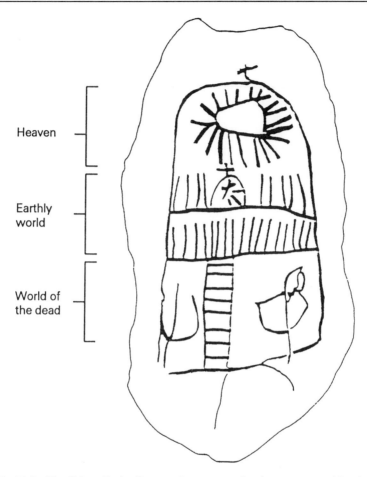

Figure 11.3 The Triora Stela. Drawn after a reproduction suggested by Anati in 'Bollettino de centro Camuno di Studi Preistorici'. A tripartite prehistoric concept of the world

where, metaphorically speaking, a person 'really' lived and hoped to move to. Surprisingly the highly practical route map of the day becomes a cosmological map, when seen from today's point of view. *This is taken as a reminder that despite the general usefulness of classifications – be it of maps or of ailments and remedies – the historical view must be taken into account* (see also legend to fig. 12.3).

3. Thematic maps

Although this kind of map has been known since the seventeenth century, the term has only been in use since 1953. It concerns a vast category of maps primarily designed to delineate individual categories of phenomena such as the geology or the animal or human population of places (Robinson, 1982). The number of uses to which thematic maps can be put is virtually unlimited and thematic mapping as a heuristic device coincides with a technical revolution in the history of map-making. In contrast to early world maps which were global and encyclopedic, thematic mapping reverses the trend and leads to ever-increasing specialization.

Because of its great flexibility, this category is potentially the most useful one for analytic mapping. 'Thematic maps differ from descriptive, and special maps in depicting not reality but ideas about reality' (Wallis and Robinson, 1987); the same applies to analytic case reports. As the thematic map is particularly important to the mapping of analysis it is appropriate to recall the relation of this to other kinds of maps by quoting Robinson who enumerates three general functions which maps have served from early times.

1   A record of the location and identity of geographical features.
2   As a guide for the traveller.
3   As a vehicle for the figurative expression of abstract, hypothetical, or religious concepts (op. cit.).

The above enumeration follows an order of increasing importance in the construction of analytic maps. Furthermore, 'the pure thematic map focuses on the differences from place to place of *one class or feature*, that class being the subject or *'theme'* of the map' (ibid.) (emphasis added). Examples can be drawn from a range of almost unlimited width such as maps showing magnetic compass variations, the depth of seabeds, the distribution of plants or animals, density and poverty or wealth of a population in any part or all over the whole world.

The problem in the adaptation of thematic maps to analytic mapping is what to choose as the 'base map'. By this is meant that the information to be mapped has to be put on a general map about which there is general agreement. In cartography that represents no problem now that the whole of our planet has been surveyed. *In the mapping of analysis no such certainty exists.* This absence does not need to be a bar as long as the fundamental assumptions and intentions with which the mapper sets out are clearly stated. And the difficulty with that is that analysts may regard their own point of view as having been verified to an extent that they can treat it as if it were generally accepted by all right-minded colleagues and by all 'successful' patients.

Because of the potential importance of the category it needs only to be added that modern printing techniques and none more than colour, have greatly facilitated progress in thematic mapping. No example is required, as readers will be familiar with this type from their school atlases as well as from its use in advertising.

4. Fantasy maps and maps of fantasy and dreams

Fantasy maps are maps of places which are wholly or partly imaginary. As for fantasy: there is a convention in British psychoanalytic circles according to which *phantasy* was used to indicate that the imagination was deliberately rather than fancifully or whimsically used (Rycroft, 1968). Being of the opinion that this requires very nice judgement indeed, I have used 'fantasy' for every kind of imagination.

This rough and ready definition gives little idea of the range and special qualities that are covered by 'wholly or partly' in the definition, nor of the kind of imagination that is expressed by the mapping. Wallis and Robinson, for example, recognize the 'satirical map' and the 'symbolic map' as allied but special categories (op. cit.). In the previous chapter I also gave an example of a fantasy map as a map invented in support of a story or to carry a symbolic message in the form of an allegorical figure (see previous chapter, fig. 11.1). It is *the maker's intent* that determines whether the special sub-type of fantasy is 'allegorical'. It depends on *the classifier's judgement* whether he/she calls a map, say of the Garden of Eden, a fantasy map or a 'religious map', as Wallis and Robinson do (ibid.), or a 'symbolic map'. And we, *the viewers*, may finally *decide* to put this map into yet another category and refer to it as a map of 'Utopia'.

Unlike the verbal description or interpretation of a fantasy or dream, the fantasy map is designed to 'make visible' both the content and the observer's standpoint in the particular spatial way we associate with maps (see definition). 'Fantasia', be it noted, originally meant 'a making visible' (Shorter Oxford English Dictionary).

But what exactly is it that the fantasy map makes visible? First, the constituents, second, the intent.

Here the note on memory as a new construction made of old building material is applicable. Even if the source of the fantasy or dream is derived from someone other than the mapper, it is the latter's imaginative construction that does, in my view, contribute and add a dimension to our understanding. To anticipate the example in Chapter 12 (figs 12.5–12.7) I do just this when I map a patient's dream. All I need to add to make an 'honest' map of it, is to let the viewer know what the facts as reported had been, so that it can be seen what I have done with the information. This treatment is not unprecedented, only the explicit distinction between the material and the interpretation is often lacking. For example: Daniel's dream (The Book of Daniel 7: 2–14) was published by Hans Lufft in 1530 to illustrate Luther's commentary on and translation of the Book of Daniel (fig. 11.4). Four years later it was inserted into the Wittenberg Bible of 1534. The main attractions are the four mythical beasts. But their relation to the rather crude background contours of the continents of Europe, Asia and Africa had been given a new significance. Both Luther's commentary and the Bible text are used to illustrate the threat of the

Turks assaulting Christian Europe. After an important victory, in 1529, the Turks were close to the gates of Vienna. It is particularly relevant that although the subject of the map is Daniel's dream (vision or fantasy), the mapper's instruction may have been to use the prophet's description in order to lend authority to political propaganda. Seen in this light it may be regarded as an illustrated map used for propaganda. We become aware that the mapper's cosmos can easily be used to 'spread the gospel'.

This leads us to the kind of fantasy map with which readers are likely to be familiar. I am referring to a subgroup of the fantasy maps, namely the *allegorical map*. Here too the mapper's intention plays a major part and therefore leaves little space for the viewer's interpretation. Let us look at two fantasy maps reproduced here, Figures 11.5 and 11.6, and compare these with Luther's map which used Daniel's dream of a biblical prophecy, as such of cosmological significance and also as a dire warning. In our time we look at the selfsame map as more allegorical than anything else. *Therefore as the 'vertex' shifts, so does the classification* of the type of map we are dealing with. For example, the map illustrating Bunyan's *Pilgrim's Progress* as well as the jocular *Map of Matrimony* is based on the Christian orientation which for the designers and viewers expresses *a world order, a cosmology*, although in two very different moods, see Figures 11.5 and 11.6, *the cosmological symbol* in the one being the rather large cross, in the other the Church with a minuscule cross. These *and the explicit journeys* made me call this kind of map 'inner', see next section. The viewer is appealed to in very different moods, the one serious, the other jocular. Yet the cosmological symbol appears in both and the sense of *commitment* as meaning and message joins both maps.

The intention is very different in fantasy maps like that of Stevenson (see fig. 11.7). Stevenson tells us that he had designed the map first and written the story of *Treasure Island* later. However this may be, the device using an invented map to increase the plausibility of a story has often been employed in modern fiction. I shall do something similar when in the next chapter I use my imagination to make a map of a patient's dream: a fantasy map about a dream. Only the intention is different. Mine is to throw light on the little noted feature of location.

To sum up: a map of fantasy mediates between two kinds of reality: it offers us a view *from* and also *of* a bridge between two worlds; worlds which we find convenient to treat as if they were separate, like art and science.

So much for a description of four cartographical types that can serve as models in the construction of analytic maps. Now for the additional type which we need to make the connection between cartographical and analytic maps.

Figure 11.4 'Daniel's Dream Map'. After an original woodcut (Wittenberg 1530) later included in Luther's Bible

Figure 11.5 John Bunyan's *Pilgrim's Progress* illustrated by Robert Lawson 1939. A fantasy map (allegorical)

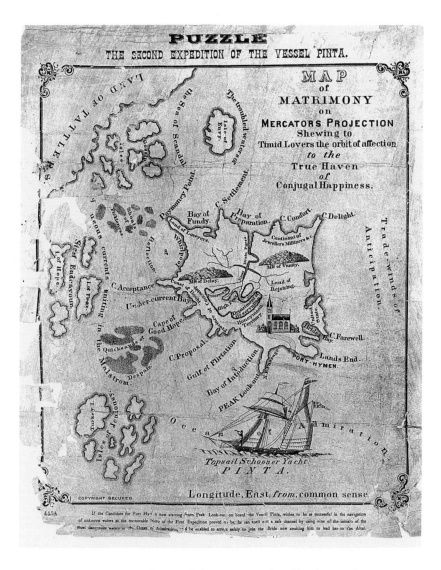

Figure 11.6 Map of Matrimony. A fantasy map that, like the previous one,
refers to an allegorical journey. The cross on top of the church spire is only just
visible. By courtesy of the Library of Congress

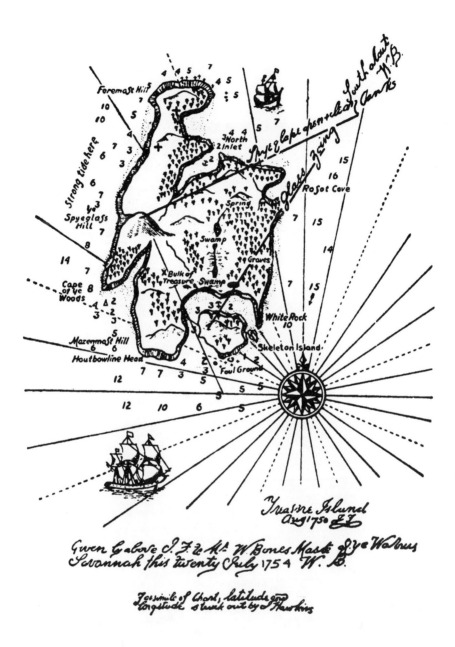

Figure 11.7 This fantasy map accompanying *Treasure Island* was needed by Stevenson not to get lost in his story. It guides the reader and adds to the make-believe

INNER MAPS

It is not down in any map; true places never are.

(Herman Melville, *Moby Dick*)

In a sense, all maps that do not refer to a physical (outer) territory must be called 'inner'. Yet, the special category is required as a stepping stone towards the analytic map, see Chapter 12. The difference between it and a contrivance such as Stevenson's fictitious map for *Treasure Island* is that he took care to make it look like a geographical map. The inner map, on the other hand, is like a metaphor; similarity is irrelevant. The metaphor does not aim to convince by physical likeness. The intention is to make psychic contents visible and thus accessible to reflection and further elaboration. So far from trying to emulate physical features, the inner map makes use of these in two ways. The first is by selecting as building blocks those elements that appear particularly suited for the formation of symbols; examples are a rose, a spider's web or the spiral of a whirlpool. Second, it enhances the quality of these things by transforming them into sensuously appealing images. Now the metaphor and the inner map have in common that they *enlarge and thereby heighten the space* of whatever they refer to (the referent) much in the way that poetry does. That space – in contrast to a mere blank – *cannot* be on any physical map. Yet it is what Melville refers to as a 'true place' because it is where we really live when fully, that is spiritually, alive. Melville further borrows an island 'far away to the south and west' which was more truly the birthplace of Queequeg, the 'noble savage' of his story, than any place on a 'real' map could have been. Such vague islands are traditionally Utopian; the paradox we shall have to face is: how 'real' is Utopia? (see p. 337, below).

An additional quality of the inner map to note here is that *not all the building blocks* are taken from nature, some are symbols specially designed and crafted by humans. Among these the cross, the labyrinth and the mandala are of particular relevance to us. But for the time being let us continue to the junction of a real and an inner map.

When in the previous chapter I referred to a sketch map of the way to my house (see p. 193 above) as an example of an itinerary map I had put myself into the position of the visitor. This meant I suppressed as unhelpful an inner map, namely my view of the road by which the visitor would be arriving but as seen from my bedroom window. So the inner map says something about what it actually feels like to live in a certain space: the house. Where I live has to be taken literally as well as metaphorically: my daily round and my little universe. We may assume that Melville's remark about true places means that no ordinary map can actually convey what it feels like to hail from and really live on that island.

Another example: if I had been given a sketch map to my analyst's consulting room, I would still not have had the slightest idea what the vicinity of her house looked like when I actually got there, nor would I have been able to visualize the room with its special ambience: that room that would become so closely associated with all the inner rooms I would discover and live in during the years that followed the first visit and that would figure so large on my inner map. A small space in reality, it would become the centre of my cosmos for many years. Of course, there are other potentially cosmological maps, not mine yet part of traditions in which I knowingly or otherwise participate. These too would be illuminated in the course of an explorative, analytic journey.

Although it is obvious that inner maps must borrow from outer perceptual reality, yet after they have become 'inner' their influence on what can be perceived is as great as that of a chemical stain on a tissue for microscopic examination: without it many structures cannot become visible while others become invisible. What is it that would correspond to the stain enabling us to differentiate between 'inner' maps and other categories? Three exclusive or *negative criteria* may help to explain.

First, it must be recalled that there is nothing preordained about the four cartographical categories that I adopted for the purpose of introducing a preliminary classification of analytic maps. More and other types could serve as models. For example, the sub-category of the *mappa mundi* (see Glossary), known as a *Climate map* (see Fig. 11.1b) could be adopted as a model by an analyst who wanted to construct a map showing variations in the transference climate. Then again, there is no reason why analysts should not in due course cut themselves adrift from the cartographical model altogether and invent their own categories and methods of representation, Fig. 12.8 is an example.

Second, the history of cartography is full of examples of the mixture of fact and fiction. Moreover, in the above glossary on 'Early world maps' I differentiate between preconceived world images of a cosmic order and maps based on the recorded observations of actual voyages. For example, not a few of the *mappae mundi* incorporate both new geographical items as well as encyclopedic, legendary and mythological features. These were gradually extruded into the margins of maps and charts where they figured as entertaining or decorative elements. In short, the presence of such mixtures can be defended as a compromise with popular taste and are insufficient reason for referring to a map as 'inner', for example Fig. 11.14.

Third, there are further subtle distinctions. To repeat the Utopia question raised earlier: is a map about paradise a religious map or a fantasy map? The criterion must depend on whether the fantasy used is that of an individual or whether it is of a traditional belief which is real enough at one time and becomes classified as symbolic or fantasy at a later epoch. Thus Wallis and Robinson observe that some pictorial maps of imaginary or legendary places can be traced back over many centuries in association with religion, which were not *intentionally* (emphasis added) imaginary before the sixteenth century (op. cit.). Bearing the mapping of paradise in mind, I would add that attempts to put it on the map, albeit in different geographical locations, continued right into the present century as I have described in 'Where is paradise? The mapping of a myth' (Plaut, 1981). But when the *traditional* belief in the earthly paradise as a geographical place waned, the individual attempts to map it were regarded as fanciful and the maps were correspondingly classed as fantasy maps or maps of Utopia. Nevertheless, individual designers of religious maps were, so far as we know, sincere believers in the literal interpretation of the Scriptures, mapping to spread the Gospel. Quite the opposite of Thomas More, who, in 1516, wrote down, tongue in cheek, unworkable instructions for mapping of the island of 'Utopia', that became popular as a political satire.

What is needed next are *positive criteria* whereby the usefulness of a separate type of map called 'inner', not only as distinct from outer or real, but also as different from 'fantasy' could be established.

On spatiality and 'islomania'

It was at a meeting of the Medical Section of the British Psychological Society in the 1950s when, after a presentation by a Jungian analyst containing fascinating mandala symbolism, Winnicott got up and asked whether his colleague could show why the drawing of the small circle in the middle surrounded by a larger one outside, did not represent a breast and nipple. The assumption had been that it was a symbol of the self which was regarded as the unifying principle of the personality. It is pertinent to the present theme that for Jung symbols of the self arise in the depth of the body and express its materiality every bit as much as the structure of the perceiving consciousness (*CW* 9, I: para. 291). This statement linked with the anecdote led to my *hypothesis that a primary spatial consciousness is the common source of both the baby's rooting (for the nipple) reflex and of the impulse in humans and other animals to orientate themselves in relation to their living space, both real and imaginary.* The specifically human capacity to make maps consists, first of being able to combine spatial awareness arising in the body with observations about the heavens and earth; and more specifically the ability to project the inner image on to a flat surface and to keep it there with the help of drawings. This combined capacity existed already in prehistoric societies, as star maps and settlement plans show. It is further possible to demonstrate that the creation of an imaginal world (the cosmos) received just as much and as early attention as practical topographical maps. It is a thesis that receives support from three separate sources, namely, ethnography and prehistoric cartography (Delano-Smith, 1987) as well as from the researches of Piaget in *The Child's Conception of Space* (Piaget, 1955). Piaget found that closed shapes, such as circles and rectangles and the topological concepts of inclusion and separateness are among primary spatial concepts.

The theme of enclosed spaces in which balanced, symmetrical states reign will be taken up once more under the heading of Utopia (see p. 337 below).

The island as a cosmological symbol in early cartography is easily recognized as an irregular shape or cluster of such shapes surrounded by whatever word or ideogram means water. As for analysis, whether looked at as an individual session or as a whole, the metaphor of an island – perhaps connected with the mainland of everyday reality by a bridge or a ferry – and mapped as such, does not overtax the imagination nor skill of most people.

The quest for both inclusion and separateness is well represented by the cartography of islands which for many centuries have had a chequered career of discovery and loss. One only has to recall the legend of St Brandan, an Irish monk who discovered the 'Island of the Blessed' (told by Beazley in *The Dawn of Modern Geography* (1949), Defoe's *Robinson Crusoe*, Jules Verne's *Mysterious Island* among others, to realize that Durrel's definition of an *islomane* as a person afflicted with a powerful attraction to islands, refers to a fairly widespread psychological phenomenon (Durrel, 1953). As a phenomenon it is closely linked with mankind's longing for *Utopia*, an illusory place where ideal conditions prevail, including, possibly, eternal life, as in the story of the Garden of Eden which was also placed on an island by some latterday searchers and cartographers (Plaut, op. cit., see also p. 148, above). At any rate, Stommel, a sea-going oceanographer, in his *Lost Islands, The Story of Islands That Have Vanished From Nautical Charts* is well aware of the human reasons that account for the persistence of these island entries on charts and globes right up to 1982. He too confesses himself to be an islomane in private life (Stommel, 1984).

Analysts should have no difficulty in recognizing the aspect of denial of harsh reality as part of the attraction and will attribute the fascinating and illusory aspect of 'islomania' to mankind's recurrent longing for blissful regression on the one hand, and, on the other, to the defence mechanisms of dissociation and 'splitting', that is the good from the bad object. Nevertheless, the longing for the proverbial South Sea island and other remote spots continues unabated, analytic sobriety notwithstanding. Analysts themselves are not immune to it. The implicit and not entirely Utopian hope is that there could be a 'new beginning' (Balint, 1968) or a rebirth (Plaut, 1977).

Despite the undoubted truth contained in the analytic interpretation of denial of reality, illusion and so on, I would claim that the phenomenon is also a manifestation of our primary spatial consciousness, 'spatiality' in search of a safe and secluded place. Just *because* it is *limited*, space can be found for the *expansion* and replenishment of body and spirit in conditions which facilitate the deferral of daily cares. Obviously, if it were demanded or even expected that such replenishment must produce demonstrably useful results, such as an outburst of 'creativity', the object of the search would have been defeated by starting at the wrong end. A religious retreat may provide such a space and could be regarded as Utopian, were it not for the imposed obedience and Spartan conditions designed to act as a discipline and brake on bodily indulgence and idleness. This description bears a functional but superficial resemblance to Winnicott's transitional phenomena and the place of illusion in developmental history (Winnicott, op. cit.). But I arrived at this view by a different route and differ from Winnicott in one essential respect. For Winnicott, fantasy is prior to reality; when enriched it leads to the experience of illusion. In my view, spatial consciousness is the primary driving force behind the search for cosmos and centres. *It is surprising that we do not make use of innate spatial awareness, 'spatiality', and our capacity to map in the recording and investigation of procedures such as analysis.*

It must be added that other psychotherapeutic methods, notably psychodrama and family therapy have adapted spatiality to their diagnostic-therapeutic techniques. For example, use is made of the physical distance at which various members of the family put one another from which the emotional pattern of relationships can be deduced (Constantine, 1978). In general, it can be said that analysis has devoted more attention to the time- than to the spatial-dimension of the mind. In order to remedy this we have to find suitable symbols that can act as 'landmarks' in, as well as delineations of, space.

COSMOLOGICAL SYMBOLS

These symbols deserve special consideration because of the important role they play in maps referred to as 'inner'. Although the analytic maps to be described share the quality of 'inner', cosmological symbols can help us to diagnose an inner map, see criteria, above. Their timeless quality reminds us that they existed long before analysis. In Chapter 12 I shall show of what diagnostic and (self)-analytic use such maps may be. But first, the following.

What are map symbols?

No map can be constructed without the use of symbols. What are colloquially referred to as map symbols are actually signs or *ideograms* which have become fixed, adopted by convention and therefore stereotyped. Some of these have already been referred to, see 'Itinerary maps' (p. 211). Others come closer to symbols in Jung's sense which is that the meaning of a symbol cannot be rationally explained. Its message, however, appeals on a level where chords are struck in the beholder whose mind is or can be attuned. The cross or a national flag are examples of *signs that can become symbols* under the right conditions. So is the humble dot: by itself it may not mean more than a place on a map. But in relation to other dots it may mark a celestial constellation and thereby indicate the relation of the observer to the cosmos. For present purposes I am making no distinction here between celestial and cosmological maps, although Delano-Smith in her excellent account of prehistoric maps does (op. cit.).

Figure 11.8 A circular map of the Garden of Eden. This is a symbolic representation of various philosophical and theological ideas. The innermost circle is the fountain or spring, situated on an island. The square seems to represent a temple built over the fountain. The four rivers (named) issue towards the four corners of the temple. The outer circle contains the inscription 'Paradisus Terrestis' but the wavy lines are reminiscent of the traditional circumfluent ocean. A cross at the top signifies the Christian orientation. By courtesy of the Biblioteka Jagiellonski, Krakow. codex 1453

How do cosmological symbols look?

For convenience sake the following broad classification of cosmological symbols would distinguish between the following: (a) emblematic; (b) naturalistic; (c) abstract.

(a) The reader has already been introduced to the first when the allegorical map of Europe was mentioned (fig. 10.1 on p.196). Here the crown, sceptre

Figure 11.9   This paradise symbol, enlarged and redrawn, comes from the eighth-century copy of Isidore of Spain's *Etymologies* in the Vatican Library. It illustrates a cosmological symbol of abstract design. Isidore lived in the sixth century

and orb are the symbols of worldly power. In other maps coats of arms have a similar significance, indicating a world order. In the seventeenth and eighteenth centuries it was customary to decorate maps with emblems which would attract patronage. It's the way of the world.

(b) A multitude of objects belong to this category varying from animal and human figures, sometimes distorted into monstrous shapes, or given the attributes of divinity, to exaggeratedly large mountains and lakes, also islands, trees and towns. Man-made objects, such as dwellings, decorated compass roses and ships are evidence of the human spirit of invention and enterprise. Allegorical representations of celestial bodies and of the winds point to the powers of both observation and imagination and the wish to combine the two.

(c) This large category is distinguished from the others by its style of representation and generally consists of some geometrical arrangement of circles, semicircles, rectangles and triangles around a centre or axis. Figures 11.8 and 11.9 belong to this category as does also the paradise symbol in one of the Beatus maps, Fig. 11.10, in contrast to the usual naturalistic Adam and Eve representation, complete with tree, apple, snake and the four rivers in the other Beatus copies and also in the maps of Ebstorf and Hereford (Fig. 11.11). We do not know for what reason the one or the other style of symbolic representation occurs. The preference of individual copyists (their psychology and drawing ability included) may have been the deciding factor.

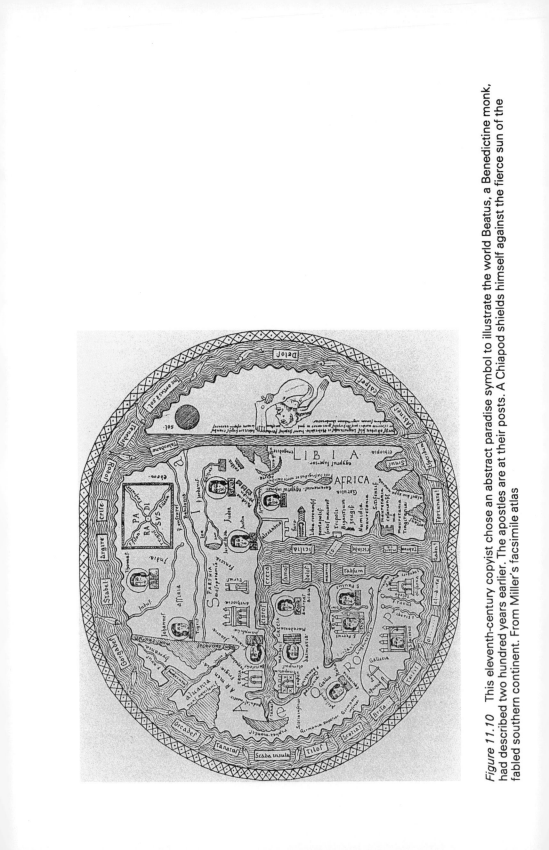

Figure 11.10 This eleventh-century copyist chose an abstract paradise symbol to illustrate the world Beatus, a Benedictine monk, had described two hundred years earlier. The apostles are at their posts. A Chiapod shields himself against the fierce sun of the fabled southern continent. From Miller's facsimile atlas

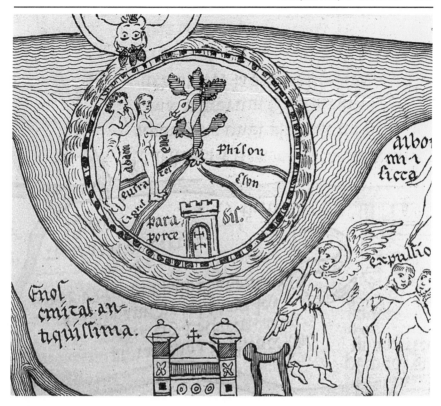

Figure 11.11   A paradise symbol of naturalistic design is found in the thirteenth-century map of Hereford. Enlarged after Jomard's facsimile. By courtesy of the Royal Geographical Society

In compositions of the first type the symmetric structure conveys a static order, balance and harmony. Fig. 11.8 especially reminds us of the *mandala* which Jung describes as a protective circle, 'the traditional antidote for chaotic states of mind' (*CW* 9, I: para. 6). Other specific cosmological symbols already mentioned are the island and the spiral. The labyrinth will be further referred to (p. 233f) below.

The usage of cosmological symbols in cartography and analysis

Let us consider various paradise symbols in manuscript maps appearing between the eighth and sixteenth centuries as models of secluded places, separated from the world by various 'defences' that make access difficult, illustrated by an island position, inaccessible mountains, walls and moats and walls of fire on the one hand, and/or by geometric designs on the other. The importance of the paradise symbol in these Christianized maps is also shown by its large size in relation to the rest of the map as well as by the position of honour on top of the map, that is in the east. For this reason such early maps were commonly 'oriented' (=East on top) reminding us of the beginning of the creation of mankind which according to Genesis 1:8 had taken place in the Garden of Eden *'to the east'*. In contrast to some world maps informed by eastern religions the Christian paradise symbol is *never in or near the centre* of the map, although Jerusalem often is. This city symbolizes the union of knowledge of the inhabited world with religious belief because Jerusalem's position had also been ordained (Ezekiel, V:5). It was in the world but unlike the safely remote paradise, destructible. We can assume that the representation of both centres was equally important and real to the mappers of the day. How did they manage to live in a unified world? How do we manage without? Has our world got no navel? Can the striving for a central self as aim of analysis be regarded as the outcome of an (unconscious) search for a unified state of affairs, Blake's *New Jerusalem* so to speak?

What I mention under global aims (p. 53 above) and mysticism (p. 310, below) would confirm this view. It is further supported by Jung who regards symbols of the centre as fascinating and therefore dangerous. What happened to him when he had finally managed to buy a ticket to Rome, Christianity's other central and holy city, and fainted can be regarded as further evidence. Jung himself interpreted the incident as his not being up to the overwhelming impression that Rome as a symbol of the centre would have made on him (Jung, 1961).

In lieu of a definite answer let us return to *the quartered circle* in prehistoric rock art (fig. 11.12). This symbol has been interpreted as a representation of the cosmos by some authorities, and of the sun by others (Kühn, 1966). Jung reminds us that it occurs as an alchemical motive and that it is also the basic structure of the Lamaistic mandala which is used as a ritual instrument of meditation and concentration and that this basic structure occurs in the dreams and drawings of many people, himself included (*CW 9, I*: para. 707–8). In his *Memories, Dreams and Reflections* he described how after his parting from Freud and during the First World War, the painting of mandalas assisted his self observation and saved his sanity (op. cit., 'Confrontation with the Unconscious'). The 'antidote' relieved his anxiety without inducing anything like a blissful, paradisaical state of mind. Looking back we may regard the work he did then as a piece of self analysis leading to a reorientation. His further writings show that he had found nourishment within the new or regained cosmos.

It is worth staying with this simple cosmological symbol appearing double in fig. 11.12 and looking like the cross within a telescopic sight, but also the

Figure 11.12 Prehistoric design found in a barrow at Kivik, Sweden, estimated age 1500BC, showing two quartered circles and regarded by some as a representation of the cosmos. Others think it represents the sun disk. It is also the basic form of the mandala and of the innermost structure of the labyrinth. The latter has been found in tombs and is widely regarded as a symbol of death and rebirth

basic structure of the mandala as a cosmic image, because it could provide a clue to our quandary of living in two worlds. For Jung it is a symbol of original 'wholeness through the union of opposites' (*CW 13*: paras 456–7). The global concept of opposites has played an influential role in Greek and later philosophy, from Heraclitus and Plato to Hegel, and certainly in alchemy and Jung's psychological interpretation of it (cf. p. 136 above). He writes 'the four points demarcate a circle, which, apart from the point itself, is the simplest symbol of wholeness and therefore the simplest God image' (ibid.). From the spatial point of view, Jung's example of two pairs of opposites left/right, above/below in the preceding sentence is of interest. *This axial system* is in keeping with our experience of the body and its *apparent* symmetry of left and right halves and (partly) paired organs. It would also correspond to the infant's assumed qualitative division into experience of a pleasurable, satisfying good breast and its opposite. In fact, however, left and right hand are much more easily confused than above and below where our bodies are obviously *a*symmetrical. Here opposite functions, feeding and excreting, for example, help to distinguish above and below, as a little later on in development does standing up and lying (or falling) down. And later still the observation of the sky and celestial bodies in contrast to our earth-bound and finite existence makes for an unmistakable axis between above and below which also links birth (or rebirth) and death. Hallpike writing as an anthropologist supports Piaget's findings and makes a relevant observation concerning the point of intersection between left and right, head and feet (Hallpike, 1979). In his chapter 'Primitive Spatial Concepts' he cites Indonesian villagers who regard the centre of the village as the navel, 'a place of great symbolic importance, being marked by a flat offering stone'. This stone is quite different from another, named *koda* after their mountain of origin. The koda stone is also an offering stone 'placed somewhere at the top of each village' (ibid.). The similarity between paradise at the top and Jerusalem at the centre of the *mappa mundi* seems rather striking: *two places of 'central' significance, two worlds between which we live.*

The longing to experience the space in which we live, no matter how divided our lives may be, as *one* in which one can feel at home and undivided, accounts, in my view, for ideas of symmetrical opposites which recur in the form of 'correspondences', such as 'as above so below', 'as in heaven so on earth', or, microcosm corresponds to macrocosm; in short, the ever longed-for union of opposites. It is this illusory conflict-free zone which is suitably mapped by symbols of paradise with their strikingly symmetrical design; for examples refer to Figures 11.8 and 11.9.

We therefore notice that Jung's mandala as symbol of the self and its connection with the individuation process as a goal of psychological transformation are differently expressed hopes of redemption sharing the same symbol. The relation between these hopes is ably described by Jacoby in his *Longing for Paradise*, especially Part III, 'Paradise as futuristic expectation of salvation' (Jacoby, 1985). The fascinating power of ideas as expressed as principles such as the opposites or 'correspondences' is well illustrated in early cartography. The great Mercator himself, in his world chart (1569) commented that the landmasses should be equal in weight, thus supporting the belief that, without the counterpoise of a large southern continent, the landmasses of the northern hemisphere of the earth would not remain in equilibrium: a good example of medieval thinking by correspondences, 'as above, so below'. The insistence of analytical psychology on opposites and their union as the way of dealing with conflicts and the road to individuation represents a comparable idea. In practice, that ideal can inhibit the discovery of what is 'real' in the sense of unchangeable in a person (cf. Chapter 9, p. 178).

At this point I must confess that I found that I had used symbols for enclosed spaces *after* I had tried my hand at *drawing analytic maps* (see below, figs 11.1 to 11.7). I think the latter were the outcome of my own playfulness combined with the intention of representing concisely something for which I either found words in well-known but threadbare theoretical terms, in which case firm outlines resulted; or, the outlines were irregular, asymmetrical and of uncertain and broken appearance indicating something vaguely and possibly wrongly intuited, awaiting further clarification.

This links my attempts with those of the cartographers of old who apparently used a number of devices to hide their ignorance – but was it necessarily ignorance? Or is it arrogance that takes possession of us when we look at early world maps, schematic types of images and think of their makers as having been ignorant or dishonest? Because the maps were based on the then available knowledge and systems of belief and a network of myths and legends, mapmakers were sometimes prompted by wishful thinking, travellers' tales and analogical reasoning. Such was the case with the vast southern continent; although often referred to as *terra incognita* or, more hopefully, *nondum (not yet) cognita*, it was nevertheless given quite definite outlines, especially where it approached Cape Horn and in the region where Indonesia and Australia are situated. Although the shape of 'terra australis' itself is quite irregular, the stipulated existence of this great southern continent is in keeping with the rule of symmetry as a balanced state.

In the early days, blank spaces on maps were sometimes filled in by monstrous animal or human-shapes of legendary origin. A comparable phenomenon happened in the history of analysis when protagonists of one 'school' attributed comparable characteristics to the protagonists of rival theories or to heretics within their own ranks. I found these monstrosities, or caricatures, technically too difficult to put down on any map, but comfort myself with the thought that in the long run they proved to be unimportant. However, analysts could do well to remember the apocryphal story of the explorer who said to his map-maker: 'Where unknown, put dragons'.

SPIRALS AND LABYRINTHS

The reason why these symbols are worth studying from various angles is that were analysis to be regarded solely as a method of therapy, a cure for sick minds, it could not survive. As has been pointed out by Jung and post-Jungians, these minds may be sick *because* they are isolated, culturally and socially. In which case, the rarefied air of analysis could make matters worse.

Spirals and labyrinths were fascinating to the medieval public of Richard of Haldingham, author of the thirteenth-century *Hereford map*. As cosmological symbols they remain so to this day (fig. 11.13).

The map is strewn with many other illustrations of mythological or legendary origin. For instance, in the section of the Mediterranean reproduced here, we see a mermaid complete with fishtail and mirror near Delos. The spiral is meant to illustrate the whirlpool of Charybdis between the rock of Scylla and the mainland of Italy. The head with open jaws tells us, in case we have not got the point, of the fate awaiting the unwary mariner.

On Crete the labyrinth of Knossos is the centre of attraction, filling nearly the whole island. According to the myth it had been constructed by the skilful Daedalus, quite different therefore from the natural phenomenon of a whirlpool or the 'supernatural' mermaid.

Spirals and labyrinths have been repeatedly mentioned together as if they were synonymous or interchangeable. One reason why the differences are sometimes slurred over is that the adjective 'labyrinthine', meaning tortuous, intricate or complex, is taken as if it were a sufficiently accurate description of the labyrinth. For example, Freud in his *Revised Theory of Dreams* writes how often mythological themes find their explanation through dream interpretation and instances the story of the labyrinth, which turns out to be a representation of anal birth: the bowels are the tortuous path, and the thread of Ariadne is the umbilical cord (*SE 22*: p. 25). Freud's 'explanation' does not take any account of the construction of a labyrinth: he merely makes it fit into his theory.

A different kind of error is due to a certain superficial similarity of these symbols. Thus Purce in *The Mystic Spiral* mentioned that both appear in tombs and also express concentration of energy and rebirth (1976). Moore writes: 'Mazes (here = labyrinth) and spirals are symbols of the unfolding spiral of life, of the path from the cradle to the grave, of the path to the inner mysteries' (Moore, 1983). When Henderson in *Thresholds of Initiation* writes about a patient's dream of a 'serpent coiled in a complicated knot suggestive of a labyrinth' he seems to ignore that coils, spirals and labyrinths are of fundamentally different structure (Henderson, 1967). Later he uses the labyrinth again, this time metaphorically, when he writes of a mother preparing her daughter 'to find her way through the labyrinth of marriage' (ibid.). Perera, in her 'Dream design: some operations underlying clinical dream appreciation', rightly emphasizes the kinaesthetic component of imagery (Perera, 1988). Although she mentions it, she does not differentiate between the symbolism of related patterns, i.e. the spiral, the maze and the interlace. Kerenyi (a mythologist who agreed in many ways with Jung's views) in his *Labyrinth Studien* reminds us of a Greek poet who referred to shells as 'the labyrinth of the sea' (Kerenyi, 1950). But I think we have to distinguish between the poetry of the soul and analysis as a rigorous procedure.

The similarity in the structure of these symbolic configurations consists of their concentric patterns. But, as shown in Table 4, the differences are psychologically relevant.

Focusing now on the above table and the analytic implications of these

Table 4   Structural differences

Spiral	Labyrinth
The spiral runs in one direction without any break and in the opposite direction in case of the double spiral.	In the labyrinth the direction of approach to the centre follows a pendulum movement as the direct passage is blocked.
The path and the line are identical.	The path lies between the two 'walls'. Entrance and exit points are the same and usually in the West in Christianized maps, at the bottom of the labyrinth.
Spiral formation occurs in nature, e.g. whirlpools, ammonites, galaxies.	The construction of labyrinths is complex yet precise. Labyrinths do not occur in nature, *nor in dreams*.
Upper and lower half are the same.	Upper and lower half are different.
The centre is a virtual point.	There is a definite space in the centre.

symbols, with particular reference to image-oriented Jungian analysts, I should like to evaluate the list of differences in terms of (a) movement, (b) structure and (c) functions. The analytic applications and interpretations will be noted under each heading.

(a) Movement

I am taking the concentricity of both symbols first because it is the most striking characteristic and also because of the link with the quality of 'tangibility', referred to on p. 205, above.

Looking at either spiral or labyrinth, the viewer is practically compelled to follow the windings to the centre with the eyes. But in the case of the labyrinth this is more difficult and so viewers are tempted to trace the path with the finger or pen.

This effect is in itself a clue to one of the roots of these symbols in the form of dances, which, according to Kern, is well authenticated (op. cit.). In the case of spirals the winding and unwinding of the dancers is easy to follow by comparison with labyrinth dances and games which probably required a drawing on the ground so that the dancers could follow. Another enactment was 'the Game of Troy' where the labyrinth figure was walked or ridden over, as originally described by Virgil (*Aeneid*, first century BC). The importance of the differentiated movements in this and other reported labyrinth dances was an essential element, in two ways. They conveyed a memorable visually and bodily moving sensation and feeling which gripped both dancers and onlookers on certain ritual occasions to be mentioned under (c) below. But *the*

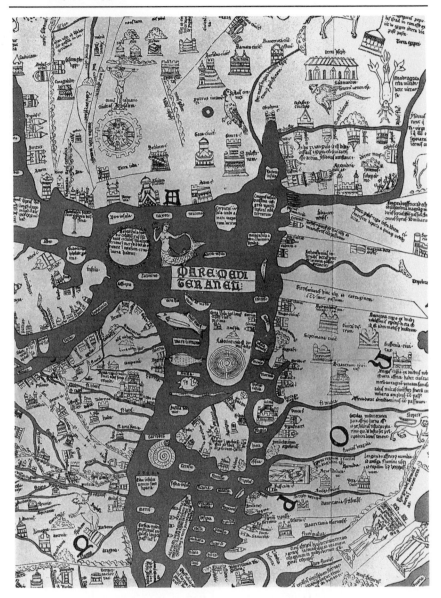

Figure 11.13 Section of the Hereford map, showing the labyrinth of Knossos and the spiral-shaped whirlpool of Charybdis. In the upper (eastern) portion of the map is the eight-spoked wheel-shaped city of Jerusalem and Calvary

movements themselves were a contribution which along with the literary, or more likely oral and visual tradition, went to shape what Kern calls the 'Ur-labyrinth' (op. cit.). Differently put, the archetypal idea 'labyrinth' could not have materialized without *the kinaesthetic contribution* and modes of expression. Once in existence the labyrinth could acquire further symbolic and ritual functions. Despite my putting it this way it is not all that important which sensory contribution can claim primacy. The main point is that the labyrinth still has the aura of a living symbol and that both finished products, spiral and labyrinth, still 'move' the beholder.

As to the analytic application of movements the 'circumambulation' of the centre has received much attention from Jung and post-Jungians. The term, although self-descriptive, is borrowed from *circumambulatio* which was a technical term in alchemy meaning concentration on the central point of transformation or change. Jung noted that the same happens when dreams are viewed as a series (*CW 8*: para. 550). A similar spiral design was chosen by the mapper of the tenth-century world map (fig. 11.14). There can be no doubt that the spring of the four traditional rivers, the 'Fons Paradisi', symbolizes a source of energy. Jung associates the snake in his patient's painting with that of Kundalini yoga that winds three and a half times around the centre (*CW 9, I*: para. 648). The spiral symbolizing the spring seems to have the same number of windings which may or may not be significant. Elsewhere Jung refers to the unconscious processes as moving spiral-wise around a centre symbolized for example by a spider in its web or a serpent coiled round the creative point, the egg which also represents a cosmogonic symbol (*CW 5*: para. 589).

The significant difference between the movement of the spiral and that of the labyrinth is that in the latter the line to and from the centre is not continuous and direct but broken up. The movement swings from side to side like a pendulum while at the same time taking a decidedly circuitous route (see also 'Structure', (b) below).

Seen from the analytic point this pendulum movement is comparable to a natural rhythm, like breathing or the contraction and dilation of the heart (systole and diastole). The to-and-fro of the labyrinthine windings further seems to reflect Jung's use of the principle of the *enantiodromia*, meaning 'running counter to'. He had observed that movements were often phasic, so that if one direction had reached an extreme point the opposite could be expected to emerge, as if by 'the swing of the pendulum'.

Neumann in *The Great Mother* is one of several analytic writers who quote Layard's anthropological studies on Malekula with special reference to labyrinth drawings and initiation and death rituals (Neumann, 1949). In the present context the important characteristic is that the labyrinth is walked through, or the labyrinth design walked over, by men. Kern is quite clear that the highly complex sand tracings of the Malekulans do not conform to the characteristic features of a labyrinth (op. cit.). But the intricacy of design and a superficial

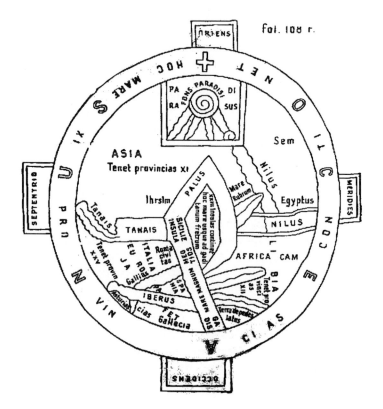

Figure 11.14 This tenth-century copy of the *Etymologies* (cf. fig 11.14) shows an abstract paradise symbol. In the centre is the spiral source from which the four rivers issue. Only the Nile, traditionally, connects with the real world. In other respects too the map represents an example of compromise between an imposed, symmetrical world, as shown in figs 11.1a and b and geographic reality. Manuscript in the Academia Historia, Madrid. Reproduced by Menendez Pidal (1954)

resemblance as well as its ritualistic usage relate Layard's studies closely enough to be mentioned here (Layard, 1931).

All Jungian studies of the labyrinth make reference to clinical phenomena associated with the archetypal 'great mother'.

Although remote from the symbol of the labyrinth, Fordham's concept of integrative and de-integrative processes of the self should be mentioned again, although it relates to individual psychic development. The concept shares with the labyrinth only the characteristic pendulum or phasic-movement by which the centre or growth point is approached (Fordham, 1969, 1976). Free from any sensory imagery the abstract has the advantage of being applicable to many situations. On the other hand, the very lack of an image exposes the concept to the dangers of reification and is easily mistaken as if the concept itself could be observed.

(b) Structure

As readers we are used to keeping our bodies still while the eyes scan the printed page and illustrations. Our habit does not have to change in the case of the spiral where we can follow the direct line to and from the central point. But matters are very different in the case of the labyrinth, as we saw in table 4. Therefore, to appreciate the better both movement and structure, I would ask the reader to use his/her hand as well as eyes by actually drawing the design of a labyrinth with the help of the illustrations, *diagrams* 11.16a and 16b to get into the 'swing of it'. See *Appendix* at end of the chapter.

In all variants of the shape the axial system of the labyrinth, mentioned on p. 282, remains of central importance. According to Kern the basic structure of the labyrinth is a combination of square and circle (op. cit.). The four points inserted into the corners of the central cross, make up a square, constructing a labyrinth. The circle is composed of a series of semicircles, leading to the round appearance of the labyrinth. The circle then represents the field of vision which contains the four basic directions. Kern considers that this combination of cross and circle establishes the basic cosmic image of order and orientation.

Jung reached a comparable conclusion when he investigated the structure and dynamics of the self as based on alchemical and Gnostic sources: 'The quaternity is an organizing schema par excellence, something like the crossed threads in a telescope. It is a system of co-ordinates that is used almost instinctively for dividing up and arranging a chaotic multiplicity, as when we divide up the *visible surface of the earth*, the course of the year, or a collection of individuals into groups' (emphasis added) (*CW 9, 11*: para. 381).

I would call the quartered circle a first attempt at orientation, that goes back in prehistory, to a time before there was as sharp a distinction as there is today, between what I earlier referred to as the two centres: 'where you live' and 'where you really live'. But with the help of the labyrinth it becomes possible to make the distinction visible. Although it is not a complete inner map, it is at least a symbol of the cosmos in which the analytic journey takes place. Although built on a simple spatial perception of order and orientation, its complex construction is indicative of a significant increment of cognitive intelligence. The labyrinth still conveys more about the human situation than any other living symbol. No wonder it was adopted by the churches. *How is it that this highly crafted symbol cannot be dreamed?*

Perhaps a tentative explanation can be found in Matte Blanco's bi-logic (1975). He replaces Freud's 'primary' and 'secondary process' (*SE 12*: p. 213) as well as the old division 'conscious–unconscious' and, I would add, Jung's 'Two kinds of thinking' (*CW 5*: paras 4–46) with the terms of 'symmetrical' (=symbolic) and 'asymmetrical' (=discriminating) order and 'logic', each requiring the other. Matte Blanco's *combination of a symbolic and a discriminatory order is represented in the construction of the labyrinth*. I suggest that the reason why it does not appear in dreams can be attributed to their lacking the asymmetric, discriminatory order. However this may be, Matte Blanco's hypothesis of multiple spatial dimensions does stimulate dream theory, as Jiménez has shown (Jiménez, 1990).

It would be tempting to regard the spiral-shaped line as the path that leads to the centre, the Jungian self and goal of the individuation process. When Ariadne gave Theseus the thread she knew the path would not be straightforward. Nevertheless the spiral remains a pattern of fascinating simplicity inspiring Utopian hopes of cure and salvation. Analysts know that the labyrinth with its blind alleys and ninety degree turns symbolizes the analytic process more appropriately than the spiral. But even that knowledge does not prevent the vast majority of analytic journeys from being reported as 'point made' or 'mission accomplished'. Following Ariadne's thread the centre was reached and, the monster slain, an exit having been made good, a rebirth or a new beginning occurred – *after* analysis, so to speak.

Reality is very different. Although this has been pointed out by analysts, for example Blomeyer in his chapter 'The School of Individuation' in *Spiele der Analytiker* ('Games that analysts play'), I should like to take the point about the persuasive power of both cosmological symbols and analytic theories and aims a little further by arguing that this is due to their symmetrical construction (Blomeyer, 1982). That is, the balanced arrangement around a central point at the intersection of axes makes it appear as if the quadrants were equal and mirrored each other, as is the case with Lamaic mandalas. The roughly circular (or square) appearance of the labyrinth may, at first glance, also give the impression of symmetry, but on closer inspection the two halves turn out to be different, that is *asymmetrical*. I shall return to this point under 'function'. For the present it needs to be added that the labyrinth became a completely rounded figure only in the ninth century when, under Christian influence, the inner space shifted from one of the upper quadrants to the centre so that the labyrinth became properly concentric. This emphasized the central, or intersecting point of the cross and the symmetry of designs around it. The central space further permitted Christian symbols to be inserted. The feeling communicated both by the mandala and the Christianized labyrinth can be epitomized in Browning's words 'God's in his heaven – All's right with the world!' Or, if not now, then in future. Knowing this feeling to be illusory does not prevent us from wanting to return to Utopia from time to time.

(c) Function

Under this heading I consider various interpretations of the ideational content and practices associated with the labyrinth symbol.

By referring to it as a cosmological symbol, I have already pre-empted its order-creating function. The same could be said of any symbol because symbols are, according to Jung, transformers of energy, for example from an instinctual to a more conscious and spiritual level. In the case of the labyrinth the symbol mediates between states of orientation and disorientation. This function can be easily understood in a general way on the basis of what has already been said above under movement and structure. But how does it operate in detail?

Anyone trying to answer this question will arrive at Kern's conclusion when he writes about the essential quality of a living symbol as something that cannot be reduced to having a single meaning (op. cit.). It is a conclusion with which Jung would no doubt have agreed. Meaning and function become closely related in *ritualistic practices* and I shall, in trying to tease out details, start with the latter, disregarding, however, strict chronological order.

RITUAL AND SYMBOLIC USAGE

1. Labyrinths in churches

Although earlier examples were known, these flourished during the Middle Ages, but late constructions date back to the nineteenth and even twentieth centuries (Köln (Cologne) Cathedral). The best known of these is the floor mosaic at Chartres, apparently the prototype of several others. English turf mazes follow the same pattern and are also large enough to walk through. Why the labyrinth should have found its way into churches at all remains puzzling, because it did *not* exist in pagan shrines, but only in the profane buildings of antiquity. Nevertheless the Christianization of the labyrinth was accompanied by important changes in structure as well as content. Jerusalem was sometimes put in the centre, as it was in the *mappae mundi* referred to earlier. It is reported that those who could not participate in a crusade were credited with an equivalent penance if they walked through the labyrinth as at Chartres on their knees. Hence the 'Road to Jerusalem' as a byword for the labyrinth, but also known as '*Maison Dédalus*'.

Under Christian influence the mythological figure of Theseus was replaced by Christ or a symbol of Christ. The minotaur became Satan, Ariadne's thread the Christian faith.

Certainly, the Church at the time seemed to have been wise rather than to banish it, to adopt the labyrinth of pagan origin into the Christian cosmos. After all, the 'language' that the labyrinth used referred to a spiritual journey and the rituals which accompanied it were about birth and death, initiation and rebirth. So the renewal of life through faith in the resurrection and surrounding rituals, fitted in quite well. There was also nothing alien about the labyrinth that symbolized a life that was full of hardships and setbacks. Nevertheless, if faithfully conducted, the labyrinth symbolized hope of salvation. Similar hopes implicity surround the analytic journey.

No specifically Christian rituals are reported, other than the rather unimportant 'Journey to Jerusalem', see above, and the Easter dances around the labyrinths in the cathedrals of Auxerre and Sens (see Kern, op. cit.). One may assume that the symbolic significance did not necessarily have to be expressed as liturgy. A special case was the cathedral of Lucca where a labyrinth is placed upright near the western door. The faithful were reported to follow the windings with their fingers.

2. Analytic usage

It is significant that labyrinths appear as emblems on the front cover of two Jungian publications. One is the quarterly German journal *Analytische Psychologie*, the other, an American publication entitled *Jungian Analysis* edited by Stein (1982). Beneath the (Hopi) labyrinth of the latter, Jung is quoted: 'The right way to wholeness is made up of fateful detours and wrong turnings.' Image and words are congruent and nobody would argue with the truth and wisdom of the message. However, the details *can* be questioned. For example, does wholeness mean anything other than an ideal state? How do we recognize it? Does anyone 'really live' there? Does it mean anything essentially different from Christian ideas of salvation? These are questions I shall return to, see 'Utopia' (p. 337).

The wide range of phenomena around this symbol is shown by magical, mythological and religious rituals. A definite rhythm is indicated by dances which alternately seek the centre and escape in the opposite direction. And so powerful and fascinating, so 'numinous', is this symbol, so hopeful the aim of the journey with its liberating effect, that the actual way to get there (the asymmetric, pedestrian and multidimensional itinerary) could easily be neglected. The comparison with the medieval world image of the *mappa mundi* springs to mind: If any pilgrim had used it as a road map, he would never have got to Jerusalem (see fig. 11.10). Translated into analytic terms, this means that technique and the cognitive contribution to analysis are in danger of receiving short shrift at the expense of enthusiasm about the universal, the cosmic, or global aim of attaining the wholeness held out by symbolic images in dreams and fantasies. If a slogan like 'the way is the aim' were adopted indiscriminate-ly, analysis would be in danger of deteriorating into a cult of wholeness via conjunction of opposites or by whatever name the universal or global aim be known. *I regard such 'symmetric fallacies' as a potential brake on discovery, comparable to the balanced state of the medieval world image of the mappa mundi.* No practising analytic psychologist is likely to disagree with this in principle, but judging by the enthusiasm about the unconscious producing mandalas, spirals and so-called 'labyrinths', the aesthetic and fascinating aspect of these symbols can make us overlook the fact that there are also considerable complications and obstacles. The devout attitude toward the unconscious goes back to Jung whom I would like to quote in this context from his essay on 'Psychic Energy' (*CW 8*: para. 92). 'Symbols were never devised consciously, but were always produced out of the unconscious by way of revelation or intuition.' However, the case of the labyrinth shows that a conscious contribu-tion must be included. Alternatively the division conscious/unconscious has to be drastically relativized.

There is something to be learned from the history of discovery of our own planet that can be applied to analytic theories: the loss of a deo-centric universe – like that of an ego-and-self-centric analytic cosmos – is painful every time it occurs. I would therefore reformulate the Jung quotation below the labyrinth of Stein's book (see p. 242, above) as follows: 'The road to reality turns to and fro, from symbolic wholeness to discriminating asymmetries and back again. Theoretical universes met on the way are only of short-lived heuristic value.'

3. A variety of secular applications

There may well be an additional link between analysis and the renewed interest in labyrinths. Kern, in reviewing the contemporary scene, refers to the enthusi-asm and excitement that surrounded the Milan labyrinth exhibition of 1981, which was seen by 120,000 visitors (Kern, op. cit.). There he also draws attention to the aura of the mysterious that surrounds the labyrinth along with the general increased interest in the '*occult*'. In his opinion the image of the labyrinth is associated with our longing for a mysterious unity. He considers that the way through the labyrinth is a road to individuation, of concentration and a means of unification of the person. (Curiously enough, Kern makes no reference to Jung.) Popular literature such as Umberto Eco's books *The Name of the Rose* (1983) and *Foucault's Pendulum* (1989) may also be called to mind. Here the connection with evil is quite prominent.

One of the earliest known labyrinths, 'Cretan' in type, dates back to about 2000–1000BC and is a rock carving on the wall of a burial chamber in Sardinia. We don't know what rituals accompanied these burials. Quite likely similarly situated labyrinths were meant to be instructional maps for the departed and a *memento mori* for the living. In that way they fulfilled their function as cosmological road signs.

After these references to death and the occult let us return to the living and some vital functions such as civilization, sex, love, marriage and birth in relation to the cosmological symbol.

Civilization

The placement of labyrinths at the entrance of caves and constructed dwellings is well authenticated. It was said that evil spirits could only fly in a straight line and would therefore get confused and distracted by the windings. Apparently good ones were undeterred by the circuitous route. In a practical way, this suggestion was taken up in building plans of fortifications along the lines of a labyrinth (Kern, op. cit.).

The ritualistic use of labyrinths as outline for games and dances at the foundation of towns and the delimitation of space in general could also have been referred to under movement. There is also a protective aspect to this function which resembles the implicit but not unimportant rituals that accompany *the analytic procedure* with its set space and time as referred to in Chapter 9.

Sex

There is no doubt that the labyrinth in various cultures symbolized the womb, as well as the tomb. An illustration in Kern's book shows a bronze age rock-carving from Spain. The man-like phallic figure penetrating into a labyrinth-type structure has been interpreted as intercourse (op. cit. fig. 11.14, here redrawn as fig. 11.15).

Love

Literature provides reliable evidence about love labyrinths in gardens, especially in the sixteenth and seventeenth centuries. Some resemble those used in alchemical texts and a tree is often found in the centre. This in the case of love labyrinths may be surrounded by a summer house. There can be little doubt that it symbolizes fertility. Equally, the tree in the centre is the tree of life like the second of the paradisaical trees. There are also hints in literature that the love labyrinth, the walls of which consisted of hedges, symbolized the complications and ambivalences of erotic relationships.

Cosmic marriages

The anthropologist Eliade, who, like Kerenyi was close to Jung, in his article 'Terra Mater and Cosmic Hierogamies' (divine marriage) refers to the labyrinth as a symbol of the Earth-woman and the location where some famous mythological marriages were celebrated (Eliade, 1954). It is not difficult to

Figure 11.15 Conception in the labyrinth? After a rock carving dating from ca. 900–500 BC. Showing a labyrinth-type structure into which a man-like figure seems to penetrate. Drawn after a photograph by Anati, 1968

imagine the rituals that accompanied such celebrations for which the labyrinth in or as a cave represented the womb for the creation of both, the universe (cosmogony) and of ordinary life by conception and birth.

Further evidence from a different culture, that is the Hopi Indians of North America, comes to us in the form of the labyrinth which symbolizes mother earth in conjunction with father sun. Another version shows mother earth containing a child. It symbolizes, according to the anthropological report of Waters, the spiritual rebirth from one world to the next (Waters, 1977).

To proceed in proper order we leave marriage and arrive at birth.

Birth

Although this example would from our point of view be classified under 'magic' this was not the case in Rajasthan where the following procedure fitted in with the local cosmos and was meant to aid women in labour. The thinking behind it was that the pendulum movement of the labyrinth would influence by sympathy the womb to adopt a similar rhythm of contraction and relaxation (Kern, op. cit.). Herewith the recipe: a tantric drawing of a labyrinth was reproduced on a plate with a special paste. When washed off with water from the Ganges and given to a pregnant woman to drink there was no further trouble with labour pains and birth. The womb, as in western antiquity, was presumed to be divided into seven compartments corresponding to the seven windings of the classical labyrinth, a 'knowledge' that found its way to India some two hundred years after that fallacy was exposed by Leonardo's dissection (ibid.).

To sum up: The incomplete outline of secular ideas and applications of the labyrinth shows links between the earliest and the latest. The most important of these seems that this symbol conveys an understanding of the journey through life and its turnings which take us from seeing the road ahead to losing and finding it once more. While going through these cycles of clarity and confusion, we are guided by the hope that they will lead eventually to some centrally significant encounter from which we hope to emerge, revitalized.

An aura of mystery surrounds the cosmological symbol which has retained its appeal. Ashamed as we may be of our superstitions, we must concede that they are part of our cosmos, the more so as faith in the Church as symbol of an established order and authority has waned. It has frequently been suggested that analysis in our day offers an alternative cosmos or 'universe', one that does not depend on revelation so much as on systematic study of the determinants of human behaviour. We may consider these as instincts or a hierarchy of archetypes, of object relations or self psychology, or the windings of the labyrinth to which we are merely adding. Obedience to divine laws and mandates has been replaced by appeals to sensibility of the human condition with its pitifully weak cortical control over older and 'lower' cerebral centres. The corollary is that the cognitive study of our itinerary, where we come from, what we actually do and where we might be going to, must be advanced in order to catch up with the symmetric–symbolic but idealistic longing for 'wholeness'. Were we to concentrate on the inner space alone at the expense of studying the details or 'logistics' of the expedition, we should lose Ariadne's thread. Differently put, *I have made use of the symbol of the labyrinth in order to register a plea for the study of the matrix or epistemology and aim of analysis.*

Comment

The difference between Jung's finding a parallel to the analytic process in the alchemical opus and the point of view I advance here, is as follows: I find in early world maps and cosmological symbols like the labyrinth evidence of a search for orientation in the living space between birth and death. This searching cannot usefully be divided into categories such as conscious–unconscious nor somatic–psychic. It is present from birth. In humans the drive for orientation receives additional impetus from wanting to know about the environment which we customarily divide into inner and outer (see also 'two worlds', pp. 21, above and 304, below). The inner I referred to as where we 'really live', also as inner world and as 'intrapsychic' space. To discover it we require the freedom of space, the feel of 'spatiality' that locality-bound existence alone cannot give.

An everyday example of memory and recognition being linked, as if by a map of *spatial order*, would be when I go to the right room or drawer, *before* knowing what it is I am looking for. By 'following my nose' I go there, remember what it was I searched for and often find it. There are other ways of looking, searching and finding which also do not fit into such categories as conscious or unconscious as when, for example, I let myself be guided by the colour of a lost article or by a sudden association or intuition. The rational 'When did you last use it?' seems less often helpful to me. The point is that we know enough about Freud's discovery of everyday psychopathology and the role of repression, to nowadays consider some of these examples as evidence of *unexpected everyday sanity* for which neither repression nor unconscious, nor 'pre-'or 'sub-'motives seem the right or necessary differentiation; 'spatiality' allowing for overlapping systems of orientation seems to me closer to the mark.

SUMMARY

In this chapter the theme of constructing analytic maps is continued by examining the potential means or tools needed for the job of transforming metaphorical into real maps in the following sequence.

1 Introducing the reader by means of a glossary to four cartographical types of map intended to serve as models or templates for analytic maps.
2 Another map category called 'inner' was required to adapt the medium (mapping) to the analytic territory: our observations are based on finding the kind of space into which the map might fit.
   The space is in the first place of a general cultural rather than specifically 'analytic' nature. It is further suggested that the spatial dimension of analysis has been neglected by contrast with the temporal dimension.
3 To express the perceptual and cognitive capacity for orientation a special concept, 'spatiality', has been coined. It is neither 'conscious' nor

'unconscious'. The soma–psyche combination is not helpful, either. The concept is meant to link the infant's rooting reflex with later and increasingly complex schemata of orientation that are evidence of mankind's relation to the cosmos. The general tendency to hanker after enclosed spaces has been referred to as 'islomania'. Enclosed spaces often signify a Utopian or idealistic tendency (see also the romantic vision, p. 33).

4 The reader is introduced to the cartographical category of cosmological symbols the design of which is either abstract, geometric and often symmetric or representational and may then be in layers showing stereotyped figures and objects.

5 A symmetrical design based on an axial system such as a cross seems to be best suited to a primary orientation. Other geometric preconceptions are evident in the design of the *mappa mundi* which is based on the number concept of three. The concept of four is reconstituted in the form of paradise which was frequently put on top of the *mappa mundi*, thereby re-establishing the balanced axial system of four.

The outcome can be seen in a cosmological order of satisfying balance and harmony as in the cosmic mandala. But this tends to become a closed system which inhibits further discovery. More often than not, actual exploration results in a change from a symmetrical world order to an asymmetrical world map. With this in mind I compared the cosmological symbols of the spiral and the labyrinth and referred to Jung's preference for symmetrical schemata based on the theory of 'opposites' and the figure four or multiples of four, betokening wholeness but also fostering the illusory aim of wholeness.

6 The labyrinth as a cosmic symbol and inner map of great analytic significance has been described in its various aspects.

We are now ready to look at a pilot study of how an analytic map might be constructed in Chapter 12.

APPENDIX: HOW TO DRAW A LABYRINTH (Cretan type)

The instructions which follow serve a dual purpose. First, to counteract the objection that the differences between the spiral and the labyrinth are merely intellectual, not worth quibbling about since they are symbolically equivalent. Words alone may not be sufficient to counteract the generalization. The act of drawing based on a different kind of awareness may however persuade some readers that the construction of the labyrinth is deliberate and specific, involving more than an 'unconscious' rhythmic, centre-seeking and fleeing impulse. Indeed, the cognitive component is very much to the fore. It touches on the old problem of squaring the circle. But therefore to call it 'intellectual' is surely dividing mankind along the lines of a typology which has no universal application. Did only 'sensation types' take part in ceremonial dances?

(a)

(b)

Figures 11.16a and b   (a) (1) The top of the cross is connected by a semicircle with the upper arm of the left right angle. (2) The point in the left upper quadrant is joined to the vertical arm of the right upper right angle (always by a semicircular movement). (3) The point in the upper right quadrant is connected with the arm of the left right angle. (4) The left arm of the central cross is joined up to the horizontal arm of the right upper right angle. Continue as illustrated, rounding out the corners. (b) The job would have been simpler if, instead of the right angles, we would only have inserted points into the four corners of the cross and proceeded along the same line of movements as above. In that case a labyrinth with only three windings instead of seven as in the classical Cretan type would have been the outcome
Source: H. Kern, *Labyrinthe*, Munich: Prestel, 1986

Evidence quoted by Kern and Kerenyi suggests that the choreographic element was of primary significance in the evolution of the labyrinth (op. cit.).

Second, and closely connected with rhythmic movement, is the orientation in space which leads to a kind of awareness which taking thought alone cannot give. Tracing the way through the labyrinth with the finger makes one appreciate the symbol rather more, yet probably not as much as being one of a group of labyrinth dancers would. Failing that, the construction of the labyrinth which the reader can practise will open up a dimension of knowledge, 'spatiality', which exists alongside the visual–verbal and other modes of communication.

Chapter 12

Analytic maps: a pilot study

Analytic maps cannot portray the passions which are the raw material of analytic experience. However, spatial symbolism *is* suited for the recognition and portrayal of the psychic territory traversed. Therefore analytic maps can be seen as fulfilling a dual function, first, as a system of notation of the journey and the problems encountered; second, reading analytic maps can point the way to further work and, possibly, remodel it. The second function has to be restricted: the model must neither be mistaken for the work itself nor as an explanatory theory. As models the maps are thought of as stepping-stones on the way to wider understanding and better communication. In *Learning from Experience*, Bion calls this an increase in 'K' which stands for knowledge (Bion, 1962). 'K' is thought to come about through an improved relationship between a person and the object, for example an infant and the breast. As long as the relationship is 'bad', because the object is very much needed yet cannot be possessed, there cannot be any increase in knowledge about the relationship. The road is barred by the passions of hate and love. Some mediating steps are required so that even a temporary 'bad' relationship can be tolerated. Most mothers know instinctively how to help their infants over this hurdle and some psychoanalytic techniques try to emulate their approach. Needless to say, maps cannot be of direct help here. But maps as models can point to areas of ignorance or confusion and pseudo-knowledge just as they did in the age of geographical discovery. It is essential for such models to remain flexible which in practice means that we have to employ more than one map category to represent an analytic situation and to point out possible directions, or, briefly: '*How did we get here and where could we go from here?*'

As mentioned already, no type or category of map is monolithic; maps do different jobs at different times. But on account of the fluidity of the analytic 'territory' the orientation and understanding conveyed is particularly short-lived while the analysis is in progress. Accordingly, an analytic map that has served its purpose is of no further use and would best be discarded to prevent the 'rear-mirror' effect referred to earlier (p. 204). Even the maps drawn up when analysis has ended should be treated with caution, allowing for future changes to occur.

ANALYTIC MAPS 12.1–12.7

It seems right to remind the reader that the design of analytic maps is in the experimental stage. Like early cartographical maps they are of necessity crude in outline and naïve, even comical in the manner of cartoons, lack standardization of symbols and are, above all, devoid of a grid and scale. If the idea of the project is sound enough these flaws can be amended in due course.

A time scale from left to right is sometimes implicit. Movement is also thought of as going from the periphery to the centre and back. Importance can be inferred from size and type of lettering; distance from the placement of descriptive words or the placing of map symbols (ideograms), also closeness to the centre as for example the cave in Fig. 12.7 (see below, p. 267).

The style obviously varies according to subject and purpose as is the case in cartography. The intention has been to keep to methods that are within everybody's scope. Where words are used as ideograms the spatial arrangement and connections with lines, circles and the like matters. This is specially noticeable in the case of Fig. 12.2, which is meant to outline a post-analytic situation. In this instance the addition of a 'key' as part of the map is permitted, as it is also in cartographical practice. Sketches used for analytic maps, Figures 12.5–12.7 are thought to be within the 'artistic' limits of most people.

Figures 12.1–12.7 are presented here as examples of analytic maps. They are modelled on the four types of cartographical maps described in the glossary of the previous chapter. Each comment on analytic maps is preceded by a reference to the cartographical type it resembles. The additional type of map I called 'inner' (see p. 216), will be specially relevant when we turn to the 'interactional map' as model and orientation in the case of an individual situation, see Figures 12.8–12.11. In Chapter 14, 'Where does analysis stand?' (see p. 306 below), we shall look at a map constructed so as to represent the place and functions of analysis as a whole, but in the context of our social and cultural environment.

Comment on Fig. 12.1 (type: early world)

When drawing up this 'world map' I tried to recall how it felt when I started my first analysis. The map cannot reflect the mixture of feelings such as apprehension, anxiety even, as well as curiosity and hope. But I think these and many more can be deduced from the map which shows the initial situation from the patient's point of view. The semicircles containing triangles and other fragments stand for all manner of loose ends, not only broken off triangular relationships. The amoeboid shape behind the semicircle, indicating a shield or 'defences' facing the analyst, is the uncertain middle of the patient's psyche. The burden, the 'symptom' of clinical description, is the official reason for seeking help. It is indicated by the cross that is held out in front of the hole in the partition through which the analyst is allowed to look. The patient also has

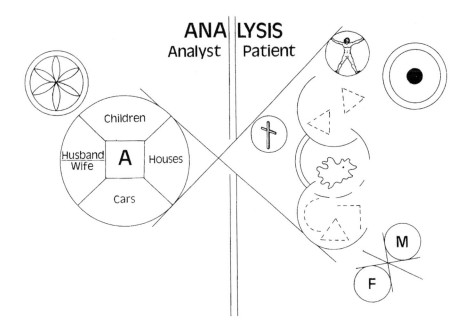

Figure 12.1   Analyst's and patient's expectations

another image of him or herself which *can* only gradually be revealed, but is all the more important for that. I tried to portray it by the suspended, apparently balanced figure within the circle on top of the map, signifying both an imprisoned state but also a guard against anxiety. A balanced state may be what is hoped for to evenuate. A virtual, but as yet vague idea of how a fulfilled life might look is shown by the black centre and white circles, top right. (The traditional Yin-Yang symbol could have been used here.) The separated circles, bottom right, are meant to reflect the patient's as yet barely expressible image of the parents in their united (fulfilled) and separated (frustrated) state.

By contrast with his/her situation the patient pictures analysts firmly established within their world of which 'Analysis', the big 'A', is the centre, the alpha and omega. All desirable possessions, signs of success and affluence are gathered around: the links with the centre are symmetrical and harmonious. In the top left-hand corner the patient perceives a rosette-like symbol which I selected from an early world map where it signified paradise (see fig. 11.9). The Jungian analyst may think of it as a mandala, or a symbol of the self, the Kleinian of an idealized breast; the patient may see it as an ornament.

What I learned from drawing this map was to recall the age that I was when I started analysis (thirty-three) and how wise, old and established all analysts then appeared to be. Strange that one should be able to forget that, when sitting, years later, in the analyst's chair. I knew it in a way, but *mapping brought that knowledge back to life*. The predominance of geometric shapes seen here is in keeping with early world maps which had already been referred to in the previous chapter.

Comment on Fig. 12.2 (type: early world)

This map is designed to show the state of affairs at the end of a reasonably satisfactory analysis. Like the previous map, it includes my views both as a former patient and present analyst. (I did compare notes with colleagues before drawing the map.)

If the map looks more like a mixture between a diagram and a table, it is because only a few map symbols appear in comparison with the number of printed words denoting that their position may change. What makes it nevertheless a map is *the uneven and largely asymmetrical distribution* of words and spaces between the words. Their spatial relations indicate the potentials of movement and linkage.

The circle in the centre represents the meeting ground in two senses: first, the physical room in which analysis took place; second, the analytic territory which is formed by the analyst's professional and human equipment as well as the patient's potentialities and handicaps as assessed by dreams and fantasies in combination with events inside and outside the analytic space. Marriage or comparable partnerships symbolize possibly the only other situation which offers similar opportunities for shared intimacy. The dissimilarity is stressed by the exclusion of sexual contact as well as by the payment. Therefore, the meeting ground delineated over the years during which the analytic pair got to know each other is unique in that it represents a paradox of illusion and disillusionment, of sharing and remaining separate. In this respect the analytic relationship reflects everyday reality to such a degree that one can understand why it could be mistaken for an actual life situation. The inner circle further symbolizes the alchemist's hermetic vessel to which Jung draws attention in 'The Psychology of Transference', as the place in which transformation takes place (*CW 16*: para. 454f). Although the vessel must remain sealed during the process, the reason for bringing cognition to bear on it afterwards is that the container can turn into a prison. I want to assure those who are still in it and afraid to come out that dreaming as a form of unconscious thinking and self-analysis can to some extent replace analysis. Moreover, the analyst will also continue to exist for a while after the analysis as a point of reference on the inner map, as an 'internalized object'.

The crossed lines in the centre of the inner circle are meant to show that the

Patient's assessment

KEY

Similarities
as human creatures

Nourishment
Confidence in being
able to survive

Differences
regarding special
episodes in analysis

HOPE for FUTURE
Can entrust
him/herself better

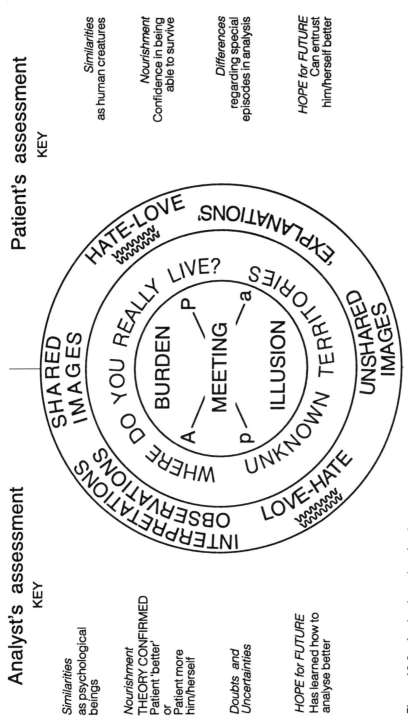

Analyst's assessment

KEY

Similarities
as psychological
beings

Nourishment
THEORY CONFIRMED
Patient 'better'
or
Patient more
him/herself

*Doubts and
Uncertainties*

HOPE for FUTURE
Has learned how to
analyse better

Figure 12.2 Analyst's and patient's assessments

patient also gained a limited view of *the patient inside the analyst* and, further, that there is an analyst hidden within many patients.

The next circle is envisaged as the surrounding territory, the place where each of the pair really lives separately. Space has been designated for undiscovered and unknown territories. There is more of it than the reports on successful cases would suggest. This information like that concerning remaining differences in viewpoints is based on former patients' publications inasmuch as they are relatively unbiased. (See Chapter 5, 'The Patient Speaks', p. 75f.) Writing as a former patient I can confirm that undiscovered territories as well as differences will remain.

Let us now turn to the 'keys'. The 'Explanations', see outer circle, from the patient's point of view correspond to the analyst's 'Interpretations' and 'Observations'. These are closely connected with the emotional climate of the transference which is of the essence throughout the analytic process. 'Explanations' are in quotes to indicate the remnants of hate that surround this area especially when the analysts always seem to get there first, not surprisingly as they are on their professional home ground.

Other words within this circle indicate the flow of emotions. They may be regarded as the equivalent of the circumfluent ocean in medieval world maps, see Glossary. The need for their *partial* transformation into knowledge has already been mentioned.

On the analyst's side of the map we read 'Doubts and Uncertainties', an allusion to Keats's famous 'negative capability', 'that is of being in uncertainties, mysteries, doubts, without any irritable reaching after fact and reason' (Keats, 1952). This is a most valuable quality for analysts to acquire, as both Bion and Winnicott have pointed out. On the opposite level of the map we find a reference to disagreements which have remained in the patient's mind. These are often more valuable than areas of agreement. (If *nothing* has been agreed on, the analysis never got under way.)

Again, it should be noted that the map is asymmetrical: the patient's 'differences' do in no way correspond with the analyst's expectations. This is not easy when the events in question involve the analyst's emotional reactions as well as indispositions and personal problems which patients can frequently intuit. Let us assume that the 'truth' of the matter cannot be ascertained, not even with the help of video-tape recordings. What really matters is that some disagreement is essential to the patient in the process of sorting him/herself out in order to become able to separate. It must therefore be allowed to persist without any indulgent or patronizing reservations. Oversimplified and expressed in practical terms, this demands of the analyst that they should be able to listen receptively without having to demonstrate their analytic knowledge by clever interpretations, remembering that their understanding must remain restricted and that 'ultimate reality' is unattainable (Bion, 1970). If their desire for nourishment in the form of 'theory confirmed' etc. is very great, they cannot exercise the art because desire gives rise to illusions.

What I learned afresh from designing this map is that the outcome of analysis depends more on whether true meetings, the product of two personalities, have taken place than on what theories were in the analyst's mind. Being able to end analysis depends on being able to bear disagreement and frustration, especially that about ending.

It would require another kind of map, designed for the general background of the history and aims of analysis, to demonstrate that analytic theory and methods are essential for 'meetings' to take place at all. Without an illuminating theory and a method to put it into practice the couple would remain in a befriending situation. Desirable as this is as a permanent *background,* a theoretical vertex is as crucial as a focal beam of theory without which analysts and patients would be in the dark.

Comment on Fig. 12.3 (type: itinerary)

The patients to whom this map would be applicable were men haunted by a sexual addiction. They functioned quite well in their daily lives but in a machine-like way. Although reasonably efficient in their work, they felt empty and experienced their environment as boring and humdrum. One explained that if I had a town plan he could draw his movements in a line leading from his home to his work, from his work to the college, from the college to the brothel, from the brothel to his eating place and back to his home. Every day was the same with only few exceptions: during the summer the centre of his life was bathing huts. Here I have drawn two pairs of bathing huts to indicate the major itinerary which connected their location with my house and the analytic work which as a subsidiary centre for all seasons, was in competition with the first.

The pair of bathing huts on the left showed the scene of his greatest excitement, 'like being on a hunt', he said. The huts were separated by a wooden partition in which there were holes. What he hoped for was that a pre-adolescent girl in hut 2 should want to see him naked and get a fright at the sight of his penis. He did not say anything nor even make his presence known. *She* should want to see him. Later, that is by the time he told me about this, he added to the fantasy that he would make his presence known by clearing his throat. However, the wished-for event never happened.

Another patient wanted that a fully adult woman should enter the bathing hut 4 next door so that he could spy on her nudity. This plainly showed him as a voyeur in contrast to the first who was a potential exhibitionist. Some 'progress' in the direction of taking the initiative rather than passively waiting is mapped as leading to the huts on the right. However the details of the symptomatology and the different kinds of sexual fantasies are of minor importance compared with the central position the compulsions played in the patients' lives. The huts had acquired magical status, being equivalent to a temple, shrine or seat of power such as can be seen in early world maps

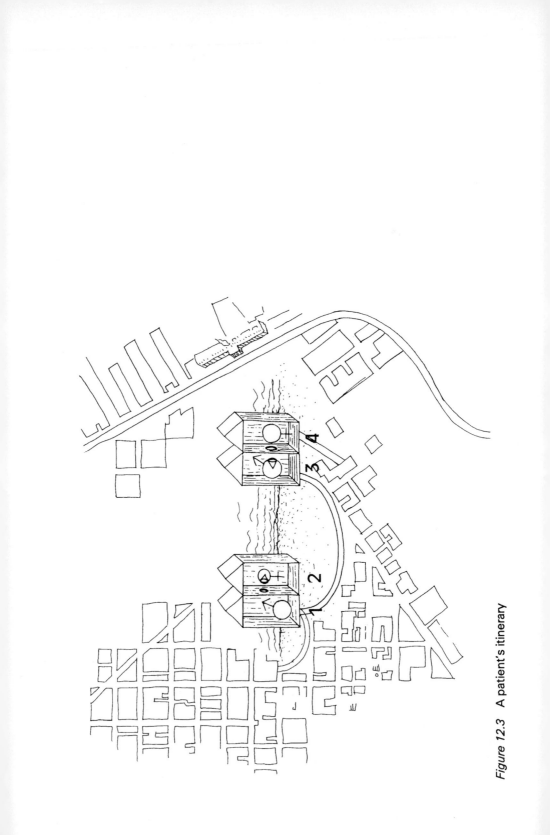

Figure 12.3 A patient's itinerary

representing cosmic symbols. It was the fascination by and concentration on illusory fulfilments which excited both depressed patients. This amounted to an addiction.

Mapping the situation made me aware that the comparison was not too far-fetched. Certainly, the attachment to a location of central importance in the life of people with a sexual compulsion is comparable to the central role a drug plays in the life of an addict. The hub of such ever-narrowing worlds devours all energy. Such narrow lives as addicts can still lead are paid for by immobile mindlessness. Their fear of arrest and imprisonment is justified, *symbolically*, not only literally.

In these circumstances, the analytic map then looks like an itinerary to nowhere. It represents the small world or cosmos in which the relation to a part-object has become hopelessly stuck, as is the case in pornography.

As the relationship between itinerary and inner maps has already been referred to, it only needs to be added that the itinerary map illustrated has, in principle, much in common with the medieval pilgrim's map, no matter how benign the latter appears by comparison. For whether the centre is of the sexual-addictive kind, or spiritually important like the place where a beloved person lived or is buried, or of religious significance, be it Bethlehem or Mecca, the itinerary map connects the world of harsh reality with the centre of a personal map. It gives a clue to the motives for the journey as well as the context. If the emotional environment is bleak but the potential for working on it nevertheless exists, the centre may shift. Interestingly enough, the first patient who had described his map to me had already begun to move from an energy-devouring to an energy-replenishing centre in his life. Analysis had been the stepping-stone.

Comment on Fig. 12.4 (type: thematic)

The following was a first attempt to draw a thematic analytic map. As it happened it failed on analytic grounds. But it is shown here to illustrate why it had to fail. (The map was replaced by the interactional analytic map (see p. 269, below).)

The theme of the map is (male) homosexuality. Development is thought of as taking place from left to right.

Theory one assumes that there is a powerful mother who contains the *father* and also has an imaginary penis – here the arrow – inside her. The result is that in the subsequent triangular inversion of the Oedipal situation, the *son* and not the father is defeated or 'castrated'. Further development shows (a) the son sharing his life with another man in mutual idealization (ladder into the sky) with the female aspects of their personalities being suppressed in the cellar whence they exert a powerful influence on their relationship; or (b) sharing his life in asexual union with a woman; their sexuality is not available in the living space. The hedge speaks for itself.

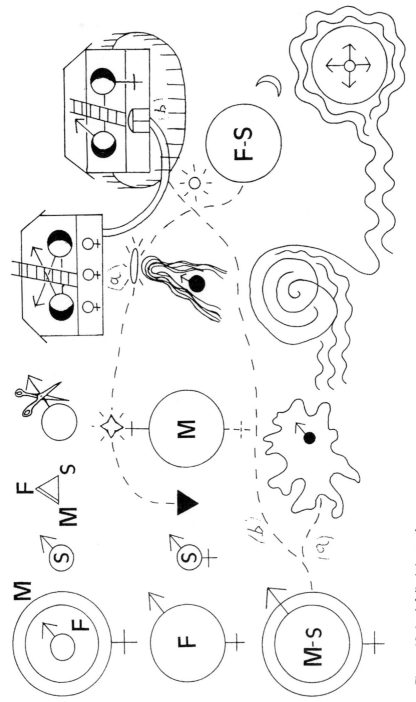

Figure 12.4   A failed thematic map

Theory two assumes that a solitary father with bisexual tendencies looks after a son who becomes identified with his father. No Oedipal triangle develops. Spiritual love is vested in a woman, a 'holy' mother, to whom the son becomes devoted, living, figuratively speaking, inside her. Alternatively, he just continues the father–son union in some other form. The celestial bodies are meant to symbolize the unearthliness of their cosmos as seen by others.

According to the third theory there is a bisexually disposed mother who, in the absence of a father, 'contains' her son to such a degree that his masculine identity fails to develop. This was the case with a young man whom his mother had brought for therapy in late adolescence because he did not seem to be interested in girls. My impression of his 'amorphous' state is depicted here as amoeboid. When analytic therapy was started he seemed to become livelier and for a while his condition fluctuated, as the labyrinth into which he seemed to float is meant to illustrate. Whenever it looked as if we were approaching the centre, scene of the classical combat and separation from mother, he refused to join battle. The monster had defeated an all-too-reluctant hero. Finally, he emerged having become, if anything, more withdrawn. Mother said the treatment had not helped. The last scene pictures him as if in a capsule or on an island where he could dream about young boys. *Drawing up the map has made me more aware* that I had been here before and that it was based on the following questionable assumptions:

One, there are no other causal factors than the parental constellation. Even if the 'dominance' of one or other parent were more influential on the formation of sexual identity than all other factors, the map ignores the analytic hypotheses of multiple causality and 'overdetermination' (see p. 46).

Two, the models here drawn up, from 'theory' to 'outcome', demonstrate that the undue influence of one or other parent brings with it a deformation of an early 'triangular' relationship, such as an 'inverted Oedipus complex' which damages the potential for heterosexual relationships. Alternatively, the triangular situation is circumvented altogether as the blacked-out triangle is meant to suggest. The result is the same. Now, the ability to form satisfactory relationships of any kind may be damaged in more than one way. Although clinical observation strongly supports the assumptions regarding the origin of homosexuality, it has to be admitted that there are other conditions, such as narcissism in which homosexuality is not a regular feature although the relational disability we find in narcissistic conditions facilitates it. Conversely, not all homosexual relationships are unsatisfactory, even when seen in the long term.

Spence, in his criticism of analytic interpretations, remarks that too many different results are 'mapped' on to too few causes (Spence, 1982). Our map shows that the reverse can also happen: different 'causes' may have the same outcome, see the dotted line on the map indicating an alternative path. Furthermore, what I have called 'theory' consists of generalizations, based on the combination of analytic theory of sexual development supported by clinical observations. Although there may be no other way to lay bare such 'causes' as I have grouped together, there remains the danger of a theory becoming self-validating, that is the observer finds what he/she expects to find. In addition, we have to remember that generality tends to compensate for improbability, as Spence wryly observes (ibid.).

Last, but not least, as there is no definite evidence that analysis or any other form of therapy makes any difference to the ill-defined condition we call 'homosexuality', the question has to be asked: how do we look upon homosexuality? Is it to be regarded as a disorder, a disease, a perversion or, as I have just done, a 'condition', meaning a natural state of being? Are there merely homosexual impulses, such as everybody would experience on account of our 'psychosexual bisexuality' as stipulated by psychoanalysis and frequently encountered in adolescence? And, further, if everybody is to a varying extent prone to such impulses, how can their intensity be measured? If it cannot, then who is a 'homosexual'? That question has not always been quite as difficult to answer as it is today. *It is becoming clear that we cannot assume that there is a base map in the form of a standard sexual development on to which the theme of homosexuality could be mapped.* Furthermore homosexuality is not a sufficiently well-defined entity to be used as a theme for a thematic map. How could we have been so misled as to think that it was ?

In the chapter called 'Psychoanalytic Research on Homosexuality: The Rules of "the Game"?' Stoller comes to the conclusion 'that there is no such thing as homosexuality and therefore there cannot be a unitary theory for etiology, dynamics and treatment' (Stoller, 1985). He goes even further when he explains that he has only used homosexuality as an example to illustrate that psychoanalysis has, so far, failed to establish itself as a science. My position differs from Stoller's in ways that are relevant to the present context.

In the first place the map need not be discarded altogether as long as one remembers that it is based on a myth (Oedipus), its variations and applications from the analytic point of view. It offers *a way of understanding* situations which are met often enough in practice to make it appear *as if it were a causal = 'scientific' explanation* which it cannot be, referring, as the condition does, to overlapping explanatory systems, including the social and cultural.

Second, the importance of a person's motivation in seeking analysis must be considered within a given social context. For example, when Freud began psychoanalysis, it would have taken a brave person to come for treatment for no other reason than homosexuality. In many countries homosexuality was at that time still an indictable offence. It is not surprising that Freud introduced the subject of 'inversion', as he called it, by referring to Plato's fable of the originally bisexual human being. Significantly, he wrote in 1905 that although there were a considerable number of such inverted people there were difficulties in finding out about the exact incidence (*SE 7*: p. 136).

As long as there is a social stigma attached to being homosexual, a person who wishes to be treated for it will to some extent be motivated by social reasons. Alternatively, he may take a pride in belonging to something like a select club and therefore resist change, even if it were theoretically possible. In our day, however, the attitude of more and more people towards homosexuality is becoming almost as tolerant as it was in classical Greece. Although the adolescent whom I mentioned earlier had himself no motivation to change, his mother's reason was that she did not want him to be different from other boys; a purely social motivation.

Third, if motivation depends to some extent on the degree of suffering and suffering on the social climate which, in turn, interacts with a myth (Oedipus and the incest taboo), then 'homosexuality' as a theme on an analytic map can only show up the vagueness of a meaningless label. On the other hand, the idea that an accurate diagnosis depends on recognition of the cause which will lead to successful treatment, stems from an idealized medical model. Logical though the sequence may be, it is not borne out by the history of medicine itself: the successful treatment of malaria with quinine preceded the discovery of the causative parasite.

Four, it is still true to this day that analysts, when in difficulties, tend to fall back on a psychiatric, that is fundamentally medical diagnosis. This is particularly true in the case of 'narcissistic personality disorders' and 'borderline conditions' for which a number of descriptive synonyms and syndromes have been coined which sound as if they were explanations. The first criterion mentioned by the American Diagnostic and Statistical Manual, DSM-III, as quoted by Kernberg in his *Severe Personality Disorders* is 'Clinical usefulness for making treatment and management decisions in a variety of clinical settings' (Kernberg, 1984). Such examples of pragmatism make it hard to understand why Stoller should have singled out analysis among the helping professions for having failed to establish itself as a science (Stoller, op. cit.). However, I find myself in sympathy with him when he castigates analytic colleagues who use pretentious language in their publications in order to appear 'scientific'.

My attempt to make homosexuality the subject of a thematic map had shown up both the vagueness of the diagnostic term for analytic purposes and the absence of a 'base' map of 'normal' sexual development. However, the failure led to the adoption of the interactional map with a temporary theme in the centre (see fig. 12.8, p. 271, below).

Comment on Figures 12.5–7 (type: fantasy)

It is not on account of the dreams on which they are based that these maps qualify as fantasy maps. True, from the dreamer's point of view the topography was partly realistic, partly distorted and partly 'dreamt up' close enough to the definition of a fantasy map (see p. 214). The dreamscapes evoked visual images in me, a common enough occurrence in anyone who listens attentively be it to a story or a dream. The mapping can therefore be regarded as a fantasy about

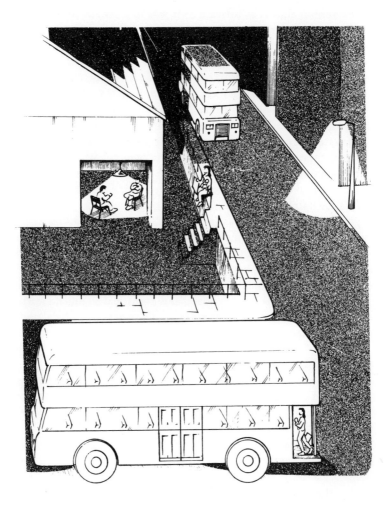

Figure 12.5   A dream map. The dreamer is talking to another man in a basement. A woman is sitting on the pavement, holding her baby in one arm, a manifesto in the other. A conductor is guiding the woman towards a bus. It is night-time

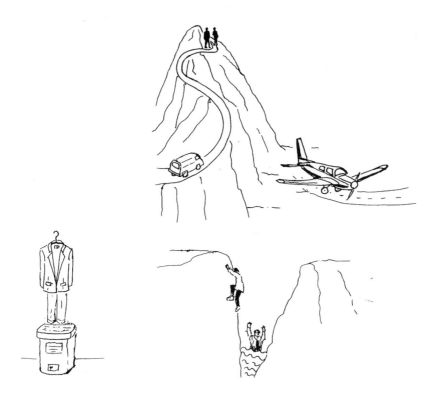

Figure 12.6   A dream map. Two mountaineers have been climbing. One fell into a stream; his suit had to be dried. Then they were on top of a mountain. A bus took them down just in time to catch a plane

a patient's dream. By making my maps public I invite the reader to share in the dream-cum-fantasy product and to make up his/her own fantasy about the illustrations.

I reduced the usual verbal report to a minimum in the legends, the reason being that I wanted to emphasize the spatial and environmental 'feel' of the situations. Another way would have been to encourage the patient to illustrate their dreams. This is not uncommonly done by analytical psychologists, and some patients will do it spontaneously. It can happen that the dream gains new dimensions and significance in this way. But the intention behind my fantasy mapping is different: it is to enable the analyst to enter the dream in a way that differs from the usual empathy, reverie, associations and thoughts. The maps of the dreamscapes help me to get to know where the dreamer really lives, that is in what sort of space rather than location, and where I therefore have to go to meet him/her. The method is therefore more restrained than Meltzer's 'While you were telling me your dream, I had a dream...', quoted on p. 36. *I had kept these fantasy maps to myself in order not to prejudice the events and conditions of the journey ahead.* Maps and prognostications that prove wrong can be a useful aid to self-analysis.

If I had not drawn up the fantasy maps relating to the dreams I would have paid little attention to the town-and-landscape aspects, nor to the time of day and the relatively large part that the 'elements', earth, air, water and fire play. The three levels on which the dreams took place, below, on and above the ground and their relationship to each other might also have escaped my notice, and also the emphasis on vehicles, bus, coach and plane as means of public communication. Instead, the human figures and animals would have been the primary focus of my interest. Indeed, without these there would have been no movement or action. But if the three dreams are looked at together, the three-dimensional topographical element becomes striking. Jung wrote about dreams which seemed to belong together, as a dream series. In the present context it is of particular interest that Jung had observed the water motif recurring in one patient's dreams twenty-six times over a period of two months (*CW 16*: para. 14).

According to an analytic tradition, the manifest content of dreams, hence also the topography, would be of little importance other than to disguise the true but latent meaning. However, Jung's notion that dreams are sometimes better understood as metaphorical statements about the dreamer's *present situation is now more widely recognized.*

My proposition that the location of dreams points to an ancient mode of orientation is supported by the poetic language of the *I-Ching*, the Chinese oracle or 'The Book of Changes' (*I-Ching*, 1951). (When consulted the oracle responds by means of ideograms composed of eight 'male' and/or 'female' lines'. These are combined into hexagrams and transformed into images from which the oracular 'judgements' are derived.) What matters here is that despite the intricate construction of the oracle the essentially simple imagery is composed of nature-given elements, such as heaven and earth, thunder and water, mountain and wind, fire and lake in their ever-changing *spatial and seasonal relation to each other.* In addition, these elementary units are not only endowed or compared with human qualities, but also linked with the relative position and characteristics of eight members of the family to each other. For example, heaven is associated with 'strong' and father, earth with 'devoted', 'yielding' and mother. Whatever we may think of these stereotyped attributes, there can be no doubt that the ideographic combinations of natural elements which make up the images of the *I-Ching* are in keeping with the significance of cosmological symbols discussed and illustrated in the previous chapter. The

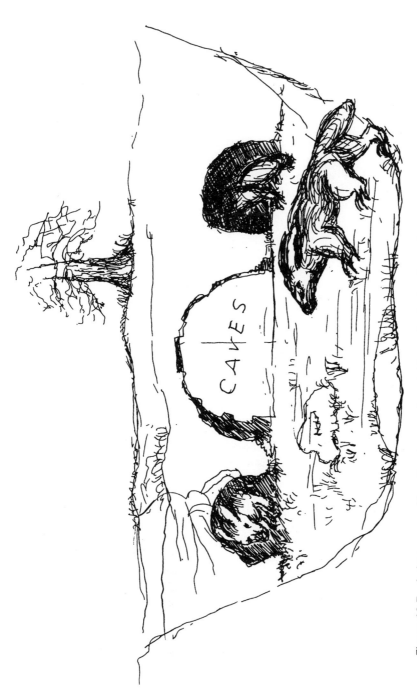

Figure 12.7 A dream map. Here the dreamer is watching animals, 'a mixture between a hare and a fox' going in and out of underground caves, really a warren. He calls his son to come and watch (The dreamer was a town dweller)

images by which the oracle answers the enquirer can be regarded as 'inner maps' because they are built up of cosmological symbols and refer to changes, that is movement; travelling as such is often referred to. It will be recalled that both were among the criteria of inner maps discussed in Chapter 11 (p. 216, above). It can now be claimed that the kind of situational dreams here mapped are the equivalent of the dreamer's inner map and search for orientation. This seems to justify the conclusion that we are still connected with a part of humanity's early orientating equipment to which I referred as *spatiality*. It seems possible to re-enter this domain by means of one's imaginative participation and, in particular, by using one's fantasy to design maps.

However, the role of humans other than members of the 'family' both in the mapped dreams as well as in the *I-Ching* is not to be overlooked. In the book they play archetypal roles, for example princes, wise men and fools. Animals too play an important part. These, as indeed in western fables, are often endowed with human characteristics, but caution is indicated: the attributes can differ from the conventions to which we are used. Who, for example, would have associated the cock with 'the Gentle' but with pervasiveness and penetration too and therefore with the wind; and even more surprisingly, also with the eldest of the three daughters? It follows that one has to be conversant with the cosmology one is dealing with. Certainly, the mixture of fox and hare represented in fig. 12.7 would be hard to place into any ready-made context. I have quoted the *I-Ching* as representation of a cosmos that is vast and comprehensive and, like analysis, focused on human relations. Neither can be understood outside their context, be it western or eastern, including the natural and political environment.

A little nearer home and closer to analysis is Searles who drew attention to the importance of the subject of locality in his *The Non-Human Environment* and to the role the natural environment plays in mental imagery. He recalls how vividly he experienced grief during his analysis when he became aware that the house in which he had grown up was lost to him for ever (Searles, 1960). Analysts would have difficulty not to interpret this as displaced grief about the loss of his mother. It is not that they are mistaken in their interpretation, but by excluding the significance which the *house as such* had for the patient, their understanding of the patient's inner map is reduced. Searles goes on to speak of our love of gardening and frequenting the familiar haunts of nature, and the enjoyment of active sports which bring us closer to it as well as the landscapes and animals, in fact, all features that 'well up in our dreams from our innermost beings' (ibid.).

Although analysts would agree with Pope that 'the proper study of mankind is man', it is also true that our very beings are inextricably bound up with nature which is not only made use of as building blocks for dream- and fantasy-images, but also inseparable from our emotional life.

There is evidence of a biological and embryological kind which shows that in the process of our evolution not all our past equipment has disappeared. For better or worse, without it we cannot only function on the cortical level of our brains. No matter how we think of the body–mind connection, it would seem rash to assume that the phenomena we call psychological are not also emotionally linked with our natural environment. Like the impulse to orientate ourselves in space (spatiality) our reaction to that environment is not merely 'primitive' or atavistic, to be excluded from the 'proper study', just because such phenomena are not transformed by verbal interpretations from 'unconscious' contents into reasonable, secondary mental processes.

AN INTERACTIONAL MAP FOR OBSERVING MOVEMENTS WITHIN THE ANALYTIC PROCESS

Although attempts have been made to analyze individual analytic sessions by means of vignettes, possibly aided by mechanical recordings, there is an important distinction to be made between using such case illustrations in support of a theory or, vice versa, to illustrate a point of view (vertex) from which the phenomena were looked at. (It is the latter I am concerned with throughout this book.) Even the most vividly described dream followed by ingenious and convincing interpretations, all of gem quality at the time, often turns out to have no lasting effect and few are actually remembered after some years have elapsed, as reviewing one's 'dream books' shows.

If we find ourselves as previously mentioned, on shifting sands (see p. 59), how can we get on to firmer ground? The recognition of a general recurring pattern of interactions between various 'layers' and centres within each person (intrapsychic) as well as of the conditions required for intimate meetings between the persons (interpersonal) seems to offer a more enduring basis for the observation and understanding of individual variations. The interactional map of analysis is more solidly based than different analytic theories regarding the meaning of 'unconscious' material, such as dreams, would lead one to believe. Thus when analysts meet in a relaxed private atmosphere they all appear to have met the same patient, that is the problems met in analysis are comparable. When they defend established theories on a public platform, the area of agreement appears to have vanished (see Table of Equivalents, p. 331, below).

This comment on patterns of interaction in which agreement among analysts can be found, is not meant to fudge existing theoretical differences, nor to suggest that it would be a good thing if all differences were suddenly to disappear. But what happens among analysts can be taken as a model of interaction that varies with the circumstances, including the location of the meeting. At any rate, the happenings I described are common enough not to be regarded as pathological. Now, in analysis the environmental conditions are kept as steady as possible, the better to observe the variations. Such variations can then be looked at as functions of the intricate pattern of relationship between the participants which can be graphically recorded without however becoming 'objective'.

In the intricacies of the analyst–patient interaction we have a situation which begins with the unfolding of an intrapsychic theme in the patient. Whether this be regarded as 'a complex', 'a conflict', a mythological motif or an 'unconscious fantasy' does not appear as important as how, in detail, by what technique, it is negotiated in practice. Are the patient's eyes to be opened by the analysis of resistances that have made illusions preferable to seeing a painful but potentially liberating reality? Or is it hoped that the patient's eyes will be opened by the truth of a metaphor or parable, such as the beam and the mote of self-knowledge and its application to the present situation?

If the way I put these questions is taken as a rather pointed indicator of the difference between a 'Freudian' and a 'Jungian' or any other vertex and technique and yet agreement can, as I suggested, prevail over *fundamental patterns of analytic interaction*, then the latter must, in practice, be more important than the differences. An attempt can therefore be made to map the hypothetical processes of interaction.

Comment on Figure 12.8 (the interactional map)

Technically speaking, this map, like the map in Fig. 14.1 (p. 322 below), is a 'cartogram', that is a mixture between a map which refers to some territory and a diagram where the space available is subject to arbitrary utilization. Here I am following cartographers Robinson and Petchenick's definition and find myself supported by Arnheim whom they quote: '*All perceiving is also thinking, all reasoning is also intuition, all observation is also invention*' (op. cit.). At this point the main purpose behind the mapping of analysis may well bear repeating. *By making use of an unaccustomed method of graphic representation it is hoped to make recognizable what happens in practice, to make visible the aims and means of our explorings so that they can become communicable to other interested persons.*

As mentioned earlier the interactional map resulted from the failure to construct a thematic map (cf. Fig. 12.4). The latter, it will be remembered, had been designed to be a map on the theme of male homosexuality and was based on the notion of a 'normal' sexual development from which it was a supposed deviation. In view of the theoretical considerations, it seemed at first possible to construct a map based on the notion of intrapsychic processes in the patient combined with the fluctuating transferences between analyst and patient on the other. Eventually, the interactional map (see Fig. 12.8) became the base map and the constellated theme (T), the focal point of the map would, for the time being, replace the former diagnostic category, such as homosexuality. The difference is that the name of the theme would not be a ready-made diagnostic label, but rather the specific product of the analyst–patient interaction. It is referred to as the 'thematic centre' and surrounding territory, to be presently

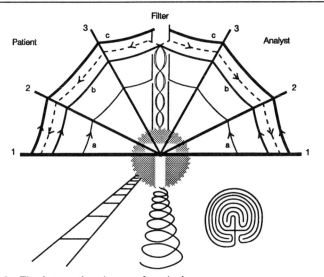

Figure 12.8   The interactional map of analysis

described in detail. The lower half of the map will be referred to under 'How to get there' (p. 281).

The upper part

The upper half of the map represents *a relational matrix*. This term was coined by Mitchell in his *Relational Concepts in Psychoanalysis* (Mitchell, 1988). Here I am applying it to both the intrapsychic and the interpersonal area of observation. For the sake of simplicity this portion of the map has been divided arbitrarily by six lines, three on either side of a double line which divides the patient's side from that of the analyst. Let it be called after its function 'the filter'. It involves the transference but also the analytic relationship in a wider sense. (More about the filter on p. 274, below).

There are three lines on either side of the filter which meet at a central point of the T (theme). They represent 'levels' or layers of the mind and are potentially connected with each other by a series of loops, here three (a–c). Communication within each layer is limitless. The lowest of the three horizontal lines is heavier than the others and meant to represent a layer of the 'mind', a reservoir which is image- and therefore name-less. This is in keeping with Jung who infers that there are 'psychoid functions', no more capable of consciousness than the archetype as such (*CW 8*: para. 382). Bion's 'beta-elements', which are 'extremely primitive', mean much the same thing (Bion, 1963). We may think of it as the physiological substratum to all mental activity. It is implied that hypothetical driving forces belong here such as instincts and archetypes, not directly perceptible by the senses. If they were, the kinaesthetic would, in my view, be the first. Phenomena such as some physical illnesses have been postulated to arise from this region of psychological invisibility.

When these 'elements' become representable in the form of images that can be shared, we are in the realm of the second layer of mental phenomena. Their first appearance may be, as Jung describes, in the form of relatively fixed symbols the appearance of which in dreams can be of great diagnostic and prognostic value and point to a connection with the psychoid substratum. Jung gives the example of a horse jumping out of a window in the anxiety dream of a young girl which made him diagnose organic disease correctly (*CW 16*: para. 343). At any rate, the second or middle line on *the patient's side* is meant to represent dreams, fantasies and the like.

The second is linked with the third layer at hypothetical points by a heavier connecting loop or cable which represents selected as well as spontaneous verbal and non-verbal communications made in the course of an analytic session. This 'material' may vary widely, ranging from dreams to reports about the weather and traffic, reasons for being late or early, people and things encountered on the way, thoughts and feelings about the previous session or meeting with others, and what they said and how the patient felt and reacted. Further belonging to this category are actions, reactions and occurrences, for example events at the place of work. So does the patient's 'input' by way of media which affect patients, arising from outside their personal surroundings. All these demand to be assimilated as for example an assassination or a war. Compare, for example, Hubback's 'The assassination of Robert Kennedy: Patients' and analysts' reactions' (Hubback, 1970). If I enumerate this category of events here, it is because it is not analytically recognized unlike the fascinating staple diet of dreams. Yet the way the events are assimilated (digested) or got rid of (excreted) is analytically as important as the most ingenious interpretation of dreams.

In a case I have in mind, there seemed to be a missing link (b) between layers 1 and 2. The usual transformation from the nameless and imageless layer 1 to that of images 2 appeared to be defective. An existing connection from 1(a) was inferred because of psychosomatic symptoms and from 1(c) because the patient regarded symbols as having a fixed meaning which one could look up in a book. In the example, neither loops (a) nor (c) really made contact with the other, that is the analyst's, side although attempts to 'get through' were noticeable. What did get through is line (b), the dreams. The crucial line is the dotted one which runs as a feedback in the opposite direction through all the layers to the psychoid 1. When this happens it appears as a significant event in analysis.

Turning now to the lowest line on *the analyst's side* it will be seen that it corresponds exactly to its opposite number on the patient's side.

The second line represents the analyst's personal life. I call it that in contradistinction to the corresponding category on the side of the patient, not because analysts are in any way different but because their dreams and the like do not overtly become part of the interaction which is primarily designed for the patient's benefit. The personal life does, however, willy-nilly enter, if only on account of sickness, holidays and family matters. If there is a major crisis in the analyst's life, for example, serious illness, death or divorce and he/she nevertheless decides to carry on working, it would in some cases be essential to let the patient know what is up and decide whether it is possible to continue or whether the patient would be better advised to wait or to work with another analyst. In any case the analyst must consult a colleague, either for supervision or a period of further analysis.

The contingency is mentioned here, because the interactional map would then have to be connected with a second identical map in which the analyst is the patient, working with another analyst. This is in any case the situation when analysts are in training and patients know about it, as I think they ought to. (I do not know of an instance where such knowledge has prejudiced the analytic work.)

Ordinarily, however, the analyst's private life is regarded as a taboo area because any information arising from it may well interfere with the proper concern of the patient's analysis, particularly transference projections. Nevertheless, patients are as curious and shy about it as children are about the sexual and emotional life of their parents and for much the same reasons. The case of the sick analyst also illustrates the close link between the data represented by all (three) layers of the map and their influence on each other as well as on the data fed through to the filter of communication and back again.

The third line on the analyst's side is called 'professional equipment' and deserves special consideration, although ordinary human 'empathy' remains quite the most important item. For practical purposes I mean the ability to remain aware that the patient, no matter how different, is above all a suffering fellow creature. The additional implements consist of theories and analytic rules and techniques, as well as digesting one's reading, participating in seminars and discussions with colleagues; also, reflecting on the context of the work, special points of interest and writing.

In the situation mapped here I have assumed that the professional equipment had become too heavy. Consequently, line 3 did not get through the filter any more than the corresponding line of chatter on the patient's side; both remained barriers. What did get through is line (b), the dreams. This is more likely to happen when all the analyst has learned and absorbed from his/her own analysis has been amalgamated with the professional equipment so that it is now part of him/herself. Even though this self remains subject to (a) varying influences arising from the first and second lines or categories and (b) whatever his/her feelings, intuitions and so forth, about the patient are. It is therefore unrealistic to think of the analyst as a well-polished mirror or in terms of similar metaphors which are meant to convey that he/she is or tries to be in a state of perfectly balanced neutrality and also 'without memory and desire' towards the patients, as if he/she had no spontaneous recollection of previous sessions nor any fantasy or wish regarding favourable developments. She or he is merely *prepared* to know about such desires in order to be able to suspend them. Nevertheless, fear of the unknown attacks the analyst almost as much as the patient and can cause him/her to use the equipment as an armour, to paraphrase Bion (1963). When this happens, patients are frequently able to spot it, although they do not necessarily say so at the time, any more than children do at the stage when they identify with an anxious or embarrassed parent.

The filter of communication

The filter is an imaginative construct designed to make the circumstances visible in which real communication between patient and analyst can take place. It is mapped here as a double membrane the permeability of which on either side is symbolized by openings at irregular distances (refer to the enlarged insets, figs 12.9 and 12.10). It is essential that the position of the holes is not fixed but varies according to a relatively small number of criteria of which examples shall presently be given.

When there is no corresponding opening on the other side the loop carrying a message remains as a 'loose end' in the filter or becomes transformed into another mode of communication to join up with the opposite side when an opening occurs. This may come about for example when the analyst acquires a new viewpoint or 'vertex'. A communication is then established that can flow back to and modify all other strata. The plaited vertical line from the node of communication to the thematic centre is discussed below.

Determinants of communication

The advantage of visualizing and thinking about communication in terms of openings or blockages in both membranes of the filter is that it helps to cut down a multitude of theoretical possibilities to only a few which are deemed relevant in the current case. In my view psychoanalytic theories can account for blockages more easily than for passages; in analytical psychology the converse holds good. The reason why a blockage is easy to spot is because 'defences' and 'resistances' are the theoretical stock-in-trade explanation. The relational matrix on the other hand helps to focus on conditions in which relevant communication *does* occur. The 'feel' of the transference is not of itself a reliable guide. Is it to be called 'positive' when the patient is in a highly suggestible state and seems to swallow everything the analyst says? (See also 'Suggestion', above, p. 69.) Or, conversely, 'negative' because nothing I say seems to be right but when I say nothing it is certainly wrong. The labels 'positive' and 'negative' are merely descriptions of prevailing affective states, but give no indication of the complex psychodynamics which they apparently

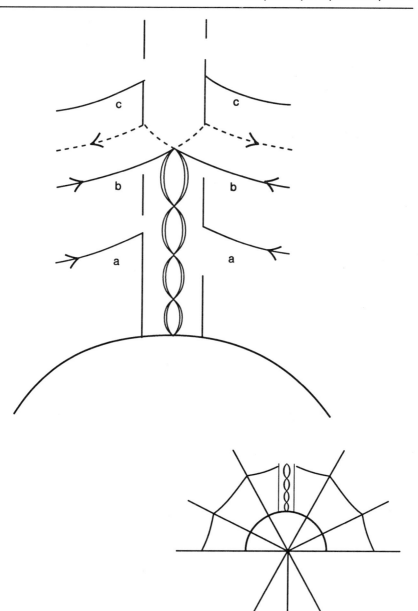

Figures 12.9–10   Details of fig. 12.8

summarize. I shall therefore return to the interactional map in which the filter plays a crucial part and use a narcissistic state as an example of extremely limited communication. In this state the aptness of an analytic interpretation is not the decisive factor for getting through, no matter how well founded it may be. The opening of the filter is contingent on the simple perception: 'does the analyst say he/she likes or dislikes me?' The response varies accordingly in that the filter either opens or shuts.

Equally typical responses on the analyst's side would be not to take in anything the patient says when it does not seem grist to the analytic mill, as, for example, when the patient's message is classified as merely conscious material, defensively camouflaging the guarded, unconscious meaning. Alternatively, an interpretation that the analyst offers which falls either on deaf ears or is vehemently rejected could easily be regarded as having been to the point, just *because* it was rejected. True, the interpretation must have been received to meet with a negative response. But it is not warranted to conclude that therefore it must have been right, thus confirming the theory of 'resistance'.

Some questions outstanding can no longer be shelved. These do not concern the therapeutic result of analysis, nor *whether* transformations or 'change', as always assumed to be change for the better, does come about but: *how, in detail, does analytic communication work?* A second and closely related question is: *If anything that can be called an aim has been achieved, how, if at all, is it related to the communication between the partners?* Of course, there are plenty of answers available such as making the unconscious conscious, strengthening the ego, resolution of conflict and of the transference, and so on, but these are no more than restatements of analytic preconceptions. Or, alternatively, the assumption is offered that the personality of the analyst is more important, contributes more to the outcome, than any particular theory or technique (see p. 119, above). There is truth in all of this, but it leaves curiosity totally unsatisfied. As no agreed or generally acceptable answer has so far been forthcoming, a speculative map such as fig. 12.8 may help to clarify the above questions and conceivably point to fruitful areas of research.

A note on the graphics used

It is in the nature of this medium to produce regular symmetrical outlines, when irregular, broken up and asymmetrical shapes would be much more in keeping with the course of analysis. Symmetries are indicative of abstract thinking and should therefore be regarded as artefacts. However, computer graphics tend to produce straight rather than broken irregular lines, and geometrical and symmetrical rather than irregular shapes.

The thematic centre

The significance of the thematic centre is two-fold:

1 as a temporary theme or topic of analysis which is variable, while the 'matrix' surrounding it is regarded as a constant;
2 the theme is also the analytic working pattern characteristic of the individual patient and analyst. It can be thought of in terms of a person's reaction pattern or type according to Jung's typology;
3 the thematic centre is frequently related to the 'mutual transference' first described in Chapter 2 (p. 27f above).

It must be recalled that this map remains nothing more than a graphic expression of speculations about the detailed steps which make up the analytic process. There is, nevertheless, an observational underpinning to the speculations.

Let us assume then that the kind of interaction to which the upper half of the map refers has been in progress for some time and that a steady frame for analytic exchanges has been built up. The interactional map, Fig. 12.8, shows that the loop which got through established contact. A new cable arises at the nodal point of crossing, shown plaited here to indicate that it is composed of contributions from both partners. This joint cable continues toward the small innermost circle at the junction of the 'T', standing for theme, where layers 1–3 also meet. It represents the germinal point of the thematic territory which accresces around it. It is aided by the centre- and meaning-seeking intrapsychic and interpersonal contributions which, acting like intense focusing beams, seem to stimulate the specific growing point. Having been constellated in this fashion, the thematic territory seems to gain an autonomy of its own. Everything that happens in the analytic session now appears for the time being to have a bearing on the central theme.

Jung refers to this phenomenon as *'synchronicity'* which he describes as an a-causal connecting principle of *meaningful coincidence* (*CW 8*: paras 816–968, see also p. 31). Such coincidences occur also outside analysis and can be truly startling. But analysis offers the better facility for observing and connecting the events with the psychological state of the experiencing person(s). I think it is often possible to discover a complex but nevertheless *causal network that accounts for apparent coincidences*, although precisely *why* a thematic central territory should gain dominance is not explained by mapping *how* a hypothetical interaction works.

An example

Here is a case in point which will to some extent flesh in the interactional map. The illustration is shorn of most of the colourful detail for reasons mentioned earlier. I have also omitted the history of the patient and her ailment in order to prevent identification and to concentrate on the origin and effect of the thematic centre as observed in analysis.

The difficulty in this case was that no thematic centre could be established because I could not say anything at all that would be acceptable to the patient who had a way of demolishing all my words. The theme was hidden behind the transference. If my words conveyed any understanding she would reject the implicit sympathy by saying that my feelings were a sham and what I was really interested in was her money. At other times the interpretations I offered were taken as a criticism to which she reacted with pain and rage, as described above. When occasionally I was able to strike a note that seemed neutral enough, the patient replied that she knew all that from her own reading. When I tried to make our lack of communication into the theme, the patient retorted that I was unable to bear my frustration of not being able to help her. It looked as if I were limited to functioning as the recipient of her anguish and rage and this state of affairs continued for many months. In terms of the interactional map, the filter seemed impermeable.

Intrapsychically, there was a curious gap between the patient and her dreams of which she reported many with detached curiosity. She also had associations. But when I tried to make links between her dreams and waking life the patient repeatedly said that she could not understand what I said.

Yet there were signs that she depended on me and of great anxiety about losing me, either by my throwing her out or by dying. This and the development of a distressing psychosomatic symptom, told me that something was stirring in the psychoid layer of her personality. But how to translate these signals into a communication that could be further transformed into imagery and words that might serve communication and allay her anxiety? Time and again any attempt to do so fell prey to formidable intellectual reasoning.

Her relation to her own body was so poor that, if it was not causing her distress, she experienced it as if it did not belong to her. Certainly she felt no joy in it.

Similarly, her movements and gait were unrelaxed. When one day during a crying spell I touched her shoulder in a comforting gesture, it felt as if I was touching a statue. The unspoken message was paradoxical: a craving for warmth combined with a touch-me-not attitude. Yet in her ordinary dealings with impersonal situations she had achieved a mastery which had earned her the praise of her parents and teachers. She had no recollection of ever having played imaginatively with other children.

A gradual change could be dated back to the time when once before my holiday – a time she particularly dreaded – I lent her something for which she had expressed a liking and which she could accept with a smile. She had guessed that I had made an exception to the analytic rules, see line 3 on the analyst's side of the map. My action was informed by line 1, the psychoid layer of Fig. 12.8.

As the result of my drawing up this map it dawned on me that the patient's fury had been directed against the communication between the layers of the psyche that functioned within me but not in her. I was reminded of Bion's famous paper 'Attacks on linking' (Bion, 1959). It was a degree of integration she desperately wanted but she had no means of expressing her need other than by destructive attacks. When I had allowed myself to act in a way that showed a certain spontaneous functioning by forgetting about a rule of analysis and lent her a personal article she felt relieved and less isolated than before. *By mapping I gained a deeper understanding of the interdependence between what happens within a person and between persons.*

Taking theory into account, it can be seen that my 'discovery' is in agreement with what Bion further wrote concerning 'attacks on linking' (Bion, 1965). But the way I arrived at my conclusion is significantly different. Bion's argument starts from the Kleinian view of an infant who, unable to bear the frustration of an absent breast, reacts by reducing it to a mere position where the breast had been, a 'no-breast' represented by the visual image of a point, as Bion writes (ibid.) (see also 'no-thing', p. 315 below). In my view this is an explanatory myth which is plausible because it apparently begins with the mental life of the infant and leads via analytic theory of mental growth to a personality that can appreciate time and space. My appreciation of the problematic which Bion refers to begins with an infant who has got a rudimentary sense of space. It leaves the causal explanation uncertain. My assumption is that even before birth, infants and their expectant mothers too, vary to a considerable degree in their disposition to tolerate frustration. What really matters is that despite different theoretical positions the crucial practical point remains how the patient's ability to tolerate the frustration of absent objects could be increased. Significantly the subject of tolerance is mentioned twice on the same page of Bion's book (op. cit.) I have already referred to this in connection with individuation (see above, p. 182).

Returning now to the situation with the patient I had used to illustrate my viewpoint. It seemed remarkable that when we resumed after the break she was able to speak of fantasies about which she had felt too ashamed to speak. What is more they were not just dumped as before, when she had treated such matters as if they had nothing to do with her. At that time she also asked for a particular blanket to be put back on the couch that had been lying there earlier on. She also became less punctilious about time and payment of fees. Although I am aware that this could be classed as 'regression', I regarded it as progress towards greater tolerance of the limits imposed by the analytic relationship.

As to my own contribution to the previous stalemate, the patient had not been altogether wrong: I had frequently felt persecuted by her and helpless, as well as driven to the edge of despair and angry about her destructive attacks on the analytic work. At one time I had become seriously worried about her destructiveness and my sleep became disturbed.

The patient had also been right in that I did occasionally feel the impulse to stop the analysis but never actually planned to do so. What stopped me was not so much fear of the consequences as the frustrating combination of an enduring interest combined with the knowledge that she was suffering, not least of all from remorse after her attacks. I had attempted the usual interpretative work intended to create links between past and present experiences as they became noticeable in the transference situation. But no corresponding opening on both sides of 'the filter' could be found on any level until the turning point mentioned had been passed and she felt sure that I was adequately involved and she was accepted by me as she was, without having to please. This brought about a considerable change in her self-image and in the working alliance.

We are now ready to *sum up the upper half of the interactional map of analysis* in general and with particular reference to the example, it consists of the following:

1   A relational matrix, comprising intrapsychic and interpersonal communications. These form a network that is assumed to be present even at a time when apparently no link between the layers of psychological functioning exists and no working alliance has been established.

2   A hypothetical filter, the permeability of which varies according to certain conditions. Being linked is frequently an essential criterion on the patient's side, although the example was an extreme case. Analysts, by virtue of their position and knowledge, are better equipped to remain receptive under various conditions and to find something likeable in most patients as they get to know about their mutuality.

3   A 'cable' of joint contributions has been imaged to run between the layers of the filter towards a central point or focus of the theme. The lines of separate psychological functioning are also seen to converge toward this point from both sides. *In the example the theme is the quest for basic trust.* (The genetic basis of distrust has been omitted from the example.)

   From this point a surrounding area of influence develops until it seems to dominate the whole of the map. In this case a feeling of cooperation and partnership gained ascendancy over disruptive emotional flare-ups. Another criterion was that various events, such as a series of dreams or spontaneous, unaccustomed behaviour began to spell out the same message of relief. The gain does not always last. Other themes are likely to turn up in due course. But whatever the central theme may be, it influences and often nourishes in its turn the relational matrix from which it sprang. Differently put, the theme can exert a beneficial influence by holding the patient together, promoting at the same time real communication between the two persons involved.

4   The interactional map has replaced thematic map 12.4. A relational matrix has taken the place of the base map (p. 270, above). The specific theme is represented as the central territory in the interactional map.

Finally, a caution about my gesture that became the undramatic turning point in our example. It must not be taken for a recipe or short cut: without wading and working through the slough of distrust we could not have reached that point.

HOW TO GET THERE

The lower half of the map illustrates three spatial models of the analytic process. The three I have selected are already known to the reader as cosmological symbols (see p. 225, above). These models must not be mistaken for theories of which there are plenty and new ones are spawned at frequent intervals. Some of these have been mapped under the heading: 'Where does analysis stand?' in Chapter 14 (see p. 306). But let us look first at simpler notions about how analysis is envisioned, including some barely formulated assumptions which nevertheless exert a subtle control over the relational matrix. However imprecise these may be, it would be unrealistic to expect patients not to have some basic assumptions about progress in analysis, what the way to the centre looks like and what it feels like to reach it. Some assumptions can be seen as a continuation of those anticipated in the beginning in Fig. 12.1 (p. 253 above). It is not as if analysts were free from comparable assumptions and simplifications. The 'global aims' described earlier belong here. But analysts have also given thought to repeated relational experience and built up central concepts and personal variations of vertices of greater variety and complexity than can be shown on any single map.

Although the lower half of Fig. 12.8 appears to be quite different and separate from the top, it should be regarded as being part and parcel of it. The appearance is due to my not wanting to clutter up the map with models that suggest how communication between the hypothetical layers of the psyche may be thought of. The three cosmological symbols are regarded as models of the analytic process. Thus we have the ladder indicating linear ascent, the spiral standing for concentricity and the labyrinth as a composite of centripetal and centrifugal movements.

The ladder has been placed on the patient's side of the map because it represents the idea of a straightforward ascent, that is from a state of disorientation upwards by a number of rungs of learning/living experiences on to the heart of analysis. If this notion appears naïve to analysts, I shall want to recall how after a few months of my first analysis I asked my analyst when we would come to the archetypes. At that time this meant promotion to a higher rung of the ladder.

Analysts would be more inclined to look upon a *rising spiral* as a model on which progress could be marked by a point on the spiral that appears time and again in circular fashion except that the diameter of the spiral constantly narrows as the virtual centre is approached. The concentric movement, so it was hoped, would bring with it an increment of consciousness, an integration

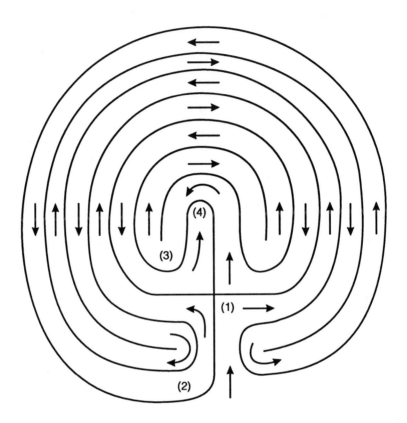

Figure 12.11   Directional changes in the labyrinth

of the personality and eventually individuation or by whatever name the ultimate goal of the process be known.

The *labyrinth* represents a much more sophisticated model of approach to the centre and one that corresponds more closely to the course of events in and out of analysis. The labyrinth, see fig. 12.11, is of the Cretan type, with seven windings. Many more would have to be added if one wanted to chart a whole analysis, but the principle would be the same, that is a path marked by pendulum movements represented by the turnings in the structure on the way to a virtual centre. Three phasic movements of the path have been mapped.

1   The entrance in the right lower quadrant leads past two windings straight up to the corner of the central cross. This is reminiscent of some analyses when right in the first session the central theme becomes noticeable,

although the full significance can only be appreciated in retrospect. After the first winding the path becomes centrifugal, i.e. it opens outwards as if surveying the periphery, comparable to telling a life history or background.

2   Next, a new inward movement begins in the left lower quadrant and spans both upper quadrants until the path is only separated from the centre by one partition. Suddenly, it seems to have dawned that the inner life of dreams and the like was at least as important as the description of parents and all the outer circumstances.

3   A further centrifugal movement takes the path through two windings in the upper quadrants before the final turning inward ends in the centre. It looks as if the patient had taken fright about getting into deep waters but then realizes that there is no escape.

Commenting further on the labyrinth as a model of the analytic path, we note that it has much in common with other rhythms occurring in nature such as the ebb and flow, contraction and dilation, inhalation and exhalation, the systolic and diastolic movements of the heart muscle etc. Fordham's hypothesis of integrating and deintegrating phases of the self (see p. 23 above) suggests how the movements in the labyrinth can be related to analytic observations. The outstanding questions remain: what constitutes a centre in the analytic sense and what happens to a person who reaches it? The short answer to both questions is that the analytic centre is a Utopia, a non-existent place (see 'global aims', p. 53f, also 'individuation', p. 145). If we were to look at the fate of the hero and heroine in the drama of individuation as portrayed in Chapter 9, we would answer the second question by saying that arrival at the centre coincides with death. No wonder we try to 'resist' such arrivals.

Chapter 13

Some reflections on the Klein–Jungian hybrid

This chapter is based on an unpublished paper read thirty years ago to the Society of Analytical Psychology, London, at one of the monthly meetings open to members and trainees. A change in the orientation of that group of 'Jungians' had begun as they became more and more interested in the psychology of Melanie Klein. I was, and still am, part of the experiment – never designed as such – which seemed to me an attempt at hybridization, the outcome of which is still uncertain. It is, however, continuing as Zinkin's recent paper 'The Klein connection in the London school' shows (Zinkin, 1991). Whatever it was that gave rise to the experiment, the unscripted hypothesis seemed to be that two schools of analysis could be combined by 'cross-fertilization' and that the upshot would be better than each of the constituents. The 'experiment' was however unofficial and then only undertaken by one of the parties although, still more unofficially, an interaction is likely to have affected the other (Kleinian) side as well. The paper was written at the time strictly for 'home-consumption'. As it happens, the issues involved, that is the choice between splits and amalgamations have begun to affect other institutes of analytical psychology as well as the wider world of psychoanalysis, as Wallerstein's paper quoted earlier and the search for common ground among the different 'directions' bear out (Wallerstein, op. cit.).

Except for some subediting, rephrasing and abbreviating I have not changed the content of the paper. Instead it has been updated by means of interspersed comments set in and printed in italics. The reason for putting the paper into Part III of the book is that in several respects it will serve as a case in point for the subject and mapping of the last chapter 'Where does analysis stand?'.

A hybrid is supposed to be the offspring of two beings of different species; another definition has it that it is a thing composed of incongruous elements. It is my object to examine to a limited extent the nature of the mixture of Kleinian and Jungian psychology which is prevalent in our Society today. That this is an accomplished fact may be doubted by some but I shall briefly present what I regard as evidence of it being the case.

In recent years there has been an increasing amount of interest expressed by our trainees in Kleinian psychology. This sometimes takes the form of requests for translating from one terminology into the other. There have also been a considerable number of references to the Kleinian school in publications by our members. Thirdly the language by which we communicate with each other, i.e. in the Professional Committee, has changed very considerably in the direction I indicated. Making a summary of the expressions used I found a pretty full inventory of Kleinian terms, in addition to a few psychiatric labels and Jungian concepts. The latter still include expressions like 'symbolic' or 'analytic' attitude and some references to Jung's typology but only a few expressions of archetypal imagery referring to anima, shadow and the self, of which one used to hear a great deal more in the years gone by. It is as if the Kleinian language has become the vernacular while Jungian is spoken on high days and holidays by which I mean when communications are intended to reach ears other than our own.

This tendency has increased during the past thirty years. In 1962 there was a conflict of loyalties involved resulting later in a split similar to the one threatening the Institute of Psychoanalysis and for much the same reason, i.e. the Kleinian development. I felt at the time that the Kleinian tail had begun to wag the Jungian dog, hence also 'Klein–Jung' in the title and not the other way round. Nowadays terms used by Bion, Segal and Meltzer (all in the Kleinian succession) such as vertex, beta- and alpha-elements and the depressive position are freely used by analytical psychologists ('Jungians') publicly and without quotation marks. Perhaps it does not matter much in which language we express ourselves, as long as we can be sure that we mean the same thing. So far it may look as if a developmental (psychoanalytic) vertex could be grafted on to Jung's archetypal psychology. Parallels I have drawn between Jung's luminosities and Klein's part-objects are an example (Plaut, 1974). It is a comparison which relativizes the significance of 'consciousness' as a much-used concept in analytical psychology. There is further the close similarity between Bion's 'preconceptions referring to certain inborn capabilities and expectations', e.g. of mouth meeting breast, and Jung's archetype (Bion, 1967). But the question is whether the theory of archetypes still remains relevant for the practical purpose of analysing when Kleinian terms have become the vernacular. Judging by the technique recommended for training at the Society of Analytical Psychology, London, this has changed from sessions twice a week to four times a week, from chair to couch and, in the case of children, the limited equipment is used which Melanie Klein recommended. What really matters is that we (SAP, London) took over the post-Kleinian interpretative technique to the best of our ability, that is considering that we had not undergone a Kleinian analysis. Whether a separate and distinctly 'Jungian' training institute can survive in these circumstances seems doubtful. But in the event, hybridization may take several generations to devolve.

However, if we look further afield to art, literature, philosophy and other cultural and social disciplines, the theory of archetypes remains invaluable. So it seems as if the branches of analytical psychology had begun to nourish the tree of its knowledge, functioning, as it were, like air-roots. But investigations are also going on at the analytic roots. These take the form of microscopic observations concerning the effect on the patient (and analyst) of interpretations, including particularly transference phenomena in the analytic session. We note that this concentration on small segments also goes back to Bion (op. cit.). It has been taken up by Kleinians as well as Jungians, particularly in cases of 'borderline' psychotic patients.

I take no exception to this changing climate but regard it as a fact which requires our attention. I mean that the background, as well as details resulting from the application of Kleinian terms and the influence on our own attitude and outlook should not be slurred over. If I find Kleinian formulations useful I might easily and not always very consciously take these over into my own way of analysing, but I should consider it my duty to review as soon as I can whether and how my previous frame of reference has been altered by the new incorporations and whether they are in fact compatible with what I previously held. I am not greatly worried by who said this or that first, but I would regard it as slurring over of a difference, if I tried to read into one of the many profound but general statements of Jung's that in fact he meant the same as Mrs Klein's detailed techniques imply. Only an overall assessment and appreciation of the general background to these statements can help one to decide whether they are compatible or not. This is by no means an easy decision to arrive at but one which has to be undertaken for the sake of one's professional self-respect. Temptation must be in the direction of comforting conclusions of sameness or at least of complementarity. In addition, I am inclined to speculate that the different dynamic schools of the twentieth century will all appear much of a muchness to a future historian and it is, of course, commonplace to state that what attracts Jung's and Klein's followers is their common emphasis on man's inner world in contrast to the far greater significance that outer reality has in Freud's work. Why then make a fuss about differences? I already mentioned self-respect which demands an inner consistency of the frame of reference which one applies to one's work. I also have doubts whether a mixture, a form of eclecticism, is as valuable a therapeutic tool as the single incisive orientation. This view needs defending against the further tendency to slur over and be seductive. It runs as follows: 'Each patient is an individual with his different psychology and different needs. It is the psychotherapist's job to adapt himself to these to take the manifestations of health and illness as they come and to follow his patient regardless of his own preferences. These differences according to age group, temperament, upbringing etc., are far more important than the therapist's predilections. Some cases will therefore do better with this or that analyst or this or that form of psychotherapy.' Interested as I am in such hypothetical statements at other times, I regard it as a perfectly useless and indefensible argument when it is meant to prevent more conscious and precise formulations or to suppress the need for continuous research into the nature of our work. Used in this way the argument hinders real communication among ourselves, and between ourselves and other colleagues who work in this field.

Having thus introduced the object of my reflections let me make one other point. I have in mind that the welding together of dynamic schools will occur in the fullness of time, but this is a matter of speculation and of politics. Judging by some statements made by Winnicott, Little and Milner, hybridization has also affected the Kleinian school and one wonders how they manage not to give credit to Jung. But this need not deflect me from my course. What concerns me here is that the pointing out of differences and apparently incongruous elements may serve ultimate fusion just as well as direct attempts to synthesize. Murray Jackson in his address on Jung's archetype issued a warning as follows: 'The common use of such terms as 'ego', 'symbol' and 'self' may be misleading, since differences in their meaning in each school may be crucial' (Jackson, 1960).

I shall presently say more about the background but it is obviously a vast area and I must on this account ask your indulgence if I have to make some generalizations and recapitulate some well-known points. I lack the knowledge of philosophy which would be required to trace some of the roots from which the theories of dynamic psychology spring and on which they tacitly rely. Nevertheless one can sense that ideological differences underlie the apparently purely empirical and clinical case material from which the different principles and theories seem to have been developed. As if observations could be made by completely innocent observers! For the reason Jackson gave, I shall steer clear as far as possible of theoretical definitions which present the ideas *after* they have become set and refined. My plan is to weave back and forth between differences in ideological background and practical details and to see what appreciable differences, if any, will emerge from the pattern.

INNER WORLDS

When speaking about the inner world of Jung, or any other pioneer in the field of dynamic psychology, I mean the total picture which he created of man's psychic life out of the phenomena which he observed on the basis of his particular viewpoint, which in turn is related to his philosophical view of the world ('Weltanschauung'). The total picture is formed by putting the psychological phenomena observed into categories and by connecting these by means of a theory of interaction (dynamism). The endopsychic structure (= hypothetical entities of the inner world) thus created differs from that of Freud generally in that it is also given weight as a motivating force. It seems that with Freud (external) realities on the one hand and instinctual drives on the other come first and out of the impact of these two on an individual the mental 'institutions' were formed, i.e. secondarily. An example of the weighting given by Jung to the inner world would be that he wrote of 'the mother as the first incarnation of the anima archetype' (and not that the anima is derived from the child's mother) (*CW 5*: para. 508, *CW 12*: 92n).

The differences between the importance of original Freudian 'reality' and Jung's inner world have become much less marked in Kleinian psychology. This is particularly borne out by the last sentence of Heimann's paragraph, of which I shall quote more as I go along: 'In order to understand the infant's psychic development and many of his *physical processes*, (!) we must appreciate his unconscious phantasies' (emphasis added) (Heimann, 1955).

It is well known that Freud's theories about infantile sexuality were developed from the analyses of adults. Almost equally well known but sometimes overlooked is the fact that a theory – not only of neurosis – but of normal development of the personality had been born. So that if psychoanalysts now speak of an inner world *we* mean man's inner world and do not imply that it must necessarily be pathological. For Jung, of course, the existence of an inner world was a natural state of affairs and had never been in question and what was later called introversion never had the pathological significance which it had and still has in psychoanalytic quarters. Although he made many discoveries about the psyche which were awe-inspiring, Jung made them on what was by temperament, his home ground. It was a world peopled by images, more real in their effect on humans than the apparently real people in the outer world. I think that his being so much at home in the inner world accounts for the way in which Jung often personifies his theoretical entities, e.g. ego and self: it explains to some extent why there seems to be no clear division between imagery and hypothetical structures. (Psychoanalysts use a special word for this branch of knowledge: 'metapsychology'. Significantly, this is not differentiated in Jung's writings.) This is also the reason why to the less introverted critic a sense of animism adheres to Jung's formulations. I find myself in agreement with Fordham who pointed out that abstract theory and metaphor are frequently intertwined in Jung's statements (Fordham, personal communication).

What then are the main distinguishing features between Jung's and Klein's inner world? I shall only mention two at this juncture. The first results from the fact that Melanie Klein has remained within the psychoanalytic fold, the first and fundamental principle of which is, according to Jones, its strict determinism (Jones, 1953). No chance events occur in the mind which means in practice that the analyst must be able to explain and interpret in detail the cause of every event by means of his frame of reference. And although the centre has shifted in Klein's inner world from the Freudian genitally-determined Oedipal situation to the central relationship between infant and breast the clear relation between cause and effect has remained. The contrast between this 'causa efficiens' and Jung's 'causa finalis' point of view is very striking. Without denying the former Jung has clearly remained preoccupied with the finality of mental events, with the sense of purpose in the manifestations of the unconscious mind. The first implication – there are many – of this difference in outlook is that while a Freudian or Kleinian when confronted with a patient's statement would ask himself: 'By means of what mechanism is he trying to defend himself against a lifting of the amnesia which surrounds his infancy?' Jung would ask 'What is the unconscious trying to tell us in relation to the present life situation?' Being distanced from primary anxieties, Jung regards the territory to be explored as neither friendly nor hostile, but both. Now it seems to me beyond doubt that the Kleinian inner world is first and foremost a hostile murderous place where aggression and anxiety, greed and sadism abound (Guntrip, 1961).

This brings me to the second great difference between inner worlds, which is the degree of bodily involvement. Mental life for Klein is the direct outcome of bodily experiences and processes. It is entirely dependent on it for its image formation and in practice image formation and symbolization are never permitted to stray far from the bodily processes as first experienced in infancy in relation to the mother. Contrast with this Jung's vast and rich phenomenology of the collective unconscious which forms the reservoir on which the individual can draw in order to find his way about in the inner world. This includes, but does not stress, the experience of his own body. All this in the Kleinian view appears to be 'secondary elaboration', 'cultural end-products' etc., while for Jung the body is as real – no more, no less – as any other image in our minds. He certainly does not stress that our ability to perceive and make use of images depends on satisfactory experiences during infancy, although I think it possible that he takes this for granted. It may help to illustrate the difference, if I quoted from a passage entitled 'Unconscious phantasies' (and taken from Heimann's 'A contribution to the re-evaluation of the Oedipus conflict', op. cit.) in order to illustrate this point.

> Unconscious phantasies occur not only in infancy, they are part of the unconscious mind at any time, and form the matrix from which the preconscious and conscious processes develop.

This passage was quoted by Jackson (1960) in his address to the Medical Section of the British Psychological Society, and he wisely refrained from quoting any further, as his purpose was to show how closely the description of unconscious phantasies come to Jung's archetypal images. But for my purpose I had to read a few lines further on.

> They (the unconscious phantasies) are dynamic processes... and... influence the development of ego mechanisms. For example, introjection develops from the infant's unconscious phantasy of incorporating the mother's

breast, which accompanies the desire for the breast and the actual sensation of sucking and swallowing when in contact with it. Conversely, the mechanism of projection develops from the phantasy of expelling an object.

(ibid.)

We can see here to what extent the simple causal chain of Freud's original theories has been modified and lengthened and brought into alignment with Jung's concepts of the archetypal ('formative or spiritual') aspect of instinct. Only the causal connection with the central events at the breast without which ego development cannot proceed would be extraneous to Jung's concepts. Events, that is to say, which are significant because of their literal importance in the past as well as in the transference situation and *not* because they could be regarded as similes or metaphors etc. The practical question which arises immediately is whether the deepest layers of the patient's psyche can be reached by archetypal imagery which is not specifically contrived to reactivate the memory of these infantile events. Heimann, as we have seen, does more than describe a concept. She states the effects it has on the ego in terms of two mechanisms. Once this has been done there is a beginning of a technique, i.e. indications about use of the concept in practice. Jung must have had a horror of doing this and I think this explains why he borrowed terms from other fields of knowledge rather than tie himself to a purely psychological mechanism, e.g. 'participation mystique' from anthropology, 'numen' from theology and 'archetype' from classical philosophy. This difference, which may well be allied to the inner worlds of Jung and Klein in terms of their personal psychology, would better be dealt with under the next heading.

HOW TO REACH THE PATIENT

We saw Heimann stress the developmental function of 'unconscious phantasies' which accompany the physical acts of sucking and excreting from which the psychological mechanisms of introjection and projection are derived. Although these fantasies are close to Jung's archetypal images, the link with the physical processes is not; nor are the implications for technique. True, Jung mentions projection quite frequently and also in connection with ego development but he does not say that the origin of projection lies in the experience of expelling faeces as bad objects. The close linkage between concepts and the precise way in which they work (mechanisms) is a characteristic of psychoanalysis and *not* of analytical psychology. If, for example, I say of a woman that she is 'animus-ridden', I may have given a good description of the kind of person she is (cf. *CW 9, II*: para. 29). If I say that she suffers from 'penis-envy', I have not only added the cause of her trouble in bodily terms but I have given a directive about the practical use of the term, i.e. to bring into consciousness the desire for her father's penis which dates back to the first five years of her life. This desire has to become conscious before she can recover. Nothing else will do.

Similarly if I speak about 'repetition compulsion' in the classical psycho-analytic sense I have given a directive as to the cause and possible cure of a symptom. If I speak of an 'archetypal or 'basic' theme in a patient's life, I leave the door open regarding the possibilities of cause and cure.

As I said earlier 'penis-envy' as a term is derived from the psychopathology of adult patients, but has also become part of a theory of normal development of the structure of personality – it is the degree of envy which makes it pathological. A minus-ridden – the word 'ridden' also implies pathology, but 'animus' not being an anatomical term in the first instance by no means implies that it should not be there as part of a healthy female personality any more than that there should be no 'shadow'. I have used this example to indicate that the Jungian inner world is a much less pathological place and is first and foremost an outline of personality structure. This would seem to be in keeping with the fact that there is far less emphasis on disease in Jung's writings and there is incomparably less stress laid on the means by which we have to defend ourselves against a hostile inner environment resulting from our instinctual urges. It is not surprising since the imagery which forms the mental ('spiritual') counterpart of the so-called 'instincts' constitutes the main body of Jung's writings. What are the effects of this difference on the practice of analysis, i.e. on the methods of reaching the depth of the patient's inner world?

In order to introduce a general answer to a question which deserves to be studied in detail, let me quote Heimann again. Following immediately on to the words quoted by Jackson and myself we read: 'In the earliest stages they, i.e. unconscious phantasies, are almost the whole of psychical processes, and, of course they are pre-verbal, or rather non-verbal. The words which we use when we wish to convey their contents and meaning are a foreign element, but we cannot do without it – unless we are artists.'

Jackson, as I said, pointed out how close the Kleinian unconscious phan-tasies are to archetypal images, and I think he is right. Personally I have difficulty with unconscious phantasies because I experience a contradiction in terms as 'phantasy' brings to my mind an image of a communicable kind, be it visual, auditory, olfactory or in any other sensory form. (I think this is compatible with Jung's notion of psychoid events, i.e. events which he com-pares by analogy with physiological functions which have not yet reached a threshold by which they could become psychic processes and be perceived as such by consciousness.)

In the year this paper was written Bion published his Learning from Experience *in which the beta-elements made their first public appearance (Bion, 1962). Characteristically he referred to these as 'undigested facts' to be distinguished from memories and wrote that they are communicable by projective identification (ibid.). In so doing he adhered to the Kleinian model of the alimentary canal as the primary source of mental function but specified the mother as a suitable receptor and transformer of such beta-elements and called this transforming–metabolizing the alpha function. Jung's methods of amplification and active imagination intended to get the transcendent function going seems to serve much the same purpose. But with a characteristic difference. Help does not come from the mother, but from the teacher–analyst whose actions are deliberate and depend on the teacher being an educated person. Mothers who can fulfil the digesting–metabolizing–transforming function presumably acquired the capacity from their own mothers when they themselves had been infants by 'introjective identification'.*

This is reminiscent of the argument about early memories versus preformed images which had been taken up in connection with the Wolf Man (see p. 82). So there are two ways of reaching memories going back to the pre-verbal period. One is by verbal interpretations that arouse feelings and sensations. The other is sensations that can arouse the vague feeling of significance which then becomes structured into a fantasy. Whether or how closely the fantasy (-scene) that is (re-)evoked in this way corresponds objectively to the facts as 'remembered' must be left open.

But, again, Jung does not associate his hypothesis [of the 'psychoid'] with the notion of development of the mind from the earliest infancy and its continuity from there in adult life.

At this point it should be recalled that Jung took a keen interest in the lives of individuals who consulted him, but his primary and enduring concern was 'the history of the human mind' for which the analytic 'material' of individuals furnished important evidence. This is clearly stated in his Foreword to the third edition (1937) of the epoch-making Symbols of Transformation, *the last edition of which appeared in 1952 (CW 5: p. xxcvii). Forty years had passed since the nucleus of the 'Symbols of the Libido' had appeared in vols III and IV of the Jb. Psychoanal. Forsch., that is before the break with Freud. Significantly, the subtitle had been 'Contributions to the Developmental History of Thinking' ('Beiträge zur Entwicklungsgeschichte des Denkens'). Closely related is the subject of 'consciousness' which remained a major concept and a whole volume of Jung's late work had been entitled* Von den Wurzeln des Bewusstseins *('Concerning the Roots of Consciousness'), before the title was dropped in the* CW *edition. Although 'consciousness' does occur in Freud's work it takes up a fraction of the space in the index of the Standard Edition compared with the ten columns in the index to Jung's* Collected Works. *In Klein's work the term is not found at all nor is there an equivalent term, although 'unconscious' occurs frequently, both as adjective and noun. Bion, however, was more of a theoretician than Klein and interested in philosophy. The subject of the development of thought processes and their clinical significance was clearly important to him. He adopts the Freudian definition of consciousness as a 'sense-organ, for the perception of psychic qualities' and uses it in the chapter 'A Theory of Thinking' where he attributes a rudimentary and fragile consciousness to infants (Bion, 1967), whereas according to Jung there is no 'ego-consciousness at that stage of development' (CW 8: para. 648). It seems that the subject of consciousness has become a 'grey area' being of academic rather than practical interest.*

This historical view may help a little in our understanding why in countries like England, where pragmatism ranks highly, practising 'Jungian' analysts have found it expedient to borrow detailed analytical 'steps' from other schools, notably Klein's, rather than draw on the concept of consciousness for their inspiration.

If I read her rightly, 'unconscious' means for Heimann potential, i.e. not yet formed, not yet communicable, not yet connected with the central part of the ego but still connected with an erogenous zone. This amounts to acknowledging that the patient is not ready to express the image in words despite the psychoanalytic rule that he must try to put all that he is aware of into words. Here we have arrived at an important crossroad so far as practical application is concerned. We have to find ways of bringing something as yet unformed into a shape, image or phantasy – whatever you wish to call it.

Having achieved some degree of formulation it can be used for communication between patient and analyst and thus be brought into consciousness. The patient cannot do this alone. Heimann says 'unless we are artists'. I should say that only if he were treating an artist could the analyst possibly be satisfied with the expression or formulation of archetypal images and then leave well alone. But I think that an artist of that calibre is as rare as not to bother us here.

However, the way in which Heimann puts the problem of non-verbal communication enables us to connect it with Jung's detailed statements of his amplificatory methods of archetypal themes. I should like to demonstrate this by quoting a few sentences from 'The Transcendent Function' (*CW 8*: para. 166f). They read:

> If there is no capacity to produce fantasies we have to resort to artificial aid. The reason for invoking such aid is generally a depressed or disturbed state of mind for which no adequate cause can be found.

'Artificial aid' is right as far as the teacher-guide analyst is concerned. It would probably seem wrong to the mother-analyst who regards reverie as a natural function. A nice point. All the more so as it makes one wonder how 'natural' the analyst can be in the setting of analysis which from the point of view of a patient who is not inured, seems contrived.

Jung goes on to describe how giving expression to the mood 'reproduces the depression in some way' and that 'the whole procedure is a kind of enrichment and clarification of affect'. A practical hint is of interest to my theme:

In these cases (i.e. mild depressions) no definite starting point exists – it would first have to be created.

And Jung further asks:

What is to be done with material obtained in one of the manners described?
(ibid.)

In reply, Jung states that from practical experience and according to the peculiar make-up of the individual personality there are two main tendencies of dealing with it: the creative tendency which leads to the problem of aesthetic formulation while the understanding tendency is to know about the meaning of the product by subjecting it to intellectual analysis and interpretation. Both methods have a danger in common, i.e. a swing towards over-valuation of the unconscious products accompanied by inflation. (So much for an outline of Jung's 'Transcendent Function', i.e. a method of bringing conscious and unconscious data into a state where collaboration is possible.) Jung does not seem to have written in much detail about the effects which the methods of amplification of archetypal images can have on a particular ego. Nor has he emphasized that the concentration required for this method presupposes a fair degree of ego development. For anyone who undertakes to analyse patients in different stages of ego development these two points are of great interest. The question therefore is, whether we can take over the Kleinian mechanisms which deal with earliest ego defences and development and are based on the bodily experiences and functions in infancy, and further, if we do accept this underpinning how will it blend with the superstructure of Jung's inner world and general ideas about the function of archetypes? In order to find an answer to this question I thought it most useful to have a further look at the function of images and illusions.

THE FUNCTION OF IMAGES AND ILLUSIONS: IDENTIFICATION

A short quotation from 'Basic Postulates of Analytical Psychology' makes Jung's position quite clear. He is speaking about the concept of psychic reality:

If we try to penetrate more deeply into the meaning of this concept, it seems to us that certain psychic contents or images are derived from a 'material' environment to which our bodies belong, while others, which are in no way less real, seem to come from a 'spiritual' source which appears to be very different from the physical environment.

And again:

If a fire burns me I do not question the reality of the fire, whereas if I am beset by fear that a ghost will appear, I take refuge behind the thought that it is only an illusion. But just as the fire is the psychic image of a physical process whose nature is ultimately unknown, so my fear of the ghost is a psychic image from a spiritual source; it is just as real as the fire, for my fear is as real as the pain caused by the fire.

(*CW 8*: para. 681)

This demonstrates that for Jung 'spirit' and 'nature' are two distinct and separate sources of psychic contents. In view of this a theory which relies as heavily as Mrs Klein's on the infantile experiences at the breast for the development of the most important part of our psychic functions seems alien to Jung's basic views. But let us return to practical details. In this connection Jung's remarks about having to produce phantasies by 'artificial aids' would seem anathema to any psychoanalyst and so would, I think, Jung's method of active imagination. Listen to Melanie Klein, who writes in her *Introduction to a Narrative of Child Analysis*: 'In my interpretations I tried as always to avoid (as I would avoid with adults as well as children) introducing any similes, metaphors or quotations to illustrate my point' (Klein, 1961). However, on reading through this book, and on considering what I had read there and elsewhere about so-called 'unconscious phantasies', I began to wonder how these could be converted into the necessary imagery without interpretations which were, to my mind, similes or metaphors. If the parallel between unconscious phantasies and archetypal images (or, rather, as I said, potential images) holds good then neither the one nor the other can be brought into the consciousness of a patient who cannot transform these into actual images or phantasies without some help from outside. It would seem to follow that when interpretations are given concerning pre-verbal events, the word-images used by the analyst *must* be of the nature of similes or metaphors. The feelings or thoughts to which such verbal interpretations refer must of necessity belong to a later (verbal) period. Feelings and thoughts of later periods but comprising also the earlier pre-verbal ones are almost certainly included in the patient's response to such interpretations. Whichever way one looks at it, it seems more than likely that the analyst's interpretations help to create imagery for the patient which he did not previously have at his disposal. But whether you use 'pure' Kleinian interpretations or what Jung called amplifications I think that this is an area in which great caution is needed and that the two methods may *not* have the same effect in the end. I have implied that a lot of Kleinian interpretations are symbolizations of events dating back to a period when such modes of expression were not available. But I don't want this to mean that such interpretations cannot reach a place in the mind which could be called an early kind of memory. On the contrary, every now and again one discovers that memories are evoked by means of sensations – particularly those sensations which are not part of our conscious awareness in everyday life. A scent, for example, can bring back to mind a scene and a feeling which had long been forgotten. This would then become a structured phantasy. A potential phan-

tasy would be an inexpressible feeling of significance, the first verbally expressible quality of which might be that it is 'good' or 'bad'.

Poetry or music can, no doubt, arouse strong feelings and sensations as well,
but I think that although the responses may be similar to the re-arousal of
memories in analysis it is the context which makes all the difference. I do not
mean the transference as such (important though it is) but the general setting
of an environment created by analysis which sees to the continuity and
connectedness of the experience of archetypal images or unconscious phantasies. If the patient is seen twice a week, taught how to use active imagination,
asked to write down his dreams together with associations or to paint his
mood, then, whatever is experienced is given a different frame from the one
surrounding the patient who is seen five times a week lying on his back and
experiencing swallowing, sucking or biting sensations in the presence of his
analyst. The latter fosters the re-experiencing of an infantile dependent relationship which the former abjures. But there is no doubt in my mind that
images *are* created in both instances for the patient by the general analytical
setting as well as by the specific theoretical orientations behind the different
approaches. As regards the caution to which I referred, I venture to generalize
that however chastening the experience of archetypal imagery can be, the
greater immediate danger with the hypothetical Jungian method (as outlined
here) lies in a positive inflation – the over-valuation of the unconscious, while
the greater immediate danger with the Kleinian approach would seem to come
from depression as the result of infantile dependence and subsequent frustration and disillusionment. But we may assume that in both cases the images
created have an effect on the ego which was in a relatively stabilized condition
before analysis began. I said 'an immediate danger' because once the ego has
become labile it can easily swing from one extreme to the other – for example
'acting out' – 'manic defences' which seem so particularly disliked by Kleinians.

Now let me evaluate the functions of the images created with – but also for
the patient – from a different aspect. My own predilection for the economy
and precision of Kleinian terminology will become evident when I refer to the
topic of *illusions*. The intensity of an image – be it sexual or spiritual or both
– brings about that we become absorbed in it. This absorption or fascination
results in an illusion of oneness with the image – a fusion takes place between
ego and object, also known as identification. The words identification and
illusion tend to have a derogatory flavour both in psychoanalysis and analytical psychology. Only a few writers like Winnicott and Milner give a positive
connotation under certain circumstances. Referring to the infant's needs,
Winnicott writes that there can be no disillusionment without pre-existing
illusions, and that successful feeding which produces the illusion of oneness
must precede successful weaning (Winnicott, 1958). Marion Milner in 'The
role of illusion in symbol formation' is also very illuminating on the subject
when she stresses, 'the capacity of the environment to foster growth by

providing conditions in which a recurrent partial return to the feeling of being one is possible' (Milner, 1955). Even projection (another term with a derogatory flavour) may be seen positively by Milner quoting Fenichel: 'by putting unpleasant sensations into the external world (it) attempts to reverse the separation of ego from non-ego' (ibid.). She emphasizes the frame which the environment must provide for successful fusion between ego and object, how such a frame is reproduced by the analytical sessions and describes the damage that can result from forcing a child continually and clearly to distinguish between external and internal reality. All this is clearly in keeping with Jung's positive evaluation of regression. But Jung's descriptions are all on a plane removed from the everyday realities of a child's environment. The alchemical 'vas' and the 'temenos' give no direct information about the quality of mothering required nor of the nature of interactions between mother and child during the first few years. It is therefore quite natural that Kleinian psychology with its detailed explanations of relatedness to actual persons should fill this vacuum in our frame. These may well contain mythological elements too but her interpretations attempt to mirror the child's inner reality, it is the detail of relationship between mother and child and between the environment which creates the necessary frame to contain illusions and disillusionments and all the joys and bitter frustrations which result from it. Little or no reference is found in Jung's opus about the relations between bodily functions and maternal care as basis for mental functions. On the other hand, and as the result of amplificatory methods, there is plenty of scope for the formation of illusions of oneness which Milner observed in the form of a 'particular type of absorption' taking place when children are at play. She called it concentration (ibid.). The need for such concentration resulting in illusions of oneness is, to my mind, a recurring and a lifelong one. But a satisfying or at least tolerable relationship between the inner and outer world need not always result from such experiences. It could happen, for example, that refuge is had to the inner world as a kind of withdrawal from depressing encounters in the outer. At all events, there are indications that the two methods of arousing and dealing with archetypal images, that is by causal or quasi-causal interpretations or by amplificatory methods need not have the same outcome. Olympus, for example, may be a symbolic image of the breast: but it seems unlikely that this will arouse the sucking sensations in the mouth without which in my experience a sometimes crucial period of development cannot be brought back into consciousness.

Having said this I hasten to add that differentiated archetypal images like Olympus can also arouse bodily sensations, just as religious images can cause sexual feelings, but it is left open how much weight needs to be given to this. Whether one or other method is preferable may depend on several factors in each case. But in general I feel that the bodily causal type of interpretation leads to the analyst becoming identified with 'the object' to which the patient is directly related by way of transference, for example to the breast. Differentiated archetypal imagery on the other hand leads to an *indirect* relationship in which the analyst stands for a super-ordinate or coordinating authority, a god-image or the 'self'. The former, that is the direct object-relationship appears to be the more easily observed hence controlled [by the analyst] while the latter has greater potentialities, the realization of which is, however, left to chance or natural processes. The former (Kleinian) approach is conducive to constant interpretations; understanding silences and concentration are in keeping with the latter (Jungian) method.

OBJECTIVES AND OBJECTS

I asked myself what in broadest outline the patient's objectives – more often than not unconscious – were in coming to analysis and thought that there are two: on the one hand he wants to find his place in relation to the world, his limits as well as the realization of his potentialities; on the other he wants to be able to transcend himself, to have experiences of being able to lose himself wholeheartedly; to merge with objects in such a way that new situations are born out of it. (*For other formulations of objectives see 'Why people still want analysis', p. 313 below.*) Without the first objective being achieved, that is boundaries having been established, attempts at reaching the second, that is transcending the boundaries, can only lead to intoxications more or less short-lived, but sterile in the long run – no real transformation of the personality having been established in this way. This at least seems to me what we and our patients are hoping for when we say that someone, as a result of analysis, has 'completely changed'. There are, to my mind, two ways of distinguishing between intoxications and fusion with objects (i.e. illusions) and, on the other hand, a transformation or development of the personality. The first is in terms of object-relations. Here the question is what happens when the relationship with another person (which may or may not be the analyst) can be acknowl-edged to exist after the illusory fusion [state of identity] with that person who represented the primary object has had to be abandoned.

> *I think that Winnicott's term 'object-usage' applies here. This usually does not come into operation before the end of analysis.*

The second test can be observed in the analytical situation and occurs when a so-called big dream or other archetypal image is looked at from the causal-reductive point of view, i.e. from the point of the patient's personal unconscious. (There are nearly always some personal elements in such a dream which enable one to do so.) If the patient, who was in a state of fusion or fascination as the result of such a dream continues to value but not over-value the dream experience, I would assume that a certain personality development has occurred.

I implied earlier that it seems to be an immediate danger with the hypothe-tical Jungian patient, that he has ego-transcending experiences due to an influx of archetypal imagery. He easily loses his boundaries without the restraining effect which observation of his object relations bring about.

But the hypothetical Kleinian patient under the influence of a continual barrage of interpretations referring to his efforts to cope with anxiety, both persecutory and depressive, may not recognize his boundaries either. The highest theoretical objective of analysis remains (according to Fairbairn) a maximum synthesis of the structures into which the original ego has been split, that is to promote the development of a whole strong ego out of its components. There is a footnote in Klein's paper 'On Identification' which reads:

> I would say that however strongly splitting and projection operate, the disintegration of the ego is never complete as long as life exists. For I believe that the *urge towards integration* however disturbed – even at the root – is in some degree inherent in the ego. It is these facts which make it possible *for the analyst* to bring about some measure of integration even in very severe cases (both emphases added) (op. cit.).

This paragraph requires two comments. First, interpretations (see below). This has clearly changed. According to Spillius, some of Klein's youthful and enthusiastic followers may have acted in this way which is now recognized as detrimental to the 'recognition of live moments of the emotional contact'. Receptiveness is destroyed when the analyst is looking for evidence of his/her conceptions in the patient's material. This may be why Bion issued such a strong warning about 'memory and desire' which destroy receptivity and intuitive hypotheses (Spillius, 1988).

Second, the healing of splits and integration. The concepts can be traced back to Freud's pre–1920 'ego-instincts' (=self(!)-preservation). The measure of purpose (teleology) so strongly expressed in Jung's work is here implicit in Klein's statement. In Fordham's version the ego does not split nor is it put together again, rather it is the self which alternates between integrated and deintegrated states, both of which are required for growth to take place (Fordham, 1985). The technical difference between Klein's and what I regard as the Jungian attitude and technique is that the self does not require nearly as much help as Klein thinks the ego does. Whichever view is taken clearly influences the technique and frequency of interpretation and possibly of sessions too. The attitude of individual analysts whether 'classical' or 'romantic' also plays a part in this (see above, p. 125).

One might conclude from this that it must be a little confusing for the poor ego – which is after all also connected with the way we see ourselves – to find itself splitting, projecting *and* with an urge towards integration. But that is how it is. From the point of view of finding its own boundaries, Jung's 'self' would certainly seem to offer the patient an advantage in that he need not himself aspire to solve such complexities. If – as Storr has pointed out – the Jungian psyche can be regarded as a self-regulating mechanism with the 'self' presiding over the integrating processes, then there is no need for the ego to get confused – at least not on these grounds (Storr, 1960). And the strain on the analyst (without whose consent not a hair may fall off the Kleinian patient's head) must be considerably lessened too for he shares his burden with the self in a way that Klein's phrasing *'for the analyst* to bring about some measure of integration' (see above) does not suggest. This, too, must have a bearing on the frequency and manner of the analyst's interpretations. But before we are ready to appreciate this difference, we would do well to have another look at a subtler difference between the inner world of Klein and Jung. It concerns the relationship between instincts and dynamic structure.

INSTINCTS AND DYNAMIC STRUCTURE

I called the inner world of Klein a murderous place and this is due to the importance she gives to the death instinct, the innate destructive drive against which the ego has to defend itself from the moment of birth. Although there is also the other life – or sexual-instinct, it seems that all integrating and reparative functions are secondary to the damage done resulting from the death instinct. By giving a very important position to the death instinct as a source of psychic energy she is one of the few followers of Freud who have taken this instinct into their conceptual framework. True, Klein also endows the ego with some inherent energy as the passage concerning its tendency to integration suggests. But this seems negligible compared with the other instinctual energies. It is not really negligible but appears to be so when compared with the psychopathology the death instinct can arouse.

Jung's position seems altogether different, both as regards the death instinct in particular, and instinct as a source of psychic energy in general. As regards the latter, the concept of instinct is quite inseparable from that of the archetype, which leads to the formation of an instinctual (archetypal) image and consequently to patterns of behaviour. Energy and the configuration of energy are for all intents and purposes conceived as one single entity. Jung, like Fairbairn (see Guntrip) is much more in line with present-day scientific thought when he keeps to his theory of dynamic structure, while Freud and Klein separate energy and structure to a considerable degree. In his early days Jung accepted the Eros theory although with very considerable qualifications. Significantly he wrote: 'Libido for me means psychic energy which is equivalent to the intensity with which psychic contents are charged' (*CW* 7: para. 77n). In his later work it became more and more clear that energy, both integrating and constructive as well as disintegrating and destructive, is locked up in the archetypal image, the specific effect depending on the circumstances of interaction with particular states of ego development. At any rate Jung never recognized the death instinct as such as a destructive force. The most one can say is that he acknowledged it as a principle leading to spiritual transformation as contrasted with the biological development of life.

It is sufficiently obvious that life, like any other process, has a beginning and an end and that every beginning is also the beginning of the end. (*CW* 7: para. 34)

Here is a noticeable lack of rigorous psychological thinking on Jung's part and I suspect the 'quasi-philosophical' statement circumvents the anxiety evoked by accepting death as an instinct. Jung does, however, recognize the autonomy and moral aspect of evil and absolute evil as destructive forces both in the individual and collectively .

(CW 9, II: *para. 19*)

Nobody doubts the presence of destructive forces which assail us and against which the psyche is helpless, hence requiring protection. But the hypothetical localization and status of these forces will obviously influence the technique of analysis.

Fairbairn, for example, does not agree with anxiety as being an innate, primary phenomenon nor that the splitting of objects by the ego is required for its natural development. He dislikes the impersonal term 'defence mechanism', but allows the ego to defend itself against bad objects. The death instinct is re-interpreted by him as 'an obstinate tendency on the part of the patient to treat his psychic reality as a closed, static and self-contained system'.

An extremely pragmatic view, but hardly a psychological theory .

In all these respects Fairbairn's object relationship seems much nearer to Jung than the theories of Klein do, but I think Jung goes further in that he regards archetypal images (whether they occur in simple or in a highly elaborated form) also as objects to which the ego responds and with which it enters into a relationship. Everything depends on the nature of this interaction. If the ego is attuned to it, if the conditions are favourable, it will be constructive in the direction of ego development, otherwise destructive. One can see that in Jung's view the need for defences against anxiety (due to aggressive impulses under the sway of the death instinct) must be considerably less than in the inner world of both Fairbairn and Klein, where according to Guntrip's exposition 'the inner world is one in which only immature relationship patterns exist', the reason being that the internalized objects of this inner world have entered into a bond with infantile parts of the ego (Guntrip, 1961). If Guntrip is right then Jung's inner world is totally different from Freud's early view of the unconscious system as consisting mainly of repressed, instinctive and wish-fulfilling fantasies. However, Heimann's statement, see above, concerning unconscious phantasies forming the matrix from which pre-conscious and conscious processes develop, makes me wonder whether Guntrip is correct or whether he just disliked the Kleinian school.

My interest in all this is determined by practical considerations which at this point concerns the manner and frequency of interpretations. The archetypal image can be regarded as an object charged with an energy potential with which the ego has to come to terms whether it be a nipple or an image of the godhead. The very early ego requires help of a different kind, a different sort of frame (Milner's expression) from that required by a later more adult ego. But the principle remains the same: the more comprehensible the image, the less danger it holds for the ego. Concentration on an archetypal image, even temporary fusion with it producing an illusion of oneness – all this can be manageable by an ego that has had early experiences of such illusions as well as disillusionments and is therefore ready to go from strength to strength. It is, in fact, the comprehension of the such-ness of an archetypal image-become-object which makes the ego-transcending experiences possible of which I spoke earlier. In these circumstances ego and image do not have to be pushed together by constant interpretations concerning anxieties and defences, although help by means of elucidation and amplification, or even silent understanding is still required.

We, therefore, need to be quite certain whether the patient is one who has not yet reached Melanie Klein's 'depressive position' on account of a failure in the environment to help with the psychological development which comes about as the result of feeding and weaning. Without this having been achieved she cannot make use of the symbolization on which the amplificatory method relies.

I was wrong here. Segal in her 'A psychoanalytic approach to aesthetics' referred to a patient's failure to work through the depressive position and her inability to accept and use her death instinct (Segal, 1955). I condensed all this into 'proper feeding and weaning' and omitted the concurrent intrapsychic development.

The great merit of Jung's inner world is that it does not stress anxiety and disease to the exclusion of healthy aspects of the personality. It is in the first place an inner world of normal people who have apparently come unscathed through the experiences of infancy. Where this kind of confidence has not been established inside the ego, concentration is impossible and dangerous intoxications result from illusions of oneness. In that case interpretations *need* to be precise. There is no place for the kind of vagueness which is implied in phrases like 'something to do with'. The patient cannot be expected to choose. He is given what the analyst feels is best for him – just like an infant by his mother. Whether the interpretations are correct is not as important as that they should be easily related to the 'I–you' situation and expressed in bodily terms wherever possible.

There has obviously been a change in the climate of Kleinian analysis as indicated above. It was Bion again who seems to have been instrumental when he emphasized the mother's (or analyst's) containing function (see also my comments on the empathic model of transference–countertransference) in the next chapter (see p. 316) (Bion, op. cit.). This does not mean, however, that interpretations based on primary anxiety and aggression are compatible with the Jungian frame of reference. I also wish to add that I am more convinced of the efficacy of analysing these emotions than I am of the genetic causality as the theoretical basis on which the technique is based.

CONCLUSIONS

I shall not summarize the various references I made to theoretical backgrounds, but make a general remark about the observer's influence on the events which occur in analysis. After that I shall give a summary of the main practical points.

It seems to me that the observer's (analyst's) orientation is a major factor in determining the course of an analysis. *(Note: the course, not the outcome.)* Which implies that phenomena tend to proliferate at the point on which one's interest is focused. In the case of exceptional ability and concentration of an observer a new vista may open. This is what happens in the case of pioneers whose vision becomes also valid for others. Such major discoveries are not mutually exclusive but the areas illuminated in the vastness of our ignorance tend to make one believe that they are the whole truth and that makes for a certain fanaticism to which Jung seems to have remained much more immune than Klein. But as a therapeutic tool one-sidedness can be very incisive. The point I am making about the inevitable subjective factor does not invalidate the findings. It seems, however, peculiarly difficult to focus – as I think we are trying to do – on two areas of discovery at once without developing a squint. To bring two major contributions to a single focus is a difficult task which – if it can be accomplished at all – can only be undertaken after the differences have been delineated.

SUMMARY

The essential differences between Jung's and Klein's theoretical backgrounds are mainly reflected in their approaches to the patient and in the techniques employed. The discrepancies concern different evaluations of an inner world, the existence and importance of which is not in doubt. It is not primarily a pathological one for Jung, whose work lends itself more easily to a theory of personality structure than to a theory of psychopathology. The principles of determinism and of the continuity of mental life from infancy receive little attention by Jung.

Concerning the approaches to the patient's unconscious, I pointed out that the difference between interpretations (based presumably on free association) and amplification of unconscious products is very considerable. Yet, to my mind, both methods attempt to bring that into awareness which did not exist in a communicable, but only in a potential form before – see archetypal images and unconscious phantasies. This part of the unconscious is very different from what was understood by the unconscious as resulting from repression in the early days of psychoanalysis

All kinds of interpretations make use of images whether as similes, analogies, metaphors, symbolisms, or just images contained in ordinary language. This is explicit in Jung's case and implicit in Klein's.

The attitude towards the value of identifications and illusions of oneness with the object is not clear in either Jung or Klein. It is intimately bound up with the evaluation of regression. Although Jung seems to have appreciated positive regressions at first, his method suggests that he tries to put the brake on it in every way. The chairs, relatively infrequent interviews, encouragement of the patient to make conscious efforts, all seem to counteract regressive tendencies. Is it the result of having to see schizoid or borderline psychotic patients from abroad who could only be seen occasionally? Or did he think that nothing could be gained by an infantile dependent transference? Probably both.

A technique is required to hold the patient together who has regressed to a dependent state. All the more so for patients who are ambulatory and therefore have to live in two worlds. It is known that Jung treated such patients, but he published no longitudinal case study which would show how he prevented disintegration from occurring. Lacking the necessary concentration such patients would be in no fit state to benefit from active imagination as might be expected from other patients.

If the inner world, like the images and objects arising from it is *not* confined to destruction and immature object relationships – as does seem to be the case with Klein – then contact with the images and objects can be expected to some extent at least to have a beneficial effect on the patient. The manner and frequency of interpretations will be influenced by the different views held.

The archetypal image when adequately differentiated and recognized by the ego, so far from being destructive can have an integrating effect. This, however, presupposes an ego which has come through experiences of illusion and disillusionments. Neither fusion with an object nor separation from it can be tolerated by an ego which has not yet learned to trust.

The aim of analysis on which both Klein and Jung seem in agreement is expressed in statements about ego-synthesis and integration. Jung, as we know, takes this further with his concept of individuation.

This brings me to the 64,000-dollar question mentioned earlier about the underpinning of the Jungian structures by Kleinian methods [*particularly*] in the type of case just mentioned. Because of some fundamental differences in orientation, I think there is a distinct possibility that the Kleinian method in the hands (and mouths) of those who had Jungian training becomes something different from either Kleinian or Jungian analysis. This could, for example, amount to a relationship technique based on a 'nursing couple' model with the intention of joining it up at some future date with the archetypal world of Jung, the self and all. Depending on the circumstances of the case this may be a perfectly legitimate thing to attempt. But the welding together of two approaches differing in some fundamental ways as much as Jung's and Klein's into one consistent theoretical framework is a task of a different magnitude.

Chapter 14

Where does analysis stand?

I ANSWERING A SERIOUS OBJECTION TO MAPPING

The general objection raised at the beginning of Chapter 3 to any cognitive ('conscious') method with which to study analysis has already been met. It was that any such method would do violence to analytic data derived from the depths of the unconscious and carrying affective charges which could not be understandable by such 'head' determined delineation.

But there remains a more specific objection to mapping which can be couched in Bion's concise language as follows: the map is designed to show the state of our knowledge. But knowledge (K) inhibits the state of mind in which the analyst can *become at one* with O, that is it prevents him/her from undergoing a transformation in the direction of O (=ultimate knowledge or reality) which can only happen if he/she does not *desire* to possess knowledge (Bion, 1970). This is more forcibly stated in 'Notes on memory and desire' reprinted in *Melanie Klein Today* (Spillius, op. cit.).

We can all appreciate the intention behind Bion's injunction to be undogmatic and open-minded and so to approach the patient without 'memory or desire' other than the wish to make a fresh start every time, unencumbered by previous knowledge. Nevertheless, I regard this as an unrealizable ideal. Certainly, the analyst should try to ignore all theoretical lumber when confronted with a patient. He/she should also be unanxious about the success of their work, reputation and income. But it seems very strange that analysts who know about the strength of the unconscious mind should regard themselves immune to the wish to find their theory and previous experience confirmed. Supposing that analysts had the wisdom of not knowing, over and above all the knowledge which they do have. How can this be applied? Either the art requires the whole person – as Jung holds – which must mean that the theoretical equipment becomes an integral part of the analyst; or we have to rely on being able to suppress or split off part of our knowledge and thereby of ourselves by what Bion refers to as 'deliberately blinding' oneself. Does this not mean that we claim to have the mystic's ability to reach some state like a 'cloud of unknowing'? Can analysts pretend to be innocent of previous knowledge? The belief that they can suspend 'K' in order to come closer to 'O' (representing ultimate truth) presumes being somehow exempt from the persistence of an unconscious motive, meaning here the wish to find one's expectations and theoretical assumptions confirmed. The hope seems to be that without being very conscious of what they are, all expectations can be treated as if they could be left out. When such a belief is observed in a patient, it is called 'omnipotence' and the technical terms we use such as 'dissociation' 'suppression' and 'splitting' point to the desirability of analysing and thereby 'changing', that is stopping the omnipotence. I suggest that the belief in the powers of suppression is omnipotent. Bion, the man, was not omnipotent; quite to the contrary. He was protected against the omnipotence of 'O' by serving it with the kind of devotion and humility we observed in Gordon (see p. 168 above). And just as uncompromisingly. But for would-be imitators the question remains: how can previous knowledge be ignored after it has become part of oneself? Differently put, Bion's contempt of 'sensa' in combination with his injunction regarding 'desire' closely resembles the mystic's ascetic discipline in preparation of union with the 'Absolute'. Appealing though these notions are to some analysts, I doubt whether their practice can be limited to analytic sessions without affecting the whole of their lives. But I have yet to meet an ascetic analyst. Therefore, analysts either aspire to becoming integrated 'whole' persons or they must believe that – being only technicians – their private life has nothing to do with the job. *That* would be a clear case of splitting.

Without making a conscious effort to clarify what is in one's mind by way of knowledge and experience, I suggest that foreknowledge and preconceptions, however much disowned, will inevitably return and become mixed up with what is observed with an apparently innocent mind. The observations can be further interpreted and the resultant transformation observed once more and later still published. More often than not, the upshot is in the nature of a QED, even if the reporting analyst is sincerely convinced that what they have to communicate is an entirely fresh observation free from previous knowledge, bias and prejudice.

It is for reasons such as these that I think it better to look from time to time at favourite theories and other factors which influence one's analytic work by committing these to paper or giving them space on a map. It then becomes possible to find where one stands in relation to the wider context, that is the wider field of analytic theories and to specify the vertex in which one has put faith. Having done so one may feel free to abandon it, make forays into other areas and to tolerate the way other analysts approach the same phenomena. *Without taking one's vertex into detailed consideration it is impossible to distinguish between a reformulation and the wish to be all-inclusive or the remote possibility of an original thought.*

In view of all this it seems that a more realistic approach to 'not knowing' is to make a clean breast of where one has arrived at and what it is that one believes one knows and what one's vertex is. It is not enough to call it 'psychoanalysis' or 'analytical psychology', because it is and must also be one's own version. Whether we like it or not, we cannot pretend to be uninfluenced by the wider range of analytic theories and implicit claims of success, even if that is limited to a transformation in a small segment of an analytic hour. Focusing as we must on what seems to suit us best, we are tempted to conclude that ours is not one but the only way in the direction of 'O' and that the future of analysis also lies in that direction.

This answers the serious objection to mapping as being an expression merely of 'K' and not K that has evolved out of, or is becoming 'O'. The objection has made us curious about the relationship between mere knowledge, presumably born of memory and desire (or curiosity?) and the absolute but unknowable truth with which the analyst following Bion tries to be at one. The resemblance with the mystic's longing to be united with the Absolute is too striking to be ignored. Also the mystic's or visionary's fear lest their mission should fail which was mentioned in an earlier chapter (see p. 41, above) will presently be studied in a new light (see p. 310). But to prepare the reader for the main topic of the chapter, let us first attend to two unanswered questions.

TWO QUESTIONS, ONE MEETING POINT

The digression may seem a long way around but such answers as we can find will lead us to an outline which reflects the map in the head of at least one analyst. If that map should stimulate others to invent their own, its purpose will have been fulfilled.

The first question had been *'What is it that gives rise to the persuasive power of thought products such as ideas, concepts, theories which makes for a certain ease with which 'proof' can seemingly be found?'* (see p. 316 below). We shall see that the pursuit of this question leads us to an area in which the combination of Kleinian and archetypal psychology turns out to be illuminating. What is more, any tentative answer we may find there can help us to throw further light on the second question asked but only partly answered earlier, *'Why should people still want analysis?'* (see p. 313 below). There the answer given was in terms of the human relationship and the trust required for it which can further and create or restore the relatively independent capacity for faith. Although this is combined with the confessional and the reconstructive and constructive work of linking the past with the present, this is an aspect that also exists in less time-consuming therapies. Why then specifically analysis and not some other relationship based on self-less love which would be psychotherapeutic? But for one thing self-less love is in short supply, for another a seriously damaged person finds it impossible to accept. The offer must be destroyed and so hatred supervenes on both sides. This is why it is necessary to look at analytic theories that can throw light on the survival of unanalysed people who were severely emotionally deprived in early life. In turn, their observation could help us to formulate fresh theories on love and hatred. Unmet expectations also lead us to a possible psychological understanding of mysticism and such attenuated or distorted forms as Utopias, superstitions and the 'occult' generally.

Let us begin with the widely held assumption that in the evolution of mankind the postponement of immediate gratification of instinctual drives and desires and the redirection of the surplus energy tied up there has been regarded as a fundamental *precondition to the rise of civilization*. It is a maxim which analysis adapted by means of theories designed to investigate in detail what happens when there is too much (or sometimes too little) frustration during the first three years of life.

On the interpersonal level the hypothesis was well expressed by Winnicott's term the 'good enough' mother, meaning that an optimal balance can be found for any particular child between frustration and spoiling (Winnicott, 1965). Occasional spoiling, as for example, when a child is in pain or sick is exactly what is needed, yet some parents are afraid lest they spoil the child. The opposite expression of parental anxiety would be not being able to say 'no' and by instant and continuous gratification fob the infant and its anger off, thereby spoiling the gradual development of the capacity to cope with frustration (Winnicott, ibid.). In the event, the existence of external reality, that is of objects which constitute a world separately and outside the growing child, would have been denied. We can see why Winnicott regarded such parents as spoiling. So his 'good enough' is really the best possible mother.

The difficulty is that we cannot define, except in extreme cases, what constitutes too much frustration because we cannot dispense with the factor of individual constitution and endowment. What then are the criteria on the basis of which we come to the conclusion that in a given case there was more deprivation and frustration than had been tolerable? It is fairly easy to be sure when we know the background and meet a disintegrated personality showing features such as delinquency or mental illness and addictions, possibly ending in suicide. But the matter becomes quite complex when we assume that early frustrations and deprivations can be compensated for by a kind of self-nourishment subsequently combined with facilitating opportunities and personal stamina. Does the capacity to nourish oneself depend on inborn gifts or talents? Looking retrospectively at the career of some persons who have become famous, the answer seems to be, yes. What does that mean and how are such compensations explained by analytic theories concerning early abandonment and/or maternal deprivation?

In terms of analytical psychology a global mythological answer is provided by the archetypal image of the hero who is surrounded by dangers or abandonment at birth. It is a recurring and ubiquitous motif, particularly in the case of the founders of some of the world's great religions. A variant is symbolized by a wound which will not heal, as in the case of Chiron, the prototype of the 'wounded healer'. Acceptance of the open wound signifies receptivity to the suffering of others and to healing ideas.

But if we are not content with the 'just so' truth of a mythological motif and want to know not only that but how remarkable achievements can come about despite or because of early handicaps and afflictions, we have to look for a detailed analytic theory to reflect on and apply clinically in all but the most extreme cases. And in order to do that we can proceed in two ways. The *first* is to 'fix' the elements of a myth in their relation to each other, as Jung did in order to bring out the structure by means of diagrams in his 'An Account of Transference Phenomena Based on the Illustrations of the "Rosarium Philosophorum"' (CW 16: paras 422–37). For Bion the structure of a myth consists of a chain of causation and the myth itself reflects the moral system of which it is an integral part (Bion, 1963). But he also proceeds to use the category myth (along with dream thoughts and dreams) as an element in the evolution and transformation of thought. So much for the mythological reply to the question. The *second* way is to examine the connection between the psychology of afflicted individuals and reasons why they should be particularly affected by the hero myth and its variants. How *did* they survive? A psychological hypothesis is offered, see 'Mysticism' below and the 'Power of thought' (p. 315).

This is the point at which readers are likely to ask for examples in the form of case material with which to illustrate the point. I have taken the stance that such examples must deliberately or unwittingly be designed to support the theory and therefore lead us around in a circle. Therefore I prefer to illustrate analysis by looking at the lives of people who were afflicted in comparable ways yet apparently survived by pulling themselves up by their bootstraps (self-help). We shall take a closer look at the means which probably helped them to survive.

A NOTE ON THE PSYCHOLOGY OF MYSTICISM

I suggest that the meeting point of both questions asked at the beginning of the previous section can be found in the mystical element of analysis. Yet there can be little doubt that – as Underhill remarked – mysticism is one of the most abused words in the English language (Underhill, 1960). She lists a variety of senses in which the term has been used by religion, poetry and philosophy; and claimed, for example, as an excuse for occultism and vapid symbolism, religious or aesthetic sentimentality and bad metaphysics. I would add that the association with 'mystification' has contributed to make mysticism a term of contempt. Underhill defines mysticism as expressing 'the *innate tendency* of the human spirit toward complete harmony with the transcendental order' (emphasis added) and adds that in great mystics this tendency captures the whole field of consciousness dominating their life and ending in the experience of the 'mystic union' (ibid.). The union, or at least conscious relation is with the Absolute, called by Bion 'O', the absolute fact or ultimate truth which cannot ever be known. Small wonder that psychiatrists are not alone in being suspicious of mysticism! After all it can be clinically impossible to distinguish between hypomania or what analysts call 'manic defence' and the mystic's ecstasy in which sanity, as commonly understood, is at risk. For the sake of simplicity I would take Underhill's 'transcendental' to mean going beyond the bounds of the experience of reality which is limited by the routine life in time and space and the daily necessities. The goal itself is not a blissful, paradisaical or nirvana condition but an optimally functioning 'together' human being. The technique and theories of analysis today, however different they may be, are all designed to bring outer reality and the intrapsychic life closer together. For some this means healing–curing, for others rebirth, occasionally both. Later on I refer to the two realities, or universes as 'two worlds' (see p. 315 below).

If Underhill is right and the mystic tendency she calls innate is present to some extent in everybody but is not further developed by devotion, concentration and so forth, does it wither or does it survive in some attenuated form? If the latter were the case, not only superstitions to which everyone is prone but also occultism and oracular procedures – all common enough – can be regarded as 'mysticism manqué'. A comment by Gay in Freud, A Life in Our Time, is relevant here (Gay, op. cit.). He observes that Freud himself for all his rationality remained superstitiously anxious about certain numbers. He feared that he would die when sixty-two. When a telephone number ending in sixty-two was assigned to him that anxiety seemed to be confirmed. He died in fact at the age of eighty-two.

There is probably no better way to demonstrate how differently Freud and Jung dealt with the same subject than the case of mysticism. Both wanted to defend themselves and their theories against being 'mystical' and accused each other of mysticism meaning being 'unscientific'. Which proves that Underhill's observation is not confined to the English language. Gay writes that Freud struggled with the mystical tendency in him. He connected his superstition by self-analysis with his 'specifically Jewish mysticism'. Yet in a letter to Abraham he wrote 'In general, it is easier for us Jews, since we lack the mystical element' (Gay, op. cit.), a statement which is blatantly contradicted by Bakan's thesis in Sigmund Freud and the Jewish Mystical Tradition (Bakan, 1990). Then there was Jung who had become interested in the analysis of culture and his own mythological dreams as such, while Freud's priority remained to gain access to the secrets of mysticism with the key of his libido theory. He wrote to Jung that he should return in good time to the neuroses, as the 'mother country in which we must first secure our domination against everything and everyone' (Gay, quoting Jones, op. cit.). Here we note the hard line Freud adopted to resist his own 'wish to believe', for instance in telepathy (Gay, op. cit.).

One does not have to have read very much Jung to know of his positive psychological appreciation of mysticism, be it in his study of medieval mystics or of mysticism in alchemy and various religions. By way of classical and Neoplatonic antiquity and Hermetic philosophy he links his thesis of the human striving for wholeness, with Plato's world soul and the *rotundum* which contains the world in itself like a body. 'An image that cannot fail to remind us of the mother' (*CW 5*: para. 406). Note, not the other way round, as psychoanalysts would argue! This line together with Jung's repeated statement on the anima whose first incarnation is the mother shows that the archetype is seen as preconception, that is prior to the encounter with the personal 'real' mother (cf. *CW 12*: para. 92n, and p. 288 above). We note the stark contrast to psychoanalytic theory which follows a 'commonsense' sequence, that is mother before rotundum and anima. The exception is Bion whose 'preconception' is, like Jung's archetype, innate and has to wait until it meets with a 'realization' such as the breast is for the infant.

Whichever way we look at it, the striving for 'wholeness', Underhill's 'Unitive State', runs right through Jung's analytical psychology where it becomes a global aim, as described earlier (see p. 53 above). Here it is difficult to refrain from speculating that Jung's emphasis on the union of opposites has to do with his parents separating for a while in his early childhood. Freud, on the other hand, who had slept in his parents' bedroom up to the age of three, was preoccupied with the primal scene and the Oedipal child's attempt to separate the parents (see Mahony, op. cit., quoted p. 82 above).

A deformation of striving for a mystical state can be seen in the taking of hallucinogenic drugs and alcohol abuse, in order to experience reduced ego-awareness. The regression is supposed to lead to a conflict-free 'blissful' or 'nirvana' or 'mindless' condition. Superficially, it looks similar to the receptivity and emptiness of mind that mystics aim at by spiritual means in order to reach the Unitive-State and Life (Underhill, op. cit.). But without the safeguard of rituals and devotion to spiritual attainment the short cuts soon deteriorate into addiction. William James wrote in his lectures on mysticism that 'the sway of alcohol over mankind is unquestionably due to its power to stimulate the mystical faculties of human nature...' Similarly about nitrous oxide: 'Depth beyond depth of truth seems to be revealed to the inhaler.' And further: 'It is as if the opposites of the world... were melted away in unity' (James, op. cit.). But Underhill takes issue with one of James's 'four marks' or criteria of mysticism, namely 'passivity' although, as I read James, he means receptivity. In contrast to James she emphasizes two essential characteristics. One is that mysticism is active and practical, not theoretical (Underhill, ibid.); the other, that mystics do not, as their enemies declare, neglect their duties to the many, although their heart is always set upon the changeless One (ibid.). Underhill's point could equally apply to the aim of analysis to mediate between the inner world and outer reality. Whatever similarity there may be between the 'uniting' effect and a mystical experience, it is clearly a process that has an activating effect on the participants. In these respects the unitive effect of mysticism resembles a person's relation to a constant object and its centring effect (see p. 179 above). That both Gordon and Celia found their aim and object in their particular interpretation of Christianity seems irrelevant compared with the phenomenon as such. But if the relationship is to the changeless One – and yet if the One is not necessarily 'God' – then what is it? Underhill's *organic process* emphasizes that sudden enlightenment is not achieved without working for the art of establishing *a constant relation with the Absolute*. The similarity with Bion's 'O' and Jung's 'self' that finds completion in the union of opposites ('mystical marriage') does indeed become striking and justifies my assertion that mystical elements are found in the analytic vertices of both Jung and Bion. Seen in this light analysis is an organic process towards the ideal of a unitive state. As such it cannot be reached, only glimpsed occasionally. The intimation or intuition of the state has a powerful effect. It is remembered and can sometimes be detected in what afterwards is referred to as 'the turning point in my analysis'. This can be something quite worldly and pedestrian. We recall in this context that psychoanalysis in the early days struggled to free itself from religion – Jung's great 'psychothera-peutic' systems of a previous era (*CW 16*: para. 390). The mystical element commonly associated with religion had to be most strenuously suppressed and denied; conversely, the scientific aspect of analysis was emphasized. Had the mystical element merely gone underground? In the absence of any detailed connection between the method and the outcome, one could for instance speculate that the prophylactic effect of analysis which Dührssen's statistics point to might well be due to the partial realization of a unitive state, centred-ness, individuation or by whatever name the global but virtual aim of analysis be known (see p. 61 for Dührssen, op. cit.). By saying this I may appear to have changed my scepticism about the global and synthesizing aim of analysis, expressed earlier on. But I believe to have strengthened my position by emphasizing that there must be no such *aim* as wholeness, unitive state or whatever. All these remain an *implicit* possibility, contingent on the detailed analytic procedure.

WHY PEOPLE SHOULD STILL WANT ANALYSIS, FURTHER REASONS

Of course, there is a more overtly therapeutic side to analysis. If it were not for some evident results, medical insurance schemes would never have taken analysis under their wing and granted cover. It is my impression that this cover was and is still given grudgingly and that medical doctors suspect that analysis harbours a heresy. From their point of view the 'healthy-minded doctors' – in James's sense of the word – are not mistaken (James, op. cit.). The tendency which Underhill referred to as innate, contributes indeed to the amalgam out of which analysis was created at a time when the aim was to restore health by undoing hysterical dissociations. Any mystical trend would have been the last thing the founders had in mind for their 'talking cure'. But if we consider that progression in analysis follows a three-tiered model, the kinship with some religious and mystical elements becomes undeniable: first, the confessional with its implicit purification; second, the step by arduous step method of forging links between a person's past and present in the context of a professional and ritualized relationship; third, the patient's 'truth' clarifies with each successful level and, if accepted, becomes a nucleus around which the personality forms and becomes unified. This description comes close to Jung's alchemical parallel. Whether it is also borne out by practical experience is not as important here as whether it corresponds, as I believe it does, to a secret longing in many more people than is generally acknowledged. If so, the unitive state of the mystic is not a rare and isolated aim. As far as analysis is concerned that aim must remain implicit and the road to get there is rightly long and trying. Debased forms of 'mystical' experiences are easier to come by and some, like drugs, are destructive but that does not stop anybody from trying to get quickly to a goal that at the best of times remains both fascinating and elusive. Were it otherwise analysis, especially Jungian analysis, would soon deteriorate into a cult of wholeness.

But people, as Dinnage observes, start off on analysis at a different point in their lives. In her view they are curious about their inward relation to an environment which feels like a prison until they can make their particular sense of it (Dinnage, 1988). This view in no way contradicts my own. Dinnage's 'making sense' encompasses a wider angle than the quasi-mystical search for a unitive state. Neither are as demanding on the person's tolerance of frustration as Bion's evolution of thought and Jung's concept of individuation. This is close to Amiel quoted by Dinnage as saying that a person without relation to their cosmos feels as if *imprisoned* (cf. p. 94 above). A similarly liberating aim is formulated by Ogden, 'As analysts we attempt to assist the analysand in his efforts of freeing himself from forms of organized experience ... that *entrap* him and prevent him from *tolerating* the experience of not knowing long enough to create understandings in a different way' (Ogden, 1989, emphasis added). At this point he implicitly calls upon the virtue of patience, as Bion does overtly when he likens Keats's 'negative capability' with Klein's depressive position (Bion, 1970).

Regarding the motivation for analytic therapy Fordham mentions the individual's tendency to find out about his true nature and live in accordance with it. 'In the end he wants to know, never mind how agreeable or disagreeable that knowing may be' (Fordham, 1985). This view should be read as part of the general moral assumption regarding the civilizing value of tolerating frustration and the refusal of cheap substitutes. Bion goes into the detailed psychological processes that are set in motion when frustration is met rather than evaded. The climate then becomes conducive to the maturation of the personality and the recognition of a thought in preference to a comforting lie (Bion, 1967). The painful realizations included in Jung's individuation process underline the same ascetic trend which appears to be an essential preliminary to a mystical experience as well as to the meeting of psychoanalytic 'reality'.

I therefore conclude that courage and even an element of heroism is required for analysis to be successful and that people who are motivated to undergo it may have an inkling of this and yet decide to take up the challenge.

Although the aim in the form of a centred 'together' personality is the same, the important differences between the mystic's unitive state, Jung's 'wholeness' and Bion's being in 'O' can be summarized as follows: the unitive state arises out of frustration and the tolerance of frustration. The 'thought' in Bion's sense is a kind of illuminating and nourishing 'self-help'. It does not depend on the appearance of symbols of wholeness whether as mandala or any other symmetrical symbolic image about which Jungian analysts tend to get enthusiastic. In any case, the state (of wholeness) does not last nor need it have a lasting effect other than remaining memorable. In my view it is closely connected with the (unacknowledged) wish to negotiate between two worlds which – in contrast to intrapsychic and outer reality – cannot be united. I mean the world of 'things' and 'no-things'. That is to say fulfilment and satisfaction when the preconception (expectation) is realized, or non-fulfilment and the painfulness of dark and empty space.

'No-things' do not mean the same as 'immaterial' or 'spiritual'; they are the 'ghosts' of the place where a 'thing' ought to be according to expectation or had been as satisfaction. Now there is emptiness. But a potential space between two irreconcilable worlds appears, an unstable zone of doubt and faith in which conflicts are not solved but remain. When accepted it results in a person's feeling of security. Anything more enduring corresponds to hallucinating an Utopia. Like Jung, Bion is at pains to point out that any connection there may be between the ultimate aim, whether being at one with 'O', or 'wholeness', and something similar but stated in mystical language is purely incidental. Thus in defining 'O' as ultimate reality or truth Bion writes, 'Its existence as in-dwelling... has no significance; it is not good or evil; it cannot be known, loved or hated' (Bion, 1965). The difference then appears to be between the love language of the mystic and the passion of inspired analysts who, however, have to 'play it cool' in order not to act like teachers enthusing their pupils, thereby preventing them from finding their own way.

Armed now with some knowledge about a relatively neglected aspect of analysis, we are ready to return to our second question. We shall see how the answer is again connected with the psychology of mysticism and survival under conditions of (emotional) deprivation.

WHAT MAKES THOUGHTS POWERFUL?

Valuable as the hypothesis of thought reducing frustration is from the analytic vertex, it does not follow that early deprivations and frustrations will produce original thinkers and exceptional achievements, nor that well-fed people are barred from that élite.

The psychological conditions which expose a person to the hero myth may result in the variants of him/her becoming a mystic, visionary, healer and/or original thinker. Bion's hypothesis of 'no-thing' was taken up by Fordham in his chapter on St John of the Cross (Fordham 1985). Bion had used the infant at the Kleinian breast as his model when he described frustration as the outcome of an unmet preconception (= archetype → expected image). The possibilities vary from frustration that leads to a hallucination (escape from frustration) to frustration that is acknowledged and not explained away. If the pain involved is tolerated, a transformation into thought takes place in which the infant finding 'no-breast' can under favourable conditions nourish himself. A kind of self-feeding and self-fecundation takes place reminiscent of Jung's symbolic understanding of the Gnostic symbol of the *Uroboros*. The model can be extended to include infants that are fed without being 'held' or 'contained'. Although they do not die of physical starvation, mental maturation cannot progress without a minimum of care. Thought products are substituted which become vital nourishment, indeed 'vitamins'. If the hypothesis is valid, it becomes understandable that the mystic or visionary fight for the survival and propagation of their vision as for dear life. The acknowledgement of their particular thought products by others, followers, disciples and so on becomes equivalent to an affirmation of their own worth as 'food', which they believe to be of higher 'nutritional' value than any other on the market. It may well be that not having been adequately 'fed' stimulated fantasies about feeding (others). Consequently they depend on consumers who are hungry and ready to be fed and fertilized as well as willing to share what they receive. It is the very strength of the thought that inspires faith in the recipient. Acting like Prometheus' (Gk. = forethought) fire, it kindles a flame in other people. The truth and value of the illumination can only be assessed in the fullness of time. At the actual moment the passion of convictions is needed and decisive.

Among those whose life and work would seem to confirm the hypothesis of survival by thought products is Isaac Newton (1642–1727). His father had died three months before his birth. He was a weakly infant. Early insecurity was followed by his mother's remarriage when he was three. At the age of twenty he hated his mother and step-father to such an extent that he threatened to burn down the house. His mathematical theories and inclination towards mysticism and a world governed by providence are well authenticated and summed up by Borstein in *The Discoverers* (Borstein, 1985).

Many factors are likely to contribute to the penetrating power of a thought that is like a seed carried by the visionary, genius and the like and falls at the right time on the right soil. As for St John of the Cross and Newton, such instances could probably be multiplied and still no statistical proof be found that would bear out the thesis of optimal frustration. Certainly, not all severely deprived people accomplish a great deal in life. 'Life' here refers to the world of outer reality. But both Jung and Bion are primarily concerned with the other, the intrapsychic life. And although analysis as mentioned negotiates between the two, when we focus on the power of thought we are looking with a magnifying glass at intrapsychic processes.

In this context Bion's formulation concerning *the ratio between 'things' and 'no-things' being the invariant under analysis* is useful. It recalls the balance between satisfaction and frustration which constantly fluctuates as all analysts and successful patients know (Bion, 1965). If I ally myself with this view as basic to my further explications, it is because the 'invariant' accords with the limits set to personality development and the precondition to the rise of human civilization referred to earlier on (see p. 309). In so doing I probably come closer to Schafer's 'tragic vision' of psychoanalytic reality than to his others, notably the 'romantic vision' (Schafer, 1970).

Bion's hypothesis further suggests the means by which severely deprived people survived infancy and childhood despite their permanent handicap in relationships. But the power of thought which arises out of unrealized expectations must be distinguished from 'omnipotence of thought', a point that will be taken up under 'Utopia' (p. 337 below). For the present, a map, Fig. 14.1a will help to illustrate the relevant points of the last two sections. Map 14.1b introduces an alternative to 'O' which together with the mystic's Absolute is replaced by a triangle of equally central importance but at the same time within reach of all who are not as gifted as mystics.

Legend to Fig. 14.1a and b

Fig. 14.1 is called a map rather than a diagram because it fulfils the criteria of mobility and spatiality. It illustrates the following points and at the same time orientates us in an important region of analysis.

1   It is a *model* of the relations between 'things' (+) and 'no-things' (–). As such it is particularly applicable to infancy when the meeting of mouth and breast (nipple) appears as the primary *event* of an expectation being met. But the model of 'things' fitting together or becoming 'no-things' can usefully be extended to later life and also to the basic assumption that civilization depends on frustration tolerance. The extension of the model is not solely dependent on the quality of feeding experiences for further development: the 'thing' that was represented by the breast in the first instance, becomes any-thing that appears desirable or needed later on.

Three hypothetical phases are depicted; the middle Fig. 14.1a (m) shows the area of an individual's satisfaction (fulfilment) and frustration (unmet expectation) evenly balanced. The situation is assumed to correspond to the average expected environment in western civilization and includes a 'good enough' mother and a healthy child. The surface of the inner area of the individual's reactions and actions, seen between the + area on the right and the – area on the left is supposed to remain constant (in size, not in shape) when the conditions vary as shown on the left (l) and right (r) of (m).

2   Fig. 14.1a (l)

The desire to acquire and incorporate more and more 'things' is shown by a bulge extending in the direction of + and also a shift of the whole inner area in the same direction. A corresponding dent is seen on the left indicating that the – area has now increased meaning, for example, that anxiety about losing possessions is lurking, threatening to invade. It depicts the condition Klein refers to as 'greed' and arises presumably when 'things' are incorporated without adequate allowance for 'digestion'. They then cease to be satisfactions. The protrusion of the inner area is met by the 'thing' which at first produces satisfaction. But with the return of 'hunger', and containment not always being available, an ambivalence, ±, now develops in the individual's inner area. The fulfilment that was satisfying at first has changed into ambivalence as seen in the 'never enough' condition of things unaccompanied by emotional warmth. The resultant state of being sated may have been the point at which some mystics like St Francis

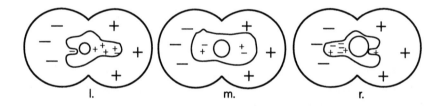

Figure 14.1a   Bion's invariant

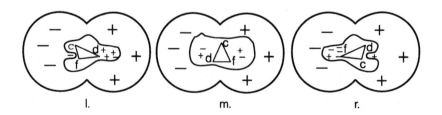

Figure 14.1b   A modification

of Assisi and the Buddha, realizing their 'starvation in the midst of plenty' turned to renunciation and detachment as shown in the phase on the right. Fig. 14.1 a (r)

Here the pull is in the direction of 'no-things' towards which the inner area has shifted and into which a protrusion extends with a corresponding dent on the other side. This illustrates a situation in which expectations have frequently not been met, resulting in pain and frustration. It is the assumed state of the mystic before he or she creates and receives unification with 'the Absolute' and when 'no-things' (fasting) become apparently secure nourishment. The threat however continues in the form of an invasion by 'things' (the temptations of the flesh) meaning a return of the longing for sensuous fulfilment. The mystic defends against this by further ascetic practices such as fasting which avoid disappointment and are designed to facilitate union with the Absolute or, in the case of Bion, with 'O'. But this is not reliable either; an addiction to 'no-things' can develop replacing the former addiction to 'things'. The clinician is reminded of the condition of bulimia alternating with anorexia nervosa. On the theoretical side Balint's 'basic fault' applies which results in 'thing-clinging' (ocnophilia) or 'thing-avoiding' (philobatism). Balint had expressed himself in terms of object-relationship and defined 'basic fault' as due to a lack of 'fit' between the infant's expectation and what the environment (people) had to offer (Balint, 1979). Gordon is seen as a 'mis-fit' who, however, exemplifies a mixed form. In the end, 'thing-avoidance' predominated, as his religious ideas and 'constant object' show. His occasional lapses into the opposite ('six dozen oysters') occurred on the fantasy level and in the form of ccasional drinking bouts.

The protrusion of actions and reactions points now into the minus area. Here too an ambivalence, now signified as $\bar{+}$ can develop. The $\bar{+}$ sign here as in Fig 14.1b (r) below, is used to indicate that the negative part of the ambivalence is stronger than the positive.

3   The individual's responses to the environmental areas of satisfaction (+) and frustration (−) are also indicated by amoeboid movements of the whole inner area. The outcome is that the area shifts and expands or shrinks and retreats accordingly. This means that up to a point *the individual influences the environment* right from the start.

4   The circular innermost 'O' is assumed to be smallest in conditions of greed, Fig. 14.1a(l). When greed dominates there can be no space for anything more 'absolute'. 'O' is largest in the mystic, Fig. 14.1a (r) who, if not actually 'at one', is in constant touch with 'O'.

5   Although treated here as having purely intrapsychic existence, it is acknowledged that 'things' do exist as such and that their physical presence or absence (as in starvation) can dominate all psychological responses. When this differentiation is not acknowledged psychotic states or, at best,

Utopias come about, as will be discussed in the last section (see Fig. 14.4, p. 339, below).

THE DEMYSTIFICATION OF 'O'

Fig. 14.1b is the same as fig. 14.1a except that the innermost area has been replaced by a triangle representing the variable reactions and actions which are set off by encounters with frustration and satisfaction. The importance of faith and doubt in analytic thought and discovery was discussed in the first chapter where the *'cultural activities'* were introduced as a third region in which both faith and doubt have a share. It is now taken up again because of its central significance in all human endeavour. The third point of the triangle is called 'cultural activities', abbreviated as 'c'. The term comprises science, art and religion. Without any further specifications it is meant to indicate that there can be no negotiation between 'things' and 'no-things' nor any balance between satisfaction and frustration in individual instances without this third factor coming into play. Winnicott's transitional phenomena as well as the child's playful experiments with losing and finding belong here. In 1951 this constituted an innovation in a psychoanalysis which true to its 'scientific' aspirations had no space for anything half-way between 'reality' and 'illusion' (Winnicott, 1958). In Jung's psychology the intermediate area between conscious and unconscious had been and remained of central importance since it was first referred to in an essay 'The Transcendent Function' (1916) (*CW* 6: para. 828). It had originally been called 'transcendent' because it represented the 'union of the conscious and unconscious'. Later this idea was to some extent replaced by the concept of the self and the 'reconciling symbol'. My own version emphasizes the parentage of faith (f) and doubt (d) giving rise to curiosity and the spirit of enterprise which are more highly developed in the human than in any other animal. But in my view 'c' also has an existence independent of its parents with which it constantly interacts, see also 'Zodiac', p. 325 below. Structurally this is expressed here by the third point of the triangle. 'C' itself being composed of science, art and religion is seen as trinitarian but without the religious aura that surrounds that term. In analogy with the human family we can say that it is in the position to feed the parents, 'f' and 'd'. Although there is nothing 'supernatural' or omniscient about it as there is about 'O', its existence is equally hermeneutic, that is it is only an interpretation, not an explanation of the phenomena. My interpretation is, however, worldly, not mystical. Whichever way we look at 'c', it requires the concentration and devotion of the individual, in short *cultivation*.

If 'cultural activities' sounds like being an indubitable support for faith, we only have to think of the ways in which both science and religion have been and are being used to destructive ends. Hence the connection with doubt is required to steer clear of idealization. At any event 'culture' like 'social' points to the individual not being an isolate. It follows that whatever thought, intuition etc. a person may have and however unique it may appear, it is sure to be grounded somewhere in the collective area of cultural activities signified by the third point of the triangle. As regards the theoretical importance of the cultural area in analysis, I find myself in agreement with Henderson who looks at it as an addition and extension to Jung's psychology (Henderson, 1991). In using 'c' in its triangular relation to faith and doubt I make no such claim.

I do however claim that it is of greater practical value than 'O'. Although put in the space where 'O' was, the triangle is no more than a temporary and rational representation of what remains ultimately unknown. The avoidance of the mystical aura of 'unknowable' is deliberate.

The fluctuating shape of the triangle in Fig. 14.1b gives information about the individual's orientation and deployment of resources between the plus and minus areas. The relation of the triangle to these areas *appears* to be determined by environmental conditions but is at least as much created by the individual him- or her-self. Unlike 'O', the triangle is unstable and, more often than not, asymmetrical, particularly by comparison with the circle, square and Jung's favourite number, four, elements which are the basis of his structural diagrams of psychological processes.

However, the main practical advantage of the triangle over the mystical 'O' is that the three points, faith, doubt and cultural activities do not require the mystic's unknowing and preparations for union with the 'Absolute'. Instead, the triangle reflects the prevalence of a condition in which the individual is in a divided state of mind, unlike 'being in "O"' or at Eliot's 'still point of the turning world'. *The strength of 'O' is that reason cannot comprehend it: that of the triangle composed of faith and doubt linked with cultural activities is that it can be grasped by reason.* And finally it can be empathically understood that 'faith–doubt' gives rise to fresh ideas which combined with cultural activities (science, art, religion) can transcend the limitations set by frustration with 'no-things' and satiety with 'things'. Cultural activities do become containers as well as the means of expression of preconceptions or, which is the same, archetypal images. But it is a medium that does not only mediate faith and doubt, but *becomes* the message and is therefore an autonomous area equal with 'f' and 'd'. For example, before America was discovered both faith and doubt about the westward passage to the Indies had been in evidence. What made the discovery feasible was, among other things, science in the form of navigation. Once on the map, the New World supplied refuge and nourishment to the old.

Looked at from another angle, the playful experiments of children are the forerunners of science as an innate cultural activity, similarly art, judging by the drawings of children and of prehistoric cave paintings. The tendency to put the product of vision and observation down on a surface we regard as innate. Similarly innate is the formation of myths and religion explaining the origin and destiny of mankind. It is not difficult to see an archetypal basis in the recurring patterns of behaviour. But the *content* and *interpretations* of the myths etc. have implications which determine our values and conduct very differently, depending on the epoch and cultural zone. Therefore 'cultural activities' rank here equal with faith and doubt in the triangle which shows the prevailing balance of our *variable* responses to frustration and satisfaction .

So where have we got to?

Earlier in the chapter (see p. 309), I pointed out that the tolerance of frustration was as crucial in the course of the analytic process as it is in daily life and in the history of civilization. It seems that frustration, tolerance and abstinence had played a part in the lives of mystics and others who had clearly been 'deprived' in early life. The question was how they coped and managed to survive and even flourish.

If we could find a vertex from which to view frustration or 'un-met preconceptions', we would probably be in a better position to answer this question as well as two others which had, in one form or another cropped up repeatedly in previous chapters. One was what was it that made thought products powerful, that is penetrating and potentially fertilizing, the other, why people should still want analysis. An exposition of Bion's view on the ratio of 'things' to 'no-things' seemed to provide a common basis for under-standing the survival under conditions of frustration and the power of thoughts that can arise if such frustrations are tolerated.

The map, Fig. 14.1a, was designed to render Bion's explications visible. It showed his hypothetical 'O' which here as elsewhere is as central in Bion's writing as the self is in Jung's. But I believe that such central and whole-making concepts, appealing though they are, could easily reduce analysis to a cult. I therefore decided to demystify 'O' and replace it by a triangle as shown in Fig. 14.1b as explained in the legend.

Map 14.1a and b will become the focal point of a more comprehensive map, see Fig. 14.3 in Part II of this chapter, showing the vertices of different analysts and one non-analytic psychotherapist in relation to each other. Before we can proceed we must choose a model (see Part II of this chapter, Fig. 14.2).

II PUTTING IT ON A MAP

CHOOSING A MODEL

No metaphorical reference to 'roots and branches', 'dream', 'myth' or 'jour-ney' can tell us what the *specific* characteristics of analysis are. Let us therefore start by assuming that a general analytic viewpoint (vertex) exists.

Next we notice that there are also several versions of it to which various groups of analysts subscribe. Taking an even closer look we become aware that these groups ('schools') are not as homogeneous as it appeared. Similarities notwithstanding, each individual analyst is also the representative of his own vertex, so that there are necessarily divergencies and dissensions. Therefore, even before choosing a model we have to bear in mind that an analytic map *cannot* meet the approval of all analysts. What is more it cannot *be* the territory any more than any other map. But Korzibsky's 'The map is not the territory' can usefully be combined with a line of Fielding's: 'Map me no maps, sir, my head is a map, a map of the whole world' (Fielding, ca. 1730). By combining the two statements we arrive at the following. *The map in the head of the analyst is the territory. It reflects his vision and is supported by his trust in a particular analytic vertex and the observations made in that light.* Like the interactional map, fig. 12.8, map fig. 14.3 bears no resemblance to what the analytic experience is like. It merely represents an attempt to show *what it is about*, that is what the guiding ideas, theories and techniques are.

As for the process of mapping, I follow Wollheim's suggestion concerning the case of the prehistoric cave-dwellers' painting (see p. 202). Which combines the preconceptions in the mind of the analyst, not only with the observations made, but also with the movements of the eye that gauges the space available on the paper and the hand that guides the pen. Thus thoughts are imaged and transformed into physical shape. During the metamorphosis thoughts become more substantial and can evolve further because the medium of mapping makes us visualize the various elements in their spatial relationship to each other.

Generally speaking, we map to clarify our knowledge of a 'territory' by making it visible and public. Moreover, maps are a medium which gets away from words that have become threadbare and inadequate. The mapper knows that his/her product looks like a final statement when it really came about by way of hesitations, adjustments and surprises. They occurred when vision, sight and movement of the hand were being coordinated in the act of creation. In addition, it is expedient that the mapper should choose a model with which he or she is familiar. The model limits but does not inhibit an imaginative rendering of several vertices. If I chose the planetary system as model, it is not because I think it represents the prototype of analysis or to demonstrate 'a profound harmony between all forms of existence' (cf. *CW 9, II*: para. 413). Jung found it 'easy to see' why the first attempts to construct a model of the atom used the planetary system as prototype (ibid.: para. 380). I have selected the model on account of the flexibility and mobility within a structure that has undergone significant revisions since it was first designed. I do not regard the model as an analogue of anything.

The model

The model for designing Figure 14.3 is borrowed from Cellarius' Celestial Atlas, '*Harmonia Macrocosmica*' (1660). The map represented here depicts a modification of the geocentric planetary system as originally proposed by

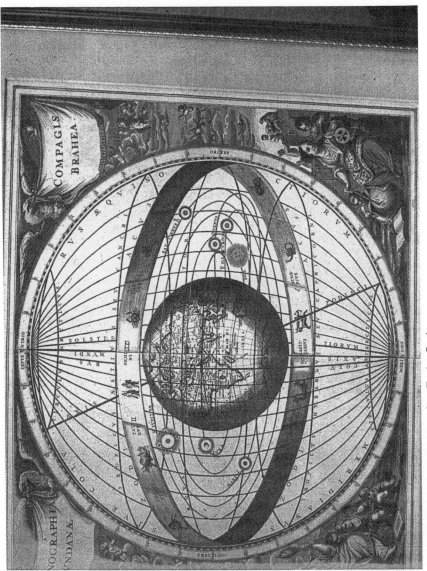

Figure 14.2 Celestial map, after Tycho Brahe

Ptolemy, see Fig. 14.2. Although technically speaking a celestial map, I have treated it here as belonging to the 'Early world maps' described on p. 208f. The cosmic relation with the centralized world justifies it being classified as such in the present context. Brahe, who designed this view of the solar system, was born three years after Copernicus' death in 1543, the year in which his famous *De Revolutionibus Orbium Caelestium* had appeared. The point is that despite all his painstaking astronomical observations which included the orbits of the planets, Brahe disagreed with Copernicus and clung to the geocentric universe. Copernicus' heliocentric universe with the earth revolving around the sun took quite some time to become accepted.

Some details of our model need mentioning so that the reader can see what has been modified or stripped away in order to adapt the map to our requirements. We note, for example, that the axis of the zodiac is shown at a tilt in contrast to the earth's axis which was still depicted as vertical. Consequently the girdle of the zodiac appears oval. It has been left that way because of the visual effect of three-dimensionality. The axis itself has been omitted because it gives the wrong impression of there being an opposite that is of constant orientational value, for example above or below, north or south; see also under 'Axes' (p. 327). The earth looks as if it were suspended in space inside a circle, formed in turn by the circle of an equinoctial meridian on the outside, while the other meridians, forerunners of the degrees of longitude, appear as vertical lines the curvature of which increases from the centre to the periphery. In combination with the horizontal oval lines it creates a network-like effect. Most of the ovals stand for the orbits, then believed to be circular but shown here as ovals because they are seen slanted. The irregularly spaced planets – the sun is included – give the whole map a rotating or at least mobile appearance which is what we need, see fig. 14.2.

Shifts in and between universes

Our model must allow for shifts within the analytic realm as well as for its relations to other universes. A comparison with the maps in Cellarius' atlas tells us that in astronomy there have been periods of pro- and re-gression. The same holds good for maps showing the discovery of our own planet. This has to be expected in any developing science and there is no reason why analysis should be an exception. It looks for example as if a *shift in the analytic universe* had taken place when the self eclipsed the ego as the centre of analytic theory. At present it may seem as if it had been all progress. But it will take time to assess whether or to what extent this constituted progress or regress. Therefore periodic surveys and adjustments are required to assess what concept is central in its spatial relation to others. The need for such surveys applies particularly to analysis because our theories are as persuasive as maps but assessment of the relations between the process and the outcome are riddled with subjectivity. However, for the sake of everyday orientation, the sun that appears to rise in the east and to set in the west did not lose its orientational importance after Copernicus' discovery had reduced the earth to just one of the planets of our solar system. But we must limit ourselves to a consideration of the spatial position of any given vertex on our map, Fig. 14.3, in relation to others. We could for instance map in what circumstances the concepts which combine to form a vertex are seemingly equivalent or differentiated and even opposed to, and incompatible with, each other.

As a particular example of a shift the case of the ego may be quoted: its practical orientating continuity creating and linking function remains as much required as ever. But the more the mechanics of living demand our attention, the more it becomes essential to know what it is all about because the 'other', the hypothetical non-ego or self cannot be dictated to, as Eliot reminds us (see p. 178 above). Getting to know this other is of practical importance since it needs to be taken into account. We learn to disregard or suppress it on account of our socio-cultural emphasis on mastery. But it is during infancy and times of emergency, disability and helplessness that the psychosomatic demands of the self become irrepressible. Hence my reminder of our living and analysing in the virtual space between two or more worlds, as mentioned on p. 311 above.

Analysis dwells in and illuminates this space and so helps us to appreciate that apparently different worlds such as psyche and soma, intrapsychic and interpersonal, or of 'things' and 'no-things', satisfaction and frustration belong conceptually to the same moiety, realm or cosmos. Both halves are contingent on each other for recognition. Sometimes they seem so close as to virtually overlap, as for instance in moments of doubt whether the acquisition of a 'thing' will contribute to one's well-being or become a hindrance. The over-riding analytic criterion for deciding whether to acquire or refrain, to hold fast or to let go, must be which decision is likely to keep open the space between as the channel of communication. Here doubt can help to make no decision which implies the freedom of the self to remain mobile, allowing the I (ego) as executive organ to follow. It is a decision made from within the open analytic space. Were *that* to collapse by a unification of opposite worlds, we would, analytically speaking, be dead. But no 'union of opposites' is required nor indeed possible, if two irreconcilable worlds are seen as two sides of the same coin, belonging to the same moiety, each defining the other. They are only separated in a potential space which is however our most important channel of communication. The analytic aim implied by Jung's psychology of the 'union of opposites' is an ideal, and as unattainable by ordinary mortals as the mystic's union with the Absolute. As long as the channel remains open, the possibility exists of discovering that the apparently disparate worlds, say of politics and analysis are not as diametrically opposed to each other as they seem. (For details see *The Political Psyche*, Samuels, 1993). Any idealistic hope and declaration that it is all one world, that microcosmos and macrocosmos are 'all the same', will effectively stifle relatively unprejudiced investigation, most of all the discovery of detailed points of contact as well as of disparity.

The mention of ego/self as alternative foci on an analytic map recalls Neumann's ego-self axis which he chose to describe as an opposite and complementary relationship (Neumann, op. cit.). Jung used axial schemata in order to demonstrate the archetypal structure of the transference, the structure of the self and the union of opposites (*CW 9, II*: para. 347ff). Axes are not infrequently used by post-Jungians in connection with psychological types, in recent years for example by Beebe (op. cit.). The schemata are said to be based on clinical experience, as is said of all intuitive insights. But because symmetries are aesthetically satisfying, the hidden danger is that events and persons are made to fit in with intuitively anticipated and symmetrically arranged schemata.

THE CONSTRUCTION OF FIG. 14.3

This map is, like all maps, meant as an aid to orientation. Unlike cartographical maps the orientation is in non-physical space and without definite boundaries. The scale can only be deduced from the position, distances and relations of the various 'landmarks' to each other. It tells the mapper and other viewers where they stand in relation to the territory from which all details have been omitted. The map is therefore a general survey conducted from the mapper's point of view at a certain moment in the life of a cosmos that does not stand still. According to the types provided in the glossary of Chapter 11, the map is a mixture of a fantasy and a thematic map (see p. 213 above). The subjectivity of the map is valuable, if agreements and disagreements about it can be balanced against each other. The balance will point the way to a differentiated and relatively objective view which could conceivably be tested by observers. The next step would be to design a large-scale map of the itinerary type on which the various steps of the analytic process could be plotted. But that is a project which must await future developments. For the time being, however, we must remember that the map may become authoritative, as all maps do. This is unwanted and I suggest as an antidote that this or any similar map should be treated with deliberate disrespect after it has served the purpose of portraying a certain cosmic orientation. But not with disrespect for the medium of mapping which has a quality in common with analysis that is of the essence and is best put in form of a paradox: the map is there and yet it is not. It is as puzzling as the 'fly away Peter, fly away Paul' game is to little children. However, this time it is not a game. In Bion's language, the map is sometimes a 'thing' but then again it is a 'no-thing', each requires the other for its claim to existence. Each is as real as the other. The paradox is that 'thing' and 'no-thing' are equally important. We are reminded of Bion's statement regarding the invariant ratio. The variable situations within the ratio are illustrated maps, figs 14.1a and b. In other words, patients in the course of analysis become accustomed to living between worlds of 'things' and 'no-things', of satisfaction *and* frustration. Individual solutions may then emerge. 'May' because the emergence must not be a foregone conclusion in the analyst's mind. That would prejudice the patient's potential and separate discovery. The analyst as pointed out can best guard against this by making his/her 'map' visible. It becomes then undeniable that he or she *has* an aim and 'desire' which can then be discarded, but not before.

The central sphere

The large sphere in the middle (corresponding to the earth in Brahe's map) represents the analytic realm as a whole. In the centre we see various lines converge where Bion's 'invariant' is assumed to lie. For the sake of simplicity it is reduced here to a focal point. We recall in passing that most of the time it is far from being like Eliot's 'still point of the turning world'. The exceptions are moments of being centred or being in *Tao*, resembling Fordham's self in an integrated state, see also Fig. 14.1a and b (m).

The 'planets' and 'orbits'

Each of the seven vertices depicted occupies a lettered place on the four orbits. The places are of the vertices most frequently referred to in these pages, that is of Freud, Jung, Klein, Bion, Winnicott and Fordham, but now there is also a non-analytic psychotherapist 'X'. It will be noticed that Freud's portion of the line occupies the widest space. It lies on the outer orbit on which Jung and Bion are also placed. (A short stroke limits the space they occupy.) Klein is on an orbit of her own; so are Winnicott and 'X'. The place where the stippled lines start from Freud are thought of as illuminating rays which touch the other vertices in different ways. For example, fairly near the middle in the case of Bion and Winnicott and at the edge of the others, even that of psychotherapist 'X'. All this is, as mentioned, highly subjective and reveals no more than the orientation of the mapper concerning the analytic territory. *The real value of the map lies in the freedom and immediacy of the method as a communication.* The mapper has toyed with the allotment of landmarks, spaces and so forth according to his predilections. Now the map makes public what had been private and personal. Once public it is open to criticism and subsequent surveys according to the 'maps' of other analysts and informed sections of the public. We may expect agreements, disagreements and evaluations which can be subjected to further study. All of this can stimulate the design of research into analytic vertices and their relation to the technique and process. For, if the discovery of the earth is anything to go by, once the existing world image and *Weltanschauung* began to be doubted, new maps followed. However inaccurate, maps can also stimulate exploration. *One wonders whether a comparable renaissance is due in analysis.*

Returning to Fig. 14.3, we note that Freud, Jung and Bion share the same orbit, namely the one that is furthest away from the centre. The three vertices

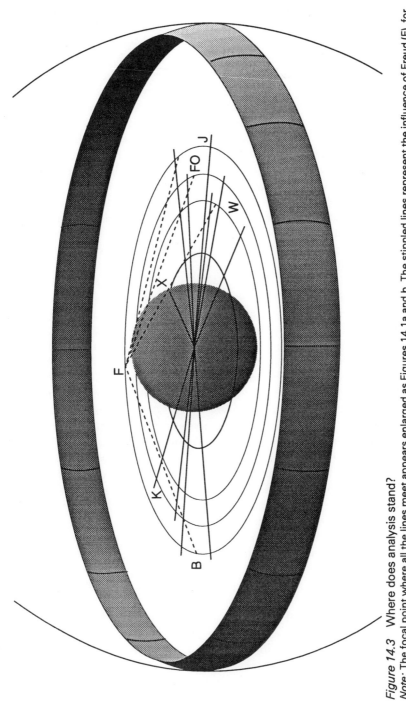

Figure 14.3 Where does analysis stand?

Note: The focal point where all the lines meet appears enlarged as Figures 14.1a and b. The stippled lines represent the influence of Freud (F), for example, on the other analysts: K (Klein), B (Bion), W (Winnicott), J (Jung), FO (Fordham) and on X (a psychotherapist) which are placed on the same orbit are meant to indicate that all three are regarded as equally 'massive' in their contribution, hence represented at the same distance from the 'earthly' centre, here the analytic sphere. Sometimes one, sometimes another can appear at the zenith. Their orbits being the longest, the three 'planets' will take longer to revolve. (They have the longest 'year', or in predictive terms, the illuminating effect of the three vertices will last longer than that of others. Being distant also implies that the exponents were primarily theoreticians, not so close to the field of observation as to be overcome by the emotional charge that emanates from it, they were deeply involved in their observations, yet sufficiently detached to formulate their vision and observation in an original way. Their thoughts were powerful with all the implications mentioned in the foregoing section.

Klein is seen to be near Bion who followed her. If her orbit is nearer the centre, it is because I see her as rather less of a theoretician. Her clinical observations and theoretical assumptions are close together which helped her to find formulations like 'the depressive position' which still enjoys widespread popularity and is used by analysts of other schools, see also Chapter 13, the Klein–Jungian hybrid. The same can be said of Winnicott who was above all an astute clinical observer whose 'transitional object' became widely known and not infrequently misused. Fordham has been put on the same orbit as Klein and for the same reasons. His major contribution, not perhaps as widely known as those of the others, is that the self begins in earliest childhood and that it can be observed in two phases, integration and de-integration.

This leaves the psychotherapist 'X' who is uncommitted to any 'school' although we must assume that his/her knowledge has not been left untouched by Freud. But in the main he or she works with common sense, empathy and 'positive thinking'. He/she leaves the analysis of the transference alone wherever possible, yet may be working very close to our sphere as a whole and to the central area as mapped in Fig. 14.1a. But his/her 'light' (= theory) does not reach down to it. It is seen but not envisioned. Just because of the closeness of the vertex of 'X' to what is physically perceptible (the expression of affects and 'sensa'), the power of thought in terms of vision cannot illuminate the realm of the invisible when it is eclipsed by 'sensa'. X's position is rather like that of the moon that, revolving around the earth at the same rate, has a 'captured rotation', thus making it impossible to see the dark side of it. Conversely the placing of the 'planets' in fig. 14.3 assumes that the distance from the centre is directly proportional to the acuity and penetrating force of the vision in contrast to 'sight'.

The relative position of the planets to each other is, like the other contents, admittedly subjective yet relevant in the present context. One example must suffice. It concerns the positions of Klein–Bion on one side and Jung on the other. Their being on opposite sides does not mean that they are opposed to each other in all respects. In fact, they do have a lot in common. So placement here depends on whether to allot priority to equivalents or differences and what criteria we chose for either.

Let us take the differences first because that will show the reader more than anything else where techniques point to innate attitudes which clash to such an extent that hybridization becomes impossible. In general, I have come to regard techniques as more reliable guides to fundamental attitudes than comparisons of concepts and theoretical statements. In other words, if we were only to look at theory for comparison, the gulf between different 'schools'

Table 5 Equivalents – apparent or real?

Example:		
Jung's *'Primary identity'* *'Participation mystique'*	*Klein's* *'Projective identification'*	
	Interchangeability:	
	Real	*Apparent*
Seen from the angle of:		
1 Phenomenal and experiential categories	*	
2 Technique and attitude, e.g. classic vs romantic		*
3 Theoretical assumptions and origin of vertices		*
In the setting of:		
4 Friendly discussion	*	
5 Public debate and publications		*

would appear to be bridgeable. Not all the differences to which I referred before, nor indeed the apparent equivalences are represented by the location of vertices on the same or opposite side of Fig. 14.3. Some details are better dealt with by text and tabulation (see Table 5).

Technique and attitude

The table is an attempt to differentiate between aspects and settings under which an equivalence or interchangeability of terms is either apparent or real. The situation becomes even more complex, when the theoretical terms used by two schools are the same but mean something different or have multiple applications. This is the case with the self, as we have just seen. Another stark example has recently come upon the scene by way of the 'psychic balance' or 'equilibrium'. For Kleinians this means a 'pathological organization' used by the patient to avoid psychic pain (Spillius, ed., 1988). For Jung 'psychic equilibrium' or balance is the mid-point of the personality – a creative centre, likened to being in Tao (*CW* 7: para. 365). The psyche maintains its equilibrium because it is a self-regulating system (the disturbance of which causes trouble) (*CW 16*: para. 330). Here opposed vertices require clear expression and different handling (technique) confirms the different connotations. The major criterion for the placement of our 'planets' was technique. It will therefore be discussed in detail. The differentiation as such explains why there can be no axis or polarization in Fig. 14.3 as there is in the model, Fig. 14.2.

It would require many axes to show in what respect different vertices throw either the same or different light on the focal centre. By not introducing an axis I am consistent with the view expressed on the *concept of opposites* referred to above (see p. 122, above). There I argued that each of the polarities contains characteristics of what is supposedly opposite. As both belong to the same category, they are merely the other side of the same coin. I have therefore assumed that there are different perspectives depending on the position in which the 'planet' is in its orbit and if the third dimension, depth, were used, it could show at what points in their orbits the planets, that is vertices, are congruent. In other words, Fig. 14.3 is really a two-dimensional snapshot taken at the moment when Klein–Bion with Jung on the other side were in 'opposition'. The moment was chosen according to the criterion of different techniques applied to apparently interchangeable conceptual terms as shown in the example of table 5. Readers are already familiar with it from our previous discussion (see p. 285, Chapter 13 above; see also p. 331 above). As the phenomena and categories as well as the setting, that is points 1, 4 and 5, have been referred to already, we can now look at differences in technique next and subsequently make some observations about the origin of vertices which cannot be dissociated altogether from the proponents' personal background.

There can hardly be a greater difference in technique than between Klein and Bion on the one side and Jung on the other. Klein, in her interpretations, avoids 'similes, metaphors and quotations' (op. cit. 1961). Bion avoids myths and dreams and dream thoughts in his interpretations and refers to *pictorialized formulations* as 'psychomorphology' (Bion, 1970). *Jung would be unthinkable without it.* Yet all three look to transformations that bring about a change, that is development, in the patient's present psychic condition and, ultimately, personality. Furthermore, the writings of all three make it clear that the intrapsychic world and dynamics are their primary concern in comparison with interpersonal relationships which are regarded as the outer and tangible vehicles of change.

This is very different in Jung's case descriptions as well as in his metapsychological language – most 'Jungians' ignoring the distinction regard it as psychological – where he makes almost constant use of images. His 'amplifications' are usually pictorial, and so are his illustrated intuitions supported, for example, by alchemical parallels to the psychological process. Sometimes the illustrations take the form of patients' paintings, sometimes of symbolic pictures taken from various cultures and from different epochs. At other times vivid word images, metaphors and comparisons are used in the 'dialectic' process of analysis. A particularly striking example is his work on the trans-ference. The state of the patient's psyche is deduced from the similarity to alchemical images including symbolism and accompanying affects. The latter may be projected on to the person of the analyst who responds affectively, by being tuned into the same motif. (See also my example of 'mutual transference', p. 277 above.) He or she can be so, not only by empathy and intuition but also because of having 'been there before'. This includes knowledge of the ampli-ficatory material, mythology and so on. That is to say the direct projections aimed at the person of the analyst do reach that person but – and now it becomes a matter of technique – are treated (not necessarily explained) via the medium of collective images. So the state of the patient's psyche is discussed on the basis of symbolic imagery. My impression is that when this was not the case, Jung used common sense backed up by metaphors and arguments *'ad hominem'*.

Winnicott, however, is very different from Klein and Bion when he uses spontaneous drawings (squiggles) as a technique of elucidating fantasy but he takes a share in it at the same time by adding to the patient's squiggle or by making his own to which the patient can interpret and add to and so on, rather like Jung's amplifications pictorialized. His attitude to 'unconscious' produc-tions in which the conscious or cognitive mind participates is also close to Jung's transcendent function. Despite their different theoretical vertices a similarity in their techniques points to a kinship in their attitudes and to a spirit which appreciates that fertile area of the mind where outer and inner realities meet and spontaneously combine. I have therefore put Winnicott closer to Jung than to either Klein or Bion or, for that matter, Freud. There is a further technical meeting point inasmuch as both use word – as well as visual – images in their interpretations. Their congruence in matters of technique seems to me of greater practical consequence than the different sources of their knowledge and theories. I think that their fundamental clinical, rather than theoretical approach to the patient is shown when they allow space for uncertainty and spontaneity. Frustrations and satisfactions, 'things' and 'no-things' become relative and less fixed when illusory and fleeting imagery is positively evaluated rather than ruthlessly exposed to the 'truth'. It is therefore consistent that both recognized and valued the intermediate area whether referred to as 'transi-tional phenomena' or as the 'transcendent function'. The difference is that in Jung's case the phenomena were considered less intermediate and often be-came of central and autonomous significance. Their symbolic content was expected to bring about changes. It was not to be reduced by taking it apart, that is analysed.

My placing of Fordham between Jung and Winnicott has been inconsistent with the criterion of technique on the basis of which he should have been close to Bion and Klein. The same applies to Fordham's astringent attitude towards imagery which remains uninterpreted. If I have nevertheless put him close to Jung, it is because that is formally correct, meaning according to 'family' tree, contribution and institution. Although much of what I said about Fordham applies also to myself, I am of the opinion that the crucial events in analysis do not depend on verbal communications. I allow images and affects to speak for themselves and don't mind so much if they are less controllable than words.

The rough and ready criteria of technique were (a) frequency of session and regular use of the couch and (b) interpretations of the transference on the personal, that is the I–you level and (c) the trust or distrust that is put into visual imagery and symbolism that does not require to be reduced (analysed) in order to be understood. As long as it cannot be demonstrated that the Jungian vertex can be implemented by Kleinian technique or vice versa, it is premature to talk of hybridization.

The criterion of technique is unequivocal because the analyst cannot do two things at the same time such as interpret verbally *and* keep silent, or make observations about the archetypal symbolism and its amplifications as represented in a picture *and* interpret, for example, that the patient brought the picture in order to avoid facing his/her sexual feelings for the analyst.

It must, however, be added that there is no homogeneity behind party lines. Kleinian analysts like Rosenfeld take issue with colleagues who like Winnicott state that the needs of psychotic patients are often not satisfied by verbal interpretations alone (Rosenfeld, 1987). He believes that the analyst's words alone can hold the patient together. However, Rosenfeld makes allowances for the analyst's 'whole attitude, behaviour and way' in which the words are communicated. (I assume that this includes particularly the tone of voice.) Among the 'Jungians' it is Fordham who in opposing Schwartz-Salant's attitude to interpretations clearly adopts Rosenfeld's Kleinian stance (Fordham, 1991). Personally, I agree with Thomä when he writes about the fanaticism that has developed about interpretation (Thomä, 1987, in Klauber and others). As Klauber, a widely respected psychoanalyst pointed out, there is a tendency to overstress the value of interpretations. He mentions Ferenczi, Michael Balint and Winnicott as belonging to a different stream (op. cit.). Spontaneity would also permit touching the patient and even physically holding a very regressed patient as Winnicott did when the occasion seemed to demand it (reported by Little, op. cit.).

My position on technique is best stated by the example of spontaneously giving a token which may in certain circumstances tide the patient over the analyst's absence. It is an example of a technique which provides a valuable criterion and pointer to where an analyst – attitude, technique, vertex and all – really stands. The hope in the case of separation anxiety is that the token, a 'thing' belonging to the analyst will function as transitional object being both a 'me' and 'not me' possession negotiating between presence and absence, after the manner that some mothers spontaneously leave their handbag as a token that they will convey to an anxious toddler that she will come back. The risk is that the token can acquire magical properties and be used as a fetish.

Technique as such is not primary but meant merely as implement of an original idea which has become a vertex. Different vertices require different technical application as the example of Winnicott's 'death' of an object in contrast to Jung's 'ghost' of an object given above demonstrated (see p. 32 above). Reasons have been shown why technique is a more reliable guide to where an analyst stands than theoretical statements and loyal declarations. But the individual analyst's innate attitude, referred to as 'classic' or 'romantic', or a particular mixture of the two, must also be a factor when we evaluate his/her standpoint according to the criterion of technique.

Finally, the common denominator between all techniques is that without adequate contact with the patient as a person they are ineffectual. Thus, the analyst's silence can make the patient feel abandoned, as if his/her utterance had been worthless. Likewise the analyst who holds forth can make the patient feel left behind or even out. *The finding of a meeting point may be a very individual matter. In importance, however, it comes even before finding 'the truth'.* This has always been acknowledged by Jung for whom the patient's immediate presence was more relevant than his/her past experience. The maintenance of contact and spontaneity when new ground is being broken and self-knowledge is added under stormy conditions and with the help of a technique makes demands which so far have remained uncharted. But in all this uncertainty certain directions and positions can be distinguished and, however tentatively, mapped.

The origin of vertices

We saw that the human touch cannot be omitted when it comes to the application of analytic knowledge by way of techniques. Likewise, the origin of a vertex cannot be dissociated from the person and background of the analyst who pioneered it. For example, the effect of Freud's Jewishness on his social background and theories has often been commented on, recently for instance by Stroeken (1991). Early educational and professional interests undoubtedly play a part in the origin of vertices and the field of observation to which they are applied. Winnicott's work in paediatrics, Jung's on schizophrenia and the development of thought and symbol-formation are clear pointers. Bion's readings in philosophy and mathematics were an obvious influence on his vertex. It is also clear that he was affected by the fossilized establishment religiosity of his childhood which made him so vigorous in his protest against 'lies'. It was probably conducive to his discovering the merits of mysticism.

Undeniably each pioneer climbed up on the shoulders of his predecessors. Having got there, they attempted to improve on their spiritual ancestors by showing up where they had been wrong, each son or daughter, so to speak, being more right than the parent. But the value of such deconstructions is that it links a theory with the social and cultural matrix. For the latter is both the background of thoughts and vertices, as well as the foreground on which patient and analyst meet. When theory does its job of throwing light on unexplored territories, the personal psychology of the explorer seems to me irrelevant.

The 'zodiac' and the outer circle

We now leave the part of our structural model that had been adopted for orientation among analytic vertices and turn towards the periphery. As we do so, fig. 14.3 becomes more speculative and changes from a thematic to a fantasy map. This seems inevitable when the referent is the context of analysis as a phenomenon in our time.

On the far side of the analytic sphere and the vertices which orbit around it we find the 'zodiac' with its twelve 'constellations' widely known on account of their astrological significance. I have used this structure to represent the encompassing cultural realm(s) as the matrix of ideas and thought products which can lead to discoveries and inventions. The apparent orbiting of the 'constellations' is meant to represent the coming and going of epochs. Their influence on human evolution and history is not questioned. It is however unevenly distributed according to geographical zones and temporal 'climates'.

The ideas – Bion's thoughts in search of a thinker – are assumed to emanate from this realm (Bion, 1970). A plausible but speculative example of the beginning of a new epoch would be to consider the intensified and systematic searches into our inner world as coinciding more or less with the completion of the discoveries of the earth. In passing we note that 'cultural' now appears in three contexts. It was first used in connection with Fig. 14.1b where it represented an individual's participation in cultural activities, one corner of the triangle in 14.1b, 'c'. Now 'cultural' refers to an epoch from which thoughts and their consequent developments originate. A further subdivision brings us to cultural zones or climates referring to the geographical distribution of cultures.

Let us now look at the outer circle of our model, Fig. 14.2, representing the equinoctial meridian. I shall treat the outer circle as if it represented the social and political system which confines our cosmos. It is yet another neglected aspect in analytic literature. This despite the undubitable influence it has on how – or even whether – analysis can be practised and taught. I referred to this as 'The presence of the third', borrowing the title from Cremerius (Cremerius, 1984, Plaut 1990, both op. cit.). Although living in the same cultural epoch and zone, Cremerius and I represent diametrically opposed but possibly complementary positions. Politically speaking, I submit that Cremerius views analysis from the position of one who works within the medical insurance system. Seeing it from without, I feel free to regard analysis, as Jung did, as the successor to a religious psychotherapeutic system, the function of which had been to help individuals negotiate between outer and inner realities. Yet in our politically different views both Cremerius and I are concerned with the population's health. As part of the socio-political system, analytic therapy depends to a greater extent than has been acknowledged on implicit moral injunctions which will be summarized on p. 344 below .

A different but related example of the point of contact between the cultural 'zodiac' and the socio-political system – the encircling 'meridian' with its influence on analytic practice – is the following. In parts of the world where the value of the individual, meritocracy and capitalism predominate, analysis flourishes. Where, on the other hand, the 'we'- or group-identity represented the greatest good, analysis, like religion, has at best been tolerated and certainly regarded with suspicion, as the 'soul' of each person was the common property of the tribe or State.

FROM DAYDREAMS TO UTOPIA

> A map of the world that does not include Utopia is not worth glancing at, for it leaves out the country at which Humanity is always landing.
> (Oscar Wilde, 'The soul of man under socialism', 1891)

The mention of political systems provides a natural transition to Thomas More's political satire from the title of which the generic term 'Utopia' is derived (More, 1516) (Trl. from the Latin and introduced by Paul Turner, 1965). Although it is not often noted that the word literally means 'Not-place', usage has made it into 'ideal-place' in contrast to the real world with which we have to put up, no matter how much we hope to transform it into a better world. We know about the seriousness with which political idealists and dictators have tried to create ideal states, no matter how much they were out of keeping with human nature and hence also economically unviable. Most of the considerable Utopian literature continues to be written in the form of futuristic fiction and/or as playful entertainment much in the vein that More wrote. Nevertheless, the toying with wish-fulfilling idealistic fantasies against a pretended realistic background is not all there is to More's Utopia. It is at the same time a criticism of the social and religious system of which he was a part. If More as a devout Catholic advocated among other things euthanasia, the marriage of priests and divorce by mutual consent, he could only hope to get away with it by telling it as a joke – the more or less of which was left to the reader. But the jibe at the existing state of affairs is unmistakable and a surefire way to popularity.

What is the significance of Utopian literature for analysis? We recall that in the case of religion Freud's statement was unequivocal. It was an illusion without a future (*SE 21*: p. 1f) The inference would be that there is no Utopian aspect to analysis itself with its emphasis on global aims on the one hand and, on the other, illusions that are unavoidably there but only in order to be analysed, that is reduced to what is supposed to be *really* there, awaiting only a 'mutative interpretation'. But illusions proved resistant and entered by the backdoor. First there was, as we saw, Winnicott with his transitional phenomena and Klauber who argued that transference was an illusion. Second, there was Freud's increasing pessimism about the outcome of psychoanalytic therapy. As regards 'Jungian' analysis critical voices like Blomeyer's have been raised, with myself also questioning the reality of 'individuation' as the end product of analysis (Blomeyer, op. cit.). The value of this global aim is undermined, as soon as we regard it as no more than an expression of faith. To think of it as realizable is an illusion, or rather an Utopia.

The setting and 'place' of Utopia

The aggressive–destructive element in More's political satire is well covered up by the amusing style of the narrative, in contrast to the Robinson Crusoe type of Utopia which shows mankind's hankering after a 'new beginning' matched by the attraction of the void. The dread of solitude and isolation as the price to be paid for a new beginning has not been left out. Nor has inventiveness and the tendency to cultivate, both apparently innate. Faith, doubt (despair) and cultural activities, the triangle in fig. 14.1b, are well represented in most Robinsonades. Characteristically, the would-be location is inaccessible, secure from the evils of the world. Islands seem to be the natural habitat of Utopias. Here the reader is reminded of the section 'Islomania and spatiality' in Chapter 11 (see p. 223f above) and also General Gordon's paradise on a Seychelle island (Chapter 9, Part I, p. 151f above).

The importance of the analyst's room as the location of analysis and the dyad which operates in solitude in the 'space' between two worlds implies that analysis facilitates the formation of illusions. True, it does not avoid the brutishness of human nature, nor does it – as many Utopias do – hold out the promise of longevity, to say nothing of immortality, as Christian eschatology does. On the other hand, improved psychosomatic health is an implicit and even officially recognized aim. True, analysts do not pretend to offer a *eutopia* (the Gk. prefix 'eu' points to good-beautiful-happy). But the conditions and the setting of analysis may speak louder to the patient than words.

There is a further resemblance to Utopian fiction in which the hero, if he returns at all, is seen to have undergone a metamorphosis or change. And transformations or change for the better are, as we saw, what analysis claims to bring about whether on the 'macro' scale of global aims or in small ways during an analytic session. In the chapter on constant objects I pointed out the frequent reality of 'no change' and the virtue of accepting it (see p. 162 above). But I do believe that we all harbour a south-sea island fantasy and that the actual location of the consulting room as well as the space that analysis gives to 'freely floating' evoke the powerful archetypal motif of Utopian bliss, going back to the Garden of Eden. Neither appeals to reason, nor can interpretations alter the longing. The analytic dyad on its 'island' does attract Utopian illusions and subsequent disappointments. Assorted group therapies offer no escape in

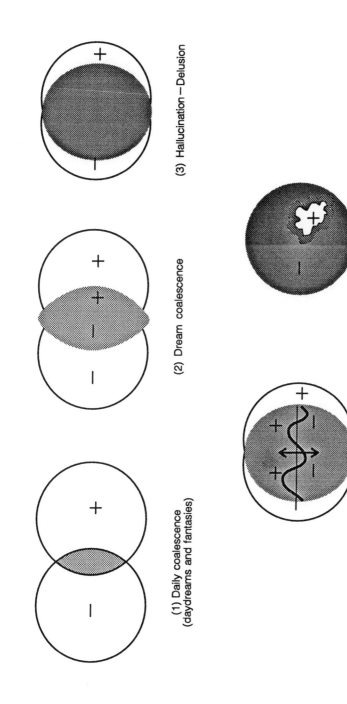

(1) Daily coalescence
(daydreams and fantasies)

(2) Dream coalescence

(3) Hallucination – Delusion

(4) Illusion

(5) Utopia

Figure 14.4   From daydreams to Utopia

as much as they nurture 'messianic hopes', as Bion had pointed out (Bion, 1961). The Utopian fantasy about analysis is further increased by the eternal hankering after a panacea. Although we can adopt a superior or sarcastic attitude to such childish longings, this does not banish and may even preserve them. Let us be clear: analysis is not an Utopia. But for the reasons given it is singularly vulnerable and exposed to Utopian projections from which illusions are the more likely to develop, the longer an analysis goes on.

In view of all this, why not make space for our ever-recurring Utopian fantasies and thereby render them relatively harmless, admitting the fantasy and enjoying the fiction for what it is, yet without surrendering to it? As a first step to acceptance, here is how I see Utopia within the theoretical frame of analysis and with particular reference to the ambivalent areas of ± and ∓ Fig. 14.1a.

Legend to Fig. 14.4

The illustration shows a hypothetical series of four common and one uncommon (3) responses to frustration and satisfaction. The five responses are not fixed. The purpose is to demonstrate the stages leading to Utopia.

1. The small shaded area shows how in the course of daily fluctuations between satisfaction and frustration an involuntarily coalescence occurs in the form of daydreams when differentiation is temporarily lost.
2. Is the same as 1 but the shaded area is considerably greater in dreams which are relatively independent of what is going on outside, as the protrusions of the shaded area beyond the circles is meant to indicate. Strong + and − feeling responses are more likely when the link with the world outside and judgement are temporarily lost.
3. An extreme or pathological state where differentiation is lost in the dark central area of false perceptions and beliefs. The condition is assumed to be the outcome of traumatic events and deprivations. The areas in which + and − were distinct has been almost totally eclipsed by the size and intensity of the overlap where + and − have lost their usual meaning. Sickle-shaped fringes of differentiated areas are seen on either side.
4. The shaded area is as large as in 3, but less intense (grey) so that the categories + and − are distinguishable. The dividing line is meant to be mobile, irregular and fluctuating. The greyness can change patchily like a fog. It is this area which has become more positively evaluated in latter-day psychoanalysis than it was in Freud's day.
5. Utopia as an island is usually treated as a 'eutopia'. It is the grown-ups' play area. Deliberately exploited in fiction, it alleviates feelings of frustration and despair and can recreate the hope of a better world; Utopias are neither meant to be taken too seriously, nor yet to be despised. Anyone can take a day off on the island and perhaps a nostalgic smile can be taken

home as a souvenir. The parallel lines of the grey area indicate an author's deliberate design to make the incredible plausible so that we can join in the playful deception, knowing that it is just that and enjoy it. Enjoyment is a word which stands for another much neglected aspect of psychoanalysis.

Summing up

In any comparison between Utopia and analysis the all-important difference is that analysis operates in a potential space with no preset limits and fast boundaries.

When this awareness is lost, the space collapses and a conjunction occurs out of which an Utopia is born. Analysis easily becomes an ideological island. Only properly analysed people and a sprinkling of artists (= professional illusionists) are allowed to live behind the walls of the island fortress. The inhabitants may even be encouraged to indulge in private feuds resulting in 'cross-fertilization' and handsome hybrids. The only condition is that they must stay on the island. No, analysis can only do its job on the mainland by mediating between worlds such as inner and outer, intrapsychic and interpersonal. These *appear* to be opposites because of our contrasting experiences, satisfaction–frustration. But the '*opposites*' are paired, and in that sense inseparable. Dependent on each other, they are *already united because they belong to the same experiential category* of utterly convincing contrasts, such as hot and cold are on the temperature scale. It is therefore misleading to speak of the unification of opposites, when all that analysis can do is to create and keep open the space between worlds which our psychological experiences alone divide. The romantic attitude with its optimistic aim of unlimited personality development leads to the ultimate expectation of a 'whole' or united personality which will emerge when conflicting interests have been resolved by a conjunction of opposites or 'when the wolf shall dwell with the lamb'. The conjunction introduces a mystical element into Jungian analysis which for non-mystics spells Utopia. What is more, if the aim of unification *were* realizable, it would close the very space in which analysis breathes. The same stifling effect can be expected, if analytic aims and boundaries were to be defined by Departments of Health.

Epilogue

Trying to clarify what analysis is about has involved examining the text, matrix and context as proposed in the Preface. I have made use of various doubts in order to strengthen my faith, that is the faith – not in analysis as it stands – but the faith required to practise it at all. Such faith is, to my mind, indistinguishable from the faith in the spirit of exploration and discovery in any sphere. It takes priority over the wish to 'help' the patient.

Critics may say that as an analyst I should have stuck to my last and have left philosophy to the philosophers. However, I have shown why I think the time has come for a drastic review of what we are doing and why analysis must not hold on to its island position. Our discoveries must be exposed to the critical view of unanalysed persons which means that cognitive procedures have to be brought to bear on 'unconscious' data. Strenger's thesis that analysis is suspended between hermeneutics and science summarizes the problematic which I tried to analyse (Strenger, 1991). This has involved taking issue with the old-fashioned detective otherwise known as the archeological model of psychoanalysis. It survives inasmuch as psychoanalysts seem to be continuously on guard against being hoodwinked by the patient. Things never are what they seem to be or the 'manifest content' of the dream is designed to camouflage the latent, the true meaning. The classical view is in keeping with the archaelogical model and the analysts who subscribe to it regard themselves as scientists. The romantic attitude, on the other hand, is closely linked with hermeneutics, the art of interpretation and meaning-finding. It is less tied to reconstruction and more concerned with construction. I am in sympathy with this view which is historically closer to Jung than to Freud but take exception to the optimistic assessment of human nature that often accompanies it.

I further agree with Strenger when he writes that the hermeneutic creativity of psychoanalysis is a precondition to therapeutic success and that psychoanalysis is one of the most important hermeneutic frames of the twentieth century. However, he comes closest to my thesis when he adds that *hermeneutic activity must have constraints*. Therefore, my aim throughout has been to add a dash of scientific rigour to the unbridled hermeneutics into which I see analysis drifting. Mapping has been proposed as a step towards better communication about analysis, leading eventually towards quantification and further dis-covery.

For too long has research been flowing in the one direction with which analysts are thoroughly familiar, that is from the unconscious or unknown to the conscious, known part of the mind. Analysis has been right to follow that direction because of the immense and unrecognized influence our unknown or unacknowledged motives have on our actions. But there is no reason why analysis itself should be regarded as exempt from manifesting signs of its own origins and motivations which are too influential to be ignored. Analysing these has involved looking into neglected aspects which for convenience's sake have been divided under the three headings mentioned.

When looking at the *'text'* I have voiced my doubts about theories, tech-niques and aims. In addition, the method of supporting theoretical views by 'case material' seems a dubious practice because of the built-in circularity. In any case the text is rewritten with every case, not only because of its individual uniqueness, but within the cultural, social and administrative *'context'*. It relativizes and determines to an often unacknowledged extent the way analysis is practised, as does also the personality of the analyst and the views of the leading analysts and their followers at various institutes of training. What I referred to as the *'matrix'* or birthplace of theories is the most fascinating and potentially richest source of information for anyone who wants to discover what analysis may be about. The passion with which pioneer analysts have fought for their convictions, the paranoia which this has spread and the bitter feuds caused among the followers would be baffling indeed, were it not for a possible explanation. Here I am indebted to Bion and the light he has shed on the psychology of mysticism as outlined in the last chapter. The subject chimes in well with Bion's 'thoughts in search of a thinker'. Very briefly: thoughts, ideas and visions and their further elaborations, perhaps as mystical experien-ces or as theories but also in the form of hallucinations and delusions can all become food to the starving, physically and/or emotionally deprived but inspired mind. It is important not to think of it as 'like' food, because for the time being it is the actual means of survival. Those who do not go mad – to put it bluntly – and have the necessary mental equipment and stamina to digest the food which has appeared like manna and further manage to transform it, say, into a theory, go on fighting, literally for dear life. They have staked their faith like mystics and, like them, they suppress their doubt. The latter is projected on to disbelievers who as the declared enemies are not as dangerous as potential traitors in the ranks of the disciples.

What the visionaries really want to ensure is that others come to share their food and find it good. In that way the 'truth' is spread. But the proponents treat the vision-become-theory all too easily as if the grain of truth were, if not the whole truth, then at least the most important and hitherto undiscovered core of it. In evaluating a theory – any theory – it is sometimes forgotten that theories are needed to illuminate dark corners or gaps in our knowledge. With the help of a theory we can see beneath the surface and make the invisible visible. It does the job, if it makes us 'see' where before we were blind. The harder the struggle that led to the 'illumination', the greater the joy when the preconception, or archetypal image, having met up with an 'observation', comes together as a conception. The analyst who has applied his theoretical vertex and combined it with an intuition may want to communicate it as an interpretation to the patient. Should the patient then respond by changing his behaviour, say relax, weep or scream, or have a confirmatory dream the interpretation appears to have been effective. But this does not amount to proof. Whether what seems to have happened is because of the analyst's verbal interpretation or whether in anticipation of a conception the analyst's voice and manner had already agreeably or excitedly changed, cannot be stated with the kind of certainty in which later publications announce the transforming effect of the interpretation. None of this means that the theory as such is worthless, only that it has suited the proponents to omit the non-specific effect of the analytic context.

My further argument has been that the greater visibility achieved by a theory must not be blurred again by assuming that analysts can proceed, as if unencumbered by theoretical knowledge. At least not without from time to time taking stock of what theories they put their trust in and, therefore, what it is they unwittingly want to happen. *After* that kind of confession, they are in a better position to make a fresh start, rather than by – *pace* Bion – simply dismissing 'all memory and desire' from their minds. I have argued that mapping is a useful aid with which to strike a balance among theories and so to find out from which vertex one views the analytic landscape.

The incisive strength of psychoanalysis has been the single-minded pursuit of uncovering unconscious motivations and dynamics. It had to be uncompromising about a 'psychic reality' that exposes not only the hypocrisies of social conventions but also illusions such as, in Freud's view, religion offered. But the very strength of that conviction has come up against parts of the personality which no amount of analysis can change. For example, to create illusions and invent Utopias are ineradicable human tendencies from which analysis itself is not exempt. But what cannot be changed can, in my view, be catered for with good humour. By taking the tendencies mentioned seriously and permitting playful outlets we may counteract their dangerous potential better than by refusing admission.

Finally, I would like to recapitulate the importance of what is generally known as the patient's 'motivation'. We are reminded that in the exchanges between Freud and the Wolf Man the tag of the un-used 'railway ticket' showed the point at issue. Without going into the vexed question of 'free will', we know that analysis is full of implicit injunctions that have a distinctly moralizing flavour. The following have turned up repeatedly: giving up hysterical miseries, accepting conscious suffering and sacrifices, preferring truth to illusions, tolerating the conflict of opposites; devotion, *agape* (=selfless love), concentration on and striving for wholeness. Analysis also demands ritual attendances which for frequency and duration are unsurpassed in the field of therapy. But perhaps the most intense of the unspoken demands is that the patient should have some of the moral courage that the analytic ancestors had. While I have no doubt that many more people have derived benefit from the analytic encounter than have not, the work does not come to fruition without the conscious contribution demanded by moral appeals. Where the demands remain entirely implicit, they are nevertheless conveyed by the analyst from whom patients learn to pick up clues and intuit what goes on in the analyst, much like children who know what their parents really feel. Such 'introjective identification' is often still present when the analysis comes to a successful conclusion. Some grow out of it and become successfully themselves.

It is true that by implication I have likened the state of analysis to that represented in early world maps. Our cosmos is still in a pre-grid state, except for Bion who like Ptolemy made a valiant attempt. Looking forward, what seems to be needed is first to design differentiated maps of the analytic complexities; second to record detailed observations about the immediate effect of the application of a theory to a momentary situation in analysis; and – this is most important – to relate the observations so made to the long-term effect or outcome of analysis. For this research, skilled involved as well as uninvolved observers are required. The job of communicating what analysis is about is too important and urgent to be left to publicity.

Bibliography

Bakan, D. 1990 *Sigmund Freud and the Jewish Mystical Tradition*. London: Free Association Books

Balint, M. 1952 *Primary Love and Psycho-analytic Technique*. London: The Hogarth Press, p. 187

Balint, M. 1958 'The three areas of the mind' in *Int. J. Psycho-Anal*. 39:1

Balint, M. and E. 1961 *Psychotherapeutic Techniques in Medicine*. London: Tavistock Publications, pp. 149–59

Balint, M. 1965 *Primary Love and Psychoanalytic Technique*. London and New York: Tavistock, p. 131f

Balint, M. 1979 *The Basic Fault: Therapeutic Aspects of Regression* [1968] (ed. E. Balint). London and New York: Tavistock Publications, pp. 110; 138f; 177; 131–48

Beazley, C. 1949 *The Dawn of Modern Geography*. New York: Peter Smith

Beebe, J. 1984 'Psychological Types in Transference', Wilmette, Ill.: Chiron, pp. 147–62

Bion, W. 1959 'Attacks on linking' in *Int. J. Psycho-Anal. 40*: 308f

Bion, W. 1961 *Experiences in Groups and Other Papers*. London: Tavistock Publications, p. 152

Bion, W. 1962 *Learning from Experience*. London: William Heinemann Medical Books Ltd, pp. xi; 6–7; 36; 90f

Bion, W. 1963 *Elements of Psycho-Analysis*. London: William Heinemann Medical Books Ltd, pp. 18; 46

Bion, W. 1965 *Transformations*. London: William Heinemann Medical Books Ltd, pp. 40; 54; 103; 139–40

Bion, W. 1967 *Second Thoughts*. London: Heinemann Medical Books Ltd, pp. 111; 143–45; 112f

Bion, W. 1970 *Attention and Interpretation*. London: Tavistock, pp. 30–1; 32; 58–99, 105

Blake, W. 'Eternity', 'New Jerusalem' in *Blake's Complete Writings*, ed. G. Keynes. Oxford: University Press, pp. 179; 480

Blomeyer, R. 1982 *Die Spiele der Analytiker*. Olten: Walter-Verlag AG, p. 251ff

Böll, H. 1962 *Brief an einen jungen Katholiken*. Köln-Berlin: Kiepenheuer & Witsch, p. 12

Borstein, D. 1985 *The Discoverers*. New York: Vintage Books, p. 401f

Brutigam, W. 1983 'Bemerkungen zur psycho-analytischen Behandlungsführung in der Eröffnungs- und Abschlußphase' in *Hoffmann S.O. (ed.) Deutung und Beziehung. Kritische Beiträge zur Behandlungskonzeption und Technik in der Psychoanalyse*. Frankfurt am Main: Fischer

Bräutigam, W., von Rad, M. and Engel, K. 1980 'Research in success and therapy in psychoanalytic treatment' 'Erfolgs- und Therapieforschung bei psychoanalytischen Behandlungen' in *Zschr. psychosom. Med.* 16:101–18

Brown, J. 1961 *Freud and the Post-Freudians*. London: Penguin Books
Carroll, L. 1962 *The Hunting of the Snark*. London: Penguin Books
Cardinal, M. 1977 *The Words to Say It*. New York: W. W. Norton & Co.
Cellarius, A. 1661 Celestial Atlas '*Harmonia Macrocosmica*'. Amsterdam
Constantine, L. 1978 'Family sculpture and relationship mapping techniques' in *Journal of Marital and Family Therapy*, Apr., Vol. 4(2)
Corbin, H. 1972 'Mundus Imaginalis or the imaginary and the imaginal' in *Spring*
Cremerius, J. 1984 'The significance of the dissidents for psychoanalysis' in *Vom Handwerk des Psychoanalytikers: Das Werkzeug der psychoanalytischen Technik*. Stuttgart: Problemata Frommann-Holzboog, pp. 364–97
Delano-Smith, C. 1987 'Prehistoric maps' in *The History of Cartography: an Introduction*, Harley & Woodward. Chicago: University Press, pp. 33; 60n; 62; 79; 81f
Denker, P. 1946 'Results of treatment of psychoneurosis. A follow-up study of 500 cases' in *New York State Journal of Medicine* 46: 2164–66
Dieckmann, H. 1980 *Übertragung und Gegenübertragung in der Analytischen Psychologie*. Hildesheim: Gerstenberg Verlag
Dieckmann, H. 1979 *Methoden der Analytischen Psychologie*. Otten und Freiburg im Breisgau: Walter-Verlag
Dieckmann, H. 1991 *Komplexe*. Berlin, Heidelberg: Springer-Verlag
Dinnage, R. 1988 *One to One*. London: Penguin, pp. 16–18
Dührssen, A. 1972 *Analytische Psychotherapie in Theorie, Praxis und Ergebnissen*. Göttingen: Vandenhoek & Ruprecht
Durrel, L. 1953 *Reflections on a Marine Venus*. London: Faber
Eco, Umberto, 1983 *The Name of the Rose*. New York: Harcourt Brace Jovanovich Inc.
Eco, Umberto, 1989 *Foucault's Pendulum*. New York: Harcourt Brace Jovanovich Inc.
Edinger, E. 1972 *Ego and Archetype*. New York: G. P. Putnam & Sons, p. 274f
Eigen, M. 1981 'The area of faith in Winnicott, Lacan and Bion' in *Int J. of Psycho-Analysis, Vol.* 62:413f
Eliade, M. 1954 *Terra Mater and Cosmic Hierogamies* in Eranos-Jahrbuch XXII. Zürich: Rhein Verlag, pp. 57–95
Elias, N. 1987 *Die Gesellschaft der Individuen*. Frankfurt (am Main): Suhrkamp Verlag
Eliot, T. 1963 'East Coker' in *Collected Poems*. London: Faber & Faber
Eliot, T. 1949 *The Cocktail Party*. London: Faber & Faber
Ellenberger, H. 1970 *The Discovery of the Unconscious*. London: Penguin Books, p. 400
Eysenck, H. 1952 'The effects of psychotherapy: an evaluation' in *J. Consult. Psychol.* 16, No. 5, 319–24
Farrell, B. 1981 'The effectiveness of psychoanalytic therapy' in *The Standing of Psychoanalysis*. Oxford: University Press
Ferenczi, S. 1955 'Problems of termination of analysis' [1928] in *Final Contributions to the Problems and Methods of Psychoanalysis by Sander Ferenczi* (ed. M. Balint). London: Hogarth
Fernandez-Arnesto, F. 1991 *Columbus*, Oxford: University Press, p. 123
Ferguson, S. 1973 *A Guard Within*. London: Flamingo, p. 24
Fielding, H. 1947 'Rape upon Rape', I. v. [1730] in *The Complete Works of Henry Fielding, Esq.* (ed. W. Henley) New York: Barnes & Noble
Fordham, M. 1957 *New Developments in Analytical Psychology*, London: Routledge & Kegan Paul, p. 131f
Fordham, M. 1963 *Contact with Jung* (ed. Fordham). London: Tavistock
Fordham, M. 1969 'Several views on individuation' in *J. analyt. Psychol.* 14:1

Fordham, M. 1979 'Analytical psychology and countertransference' in *Countertransference* (eds L. Epstein and A. Finer). New York: Jason Aronson

Fordham, M. 1985 *Explorations into the Self*. London: Academic Press, pp. 44f; 90f; 50–63; 94–114; 198–202

Fordham, M. 1991 'The supposed limits of interpretation' in *J. analyt. Psychol.* 36:165f

Freud, S.: references are to the *Standard Edition (SE)*, and by volume and page number

Gardiner, M. 1989 *The Wolf-Man and Sigmund Freud*, London: Karnac Books and the Institute of Psychoanalysis, pp. 137; 144; 148–9; 151; 210; 279–300; 283–4

Gardiner, M. 1982 *Der Wolfsmann vom Wolfsmann. Sigmund Freud's berühmtester Fall.* Frankfurt am Main: Fischer, pp. 426f; 434–5; 448

Gay, P. 1988 *Freud, A Life In Our Time.* London: Papermac, pp.58; 142; 311; 335; 444

Gordon, C. 1882 *Eden and its two Sacramental Trees*, unpublished manuscript, dated 26.2.1882

Gordon, H. W. 1885 *Events in the Life of Charles George Gordon.* London: Kegan Paul

Guntrip, H. 1961 *Personality Structure and Human Interaction.* London: The Hogarth Press, pp. 216; 222; 359

Hake, A. 1885. *The Journals of Major General C. G. Gordon at Kartoum.* London: Kegan Paul, Trench & Co.

Hallpike, C. 1979 *The Foundations of Primitive Thought.* Oxford: Clarendon, pp. 291–2

Harley, J. and Woodward, D. 1987 *The History of Cartography.* Chicago: University Press, p. xvi; 506f

Hartmann, H. 1964 *Essays on Ego Psychology.* London: Hogarth Press, p. 163

Heimann, P. 1950 'On counter-transference' in *Int. J. Psycho-Anal* 31:81–4

Heimann, P. 1950 'A contribution to the re-evaluation of the Oedipus complex – the early stages' in *New Directions in Psycho-Analaysis* (ed. Melanie Klein et al.) London: Tavistock, 1955, p. 24

Henderson, J. 1967 *Thresholds of Initiation.* Connecticut: Wesleyan UP, pp. 49; 123; 199

Henderson, J. 1991 'C. G. Jung's psychology: additions and extensions' in *J. analyt. Psychol.* 34:4 pp. 427–42

Hillman, J. 1979 *The Dream and the Underworld.* New York: Harper & Row

Hirshberg, L. 1989 'Remembering: reproduction or construction?' in *Psychoanalysis and Contemporary Thought*, vol. 12 No. 3

Hobson, R. 1985 *Forms of Feeling.* London & New York: Tavistock, p. 199

Hodgkiss, A. 1981 *Understanding Maps.* Folkestone: Dawson

Howarth, H. 1965 *Notes on Some Figures Behind T. S. Eliot.* London: Chatto & Windus, pp. 204; 205; 206; 326f

Hubback, J. 1970 'The assassination of Robert Kennedy: Patients' and Analysts' Reactions' in *Int. J. Psycho-Anal.* 15:1 p. 81

I-Ching, 1951 *The I-Ching (The Book of Changes, trl.).* London: Routledge & Kegan Paul

Jackson, M. 1960 Address from the Chair. 'Jung's archetype: clarity or confusion?' in *Brit. J. Med. Psychol.* Part 2, pp. 83–94

Jacobson, E. 1965 *The Self and the Object World.* London: Hogarth, p. 63

Jacoby, M. 1985 'Paradise as futuristic expectation of salvation' in *Longing for Paradise* (trl. title). Fellbach: Verlag Adolph Bonz

James, W. 1902 *The Varieties of Religious Experience.* London: Longman, Green & Co., p. 162; 387–8; 506

Jimnez, J. 1990 'Some technical consequences of Matte-Blanco's theory of dreaming' in *Int. Rev. Psycho-Anal.* 17,4, 455–70

Jones, E. 1953 *Sigmund Freud. Life and Work*. Vol. I, The Hogarth Press, London, p. 400f

Jung, C. Except as below, references are to the *Collected Works (CW)* and by volume and paragraph number

Jung, C. 1954 *Beitrge zur Entwicklungsgeschichte der Denkens*. Verlag Rascher

Jung, C. 1967 'Confrontation with the unconscious' in *Dreams, Memories and Reflections*. London: Fontana Library, Routledge & Kegan Paul, p. 318f

Kardiner, A. 1977. *My Analysis with Freud*. New York: W. W. Norton & Company Inc., p. 99

Keats, J. 1952 Letter to his brothers 21.12.1917, in *Letters 4th Edition*, Oxford: University Press

Kerenyi, K. 1950 *Labyrinth Studien*. Zürich: Rhein Verlag, p. 47

Kern, H. 1982 *Labyrinthe*. Munich: Prestel Verlag, pp. 16; 28; 30; 33; 37; 49–55; 59–64; 214; 430; 445

Kernberg, O. 1984 *Severe Personality Disorders*. New Haven & London: Yale University Press, p. 78

Klauber, J. *et al.* 1987 *Illusion and Spontaneity in Psychoanalysis*. London: Free Association Press, p. 6f

Kledzik, R. 1991 'Respondent to General Gordon's constant object' Chiron Conference, Glorietta, New Mexico, n.p.

Klein, G. 1976 *Psychoanalytic Theory: an Exploration of Essentials*. New York: Int. University Press

Klein, M. 1955 *New Directions in Psycho-Analysis* (ed. Melanie Klein et al.). London: Tavistock

Klein, M. 1961 *A Narrative of Child Analysis*. London: The Hogarth Press and Institute of Psychoanalysts, pp. 17–18

Klein, M. 1955 'On identification' in *New Directions in Psycho-Analysis* (ed. Klein et al.). London: Tavistock Publications, p. 342f

Kohut, H. 1971 *The Analysis of the Self*, New York: International Universities Press

Kohut, H. 1984 *How Does Analysis Care?* (ed. Arnold Goldberg). Chicago: University Press, p. 99

Korzibsky, A. 1941 *Science and Sanity*. New York: Science Press

Kühn, H. 1952 *Felsbilder Europas* (The Rockpaintings of Europe). Stuttgart: Kohlhammer Verlag

Kühn, H. 1966 *Wenn Steine reden: die Sprache der Felsbilder (When Stones Speak: The Language of Rock Paintings)*. Wiesbaden: Brockhaus

Lambert, K. 1981 *Analysis, Repair and Individuations* in Library of Analytical Psychology. Vol. 5. London and New York: Academic Press

Layard, J. 1936 'Maze-dances and the ritual of the labyrinth in Malekula' in *Folk-Lore* vol. 47,1936, pp. 133–70

Little, M. 1987 'On the value of regression to dependence' in *Free Associations*, 10.

Little, M. 1990 *Psychotic Anxieties Containment. A Personal Record of Analysis with Winnicott*. New Jersey: Jason Aronson

Lorenz, K. 1966 *On Aggression*. London: Methuen, pp. 230–1

MacGregor-Hastie, R. 1985 *Never to be Taken Alive*. London: Sidgwick and Jackson

Mahony, P. 1984 *Cries of the Wolf Man*. New York: International Universities Press, pp. 18; 33; 34; 103–5; 157

Masson, J. 1982. 'Review of Obholzer's Gespräche mit dem Wolfsmann' in *Psych. Review*. Vol. 9:p. 116

Matte Blanco, I. 1975 *The Unconscious as Infinite Sets*. London: Gerald Duckworth & Company Limited, p. 99

Mayer, J. and Timms, N. 1970 *The Client Speaks: Working-class Impressions of Case-work*. New York: Intervale Publications, p. 21

Meltzer, D. 1984 *Dream Life*. Strath Tay, Scotland: Clunie Press, p. 90; 136; 167

Meltzer, D. 1973 'Geography of phantasy' in *Sexual States of Mind*. Strath Tay, Scotland: Clunie Press, p. 180

Midgeley, M. 1988 'Teleological theories of morality' in *An Encyclopaedia of Philosophy*, (ed. G. Parkinson) London: Routledge

Milner, M. 1955 'The role of illusion in symbol formation' in *New Directions in Psychoanalysis* (ed. Klein et al.). London: Tavistock Publications, pp. 86; 101; 342

Milton, J. 1667 *Paradise Lost*. IV: 218

Mitchell, S. 1988 *Relational Concepts in Psychoanalysis*. Cambridge, Mass. and London: Harvard University Press, p. 17f

More, Sir T. 1963 *Utopia*. [1516] London: Penguin Books

More, N. 1983 'The archetype of the way, I' in *J. analyt. Psychol*. 28:2, pp. 120

Moser, D. 1974 *Lehrjahre auf der Couch (Years of Apprenticeship on the Couch)* Frankfurt am Main): Suhrkamp Verlag, p. 232

Neumann, E. 1955 *The Great Mother*. New York and London: Bollingen, Series 47

Neumann, E. 1954 *The Origins and History of Consciousness*. New York and London: Bollingen, Series 42

Neumann, E. 1963 *Das Kind*. Zürich: Rhein Verlag, p. 47ff

Nutting, A. 1966. *Gordon: Martyr and Misfit*. London: Constable

Obholzer, K. 1982 *The Wolf-Man Sixty Years Later*. London, Melbourne and Henley: Routledge & Kegan Paul, pp. 32; 33; 36f; 40; 43; 54–6; 134–7

Ogden, T. 1989 *The Primitive Edge of Experience*. New Jersey & London: Jason Aronson Inc.

Paul, M. 1981 'A mental atlas of the process of psychological birth' in *Do I Disturb the Universe?* (ed. J. Grotstein). Reprinted 1983: London: H. Karnac Books Ltd, p. 551

Perera, S. 1988 'Dream design: some operations underlying clinical dream application' in *Dreams in Analysis* (eds N. Schwartz-Salant and M. Stein) Wilmette, Ill.: Chiron Publications

Piaget, J. 1955 *The Child's Conception of Space*. London: Routledge & Kegan Paul, pp. 97–218

Plaut, A. 1959 'Hungry patients: reflections on ego-structure' in *J. Analyt. Psychol*. 4:2, p. 161f

Plaut, A. 1966 'Reflections on not being able to imagine' in *J. Analyt. Psychol*. 11:2, p. 113f

Plaut, A. 1969 'On transference phenomena in alcoholism' in *Brit. Journal Med. Psychol*.

Plaut, A. 1973 'The ungappable bridge' in *J. Analyt. Psychol*. 18:2, p. 105

Plaut, A. 1974 'Part-object relations and Jung's "luminosities"', in *J. Analyt. Psychol*. 19:2, p. 165

Plaut, A. 1975 'Where have all the rituals gone?' in *J. Analyt. Psychol*. 20:1, p. 3

Plaut, A. 1977 'Jung and rebirth' in *J. Analyt. Psychol*. 22:2, p. 142

Plaut, A. 1979 'Imagination in the process of discovery' in *J. Analyt. Psychol*. 24:1, p. 59

Plaut, A. 1981 'Where is paradise? The mapping of a myth' in *The Map Collector* Dec., No. 29

Plaut, A. 1982 'General Gordon's map of paradise' in *Encounter* June/July

Plaut, A. 1990 'The presence of the third: intrusive factors in analysis' in *J. Analyt. Psychol*. 35:3, p. 301

Plaut, A. 1991. 'Object constancy or constant object' in *Psychopathology, Contemporary Jungian Perspectives* (ed. A. Samuels), American edn, London: Karnac Books

Post, J. 1973 *Atlas of Fantasy Maps.* London: Souvenir Press

Purce, J. 1976 *The Mystic Spiral. Journey of the Soul.* London: Thames & Hudson

Racker, H. 1968 *Transference and countertransference,* London: Hogarth

Redfearn, J. 1985 *My self, my many selves.* London: Academic Press, p. 9

Redfearn, J. 1980 'Romantic and classical views of analysis' in *J. Analyt. Psychol.* 25:1 pp. 1–16

Redfearn, J. 1989 'Dreams of nuclear warfare. Does avoiding the intrapsychic clash of opposites contribute to the concrete danger of world destruction?' in *Dreams of Analysis* (eds N. Schwartz-Salant and M. Stein). Wilmette, Ill.: Chiron Publications

Robinson, A. and Petchenik, B. 1976 *The Nature of Maps.* Chicago: University Press, pp. 23f; 53; 65; 68

Robinson, A. 1982 'Early thematic mapping' in *The History of Cartography.* Chicago: University Press, p. 17

Rosenfeld, H. 1988 *Impasse and Interpretation.* London and New York: Routledge, pp. 17–18

Rycroft, C. 1968 *A Critical Dictionary of Psychoanalysis.* London: Thomas Nelson & Sons Ltd

Samuels, A., Shorter, B. and Plaut, A. 1986 *A Critical Dictionary of Jungian Analysis.* London and New York: Routledge & Kegan Paul

Samuels, A. 1985 *Jung and the Post-Jungians.* London and Boston: Routledge & Kegan Paul, p. 265

Samuels, A. 1989 *The Plural Psyche.* London: Routledge

Samuels, A. 1993 *The Political Psyche.* London: Routledge (forthcoming)

Sandler, J. 1983 'Reflections on some relations between psychoanalytic concepts and psychoanalytic practice' in *Int. J. Psycho-Anal.* 64:1

Sandler, J. and Sandler, A.-M. 1984 'The past unconscious, the present unconscious and interpretation of the transference' in *Int. Psych. Inc.* 4:3675

Sandler, J. 1987 *From Safety to Superego.* London: Karnac Books Ltd, p. 175f

Schachter, J. 1990 'Post-termination patient-analyst contact' in *Int. J. Psycho. Anal.* 71:475

Schafer, R. 1990 'The search for common ground' in *Int. J. Psycho. Anal.* 71:49f

Schafer, R. 1970 'The psychoanalytic vision of reality' in *Int. J. Psycho. Anal.* Vol. 51, p. 297f

Schwartz-Salant, N. 1988 *Borderline Personality: Vision and Healing.* Wilmette, Ill.: Chiron Publications, pp. 97–158

Searles, H. 1960 *The Non-Human Environment.* New York: International University Press Inc., p. 11

Segal, H. 1964 *Introduction to the Works of Melanie Klein.* London: Heinemann. Repr. 1988 London: Karnac Books, p. 57

Segal, H. 1955 'A psychoanalytic approach to aesthetics' in *New Directions in Psycho-analysis* (ed. Klein et al.), Tavistock Publications, London, p. 404

Spence, D. 1982 *Narrative Truth and Historical Truth.* Toronto: George J. McLeod Ltd, p. 144

Spillius, E. 1988 *Melanie Klein Today* Vol. I (ed. E. B. Spillius). London and New York: Routledge, pp. 13; 328f, Vol. II pp. 8–9; 14; 17f

Stein, L. 1982 *Jungian Analysis* (ed. L. Stein). La Salle and London: Open Court

Steiner, J. 1987 'The interplay between pathological organizations and the paranoid-schizoid and depressive' in *Melanie Klein Today* (ed. E. Spillius). 1988

Stoller, R. 1985 *Observing the Erotic Imagination.* New Haven, Connecticut and London: Yale University Press, p. 167f

Stommel, 1984 *Lost Islands, The Story of Islands That Have Vanished From Nautical Charts.* British Columbia: University of British Columbia Press

Storr, A. 1991 *Churchill's Black Dog and Other Phenomena of the Human Mind.*
London: Flamingo

Storr, A. 1966 *The Integrity of the Personality.* London: Pelican Books [1960]

Strachey, L. 1918 *Eminent Victorians.* London: Penguin Modern Classics (1980)

Strachey, J. 1934 'The nature of the therapeutic action in psychoanalysis' in *Int. J. Psychoanal.* 15:127f

Strauss, R. 1964 'The archetype of separation' in *2nd Int. Congr. Analyt. Psychol, Zurich 1962.* Basle/New York: S. Karger, pp. 104–12

Streeck, U. 1986 'Hintergrundannahmen im Psychoanalytischen Behandlungsprozeß' (Basic Assumptions in the Psychoanalytic Course of Treatment) in *Forum Psycho. anal. 1986* 2:98f

Strenger, C. 1989 'The classic and romantic vision of analysis' in *Int. Journal of Psycho-Analysis.* Vol. 70, pp. 593–610

Stroeken, H. 1991 'Der Einfluß von Freuds Judentum auf sein Leben und die Psychoanalyse' (The Influence of Freud's Jewishness on his Life and Psychoanalysis) in *Forum der Psychoanalyse,* Vol. 7:4, p. 323f

Thomä, H. and Kächele, K. 1987 *Psychoanalytic Practice* Vol. 1, Berlin: Springer Verlag, pp. 23f; 253f; 259

Thomä, H. 1987 'Transference interpretation and reality' in Klauber, J. et al. *Illusion and Spontaneity in Psychoanalysis,* London: Free Association Press

Ticho, E. 1971 'Probleme des Abschlusses der psychoanalytischen Therapie' 'Problems in ending psychoanalytic therapy' in *Psyche.* 25:44–56

Trench, C. 1978 *Charley Gordon: an Eminent Victorian Reassessed.* London: Alan Lane

Unamuno, M. de 1967 *La Agonia de Christianismo.* Madrid: Editorial Plenitude, p. 34

Underhill, E. 1960 *Mysticism* [1911]. London: University Paperbacks, pp. 81; 413f

Wallerstein, R. 1988 'One psychoanalysis or many?' in *Int. J. Psycho. Anal.* 69:1

Wallerstein, R. 1990 'The common ground' in *Int. J. Psycho. Anal.* 71:1

Wallerstein, R. 1986 *Forty-two lives in treatment.* New York: Guilford, p. 730

Wallis, H. 1973 'The map as a means of scientific communication' in *Studia z Dziejów Geografii i Kartografii* (ed. Jósefa Babicza). 87, 11–162

Wallis, H. & Robinson, A. 1987 *Cartographical Innovation: An International Handbook of Map Technology to 1900.* Chicago: University Press, pp. 132; 199f; XIV

Waters, F. 1977 *Book of the Hopi.* New York: Ballantine Books, pp. 29–30

Watzlawick, P. 1978 *The Language of Change. Elements of Therapeutic Communication.* New York: Basic Books Inc.

Wilde, O. 1936 'The soul of man under socialism' [1891] in *De Profundis.* Harmondsworth: Penguin Books, p. 34

Winnicott, D. 1941 'The observations of infants in a set situation' in *Collected Papers,* 1958. London: Tavistock Publications

Winnicott, D. 1958 *Collected Papers.* London: Tavistock Publications, pp. 68; 221; 224–42

Winnicott, D. 1965 *The Maturational Processes and the Facilitating Environment.* London: Hogarth, pp. 24; 57; 128; 181; 254

Winnicott, D. 1971 *Playing and Reality.* London: Tavistock

Winnicott, D. 1974 'Fear of breakdown' in *Int. Review of Psycho-Anal.* I, p. 103f

Wollheim, R. 1987 *Painting as an Art.* London and Princeton: Thames & Hudson, p. 19f

Zinkin, L. 1991 'The Klein connection in the London school' in *J. of Analyt. Psychol.* 36, pp. 37–62

Name index

Abraham, K. 311
Adler, A. 41, 83
Adler, G. xii
Amiel, H. 94, 314
Arnheim, R. 270

Bakan, D. 311
Balint, E. xii, 59
Balint, M. xii, 22, 35, 59, 68, 92, 112, 126, 131, 172, 224, 319, 334
Beatus 227, 228
Beazley, C. 224
Beebe, J. 327
Bernheim, H. 72, 73
Bion, W. xii, xvi, xviii 4, 9, 22–3, 35–6, 41, 45, 48, 61, 69, 95, 106, 125, 127, 128, 164, 177, 185, 190, 203, 251, 256, 271, 274, 279, 285, 286, 291, 292, 293, 299, 302, 306, 307, 308, 310, 311, 312, 313, 314, 315, 316, 317, 319, 322, 327, 328, 329, 330, 332, 333, 335, 336, 340, 343, 344, 345
Blake, W. 38, 53, 230
Blomeyer, R. 57, 240, 338
Böll, H. 141
Borstein, D. 316
Brahe, T. 324–5, 328
Bräutigam, W. 67, 76
Brown, J. 40
Browning, R. 241
Brunswick, R.M. 56, 78, 81, 84, 86
Buddha 175, 176, 319
Bunyan, J. 216, 218
Burton, R. 156

Cardinal, M. 93, 94
Carrol, L. 198
Cellarius 323, 325

Churchill, W.S. 181
Columbus, C. 40, 199, 204
Constantine, L. 225
Copernicus 326
Corbin, H. 190
Cosmas Indico Pleustes 160
Cremerius, J. 40, 41, 44, 62, 336

Darwin, C. 44
Da Vinci, L. 246
Defoe, D. 224
Delano-Smith, C. 199, 211–12, 223, 225
Denker, P. 61
Dieckmann, H. 26, 30, 31
Dinnage, R. 94, 314
Dorn, G. 146
Dührssen, A. 61, 62, 313
Durrel, L. 224

Eco, U. 243
Edinger, E. 121
Eigen, M. 4
Eissler, K. 81
Eliade, M. 244–5
Elias, N. 33, 183
Eliot, T.S. 14, 173 *passim* 321, 326, 328
Ellenberger, H. 38, 39, 44
Engel, K. 67
Eysenck, H. 61

Fairbairn, R. 299, 300, 301
Farrell, B. 61
Fenichel, O. 297
Ferenczi, S. 34, 67, 68, 334
Ferguson, S. 92, 93, 94
Fernandez-Armesto, F. 199
Fielding, H. 323

Fliess, W. 86, 89
Fordham, F. 129
Fordham, M. xii, 23, 26, 29, 30, 35, 90, 95, 125, 163, 181, 239, 299, 314, 316, 328, 329, 333–4
Freud, A. xi, 55, 79, 80
Freud, S. xii, xiv 3, 4, 6, 15, 18, 20, 23, 25, 34, 39, 40, 41, 42, 44, 46, 47, 48, 49, 50, 51, 55, 56, 60, 63, 64, 65, 66, 68, 70, 72, 73, 74, 77, 78, 79, 80, 81, 82, 83, 84, 85, 86, 87, 88, 89, 90, 94, 96, 99, 103, 111, 115, 119, 146, 163, 179, 187, 189, 190, 191, 192, 206, 210, 230, 234, 240, 247, 262, 286, 287–8, 290, 292, 299, 300, 311, 312, 328, 333, 335, 337, 338, 344

Galileo 40
Gardiner, G. 80–3, 84, 85, 86, 87
Gardiner, M. 77, 78, 79
Gaugin, P. 172
Gay, J. 37
Gay, P. 41, 190, 311
Gordon, A. 150, 165
Gordon, C.G. 145–72, 179, 180, 181, 182, 183, 307, 313, 319, 338
Gordon, E. 161–2
Gordon, H.W. 158, 167
Guntrip, H. 289, 300, 301

Hallpike, C. 232
Harley, J. 193, 210
Hartmann, H. 136
Hegel, G.W.F. 121, 231
Heimann, P. xii, 26, 288, 289, 290, 291, 293, 301
Henderson, J. 114, 234, 321
Heraclitus 231
Herodotus 121
Hillman, J. 190
Hirschberg, L. 24
Hobson, R. 65, 76
Hodgkiss, A. 203–4
Hooker, W.J. 153
Howarth, H. 175, 176
Hubback, J. 272
Hulme, D. 34

Isidore of Spain 212, 227

Jackson, M. 287, 289, 291
Jacobson, E. 137

Jacoby, M. 232
James, W. 4, 42, 312, 313
Janet, P. 31, 39
Jesus 36, 41, 150, 155
Jiménez, J. 240
Jones, E. 41, 288, 311
Jung, C. xii, xiv, xvii 6, 9, 10, 16, 19, 20, 22, 25, 26, 28, 29, 30, 31, 32, 33, 34, 35, 39, 40, 41, 42, 47, 49, 50, 51, 53–4, 55, 59, 60, 61, 65, 66, 68, 70, 73, 74, 79, 83, 90, 93, 99, 100, 101–2, 103, 104, 105, 109, 112, 114, 115, 118, 119, 120, 121, 124, 125, 126, 134, 136, 137, 138, 139, 140, 141, 142, 143, 144, 145, 146, 147, 160, 162, 163, 164, 169, 176, 177, 181, 182, 184, 185, 190, 210, 223, 225, 229, 230, 231, 232, 233, 234, 237, 239, 240, 241, 242, 243, 244, 247, 248, 266, 271, 272, 277, 285, 286, 287, 288, 289, 290, 291, 292, 293, 294–5, 297, 299, 300, 301, 302, 303, 304, 305, 306, 310, 311, 312, 313, 314, 315, 316, 317, 320, 321, 322, 323, 327, 328, 329, 330, 331, 332, 333, 334, 335, 336

Kächele, K. 49, 59, 67
Kardiner, A. 88, 89, 90, 91
Keats, J. 256, 314
Kerenyi, K. 234, 244, 249
Kern, H. 235, 237, 239, 241, 242, 243, 244, 246, 249
Kernberg, O. 59, 263
Kierkegaard, S. 144
Klauber, J. 65, 197, 334, 338
Kledzik, R. 170, 171, 172
Klein, G. 42
Klein, M. xi 11, 48, 135, 140, 164, 181, 284, 285, 286, 288, 289, 290, 292, 293, 295, 299, 300, 301, 302, 303, 304, 305, 314, 318, 328, 329, 330, 332, 333
Kohut, H. 32, 34, 35, 47, 184
Korzibsky, A. 323
Kühn, H. 230

Lambert, K. 29
Layard, J. xii, 237, 239
Little, M. 91–2, 287, 334
Longfellow, H.W. 31
Lorenz, K. 110–11
Lufft, H. 215
Luther, M. 215–16, 217

MacGregor-Hastie, R. 151, 165, 166, 167
Mahdi, the 148, 170
Mahony, P. 77, 78, 80, 81, 83, 84, 86, 312
Masson, J. 80
Matte Blanco, I. 125, 240
Mayer, J. 75
Meltzer, D. 24, 36, 144, 190, 266, 285
Melville, H. 221
Mercator, N. 232
Mesmer, F.A. 15
Midgeley, M. 48
Milner, M. 3, 197, 287, 296–7, 302
Milton, J. 155, 156
Mitchell, S. 271
Moore, N. 234
More, T. 223, 337, 338
Moser, T. 90–1

Neumann, E. 237, 327
Newton, I. 316
Nutting, A. 149

Obholzer, K. 70, 80–3, 84–5, 86
Ogden, T. 314

Pankejeff, S. (the 'Wolf Man') 78
Pasteur, L. 40
Paul, M. 190
Perera, S. 234
Petchenik, B. 203–4, 270
Piaget, J. 205, 223, 232
Picasso, P. 200
Plato 231, 262, 312
Plaut, A. xiii, 3, 16, 29, 39, 69, 130, 131, 140, 143, 145, 164, 182, 210, 223, 224, 285, 336
Pope, A. 268
Ptolemy 210, 325, 345
Purce, J. 234

Racker, H. 29
Rad, M. von 67
Redfearn, J. 30, 37, 120, 121
Richard of Haldingham 234
Robinson, A. 193, 203–4, 209, 211, 214, 215, 222, 270
Rosenfeld, H. 334
Rudolf II 151
Rycroft, C. 46, 49, 83, 118, 119, 162, 215

St Augustine 49

St Brandan 224
St Francis of Assisi 318–19
St John of the Cross 316
Samuels, A. 29, 40, 121, 190, 200, 326
Sandler, A. 42, 163
Sandler, J. 42
Schachter, J. 67
Schafer, R. 43–4, 45, 317
Schreber, D.P. 89
Schwartz-Salant, N. 125, 139–40, 334
Scott, W. 152
Searles, H. 268
Segal, H. 285, 302
Shakespeare, W. 180
Shelley, P.B. 180
Shorter, B. 29
Spence, D. 261, 262
Spillius, E. 299, 306, 331
Stein, L. xii, 242, 243
Stekel, W. 41
Stevenson, R.L. 56, 216, 220, 221
Stoller, R. 262, 263
Stommel, H. 224
Storr, A. 181, 299, 300
Strachey, J. 55, 77
Strachey, L. 150
Strauss, R. 31
Streeck, U. 203
Strenger, C. 34, 35, 37, 342
Stroeken, H. 335

Thomä, H. 49, 59, 67, 334
Ticho, E. 64
Timms, N. 75
Trench, C.C. 150, 151, 152, 165
Turner, P. 337

Unamuno, M. de 16
Underhill, E. 310, 311, 312, 313

Virgil 235

Wallerstein, R. 42, 43, 44, 97, 284
Wallis, H. 208, 209, 211, 214, 215, 222
Waters, F. 246
Watzlawick, P. 114
Wendrin, F. von 160
Wilde, O. 337
Willcocks, Sir W. 160
Winnicott, D. xii, xiii, 4, 7, 20, 22, 25, 28–9, 32–3, 35, 39, 91–2, 124, 129, 130, 137, 164, 197, 223, 225, 256, 287,

296, 298, 309, 320, 328, 329, 330, 333, 334, 335, 338

Wollheim, R. 202, 323

Woodward, D. 193, 210

Zinkin, L. 284

Subject index

Absolute, the 307, 308, 311, 313, 319, 321, 326; *see also* mysticism; 'O'
abstinence 103
active imagination 137, 292, 295, 296, 304
addiction 115, 127, 140, 182; alcohol 127, 129–33; sexual 257–9; *see also* devotion
additions, denoting 194–5
agape 15, 344
aggression 87, 110, 133; hidden 52; impulses to 301; suicide's 180; *see also* destructive
aims, analyst's 51, 63–4, 240, 304; dominant 48; global xii, 46, 47, 53–7, 106, 230, 243, 281, 283, 312, 338; inferred 49; mysticism and 311; opposites 121–2; patients' 22, 45–6, 298–300, 314
alchemy 14, 36, 51, 101, 121, 139, 230, 231–2, 314; hermetic vessel 254; Jung and 137; labyrinths and 247; and mysticism 312; opposites 121, 136; parallels xiii, xvii; temenos 103, 297; vas 297
allegorical maps 195, 216
alliance, therapeutic 67; working 99
alpha function 292
ambivalence 81, 135, 167, 181, 318, 319
ambivalent relationship 81
amplifications 24, 49, 201, 295, 297, 302, 303, 332–3; of archetypal images 294, 334
analogies 128, 158, 190, 198, 304; physical 101
analysis 341; aims of *see* aims; analysing 40; art compared 3; benefit 304; birth of 5, 105, 183; compound 38;

cornerstones of 42, 44, 48; costs of 16; cultural aim 159; as cultural phenomena 15; dissensions/distortions 41, 42, 323; dreaming compared 18–25; dreams, role of 19; epistemology 246; faith and 9; focus of 9; habit of 9; hermeneutics and science 342; historical development 189; institutionalization of 38; Jungian 34, 35, 44, 124, 126, 293, 314, 341; limitations of 64; location of 338; mapping of 192–5; matrix 246; method of application and movement 38–9, *see also* technique; mysticism and 313–15; opponents of 41; patient, effect on 8; patients' accounts of 75–88; peripheral aspects of 38; pivot of psychotherapeutic method 39–40; poeticization of 8; power, abuse of 16; prevailing trend in 34; psychotherapeutic method 40; reasons for seeking 63; religion compared 3, 5–6; results *see* results; ritualistic aspects of 101, 102, 103, 106; romantic vision of 33–7, 113, 125, 248, 299, 317; roots and ramifications 39; socio-cultural frame 18; as socio-cultural phenomenon 39; standard analytical technique 50; termination of *see* termination of analysis; time taken 15; transforming function of 114; transgressions in 16; writing about 23; *see also* psychoanalysis
analysts 5; act of faith of 4; aims of 51, 63–4, 240, 304, *see also* aims; attitudes of 25, 33–4, 125–6, 334; basic attitude

33–4, 35, 126; becoming 11; capacity
to be alone 27–8; as container 109;
dialogue with patients 43; divorce
and 12; dreams related to the patient
19, 36, 265–6; as explorer 69, 88;
generations of 6, 13, 40, 41, 79, 104,
146; as guide 126, 190; hierarchies
104; income 12; linguistic
considerations 43–4; as mirror 273; as
mother xiii, 37, 91–2, 103, 293, 302;
notes and records 22, 24; as object
32–3, 297; as observing participator
12, 19–20, 25; paradoxical problems
12; as patients 88–92; in patients'
dreams 26; personality 34, 39, 65,
125; as persons 9; pioneer 13, 15, 40,
70, 73, 87, 287, 303, 337, 343; poets
compared 7–8; power, abuse of 16;
practice of 126; preconditions for
becoming 11; professional hazards
12, 13; psychic infections 50;
relationship with patients 8, 96, 191;
repetition compulsion 52; sex of 15,
56, 63; sex with patients 16;
teacher-guide 293; technique and
125–6, 131–2, 133, 276; theoretical
position 30; theories and 119; vision
of see vision; voice of 35, 97, 120, 121,
334, 344; vulnerability of 130;
without memory or desire 4, 45, 48,
95, 177, 185, 273–4, 299, 306, 307,
308, 344; work and life of 8–11, 126
analytic criteria 180–3
analytic dyad 42, 69, 189, 203, 338
analytic family 33, 90
analytic journey 69, 183, 187, 189, 191,
192, 194, 197, 203, 210, 240, 242, 251,
322; see also journey
analytic maps see maps
analytic omnipotence 80, 307
analytic point of view see vertex
analytic situations, ineffable 134
analytic territory 197, 254
analytical psychologists 79, 125, 127,
243, 285; Society of 188, 284, 285
analytical psychology 32, 100, 124, 126,
135, 143, 162, 184, 233, 265, 274, 296,
308, 309
anima 124, 312
'animus ridden' 290, 291
Annunciation, paintings of 139
anxiety 14, 112, 136, 181, 252, 253, 299,

301–3; defences against 301; dreams
28; see also separation anxiety
archetypal constellations 49
archetypal field 31
archetypal images 123, 126, 134, 290,
293, 294, 298–9, 300, 301–2, 303, 344;
amplifications of 294, 334; self-image
11
archetypal patterns xiii, 159
archetypal school 30
archetypes 1, 29, 30, 31, 124, 134, 272,
290, 294, 316, 321; anima 124, 312; in
dreams 70; hierarchy of 246; mother
312; of separation 31; see also
preconception
art 3, 9, 136, 197; forms of 20
attitudes 125; basic 33–4, 35, 126; of
neutrality 93

base map, definition 214
basic assumption, patient's 33
basic attitudes 33–4, 35, 126
basic views, Jung and Klein 294–5
behavioural patterns 13
beta elements (Bion) 36, 61, 271, 285,
291–2; see also psychoid
biblical authority as ultimate truth 160;
see also truth
birth 93, 140, 246, 247; of analysis 5,
105, 183; as criterion of reality 163;
and death 111, 122, 247; see also
death; rebirth
bisexuality 261; psychosexual 262
border-line personalities 22, 32, 58, 60,
125, 164, 190, 263, 286, 304
breast 135–6, 140, 143, 223, 251, 253,
279, 288, 290, 295, 297, 302, 312, 316;
'no breast' 279, 316
Buddhism 106, 176, 177, 185

cartographers, Christian 159–60, 209
cartographical categories 248, 251, 252
cartography, historical development
189, 199, 214; printing techniques 214
cases, 'Celia' patients 174–5; compulsive
letter writer 129–33; girl, destructive
108; illustrations xvi, 106–8, 111;
latent psychotic 108; man lacking
definition 107; Wolf Man see Wolf
Man; young man with phobia 107;
young woman 'drop-out' 106, 108–9
C.A.T. (Classical analytic technique)

118, 126–9
catastrophic change 9, 110, 115
catharsis 46, 64
causal-determinism 46
causes 48, 49, 288–9; efficient and final 48, 51, 289
celestial maps 323–7
'Celia' 145, 147, 172–85, 313; fantasy 174; syndrome 174
centre of analysis 230, 237, 269, 283, 313, 328; of cosmos 225; personality centred cult 103–4, 105; of a person's life 100, 184; symbols of 230; thematic 263, 277
ceremony see rituals
change xv, 100, 101, 162, 169, 298; analysts' faith in xiii–xiv; catastrophic 9, 110, 115; container for 102, 115; expectation of 97, 170; obstacles to 97; see also transformation
chaos 105, 115, 121, 144; see also cosmos
charisma, success dependent on 14
Chinese oracle see I-Ching
Christianity 41, 146, 150, 216, 230, 240, 241, 242; dualism 49; Rome as centre of 230
Church 6, 49, 103, 216, 241–2, 246
circumambulation 51, 237
civilization, rise of 309, 317
Classical analytic technique see C.A.T.
clinical theory (George Klein) 42
Cocktail Party, The see 'Celia'
coco de mer 151, 153, 154, 155, 156, 168
cognition 198
cognitive processing 36
coincidences, meaningful see synchronicity
collusion 23
commensal relationships 36
Common Ground Psychoanalytic Congress Rome 1990 42
communication 19, 26, 32, 104, 293; by mapping 193; determinants of 274, 276; filter of 271, 274, 276, 278, 280; medium of 187
compensation 27
complexes 29, 30, 31, 42, 49, 126, 270; affect 29
compulsive acts see repetition compulsion
concentration 177, 185, 302; in children 297

condensation 20, 23
confessions 105, 106, 108, 111
conflict, analysis of 42; analyst–patient interaction 270; avoidance of 46; and complexes 126, 270; freedom from 232, 312; over travel ticket 83–4; as preconception 276; resolution of 276; and union of opposites 233
confrontation 109
connecting principle 32
consciousness 7, 10, 25, 46, 54, 55, 95, 96, 111, 122, 164, 185, 223, 243, 247, 276, 281, 290–1, 292–3, 310, 320, 333; Bion and 292–3; concepts and definition 292–3; Jung and 293; spatial 223, 224, 225; see also unconsciousness
constancy, object see object constancy; pre-object 141; see also constant object
constant object xv, 100, 135–44, 148, 161, 166, 178–84; as alternative path 170; different evaluation of 182; fatal 182; and individuation 178–84; numinosity of 171; preoccupation with 179; reflection of self-qualities 181
constellations, archetypal 49
constitution, individual 146, 309
construction, analysts' 74; imaginative 66; of maps 327–37; see also memory; reconstruction
contact, unique 98
container; analyst as 109; for change 102, 115; mother-analyst as 302; ritual as 102, 105, 109
context xv, xvii, 43, 45–53, 102, 198–200, 343; of analytical setting 296; historical and cultural 161
conversational model (Hobson) 76
cornerstones of analysis 42, 44, 48
cosmological symbols 225–33, 240, 246, 247, 259, 281–3; see also labyrinths; spirals
cosmos 5, 94, 98, 112, 209, 210, 216, 223, 246, 248, 327; social and political 336; see also chaos
counter-projections 26
countertransference xiv, 9, 25, 26, 27, 31, 35, 103, 108; veneration of 103
creativity, quest for 14
cult, Buddhist 106; heroes 101;

personality centred 103–4, 105;
religious 106, 107
cult-object 137, 142, 143
cultural activities 16, 320–1, 322, 336
cultural background 31, 33, 60, 102, 122
cultural conditions 137
cultural context 31, 33, 161
cultural dimension 159
cultural phenomena 3; *see also* art;
religion
cure 14, 15, 18, 22, 45, 48–53, 63, 65, 72,
73, 78, 82, 95, 96, 133; by ritual 112;
demand for 9; hopes of 38, 65, 240;
transference cure 82; *see also* 'getting
better'; panacea
curiosity 8, 11, 46, 76, 87, 88, 91, 95,
104, 127, 155, 167, 252, 276, 278, 308

death 111, 182, 243–4; as criterion of
reality 163; of object 334; suicide 180,
309; *see also* birth
death-instinct 48, 175, 180, 300, 301, 302
death-wish 166, 169, 171, 180, 181
defences 46, 47, 71, 274, 301, 302
de-integration 23, 35, 181, 239, 283, 299,
330
dependence 33
depressive position 135, 136, 147, 173,
285, 302, 314, 330; paranoid-schizoid
147, 164, 181
deprivation 309, 316–17, 322; *see also*
starvation, emotional
desire, in Buddhist world 177
destructive 110, 300, 301; activity 48;
attacks 279, 280; behaviour 108, 132;
drives 185, 300; emotions 87; ends
320; envy 41; events 15, 314; factors
97; force 301; self 132, 182, 300; *see
also* aggression
devotion 16, 56, 142, 182, 183, 185, 344;
see also addiction
dialectical process 118–19, 332
disappointments 91; *see also* frustration
discipleship and followers 6, 36, 40, 41,
87, 90, 287, 299, 300, 316, 343
discovery 40, 59, 87, 97, 143, 198, 243,
279, 303, 342; age of 160;
'asymmetrical logic' and 125;
dream-like landscape 191; enduring
98; geographical 251; Gordon's
151–7, 161; history of 198, 199; in
medicine 263; self 105; sense of 38

disgust, mother and sex 93
disillusionment 14, 46, 175, 178–9, 180,
254, 296, 302, 304; *see also*
frustration; illusion
disintegration 111, 163, 299, 309
disorientation, maps of 199
displacement 20
dissociation 64, 123, 137, 307
distortions, deliberate 127–9;
involuntary 127; voluntary 127
divisions 30; *see also* splits
doctrine 6, 113, 121
dogma 6, 103, 104, 105
dream-like 206; landscape 191
dreamer 18, 19, 20
dreaming, analysis compared 18–25
dreams 18, 22, 70, 189, 254; analysts',
about patient 19; broken 24; as drama
20; dream-censor 25; entering 19;
fourfold structure of 20; as
interpretation 26, 28, 32; interpreting
19, 24–5, 26, 32, 86; language of 23;
latent content 24, 25, 342; location of
266; manifest content 24, 25, 342;
meaning 24; memory of 23–4;
patients' 9, 19, 21, 26, 298; role of 19;
series of water dreams 266; types 20,
26; understanding 121; words in 23
dualism, Christian 49
dyad, analytic 42, 69, 189, 203, 338
dynamic structure 300

early world maps 208–11, 222, 247,
252–7
eccentricity 185
education 74
ego 30, 46, 126, 136, 143, 146, 301, 302;
American ego psychology 35, 47, 55;
archaic 132; child's struggle for 137;
constancy 142; control, lessened 23;
defence, splitting 136; development
55, 136, 180, 183, 184, 290, 294, 301;
disintegration of 163; function 54;
integration 142, 299–300; labile 296;
nuclear 131; object and 296; self and
145, 178, 183, 184, 326; strength xiii
46, 50, 276; suffering 146; weakness
control 46
elements of perception 272
emotions, aggressive-destructive 87
empathy 30, 38, 95, 96, 99, 121, 198,
266, 273, 302, 333

ending *see* termination
endopsychic structure 287–8
enthusiasm 15; success dependent on 35
environment, factors, significance of 136, 146, 268–9, 296–7, 302, 319
epistemology 199, 206, 246
epistemophilic instinct 11, 48
equilibrium 331
equipment, professional 273–4
equivalents, Jung and Klein compared 331
Eros, principle 36; theory 300
'establishment' 8, 40; mysticism and 41; values 12
ethology 104
euthanasia 337
Eve 151, 152, 156, 161, 168, 182
evolution 39, 268, 309, 336
exorcism 110, 112
experimenting, play and 4
ex-patients 75–98
explanations 6
exploration 11, 69, 78, 80, 87, 88, 97, 190, 198, 210, 248, 328, 342 ; cosmos and technology 210; self-analysis 88

failure 8, 59, 65, 70, 91, 93, 100, 128, 183, 184; Celia's 175; environmental 297, 302; explanation of 49; Gordon's 169; in mapping 263, 270; sense of 8; *see also* success
faith 3–17, 97, 308, 342; act of 4; article of 92; in the Church 246; doubt and 16, 320, 321, 322; enthusiasm distinguished 15; evolution of 4; Freud and 4; Jung and 4; religious 100; spiritual value of 4–5; *see also* trust
faith-healing 15
Fall, the 104, 152, 156, 157
fantasia (making visible) 215
fantasy 30, 70, 164, 194, 197, 243, 254, 274, 290, 292, 316, 333, 336; Celia's 174; elaborations 46; idealistic 337; incestuous 90; maps 195, 212, 215–20, 222, 263–9, 327, 336; nature of 194; reality and 195; sadistic 136; sexual 257; structured 295; theories as 94–5; unconscious 42, 270, 289, 290, 291, 295, 301, 303; understanding 121; Utopian fantasy of analysis 337
father 259; authority 89–90; figure 84,

86; transference 84
Fermentatio 139
filter, of communication 271, 274, 276, 278; corresponding opening 280
finishing *see* termination
follow-up studies 76, 97
forbidden-room motif 105
formes frustes 111, 113
'formulation' 24–5
friendship, psychotherapy as 65–6
frustration 28, 67, 111, 136, 197, 257, 278, 309, 316–17, 322, 327, 333, 341; optimal 316; toleration of 314–15; willingness to suffer 146; *see also* disappointment; disillusionment
fulfilment 10, 12, 16, 45, 48, 83, 169, 259, 315, 318, 319

Garden of Eden 148, 151–9, 224, 226, 230
genetic 47, 120, 207, 280, 303
geometric *see* symmetry and asymmetry
'getting better' 45, 98, 114; *see also* cure
'ghosts' 33, 315, 334
glossary of maps 208–20
guardian 183

hallucinosis 22, 316
healing 5, 15, 100, 106, 123, 146, 299, 311; by self-realization 6; faith-healing 15; meaning 146; 'wounded healer' 11, 310; *see also* cure; 'getting better'; health; whole-making; wholeness
health 12, 51–2, 53, 56, 57, 71, 78, 93, 112, 142, 146, 286, 291, 302, 313, 341; analysts' 12; health-giving rituals 116; meaning 146; rituals restoring 112; seeking 49; *see also* 'getting better'; healing; whole-making; wholeness
hermeneutics 43, 66, 207, 320, 342
hero 181, 309, 310, 315; as constant object 181; cult 101; death of 283; figures, need of 181; worship 159
historical context 31, 33, 161
holding 22, 108, 316; by mother-analyst xiii, 37, 92, 103
holistic medicine 56
homosexuality 162, 259, 262–3, 270; paranoia and 89; unconscious passive 89
humanization 19

hybrid, Klein-Jungian 284–305, 330
hypnosis xv-xvi, 38, 70, 72, 84, 180; link
    with psychoanalysis 210
hypothesis 32, 48, 181, 201, 206, 240,
    270, 287, 299, 309, 315, 316, 317; see
    also theory

I and you 131
I-Ching 35, 112, 266, 268
I-identity 33, 183
I–you 130, 302, 334
ideal-ego 35
idealization 36, 180, 181
identification 31, 32, 36, 55, 68, 296, 304;
    prevention of 127; see also
    introjective identification; projective
    identification
identity 33, 183; group 13, 91, 108; we-
    33, 184, 185, 337
idolatry 140
illusion 9, 14, 46, 65, 197, 225, 254, 259,
    294–8, 304, 320, 337, 344; images and
    294–8; of oneness 296, 297; positive
    296; sameness 36; surrender of 136,
    162; togetherness 28; see also
    disillusionment
images 296; archetypal see archetypal
    images; and illusions 294–8; of
    memory 4
imagination 38, 164, 165; active 137,
    292, 295, 296, 304
imitation, danger of 129
imprinting 110
incest, fantasies of 90; interpersonal
    relationships and 106; taboo 16, 263
individual 33, 35, 39, 183
individualism 183, 184
individuation xiii, 51, 54, 114, 169,
    172–3, 181, 184, 283, 314–15; as
    adaptation 163; alternative road to
    100; classical view of 162;
    concentration 181; constant object
    and 178–84; ego development 142,
    163, 173; illusory aim 183; labyrinth
    as road to 243; psychopathology of
    145–85; self-realization 6, 35;
    socio-cultural criteria 183; see also
    psychopathology
indoctrination 6
infancy 3, 15, 22, 49, 74, 91, 109, 110,
    135–6, 289, 290, 292, 296, 301, 302,
    303, 304, 309, 316, 317, 326, 330

infantile amnesia 70
infantile sexuality 19, 40, 47, 83, 103,
    139, 288
infection, psychic 10, 50
inherited component 83
initiation 105, 111
innate attitudes 331
innate cultural activity 321
innate ritualistic activity 115
innate spatial awareness 225
innate tendencies 162; see also repetition
    compulsion
inner maps 199, 221–5, 247, 259, 268
inner world 8, 247, 287–90, 303, 304;
    Freudian 287–8, 290; Jungian 287–8,
    290, 301–2; Kleinian 288–9, 290, 300;
    patients' 289; as withdrawal 297; see
    also intrapsychic space
insights 7, 13, 39, 46, 56, 78, 89, 95, 182,
    327; see also intuition
instinct 271; and dynamic structure
    300–3; epistemophilic 11, 48; spiritual
    291
instinctual drive 47
integration 22, 51, 54, 145, 183, 184,
    299–300, 330; as precondition to
    individuation 14, 173
internal object 32
International Psychoanalytic Congress,
    Rome, 1990 42–3
interpersonal relations, incest and 106
interpretations 88, 89, 94–8, 101, 111,
    125, 299, 300, 303, 320, 321, 334, 344;
    clever 97; counterproductive 53;
    long-term effect of 97; mutative 55,
    95; questionable effect 97;
    transforming effect 96; using
    analogies 304; using images 304; see
    also transference
interviews 76
intrapsychic development 137
intrapsychic space 91, 121, 163, 185,
    247, 278; see also inner world; space
introjections 31, 32, 136, 290
introjective identification 292, 345; see
    also identification; projective
    identification
introversion 288
intuition; flashes 7, 95–6; see also
    insights
intuition xiv, 4, 7, 13, 21, 36, 38, 95, 96,
    121, 156, 165, 243, 270, 299, 313, 333

island, as cosmological symbol 224
'islomania' 223–5, 248, 338
itinerary maps 199, 211–13, 221, 257–9

Janus, as constant object 143; as
    paradoxical unity 143
Jerusalem, in maps 124, 209, 230, 232,
    236, 241, 242
journey, analytic 69, 183, 187, 189, 191,
    192, 194, 197, 203, 210, 240, 242, 251,
    322; direction of 8, 191, 207, 266; of
    discovery 210; explicit 216; form of
    51; motives for 259; spiritual 242;
    through the labyrinth 242, 246
Jungian movement 42

'K' (knowledge) 251, 306–8
Klein–Jungian hybrid 284–305, 330

labyrinths xv, 51, 199–200, 221, 233–50,
    282–3; analytical usage 242–3; in
    churches 241–2; drawing 248–50;
    function 241; as model 283;
    movement in 235, 237, 239; mystery
    of 246; ritual and symbolic use 241–7;
    secular applications 243–6; spirals
    distinguished 235; structure 239–41;
    symbol 240, 243; symbolic salvation
    242; see also spirals
ladder, as symbolic device 281
landmarks 194, 225, 327, 328
latent psychosis 22
layers 273, 277; of psyche 110, 279, 281;
    psychoid 278
leitmotif 13
libido 51, 66, 300; theory 47, 311;
    transformation of 139
lies 9
light, as symbolic device 139, 140
limitations, of analysis 64
literal reality 8, 16, 180
literal-mindedness 161, 164–5, 168, 170;
    and inability to imagine 164
locality, significance of 268
love 16, 35; self-less 308, see also agape;
    spiritual 261
luminosities 140, 142, 285

magic 32, 73, 109, 116, 246, 334;
    apotropaic 107, 112; circles see
    mandalas; magical thinking 164, 165;
    see also superstition

Maison Dédalus 241
mandalas; cosmic 248; lamaistic 177,
    230; symbolizing wholeness 146; see
    also symmetry
mandalas xvii, 35, 185, 221, 223, 229,
    231, 232, 241, 243, 253
manipulation 80, 114, 192
mappae mundi 125, 209–10, 222, 232,
    241, 242, 243; design of 248
mapper 161, 323, 327, 328
mapping xvii, 30, 36, 187, 342–3;
    analysis 192–5; analytic not objective
    203; differentiating expectation,
    journey and reproduction 194;
    intrapsychic process 201–4; process
    of 323; psychology of 200–5; serious
    objection to 306–8; as
    transubstantiation 205
maps xvii–xviii, 5, 191, 198, 203, 207,
    214, 251–83; allegorical 195, 216; as
    analyst's territory 323; base 214, 263;
    categories of 248, 251; celestial 323–7;
    construction of 327–37; definition of
    193; of disorientation 199; early
    world 208–11, 222, 247, 252–7, 324;
    fantasy 195, 212, 215–20, 222, 263–9,
    327, 336; glossary 208–20; inner 199,
    221–5, 247, 259, 268; interactional
    269–81; internal 97–8; itinerary 199,
    211–13, 221, 257–9; lower half 281;
    map-making, psychology of 200–5;
    marriage 17; memory 247;
    metaphorical into literal 198–9; as
    models 197–8, 251, 322–7; multiple
    251; psychological properties of
    204–5; religious 5, 215, 222; route
    199, 211, 212; satirical 215; symbolic
    215; T in O 209, 212; tables, graphs
    and diagrams distinguished 193;
    thematic 213–14, 259–63, 327, 336;
    topographical 199, 211–13; tourist
    211; upper half 280; world 253; zonal
    211
mastery, illusion of 140
mastery xiv, 16
matrix xiii, xiv, 3, 206, 246, 343;
    relational 271, 280, 281
maze see labyrinth
meaning, quest for 14
medical model 263
meeting, location of 269
memory 136; childhood, reconstructing

14; creating continuity out of 136; dream-like 23; of dreams 23–4; images of 4; a present construct 24

'memory and desire' (Bion) 4, 45, 48, 95, 177, 185, 273–4, 299, 306, 307, 308, 344

meritocracy 184

metaphor 6, 8, 20, 23, 35, 122, 189, 197, 200, 270, 295, 333; and generic terms 315; poetic appeal of 123, 190; similarities and analogies 189–91; travel 187, 189–92; see also poetry

metaphoric language 8

metapsychology 44, 47, 99, 207, 288

method, client-orientated 75–6

mistakes, relationship of 96

model; archeological model of psychoanalysis 342; conversational 76; labyrinth as 283; map as 197–8, 251, 322–7; medical 263; planetary system as 323–7

monism 42; Christian 49; materialistic 49

moral, factors 185; injunctions 337

morality, new 41

mother-analyst 36, 91–2, 103, 293; containing function 302; holding by xiii, 37, 92, 103

motif, forbidden-room 105; leitmotif 13; Liebestod 180; mythological 270; stolen-fruit 104, 105; 'wounded healer' 11, 310; see also hero

motivation 8, 96, 110; importance of 73, 344; social 263; suffering and 263; unconscious 12, 185

mutual transference, dreams and 9, 25–33, 86, 108; example 27–9

mutuality 16, 26, 29–33, 36; archetypal encounters 31; critical concept 33; illusory sameness 36; separateness in 28; too much 36

mysticism xvi, 125, 230, 307, 313–14, 316, 326, 343; drugs and alcohol and 312, 314; 'establishment' and 41; innate 311; psychology of 310–13; unitive state and 170, 312–13, 314, 315; and unmet expectations 309; and Utopia 315; see also Absolute, the; 'O'

mythology xiii 25, 30, 51, 121, 270, 333; symbolism of 20

myths, elements and structure 310; Jung and 4; symbolism in 4

narcissism 22, 32, 58, 75, 109, 169, 181, 182, 263, 276

navigation 321

negative capability 314

negative therapeutic reaction 49, 96

'no-things' 315, 316, 317, 319, 326, 327, 333; and irreconcilable worlds 315; things and 322, 327, 333

non-specific factors

numen 185, 290

numinous 104, 143, 171, 172, 182, 242

numinous object 144

nursing couple 37, 304

'O' 35–6, 106, 306, 307, 308, 311, 313, 315, 317, 319; compared with cultural activities 321; demystification of 320–2; evolution of 177, 185; as ultimate reality 177; see also Absolute, the; mysticism

object 31, 32; analyst as 32–3; bad 136, 181; constancy see object constancy; constant see constant object; cult-137, 142, 143; death of 334; destroyed 32; encountering 31; externality of 32–3; good internal 141; as heresy 140; idealized 136; internal 32, 301; in Jung's work 137; as magic 140; objectives and 298–300; part see part object; split-off 136; splitting of 180–1; transitional 137; whole 135; whole body 136

object constancy 100, 135–44, 163, 171, 172, 173, 178–84; definition of 135; idealize 142; labile 180; see also constant object

object relations theory 31, 32, 47; British school 31; pro- and introjections 31

object-fixation 110

object-imago 32, 33

object-representation 32

objectivation 22

objectives see aims

observances, ritualistic 108; see also rituals

obsessional neurosis 78

Oedipus complex, inverted 259, 261

omnipotence 140; analytic 80, 307

opposites xiii, 49, 134, 248; in analytical psychology 124; bipolar 122–6; categories of 121; conceptual 123–5;

conjunction of 136, 243, 341; Jung's concept of xvi 100, 121–2, 125; paired 122–6, 341; union of 100, 121–2, 126, 173, 231, 233, 312, 313, 326
orientation 327, 328; theoretical 96; see also vertex
overdetermination 46, 261

panacea, belief in xv, 56; demand for 9; hope for 113, 116, 338
paradise, mapping 159–60, 161, 222, 232; symbols 229–30; see also Garden of Eden
paranoia, unconscious homosexuality and 89
paranoid-schizoid position 147, 164, 181
parapraxes 96
part object 135, 136–42, 143, 285; Lingam statues 140; perfection of 141; tantra art 140–1; Yoni statues 140
part-self, complex as 30
'participation mystique' 31, 290, 331; see also projective identification
patients, aims of 22, 45–6, 298–300, 314, see also aims; analyst as travel companion 8, 191; analysts as 88–92; analysts' attitude to 25; analyst's voice and 35, 97, 120, 121, 334, 344; basic assumptions 33; fictitious 27; getting better 45; inability to take in 131; individual 93; motivation of 71, 344; paintings 22, 332; pathology 78; personality 93; reasons for seeking analysis 63; recollections 75–85; relationship with analyst 8, 96, 191; reorientation of 49; reports by 92–4; results and 59; sex of 15
penis 140, 257, 259
penis-envy 290, 291
people, analysed 33, 57, 341; unanalysed 57, 309, 342
perfectibility, of human nature 35
permanent union, quest for 180; see also opposites
persona 11, 33
personal equation 119
personal premiss 120, 134
personality 34; structure, Jung's theory of 303; unchanging parts of 100
personification 124

phallus, independent 138–9; worship of 138, 140; see also part object
phase, object-less 135
physical love 141
Pilgrim's Progress, map in 216, 218
planetary system as model 323–7
play 3–4, 5, 89, 109, 137, 233, 240, 278, 297, 320, 321
pluralism 42, 45
poetry 6–8, 15, 39, 162, 180, 190, 197, 296; see also metaphor
poets 6–8, 9, 14, 39, 128; analysts compared 7–8
pornography 138, 141, 259
possession, states of 101, 112
post-Freudians 40, 89
post-Jungians 26, 30, 34, 40, 89, 121
Praslin, as Garden of Eden 151
preconceptions 307, 312, 321, 344; see also archetype
preconscious system 25
present unconscious 42
primal relationship 37
primal scene 83, 86, 312; dream of 83
primary process thinking 20, 21–2, 25
primitive identity 31, 32
processes; introjective 32; projective 32
projectiles 9, 10
projections 9, 26, 31, 32, 55, 183, 290, 299, 333; counter-projections 26; transference 190
projective identification xiii, 55, 291, see also identification; introjective identification
propitiation 112; see also superstition
psyche, analyst's 26; destructive forces and 301; dissociability of 137; hypothetical 281; insights and 56; layers of 110, 279, 281; patient's 26; as self-regulating system 14, 34, 331; splinter 30
psychic apparatus 14, 47, 48, 51, 52, 55
psychic blindness 10
psychic energy, transformers of 114
psychic energy xvi, 207
psychic equilibrium 331
psychic growth 30
psychic infection 10, 50
psychic make-up, unchangeable 90
psychoanalysis 308; archeological model of 342; beginnings 40; discipline, science 43; history of 87; hypnosis

and 210; technique 126, 251
psychoanalysts 39–40; title 42
psychoanalytic reality 162–3, 317
psychoanalytic theory 104, 135, 274,
 296; structural 124; topographic 124
psychoid 61, 292; functions 271; layer
 278; substratum 271, 272
psychological types 93, 120, 122, 125
psychomorphology 332
psychopathology 44, 147, 303; Celia's
 178–84; and constant object 184;
 genesis of 91; Gordon's 168–70; of
 individuation 145–85; meaning of
 147; and transformations 102
psychosomatic symptoms 93, 278
psychotherapies, proliferation of 15,
 106, 113, 116
psychotic, areas 169; latent 22, 108;
 patients 22, 164, 334

reaction formation 110, 185
reality 46, 65, 67, 164, 180, 197, 309,
 320; analyst's 109; inner 162, 297;
 literal 8, 16, 180; material 180;
 objective 162; outer 162; psychic 35,
 162, 294–5, 344; psychoanalytic
 162–3, 317; spiritual 4–5; symbolic
 16; see also 'O'
'rear-mirror' effect 204, 251
rebirth 101, 109, 140, 172, 224, 246, 311;
 see also birth
reconstruction 14; see also memory
regression 46, 91, 131, 133, 279; benign
 22, 46, 92; in dreams 21–3; evaluation
 of 304; malignant 22, 92; positive 304;
 therapeutic 92; to splitting 137; victim
 of 22
reification 124
relations, spatial 254
relationships 8, 36; analyst/patient 8;
 commensal 36; interpersonal 106;
 primal 37; symbiotic 36; triangular
 252, 259, 261
religion 3, 6, 15, 16, 137, 144, 165–7,
 171, 176–8, 197, 310; analysis
 compared 3, 5–6, 15; elements of, in
 Eliot 176–8; faith 100;
 institutionalised xvi; psychology of;
 symbols of 14; teachers of 6; see also
 mysticism
repetition compulsion 34, 96, 111, 116,
 162, 172, 291; analyst's 52; see also

rites
repression 23, 26, 28, 34, 46, 64, 66, 70,
 72, 74, 131, 132, 247, 304
resistance 24, 26, 42, 48, 52, 84, 85, 89,
 134, 274, 276; to transference 72, 96
results 5, 9, 14, 17, 52, 58–74; assessing
 59–66; motivation, importance of 73;
 statistics and 59, 60, 61, 62;
 suggestion and 70–4; see also analysis;
 success; termination of analysis
reverie 36
rhythm 115, 249, 250; bi-phasic 115;
 natural 237; ritual and 115
rite de sortie 115, 192, 197, 207
rite d'entrée 110
rites, ceremonial aspect of 102–3; as
 communication of symbols 112; as
 group experience 108; relationship to
 time 111; threshold negotiating 114;
 of transformation 101, 198; see also
 rituals
rites de passage 111
ritualistic activity 115
ritualistic aspect of analysis 116
ritualistic observances 108
ritualistic practices 108
ritualistic setting of analysis 113
ritualization 115; of sex 140
rituals 30, 102, 111; in analysis 113–15;
 analytic sessions as 103; autonomous
 99, 101–17; classification of 111; as
 container 102, 105, 109; cure by 112;
 daily tasks 112; debriefing 192;
 definitions 102; evil-averting 116; as
 habits 115, 116; health-giving 116;
 invented 114; motoric activity 115;
 numinous archetypal effect 104;
 observation of 106; physiological
 component 115; power of 117;
 recapitulate aim 111; religious 111;
 rhythm accompanying 115;
 significance of 108; as stabilizers 116;
 as therapy 113–15; transforming
 effect of 102, 106–8; unifying effect of
 112; see also rites
romantic vision, of analysis 33–7, 113,
 125, 248, 299, 317
ruminations, obsessive 111

salvation 5–6, 56, 103, 105, 176, 183,
 232, 240, 242
Satan 156, 161, 168

secondary process thinking 20, 21–2, 25
self xiii, 30, 114, 298, 299, 300, 313;
    assertion 89; de-integrated states 299;
    de-integrates of 35; de-integrating
    phases 23, 283, 330; de-integrative
    processes 239; destructive 132, 182,
    300; discovery 105; ego and 145, 178,
    183, 184, 326; Eliot's 177; false 33,
    131, 132; ideal 35; integrating phases
    23; nourishment 309, 316; objects 32;
    revelation 59; true 33, 35, 132
self-expression 23
self-image 182
self-objects 32
self-realization xvi, 6, 35, 51, 54, 55, 106,
    145, 169, 170, 184
self-regulating system 34
separation 28, 31; anxiety 13, 27–8, 334
sex 140–1, 244; between analyst and
    patient 16; instinct 48; in labyrinth
    244; ritualization of 140
sexual addiction 257–9
sexual symbolism 141
sexual union 16, 139, 141
sexuality, infantile 19, 40, 47, 83, 103,
    139, 288
shadow 32, 109, 124, 126, 162, 181, 182,
    183, 184, 291
shame xiii
shell-shock 46
social and cultural context xiii, xv–xvi, 9
social and cultural environment 252
social and cultural mileu 161
social and cultural system 262
social factor, in psychopathology 91
socio-cultural criteria 183–4
socio-cultural emphasis 326
socio-cultural enterprises 18
socio-cultural environment 39
socio-cultural frame 18
socio-cultural phenomenon 18, 39
socio-cultural sphere 49
socio-political system 337
sooth-saying 112
soul 8, 16, 337; see also psyche
space, analytic concept of 191, 193, 205,
    254; as channel of communication
    326; cultural nature of 247;
    distribution of 208; enclosed 248;
    intrapsychic 91, 121, 163, 185, 247,
    278; orientation in 249, 269
spatial awareness 225

spatial consciousness 223, 224, 225
spatial feel 265
spatial relations 254
spatiality xvii, 205, 208, 223–5, 247–8,
    250, 269
spirals 51, 233–41, 243, 281–2;
    labyrinths distinguished 235;
    movement in 235, 237, 239; structure
    of 239; see also labyrinths
spiritual journey 242
spiritual reality 4–5
spiritual transformation 300
splinter psyche, complex as 30
splits 181; historic 41; ideological 41, 44,
    183
splitting 123, 136, 137, 170, 180, 224,
    299, 307
starvation, emotional 92, 93, 316
statistical probability 59
stolen-fruit motif 104, 105
structural changes 95, 96, 97; see also
    theory
structural theory 47
structure, endopsychic 287–8
sub-personality, complex as 30
submission 166–7, 183
substitute, formation of 178
success 38, 46, 47, 49, 93, 110, 114, 183,
    184, 345; affluence 253; analyst
    unanxious about 306; claims of,
    demonstration of 308; dependent on
    charisma 14; dependent on
    enthusiasm 35; dependent on
    integration of theory 30, 308; Freud,
    Anna 79; Jungian 59; limited vi; in
    medicine 263; no criteria 169; no
    success see failure; publishing of 66;
    risk of 109; see also failure
suffering, and disease 146, 147;
    motivation and 263
suggestibility 72, 73
suggestion 72; in education 74; misuse
    of 74; as mutual influence 74; results
    and 70–4
suicide 180, 309
superego 47, 50, 133, 170; conscience
    133
superstition 110, 140, 246, 309, 311; awe
    102; see also magic; propitiation
supportive aspects, of psychotherapy
    and psychoanalysis 97
suppression 307

symbiotic relationships 36
symbolic appreciation 173
symbolic devices, ladder 281
symbolic reality 16
symbolic realization 3, 180, 183
symbolic thinking 164–5
symbolic truth, importance of 4
symbolic unification 181
symbolism 54, 68; in cartography and
    analysis 223–5; in dreams 22; in
    myths 4; sexual 141; spatial 251
symbolization 20
symbols 165; archetypal xiii;
    communication of 112; cosmological
    225–33; Jung and 14, 54, 73, 121–2;
    paradise 229–30; sexual union 16
symmetry and asymmetry xvii, 125,
    223, 232, 240, 243, 246, 248, 254, 256,
    276, 321, 327; fallacies 243
symptoms 45, 55, 78, 100, 252;
    ceremonial characteristics 115;
    formation 20, 46; language of 46;
    meaning of 51; symbolic value of 51
synchronicity 31, 32, 35, 277
syncretism 124, 125
syndrome, Celia 174
synthesis 49, 197; of analyst's and
    patient's maps 194

T in O maps 209, 212
taboo 103, 106, 109; breaking 103, 104,
    105, 110, 111, 112, 132; incest 16, 263
'talking cure' 314
Tantra art 140–1, 246
technique 125–6, 131–2, 133, 206, 276,
    299; common denominator 335; as
    criterion 333–4; as guide 126; linked
    with concept 290; not primary 335;
    related to innate attitudes 331; threat
    of termination 84–5
telepathy, and Freud 311
termination of analysis 36, 63, 65, 67,
    192; ritualistic 115; setting date for
    73, 84; threat of 84–5
territory, in the analyst's head 207, 323;
    analytic 197, 254
text xii, xvii, 45, 343
thematic maps 213–14, 259–63, 327, 336
theory 13, 14, 15, 18, 30, 47, 88, 89, 97,
    99, 113, 119, 180, 206, 259, 261, 273,
    276, 310, 344; analytic psychology
    135; as armour 274; building 47;

confirmation of 19; dreamlike 19; as
    fantasy 94–5; influence of 307; not
    worthless 97; psychoanalytic 135;
    revising 103; self-validating 262;
    structural 47; see also hypothesis
therapeutic alliance 66, 67–8
therapeutic regression 92
therapy 15, 18; as ritual 113–15
things and no things 319, 327, 333; ratio
    322, 327
thinking, literal and magical 164–5;
    symbolic 164–5
third, presence of a xiii, 39, 62, 103, 336
thought, inspires faith 316;
    metamorphosis of 323; omnipotence
    of 317; power of 315–20; primary 20,
    21, 21–2, 25; processes 20; products
    308, 316; secondary 20, 21, 21–2, 25
'thoughts in search of a thinker' (Bion)
    336, 343
tolerance 143, 146, 182, 279, 314; of
    analytic relationship 279; of
    frustration 314–15; as saving grace
    183
Topographica Christiana 160
topographical maps 199, 211–13
tourist maps 211
transcendent function 20, 25, 134, 137,
    164, 292, 294, 320, 333
transcendental 311
transference 9, 25–7, 30, 35, 42, 44, 48,
    72, 79, 80, 84, 96, 190, 271, 274, 276,
    278, 286, 297; archetypal 29, 326–7;
    complementary 29; concordant 29;
    cure 82; disposition 73; illusory 29,
    197, 337; as magic 107; metaphor,
    enlarged 190–1; mutual see mutual
    transference; negative 67, 68–9, 72,
    123; positive 68, 123; projections 109,
    190; remnants 96; resistance to 72, 96;
    syntonic 29; veneration of 103
transformation xiii, xv, 6, 36, 48, 50, 54,
    55, 100, 101, 106, 113, 276; concept of
    101; frustration of 111, 113; hermetic
    vessel and 254; of libido 139;
    mutative interpretations 55; not in
    psychotic patients 164; rebirth as 109;
    reverie and 36; rites of 101, 198; ritual
    enactment of 111; rituals and 102,
    106–8; spiritual 300; vs. change 51; see
    also change; rites; rituals
transitional object xiii, 330

transitional phenomena 20, 25, 137, 164, 225, 320, 333, 337
trauma theory 46, 64
travel, metaphor 187, 189–92; ticket 83–4, 89, 94
Treasure Island, map in 216, 220, 221
trees of paradise 151, 152, 155, 156, 244
Trinity 146
trust 3–4, 5, 16, 31, 69, 280, 308
truth, biblical authority 160; emotional 9; moments of 7; poetic 8; psychological 88; symbolic 4
types, attitudes and functions 93

unconscious xvii, 7, 28, 31, 34, 38, 45, 48, 51, 54, 55, 56, 68, 96, 101, 112, 123, 124, 126, 127, 136, 185, 192, 206, 243, 247, 269, 276, 292, 293, 298, 303–4, 307, 320, 333, 344; cultural background and 122; fantasies 42, 270, 289, 290, 291, 295, 301, 303; present 42; suggestion 73
unio mentalis 146; *see also* opposites
union, with deity 138; of opposites 100, 121–2, 126, 173, 231, 233, 312, 313, 326
unitive state 170, 312–13, 314, 315; differences from analysis aims 313; and life 312; *see also* mysticism; wholeness
unity, mysterious 243; *see also* unitive state; wholeness
unpredictability, dislike of 112
Ur-labyrinth 237
Ur-painting 202
Utopia 113, 283; belief in xv; desire for 224, 344; literature 337–41; maps of 223; mysticism and 315

vertex 45, 48, 67, 68, 125, 207, 216, 269, 270, 274, 281, 285–6, 307, 313, 315, 322, 323, 326, 328, 330, 332, 335–6, 344; essential 257; origin of 335; psychoanalytic 48
vignettes 27, 66, 145, 206, 269
virtues 183, 185
vision 13, 40, 41, 88, 96, 181, 323; romantic 33–7, 113, 125, 248, 299, 317
vocation 11, 12, 141

we-identity 33, 184, 185, 337
Weltanschauung 70, 159, 287, 328
whole-making 5–6, 51, 100, 101, 162, 322; *see also* healing; health; wholeness
wholeness 53, 54, 140, 146, 242, 243, 314, 315, 341; holistic medicine 56; longing for 246; meaning 146; search for xiii 49, 51, 312; *see also* healing; health; unitive state; whole-making
wings, as symbolic device 139, 140
Wolf Man 55, 56, 65, 70–1, 77–87, 89, 90, 96, 97, 292, 344
womb, symbols of 244, 245, 246
'working through' 27, 89, 123
world, image 125, *see also mappa mundi*; inner *see* inner world; two irreconcilable 326; *see also* maps
'wounded healer' 11, 310

Yin–Yang 121, 253

zodiac 336–7; axis 325
zonal maps 211